THE GLOBAL SPANISH EMPIRE

AMERIND STUDIES IN ANTHROPOLOGY

Series Editor, **Christine R. Szuter**

THE GLOBAL SPANISH EMPIRE

FIVE HUNDRED YEARS OF PLACE MAKING AND PLURALISM

EDITED BY
Christine D. Beaule and John G. Douglass

THE UNIVERSITY OF
ARIZONA PRESS

TUCSON

The University of Arizona Press
www.uapress.arizona.edu

© 2020 by The Arizona Board of Regents
All rights reserved. Published 2020

ISBN-13: 978-0-8165-4084-6 (hardcover)

Cover design by Leigh McDonald
Cover art: Manuscript map of Dagua River region, Colombia. 1764.
[detail] Library of Congress, Geography and Map Division.
Typeset by Sara Thaxton in Adobe Caslon Pro and Trade Gothic Std.

Library of Congress Cataloging-in-Publication Data are available at
the Library of Congress.

Printed in the United States of America
♾ This paper meets the requirements of ANSI/NISO Z39.48-1992
(Permanence of Paper).

To our respective spouses, Christian and Jill, for their love, support, and understanding as we worked on this project for the last two years.

CONTENTS

List of Illustrations   ix

Acknowledgments   xiii

Introduction: Place Making and Pluralism in
the Global Spanish Empire   3
Christine D. Beaule and John G. Douglass

1. Contact, Colonialism, and the Fragments of
   Empire: Portugal, Spain, and the Iberian Moment
   in West Africa   31
   Christopher R. DeCorse

2. Colonization, Transformations, and Indigenous
   Cultural Persistence in the Caribbean   55
   Corinne L. Hofman, Roberto Valcárcel Rojas,
   and Jorge Ulloa Hung

3. Native American Responses to Spanish Contact
   and Colonialism in the American South   83
   Christopher B. Rodning, Michelle M. Pigott,
   and Hannah G. Hoover

4. Pluralism and Persistence in the Colonial Sierra
   Sur of Oaxaca, Mexico   105
   Stacie M. King

5. A Tense *Convivencia*: Place Making, Pluralism,
   and Violence in Early Spanish Central America   130
   Laura Matthew and William R. Fowler

6. When the Saints Go Marching In: Religious
   Place Making during the Early Spanish Colonial
   Period in the Central Andes, 1532–1615   150
   Kevin Lane

7. The People of Solomon: Performance in Cross-Cultural
    Contacts between Spanish and Melanesians in the
    Southwest Pacific, 1568 and 1595   176
    Martin Gibbs and David Roe

8. Places, Landscapes, and Identity: Place Making
    in the Colonial Period Philippines   200
    Stephen Acabado and Grace Barretto-Tesoro

9. Colonial Surveillance, *Lånchos*, and the Perpetuation
    of Intangible Cultural Heritage in Guam,
    Mariana Islands   222
    *James M. Bayman, Boyd M. Dixon, Sandra Montón-Subías,
    and Natalia Moragas Segura*

10. Contested Geographies: Place-Making Strategies
    among the Indigenous Groups of South Texas and
    Northeastern Mexico   242
    Steve A. Tomka

11. Importing Ethnicity, Creating Culture: Currents
    of Opportunity and Ethnogenesis along the Dagua
    River in Nueva Granada, ca. 1764   267
    Juliet Wiersema

    Contributors   291
    Index   295

ILLUSTRATIONS

MAPS

I.1. Map of the world, indicating the location of the case
studies in this book   5

1.1. Map of early Iberian expansion in West Africa   33

2.1. Map of the Caribbean   56

3.1. Locations of selected Native American chiefly
provinces in La Florida   84

4.1. Map of Oaxaca, showing the location of regions,
places, and archaeological sites mentioned in the
text, including Nejapa   108

4.2. Topographic map of the Nejapa/Tavela study
region, showing the location of sites discussed
in the text   110

5.1. Projected urban grid plan of Ciudad Vieja   136

6.1. Map of the study area   156

7.1. The 1568 and 1595 expeditions of Álvaro de Mendaña   178

8.1. Map of the Philippines, showing the upland
area of Ifugao and the lowland town of San Juan,
Batangas   202

9.1. Mariana Islands in the Pacific   223

9.2. Map of churches and villages in Guam about
1672 by Padre Alonso López   225

10.1. Regions of Texas and northeastern Mexico
mentioned in the text   244

10.2. Map of the location of the five missions in the
upper San Antonio River basin   250

11.1. Manuscript map of the Dagua River region (1764)   268

11.2. Detail of the manuscript map of the Dagua River
region (1764)   273

FIGURES

1.1. Illustration from Pieter de Marees in 1602   43
1.2. Portuguese period ceramics from Elmina   46
2.1. Indigenous and transcultural ceramics from early
colonial contexts at Cotuí and Concepción de La Vega
(Dominican Republic)   66
2.2. Intercultural early colonial ceramic assemblages from
La Concepción de La Vega (Dominican Republic),
Nueva Cádiz de Cubagua (Venezuela), and El Chorro
de Maíta (Cuba)   67
2.3. Examples of the persistence of indigenous cultural
traditions recorded in Cuba and the Dominican
Republic   71
4.1. A locally made polychrome Postclassic International
Style ceramic vessel fragment from Colonia
San Martín   114
5.1. The *Lienzo de Quauhquechollan*   135
6.1. The site of Kipia, showing sectorization   158
6.2. Detail of Sector B at Kipia   162
6.3. Detail of Rock Face 5 at Kipia   164
8.1. The Bocos rice terraces in Banaue, Ifugao   207
8.2. A section of Structure A, one of the two
stone-based houses in Pinagbayanan, San Juan,
Batangas   210
8.3. Bottle of a pain balm and cod liver oil   214
9.1. Spanish governor's palace remnant at Plaza
de España, Hagåtña, Guam   227
10.1. Brass crucifix strung on a necklace and surrounded
by shell beads   260
11.1. View of Las Juntas   282

TABLES

6.1. ^{14}C Dates from the Site of Kipia (PUK9)   160
9.1. Generalized model of inland settlement and land
use on Guam   231

9.2. Information on selected inland archaeological sites on Guam that were occupied before, during, and/or after the *reducción*   232

10.1. Breakdown of marriage patterns among married male and female residents of Misión San Antonio de Valero   253

10.2. Breakdown of marriage patterns among married male and female residents of Misión Concepción   254

ACKNOWLEDGMENTS

This volume is the culmination of several years of hard work by many dedicated people. The idea for this volume began in the summer of 2016, when Christine emailed John asking him if he would like to collaborate on a session for an upcoming Society for American Archaeology (SAA) annual meeting. The incubation period for the session—regarding topic ideas, who we really wanted to participate, and so on—took some time, but we organized an electronic symposium at the 2018 SAA meeting in Washington, D.C. The format required participants to write chapter-length papers and submit them electronically a month in advance so that they would be publicly available prior to the session for anyone to read. The discussion that unfolded at the conference included lively exchanges both within our group and with the audience.

Soon after we all headed back to our lives after the meeting, Christine and John were notified by Christine Szuter that our session had won the prestigious SAA–Amerind Foundation Award! Unfortunately, only a subset of the original session could attend the Amerind Foundation workshop; we truly appreciate those who were part of the original session but could not continue with the project: Elliot Blair, Yasmina Eliani Cáceres Gutiérrez, Jorge de Juan, and Matthew Liebmann. The summer and early fall were busy for seminar participants, writing and revising their chapters for the seminar. Most of the senior authors (except Martin Gibbs, Corinne Hofmann, and Kevin Lane) were able to meet for a five-day seminar in Dragoon, Arizona, at the Amerind Foundation. The Amerind Foundation treated us very well, between the seminar, the setting, and the amazing food, and all in attendance readily recognized what a career highlight it was. Much to our surprise, within roughly two hours on our first day of the workshop, we realized that the organizing theme for the seminar—ethnogenesis—was not clearly evidenced in many of the papers, as we had hoped. However, two central themes did emerge: pluralism and place making. As a result, after the workshop, all participants reworked their papers into the final versions published here.

First and foremost, we thank all the participants of the SAA symposium and the subsequent SAA-Amerind workshop for their hard work and creative energy as we worked together over the last several years. Everyone has been so thoughtful and helpful to one another as we've discussed and thought through each other's chapters, and we are very pleased with the results. While some of us had known each other before, we all feel that the process produced close scholarly collaborations and friendships that we will treasure for the rest of our professional lives.

The Amerind Foundation and its president/CEO, Christine Szuter, funded our workshop and included our volume in the University of Arizona Press's Amerind Seminar Series. We are all very honored to have been invited to do a seminar at the Amerind Foundation, and we are all eternally grateful for the opportunity. We greatly benefited from Christine's valuable insights and support both during the workshop discussions and in the months since.

Allyson Carter, Scott Herrera, and others at the University of Arizona Press have been very thoughtful and supportive of this project, for which we are thankful. The anonymous peer reviews, as well as the critical reviews and thoughts by the seminar participants both in person and remotely, helped hone our ideas and made the chapters stronger both individually and as a group.

We are thankful for support from our employers for this project. John received professional development support from Statistical Research, Inc., for participating in both the SAA symposium and the subsequent Amerind Foundation seminar and for the cost of indexing. Christine gratefully acknowledges the University of Hawai'i at Mānoa's University Research Council's support for travel to the SAA symposium and her many supportive colleagues. Finally, we thank our dear families and friends for their love and encouragement, without which we could not do fun things like disappear into the Arizona desert for five days to talk archaeology.

Christine D. Beaule
Honolulu, Hawai'i
John G. Douglass
Tucson, Arizona

THE GLOBAL SPANISH EMPIRE

Introduction

Place Making and Pluralism in the Global Spanish Empire

Christine D. Beaule and John G. Douglass

The colonial empire built by the Spanish from the sixteenth through the nineteenth century was the first to achieve a global scale. Although more archaeological research has been conducted on Spanish colonial outposts and the impacts of its territorial claims in the Americas than elsewhere, the Spanish Empire also sought outposts in the Caribbean, the Pacific, Southeast Asia, and Africa, with varying degrees of success. This vast political undertaking was a crucial model for its European rivals and partners alike and was arguably foundational in launching and shaping the early modern era of empire building across oceans and vast territories. In turn, the Spanish imperial project was built on earlier Portuguese trading and colonial outposts in Africa and the eastern Atlantic, especially along the continent's northwestern coast. Spanish colonists and administrators had measurable impacts on the political organization and economic foci of the local areas where they levied colonial demands for natural resources and labor. The indigenous peoples who occupied those areas on so many continents had measurable, specific, or diffuse impacts on the Europeans in their midst as well. Moreover, indigenous individuals and groups were moved around both within regions, such as the western coast of North America, and across vast distances between regions both forcibly and voluntarily. As has been well documented by historians of the era, intermarriage between indigenous, European, African, and other groups of people begat a plethora of new racial (e.g., caste) labels. These two phenomena—intermarriage and migration—produced multicultural, pluralistic colonies within which individuals variably adopted or invented different material manifestations of identity in dual processes of ethnogenesis and cultural persistence.

The processes of identity transformation and creating and rediscovering the importance of places were organic ones for those living under

Spanish colonialism because for both indigenous groups and the agents of colonization Spanish colonies were places of cultural pluralism with a mixture of local and foreign groups living together (Cipolla 2013, 2015; Haley and Wilcoxon 2005; Hu 2013; Panich 2013; Voss 2008a, 2008b, 2015; Weik 2014). As the empire grew across time and space, so did connections between new groups and cultures. Colonialism, Stephen Silliman (2005:62) writes, is "about processes of cultural entanglement, whether voluntary or not, in a broader world economy and system of labor, religious conversion, exploitation, material value, settlement, and sometimes imperialism." Lee Panich (2013) sees the results of those entanglements on indigenous and colonists' lives as a constant process of "becoming." This process of becoming necessitated viewing the world around oneself in new contexts and with new insight and the creation of both new identities and places of importance as the result of the push-and-pull changes in everyday life and of creeping colonialism (Ferris 2009:168–170).

Archaeologically, the material residues of this cross-cultural interaction are visible throughout the regions covered in this volume's chapters (Map I.1). In addition to tackling broad questions revolving around cultural persistence and pluralism within colonialism, the authors collectively aim to broaden our understanding of colonial place making among pluralistic communities of indigenous and foreign peoples. Although we cover different regions and situations, indigenous cultures, and indices of foreign intrusions, we see manifestations of place making in each case study. The concept of place making has received much attention from scholars (Adams et al. 2001; Cresswell 2001, 2004; Johnson 2012) and is most often defined in a physical, geographic sense, as in the creation of a meaningful place on the landscape marked by cultural incorporation and ritual practice. A location in space is thus made place within a broader social and environmental landscape; this landscape can be pluralistic, dynamic, and multiethnic. The deliberative and conscious exercise of agency is fundamental to this understanding of place making. Within a colonial setting, groups rely on prior practices and ideas (e.g., *reglamentos*) to shape their response and strategies regarding place making, which in this sense can be social or political.

The second, related conceptualization of place making used in this volume involves the making of a social place within a social landscape that is marked by the materialization of changes in people's identities in

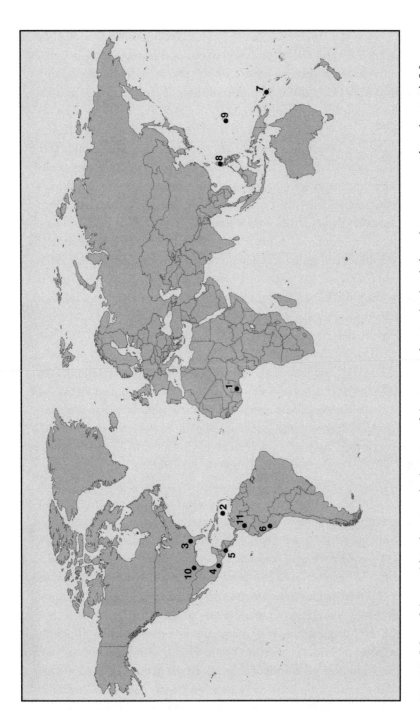

Map I.1 Map of the world, indicating the location of the case studies in this book (numbers correspond to chapters). Map prepared by Jacquelyn Dominguez.

a location on the landscape. The first, more colloquial version of place making incorporates the construction of physical features such as a mission or town, but in this second iteration, it also includes the appearance of hybrid material culture, the incorporation of foreign goods into local material traditions, the continuation of local traditions (representing rejection of or lack of access to foreign goods and material styles), and archaeologically visible evidence of opportunistic social climbing in pluralistic colonial settings. Changes in clothing fashion, culinary traditions, and other aspects of material culture may simply be adaptations of daily practices to allow the persistence of long-term cultural traditions (Arkush 2011; Panich 2013; Reddy and Douglass 2018). In some cases, changes in material culture are ways to maintain aspects of traditional culture rather than signifiers of new cultural practices. Continuities in the daily practices of indigenous peoples, including cases when foreign goods are absorbed into local material culture, belie simplistic dichotomies that equate the appearance of new goods, technologies, or material styles with replacement, domination, accommodation, or other interpretations. After early Spanish encounters in the U.S. Southeast, for example, metal axes and celts joined copper plates and armbands as prestige symbols in Mississippian chiefdoms (Chapter 3). And just 200 m from a Dominican church at Majaltepec in Mexico's Nejapa Valley, subfloor burials included a metal blade fragment and hundreds of glass trade beads (Chapter 4). These examples highlight what Kent Lightfoot (2012) and Silliman (2009, 2012) have argued, that changes in the continuity of cultural traditions do not have to be binary choices for native groups in colonial settings. Rather, change and continuity were part of the same process of responding and adapting to newly emerging and evolving colonial surroundings (what Panich [2013] has referred to as "becoming"), which included a wide variety of contexts, not just large, complex social environments like empires (see Chapters 1 and 7; see also Beaule 2017a; Voss 2015:656). Place making is visible throughout the former Spanish Empire in both these geographic and social senses (Chapters 1, 5, 6, 8, and 10).

Collectively, the authors in this volume see the interaction of pluralism and place making as conceptually powerful features of all of our case studies because manifestations of both played out in very different ways in situations ranging from brief encounters on Pacific beaches (Chapter 7) to established missions (Chapters 9 and 10) and towns (Chapter 5) over the course of four centuries and spanning many world regions (including Southeast Asia, the Pacific, the Americas, the Caribbean, and Africa). We deliberately brought together case studies from different regions and time periods and used different kinds of data, theoretical approaches, and methodologies in order to foster comparative dialogue about those themes and to explore patterns beyond local or regional ones. We aim to contribute to broader discussions of, for example, place making among indigenous peoples that necessarily incorporates geopolitical changes in relationships between the Calusa chiefdom and surrounding towns (Chapter 3), as well as locally constituted cultural exchanges between indigenous peoples in West Africa and western Central Africa and between Portuguese and Spanish individuals (Chapter 1). Similarly, first contacts included not just European voyages in the Caribbean (Chapter 2) but also later encounters in both exploratory (Pacific voyaging, Chapter 7) and organized colonial (Central America, Chapter 5) forays. The archaeological and historical remains of these encounters span not just the moments or brief periods of the exchanges themselves but also more sustained impacts. For example, the Spanish-built landscape of cities, towns, churches, roads, and other infrastructure was sometimes quite fragile; even where the colonial built environment failed to have a lasting presence, the impact of those changes in local settings may have had long-lasting consequences for the indigenous population left behind (see Chapters 5, 6, 8, and 10). Indeed, the nature of that indigenous population was often changed by the members of distant indigenous cultures, Africans, mestizos, mulattoes, and others who came to populate the world where Spaniards sought territorial control. The chapters collected in this volume thus differ from other books focused on Spanish colonialism or using global comparative approaches to historical or prehistoric case studies of colonialism (Beaule 2017a; Berger and Lorenz 2008; Falk 1991; Gardner et al. 2013; Lyons and Papadopoulos 2002; Stein 2005). This book includes regions not often included by these intellectual predecessors (Southeast Asia, Pacific, the Caribbean, and Africa), coupled with a thematic focus that integrates them despite the great variability in our chapters' geographic and temporal foci and the differences in the intensity, occupational permanence, and impact of entanglements with the Spanish.

Overall, then, this volume is designed to explore the varied nature of Spanish colonialism within cultures across the globe. At the same time, many of these chapters make wide connections between places and cultures that at first glance may not be readily apparent. In the next section, "The Spanish Imperial Project," we provide a brief sketch of this historical expansion for readers unfamiliar with the Spanish colonial empire. We intend the theoretical foci of place making and pluralism to supersede the shared feature of Spanish colonialism so that the case studies in this volume serve as analogies for colonialism's impacts elsewhere, whether those colonists were European or non-European or, as in all of the case studies, a combination of the two. In this case, the Spanish began their colonial expansion in the Caribbean and then soon after undertook campaigns in multiple portions of Central America. Within a generation, the Spanish Empire had expanded globally. Spain's inherent need for mineral wealth and natural resources and labor to extract them, combined with a desire to save souls through Christianity, led to interconnections between diverse and disparate cultures that would draw people together in new and previously unimaginable ways.

How does pluralism and place making—in cultural formations, ethnic identities, socioeconomic classes, religious ideologies, political maneuverings, economic extractions, and other manifestations—impact the archaeological record at scales ranging from the individual feature to the global? The problem of scale is particularly salient in a comparative project such as this one, because temporal and geographic scales impact one's perspective (Senatore and Funari 2015:5) on the patterns of change and persistence we aim to explore. For example, in a relatively short time after Hernán Cortés arrived in Mexico in 1519, Manila galleons and other trade ships were bringing immigrants (both freed and enslaved) to Mexico from many distant regions, including Southeast and Southwest Asia and Africa, creating extremely pluralistic cultural settings (Casella and Fowler 2005; Jamieson 2005; Matthew 2015; Russell 2005; Schwaller 2010, 2011; Seijas 2014). Rather than being brought into the dominant culture, these ethnic enclaves were strong and, as Lightfoot (2015:9217) recognizes, "remained in the voids and pockets of settler colonies." Such cultural pluralism is most visible at the site level but much less so at a larger scale of analysis.

The ability to identify cultural and personal identity through meaningful things and places is important to be able to understand its transformation in colonial contexts. At numerous sites across the Spanish colonial world, native peoples used, adopted, and incorporated European or other foreign goods and iconography for either everyday use or special purposes, but they used them in indigenous ways rather than in the ways they were originally intended. Glass beads and pigs, among other items, circulated through indigenous Caribbean trade networks (Chapter 2) and would have provided symbolic capital to their owners, much as medicine bottles and porcelain objects did in Pinagbayana in the Philippines (Chapter 8). The incorporation of glass beads, metal items (or fragments thereof), and other European goods into local indigenous material cultures and trade networks was a common archaeological indicator of colonial entanglements, ranging from indirect contact (such as the Calusa in Florida, Chapter 3) to residence in Spanish settlements (such as El Salvador and Guatemala, Chapter 5). These items represent simultaneously both residence in and resistance to colonial worlds (Silliman 2005:68).

As Mary Van Buren (2010:179) writes, some issues "require a change in scale to include the broader socioeconomic fields in which colonial groups participated. Although the sheer size of the Spanish Empire makes this a daunting task, archaeologists can broaden their scope in a variety of ways." The chapters in this volume address change and continuity on a variety of temporal and geographic scales; in doing so, they provide an opportunity for us to think critically about how those axes of variability impact our interpretations of the colonial dynamics of place making in pluralistic settings. But first, we offer a brief sketch of the history of the Spanish Empire as background in order to contextualize the book's chronological ordering of case studies.

THE SPANISH IMPERIAL PROJECT

The story of the construction and expansion of the Spanish global empire is one of repeated conquest, violence, demographic devastation, racism, economic extraction, and exploitation. It is a story of movement of Spaniards, enslaved and free indigenous peoples, clergy, and soldiers both within and between regions across the globe. However, it is also a story of exploration, discovery, blunders, and failures. Elements of all these stories appear throughout this book. Here, we aim to offer a sense of the big picture, of an expansion that was at times accidental (stumbling into previously unknown lands) and at other times deliberate, with well-organized and provisioned campaigns. The place making that occurred throughout the extremely varied global regions covered in this volume illustrate these axes of variability in intentionality and success, and the sociocultural pluralism that characterizes the whole was greatly facilitated by the movements, forced or voluntary, of the many individuals caught up in those expansive efforts.

Spanish imperialism was rooted firmly in Portugal's contacts, cultural intersections, and colonial aspirations in the African continent. The placement of Christopher DeCorse's case study as Chapter 1 reflects this chronological heritage. Although Spain and Portugal were briefly united under the Iberian Union from 1580 to 1640 and share deep and abiding cultural connections, their imperial histories and mechanisms were distinctly different. Portuguese encounters and outposts in West Africa were, in many cases, overwritten by the constructions of later European powers and African peoples, and their accommodations by indigenous locals were often more ephemeral than those of their Spanish counterparts in places like Mexico and Peru. The Spanish presence in the Caribbean (Chapter 2), on the other hand, bears some resemblance to those earlier Portuguese forays into Africa. The forced African diaspora, genocide, and disease changed the Caribbean cultural and physical landscape forever, but Amerindians and their highly diverse cultures remain an indelible part of that landscape too. This region was the initial setting of indigenous, European, and African intercultural dynamics, but it remains largely neglected in the scholarship of Spanish colonialism, which more commonly begins with Cortés's fateful conquest of Tenochtitlan. We see the chapters by DeCorse and by Corinne Hofman, Roberto Valcárcel Rojas, and Jorge Ulloa Hung as foundational to this volume, which aims to explore place making and pluralism both wherever the Spanish Empire sought to expand and throughout its imperial history. They are equally foundational to understanding the character of that empire, whose practices, understandings of indigenous others, and goals were formed in the crucibles of Iberian encounters in Africa and the Caribbean.

The colony of Mexico, founded by Cortés in 1519, quickly connected with other portions of the ever-expanding Spanish Empire. Within just a few years of the Spanish conquest of Mexico, there were campaigns to the south into El Salvador, Guatemala, and Honduras, as well as into Peru, and north into the southwestern and midwestern United States. Chapter 3, by Christopher Rodning, Michelle Pigott, and Hannah Hoover, and Chapter 4, by Stacie King, document archaeological manifestations of these early entradas (exploratory voyages). Both offer excellent examples of multicultural and multilayered settings, with highly variable impacts of foreigners and foreign goods in indigenous cultures unfolding along the way. The palimpsest nature of cross-cultural encounters and conflicts predating the Spaniards' entrance onto the scene is especially apparent in King's research. The cultural pluralism that defines these exploratory efforts with the goal of establishing a colonial presence is explored on a smaller and finer scale in Chapter 5, by Laura Matthew and William Fowler, who document San Salvador (El Salvador) and Santiago en Almolonga (Guatemala), two short-lived colonies founded in 1528. Both case studies give us a clearer sense of what *convivencia* (living together) looked like on the ground in that early historical period. These complex histories emphasize how indigenous responses to the would-be colonists, including accommodation, resistance, and co-optation, were framed by prehispanic experiences of migration, colonialism, conquest, and coexistence. Spaniards' experiences in these regions in turn informed their strategies, assumptions, and behavior elsewhere.

The Spanish conquest of the Andes was accomplished in a remarkably short period of time, from 1532 to approximately 1572, and was aided greatly by the ravages of epidemic diseases that raced south and west from various points of contact by Spaniards, accompanying both slaves and domesticated animals. However, the loci of colonial interaction with those indigenous peoples who survived the diseases and wars, displacement and enslavement, were relatively few and far between. Thus, the cultural impact of colonialism in the Andes was highly variable over space and through time in the region. Kevin Lane's research at Kipia in the north-central Peruvian highlands documents place making by the religious orders at an indigenous *huaca* (a shrine, a ritually meaningful object, or a place in the sacred landscape) and the syncretic church that was built there (Chapter 6). This site, almost 500 km away from the colonial capital of Lima, amply illustrates the physical manifestation of liminality that characterized the transition from indigenous rule to the establishment of systematic evangelization and *reducciones* (resettlements of survivors into model villages) in the late sixteenth and early seventeenth centuries.

Spaniards' efforts to expand their success (in terms of wealth extraction) extended westward over the Pacific Ocean within decades of the Mexican campaigns. Early Pacific voyages, later including the Manila galleons, were systematic expansions of the American campaigns by conquerors like the Alvarado brothers (see Kelsey 2016:59–62). In 1568 and 1595, Spanish expeditions launched from Peru were exploring the Solomon Islands with the intention of establishing colonies. Martin Gibbs and David Roe's work there (Chapter 7) draws on archaeological, ethnohistoric, and archival data to explore the transitory and ephemeral nature of encounters between Spanish ships and indigenous peoples and the former's failed attempts to establish a foothold. By 1565, on the other hand, there was a colony at Manila in the Philippines that became an economic center for trade and slavery (Seijas 2014; Tremml 2012). From Manila, groups of colonists made efforts to expand their colonial holdings and presence throughout the Philippine archipelago and beyond in order to more directly tap into well-established trading networks in Southeast Asia and China. Stephen Acabado and Grace Barretto-Tesoro (Chapter 8) present two archaeological case studies of cultural persistence among the highland Ifugao, who were not conquered, and a lowland Tagalog society that was directly administered by the colonial apparatus.

By the late seventeenth century, Spanish efforts to establish colonies and found missions had picked up steam, as illustrated in Chapter 9 by James M. Bayman, Boyd M. Dixon, Sandra Montón-Subías, and Natalia Moragas Segura and in Chapter 10 by Steve A. Tomka. Chapter 9 contextualizes early archaeological research on a Spanish mission site in Guam in the archaeological record of colonialism in the Mariana Islands (the name of the archipelago is itself a Spanish colonial legacy). Though the earliest recorded contact between Europeans, via the Magellan-Elcano circumnavigation voyages, and indigenous Chamorros in Guam took place in 1521, it was not until 1668 that the first permanent mission was successfully established. Despite great differences in scale, there are important parallels between the mission in Guam and those documented by Tomka (Chapter 10) around San Antonio, Texas. The impacts of Spanish efforts to turn indigenous peoples into tax-paying, Catholic, and loyal citizens of the Spanish Crown—part of the Bourbon Reforms in Spain, which were designed to strengthen an ailing empire, centralize control over its colonial holdings in peninsular (rather than American-born criollo) hands, and increase its profitability—lasted far longer than the occupations of the missions themselves. Founded in the late seventeenth and early eighteenth centuries, most missions were abandoned within 150 years.

Efforts to tighten control over the vast dominions they claimed continued right up until the invasion of the Iberian Peninsula by Napoléon in 1808 and throughout the rest of the nineteenth century's wars of independence in the Americas. This expansion continued within those territories as well, as colonialism was always highly variable across the landscape of any given region. Moreover, expansion efforts were not always territorial but instead were sometimes targeted efforts to extract particular resources, efforts that were framed and constrained by local realities on the ground. The final case study in this volume (Chapter 11) documents Juliet Wiersema's fascinating late case study of colonial extraction in Nueva Granada. In the late eighteenth century, the Dagua River region was a multicultural backwater inhabited by a dynamic mix of French, Italians, Spanish, and Amerindians but with a majority African population. The social mobility that African slaves and their descendants were able to achieve in this place and time presents a fitting bookend to the first case study in Africa, as well as to the volume's overarching overview of place making and pluralism throughout the Spanish Empire.

TIES BETWEEN SPANISH COLONIES

The Spanish colonial empire began with their arrival in the Caribbean, which led soon after to the establishment of the colony of Mexico, founded by Cortés in 1519, and quickly connected with other portions of the ever-expanding Spanish Empire. Within just a few years of the Spanish conquest of Mexico, there were campaigns to the south into both Guatemala and Peru and north into the southwestern and midwestern United States, all under the authority of the newly established Royal Council of the Indies. By 1565 there was a colony at Manila, which became an economic center for trade and slavery (Seijas 2014; Tremml 2012). Early Pacific voyages, later including the Manila galleons, were a systematic expansion of the American campaigns by conquerors like Pedro de Alvarado y Contreras and his brothers (Kelsey 2016:59–62).

Colonies fulfilled different goals for Spain (Douglass and Graves 2017). First, there were minerals and other resources to harvest. Once the colony in Mexico was established, for example, expeditions into the southwestern United States were launched to search for gold, silver, and other resources. Then, the Spanish aimed to convert indigenous peoples to Catholicism. The process of conversion, partially through labor at the missions, was one way to aid in also ensuring that native peoples would become good citizens of the Spanish Empire (Hackel 1998:122; Newell 2009:51–54). Lastly, as outlined by Tatiana Seijas (2014), another principal goal was the use of labor for extracting natural resources and feeding the continued colonial expansion, which, as Laura Matthew has argued (2015:84), was "a natural extension of Christian expansion." Muslims captured during war, for example, could be legally enslaved (Seijas 2014:37). This was done in part through colonies that expanded the slave trade. Enslaved people came from many categories of people in Asia, from enslaved Filipinos to Muslim war captives (Seijas 2014:Map 2.1). Based on archival records, roughly a third of sixteenth-century Mexican colonist households held slaves (Rodriguez-Alegria 2016), and they performed a wide range of tasks. During this time there were both transatlantic and transpacific Spanish slave trades, and there was also a clear program of enslaving local indigenous peoples in the Americas. Slaves also were shipped to Spain from many parts of the world, including native North America (Matthew 2015).

The Manila galleons and other Spanish ships moved diverse trade goods and slaves between colonies. These ships made many stops across the Pacific, impacting indigenous diets and material inventories of peoples such as the Chamorro in the Marianas (Bayman and Peterson 2016). Enrique Rodriguez-Alegria (2016:42–49) studied the inventories of 30 sixteenth-century Spanish colonizers in Mexico to better understand their material belongings during this early period. He concludes that roughly 60 percent of the items listed were manufactured in Mexico or elsewhere in the Americas, many likely by indigenous peoples. Although initially colonists depended on trade goods from Europe, indigenous craftspeople started copying material forms and styles fairly soon after the conquest (Rodriguez-Alegria 2016:48). That said, almost 39 percent of the items inventoried came from cities in Europe. Some items in high demand, such as European glass beads, made their way through Mexico and were shipped out to other colonies (Hackel 2016). Items from Europe, Asia, and elsewhere circulated throughout the distribution system. The colony of Manila became an important hub in preexisting trade networks linking China and Southeast Asian kingdoms, bringing varied Asian goods to Acapulco, Mexico, and beyond, but also silver in enormous quantities to the currency-starved Chinese Empire from the Spanish-American colonies (Chia 2006). Soon after Spanish colonies were established, a wide variety of new, exotic goods would make their way into the interior of colonial lands, other islands, and nations outside direct contact with the Spanish through exchange networks.

All told, intercolony trade networks facilitated the exchange of ideas, materials, and people between different environments and areas of the empire, creating pluralistic economies and societies. Oceanic shipping routes were complemented by overland expeditions and exchange networks. Colonial expansion also allowed indigenous groups to align with or fight against local Spanish powers. Spanish armed forces included relatively few actual Spaniards but contained many aligned indigenous warriors. For example, the Alvarado brothers' 1520s campaigns into Guatemala and El Salvador had just a few hundred Spaniards but up to 8,000 central Mexican indigenous warriors (Matthew 2007, 2012; Restall and Asselbergs 2007). Between campaigns, some of these same indigenous warriors were shipped to other portions of the Spanish Empire, such as South America, creating new cultural hybridity in these parts of the world. The early Coronado expedition from central Mexico into what is now Kansas, in the central portion of the United States, also had few Spaniards but hundreds of central Mexicans (Douglass and Graves 2017; Flint 2009). Of course, it was not just slaves or warriors who crossed the waters between colonies. Native noblemen and noblewomen from various portions of the empire also crossed the Atlantic to visit Spain (Matthew 2015:88–89).

PLACE MAKING

One thematic focus of this volume is on the global connection between people and places tied together during Spanish colonialism over a nearly 500-year period. The case studies presented have variable time depth, cut across time periods, and offer perspectives from incredibly diverse places. One of the important considerations in these various colonies—incorporating both people and the physical places themselves—is the creation of space and place. These spaces, as Paul Adams, Steven Hoe-lscher, and Karen Till (2001:xiv) have argued, become places when they are embedded with and represent social relations. Spaces are, they write (2001:xiii), "intangible and dauntingly infinite," and as a result, people create places from spaces that are tied to "experiences and memories of the material world that is so reassuringly solid." At the same time, places are not as tangible and pronounced as they initially appear, as social and material conditions tend to be in constant flux. In the case of the colonial world, people and communities are in a constant process of becoming (Panich 2013). In these contexts, people from diverse backgrounds—for example, colonists and indigenous groups—help create these colonial spaces that embody the social relationships between them and that are internal to those groups. Within this context, physical spaces connected with cultural interpretation help create places of importance that help these divergent groups interact. As Stephen Acabado and Grace Barretto-Tesoro argue in Chapter 8, three things constitute a place (following Agnew 1987): its location, its setting for social relationships, and a sense of place (i.e., the more intangible elements and feelings of a place that give it meaning for a particular group of people). Ideas about space and place can take many shapes, but more and more, there is acknowledgment that spaces can become loci of power and authority, gender relations, classes, factions, social memories, practices, and everyday life, among other things (Johnson 2012:275–276; Rubertone 2009, 2012). Adams et al. (2001:xx–xxii) argue that many social transformations and transitions can occur within spaces and places, including experiences, identity, imagination, and social construction. For example, any geographic space may not simply be a physical one but may have social meaning attached to it by various social agents, which helps create places. Any particular place may have a different meaning to diverse groups or individuals, especially in a colonial setting. Places are socially constructed (Cresswell 2001, 2004) and are contexts in which people help create, mediate, shape, and transform identity, likely on multiple occasions. This is place making.

Thus, we should think not only about physical or geographic places per se but also about the social setting and social relationships that help create the space that has been identified, used, and maintained by these diverse peoples. Similar arguments have been recently made regarding the creation of communities in colonial contexts; it is not the physicality but the social relations and social agency that help create, alter, and maintain communities (Hull and Douglass 2018). These places mediate and offer a social lens for viewing the surroundings. As an example, the social landscape of colonial Alta California offers important insight into this sense of place and its divergent meanings by colonists and indigenous people who inhabited the same lands. In southern Alta California, there is an area in west Los Angeles known as La Ballona that has been the home of indigenous people of the area, the Gabrielino/Tongva, for millennia. During the mission period, one native village located in this area was called Guaspet (Douglass and Reddy 2016; Douglass et al. 2018; Douglass et al. 2016; Hackel 2016; Stoll et al. 2016). This village, which we know from both archaeological and ethnohistoric sources, was a very important social and economic locus along the coast as a connection with the southern Channel Islands. During the mission period, it also contained an area in which hundreds of Gabrielino/Tongva were buried; this burial ground likely drew from a much larger population than just the village of Guaspet. This village was recruited by Misión San Gabriel, and over 90 of its villagers left to become baptized neophytes at the mission, only to return intermittently for ceremonial activities such as feasting rituals associated with the burial area and the traditional Mourning Ceremony (Douglass et al. 2018).

Within a single lifetime after the establishment of Misión San Gabriel, the village of Guaspet was no longer inhabited. The mission-period village of Guaspet and its associated burial area were constructed on an alluvial fan adjacent to the Ballona wetlands, which had been occupied as a stable surface for well over 6,000 years. This village was a persistent place on the landscape, as conceptualized by Sarah Schlanger (1992), as it was used as a seasonal habitation site for thousands of years. It is likely that this persistence helped create a sacred landscape and an important socially constructed burial place for the Gabrielino/Tongva. Through time, the concept of community changed from one focused on habitation to one more focused on ritual ceremony associated with the burial area (Douglass et al. 2018), as the mission period fragmented native communities through migration to the missions, pueblos, and ranchos, as well as through increased foreign-borne illnesses and hunger. The social memory and history of the site helped create and transform this space from one of long-term occupation to an important ritual and communal sacred place. The continuous use of the native burial area, combined with annual feasting ceremonies nearby, was a way for the local Gabrielino/ Tongva to continue their long-lived traditions in the face of colonialism, as well as connect with those members who had left for Misión San Gabriel to be baptized but who were likely to return for these important feasting and mourning rituals.

Simultaneous with and partially responsible for the decline of the native village of Guaspet, colonial rancheros developed the area for cattle range and farming activities. On the bluffs overlooking the former village and burial area of Guaspet, which likely was still partially visible as it slowly was buried by alluvial fan deposits, a horse or cattle area was developed and appears on an early map with the label "Corral de Guaspita." Although the Gabrielino/Tongva, who had occupied this land for thousands of years, no longer occupied the village of Guaspet, subsequent colonists had continued using the name, but in a transformative way, much like an analogy to the way they transformed the land around them from a sacred native place geography to a utilitarian place. While the physical location (space) remained the same in many ways, the sense of place changed dramatically from the native to the colonial occupation. That said, the location of the ancient village of Guaspet is still viewed by some native Gabrielino/Tongva as a sacred place two hundred years after the village and associated burial area were last occupied and used.

PLURALISM IN COLONIAL SETTINGS

Colonial settings are, by definition, pluralistic; they contain indigenous and foreign populations that, after perhaps a very short period of time, become intertwined in economic, political, and social realms. Each participant group struggles to find its way, and its place, in this new social order, although clearly indigenous groups struggled much more so. As described above for the Gabrielino/Tongva in what is now southern Alta California, new or altered definitions and creations of place were one of many reactions to this colonial, pluralistic reality. Martin Gibbs and David Roe's contribution (Chapter 7) to this volume tells the story of exploratory navigations from Peru to the Philippines, and there may be no better example of the pluralistic nature of colonial settings than the passengers on those Spanish ships that traveled between those locations in the Pacific: Spanish, indigenous Peruvians, enslaved and free Africans, and the list goes on. We know from the analysis of historical documents that not only were colonies pluralistic, but their ties to other colonies were as well. For example, María Fernanda García de los Arcos (1996) and Eva Maria Mehl (2014) both argue that from an early time period, Mexico and the Philippines were conjoined and historically intertwined politically, economically, and socially. From transport of Nahua warriors from central Mexico to the new colony of the Philippines in the mid-1500s, the importation of enslaved peoples from Africa, the Americas, and other parts of Asia, to the transpacific import of Mexican military recruits (including convicts and other criminals) in the 1700s, the integration of the local and foreign peoples led to a complex social, political, and economic colony. Below, we touch on elements of this pluralism as it was expressed, sometimes in diverse fashions, across the Spanish Empire.

Categories of gender and race and an individual's place within any colonial sociopolitical system, such as the caste system, were very important parts of colonial society across the Spanish world. The caste system hailed from the concept of *limpieza de sangre* (purity of blood). Legal definitions of caste groups were elaborate and complex, with fine distinctions among different classes of people. Many scholars have argued that there was little mixing between castes or races (*mestizaje*) in early Spanish colonial settings such as Mexico. Robert Schwaller (2011), for example, has argued based in part on simple demographics in these early colonies that from the outset of the colonial period, there were simply few Spanish women in these early colonies, which led Spanish men to create interethnic and interracial marriages, which in turn led to new identities and, sometimes, ethnogenesis. Using archival data, he argues that mestizas (women partially of Indian ancestry) were much more likely to marry Spaniards, while mestizos (men of partial Indian ancestry) were more likely to marry *indias*. Schwaller sees that some mestizos, even during the early colonial period in central Mexico, were able to avoid the caste limitations set on them by having strong ties with Spanish life and effectively played the role of *españoles*. Alternatively, those who had biological ties to Spaniards but were abandoned by their Spanish fathers probably identified with indigenous castes and communities. Alternatively, other scholars, such as Barbara Voss (2005:463), have argued that this system was outwardly a "pigmentocracy," with lighter-skinned people likely to be higher in the social order; castes were also related to lineal ancestry, class, and a variety of other attributes. She argues that colonial society in the heartland of colonies was very rigid in its caste system, and Spanish-colonial sumptuary laws highly restricted both upward and downward movement within this caste system by members of colonial society (Voss 2008b:413). In general, many historians likely view the situation of caste in the Americas more along the explanation of Schwaller than of Voss. In other cases, the Spanish caste system conflated ethnic groups; in the 250 years or so of the Manila galleons, migrants came to the Americas from the Philippines and elsewhere in Southeast Asia, Japan, Cathay [China], and India and became collectively known as *chinos* (Chinese) or *indios chinos* (Chinese Indians) (Slack 2009:35).

Another way of helping break the rigidity of the caste system in the core of Spanish colonies was to head toward the periphery of the Spanish Empire as a colonist or an explorer. Crypto-Jews left the Iberian peninsula for the New World to flee persecution, and many continued once they arrived in the core of Mexico and headed to places such as what is now New Mexico (Douglass and Graves 2017; Hordes 2005:89). Early overland expeditions to California were also a good opportunity for colonists to transform their identity from one of mixed race to that of *español*, far away from the colonial core (Haley and Wilcoxon 2005; Voss 2008a, 2008b). At times, people were banished to these far-flung places or otherwise fled to distant locations (Mehl 2014). The Spanish Empire was a vast network of cultures and places in which to transform oneself (see Beaule 2017b), and migration, in different forms, was an important catalyst for change (Weik 2014:198–200).

For example, at the beginning of the overland Anza expedition from southern Arizona to California in the mid-1770s, many of those heading to California were of mixed race and were willing to attempt the expedition as a way to get farther away from the harsh restrictions placed on them based on their racial category in the caste system (Voss 2008b). Perhaps to encourage them to endure the long journey, traveling colonists were sometimes issued clothing that was not allowed within the Mexican heartland. Once these same settlers arrived and were established in southern California, within a short time they had transformed their identity from Indian to Spanish, based on self-reporting in census records

(Mason 1998). In another example from the sixteenth-century British Isles, sumptuary laws were strict and restrictive, dictating what clothing one could wear based on one's status and place in the hierarchy. Audrey Horning (2014:300–302) documents these constraints in Ireland and the numerous ways people worked around them. Elites assumed that clothing illustrated established cultural meanings, but the secondhand trade of clothing allowed lower-caste people to "code switch" and appropriate a higher status. In doing so, some lower-caste individuals were able to create a new place for themselves in their respective social landscapes; this is thus an example of place making in the social sense. In the Andes too, Joanne Pillsbury (2002:78) writes of Spanish encomenderos who adopted the Inka practice of giving fine textiles as gifts to subject *kurakakuna* (indigenous nobles) on their encomiendas. Gifting textiles was, in this case, a manifestation of Spanish colonists incorporating indigenous strategies of binding subject elites to themselves in politically indigenous fashion.

Food also plays an important part in expressing identity in colonial settings. Michael Dietler (2001), for example, argues that food is an important medium during colonialism as it aids in understanding the transformative effects of colonialism in cultural identity. He argues that the adoption of alien foods is primarily through actions of individuals or social groups "located differentially within complex relational fields of power and interest" (Dietler 2007:226). That is, elites, commoners, or other groups within a culture may adopt specific foods that may, through time, be incorporated by other elements of that society. Particular foods may be used to strategically identify social roles. Peaches and other orchard fruits were introduced to the Hopi of northern Arizona by the Spanish and incorporated into Hopi lifeways. Through time, these fruits may have become Hopi rather than Spanish foods. Similarly, the incorporation of Spanish-introduced *churro* sheep into Navajo culture over time reinforced Navajo, not Spanish, identity. These sheep infused a number of activities, from food (including highly regarded mutton stew) to weaving and trade. In colonial contexts, food can be a medium of solidarity or differentiation within a group. DeCorse (Chapter 1) discusses the vast incorporation of foreign foods into local West African diets as the result of Portuguese and Spanish colonial introductions.

The examples above use specific elements of material culture, such as food, clothing, and burial goods, to illustrate the intertwined nature of this volume's two themes. Place making in the geographic sense is illustrated by the attachment of culturally specific meaning to a location on the landscape, while place making in the social sense involves the creation or modification of a group's place in a socially or politically diverse setting. In the context of the highly variable and diverse social and geographic landscape of Alta California, groups such as the Gabrielino/Tongva evidenced place making—in both senses—in this pluralistic colonial setting. The degree to which place making and pluralism are intertwined in the chapters that follow illustrates how theoretically powerful these two related concepts are for explaining some of the remarkable variability captured by these case studies of Spanish colonialism.

RECONCEPTUALIZING COLONIALISM'S IMPACTS

This volume's collection of case studies collectively reveals several patterns worth pursuing in future research endeavors. At the start, it is important to recognize that deliberative and strategic expansion efforts by the Spanish had often devastating consequences for the native populations who tangled with them and their multicultural allies. Those entanglements also had surprising and probably unforeseen impacts, too, on indigenous peoples in, for example, material culture (moving beyond discussions of hybridity and syncretic styles). The chapters of this volume illustrate great variability in indigenous and Spanish geographic and social place making in a rapidly changing landscape. In part, this included creative processes of identity formation, such as the introduction and/or manipulation of new ethnic categories and new meanings to old categories; *indios chinos* (Chinese Indians) in the Philippines and the "Spanish" on board Pacific exploration ships offer two enticing examples. Similarly, documented changes in the composition or location of pluralistic communities on indigenous landscapes illustrate place making in spaces that were themselves the sites of deep, pluralistic histories of communities.

Simply labeling these case studies "colonial" obscures the extent of misunderstandings that also shaped people's experiences of them. The ultimately unsuccessful fate of exploratory voyages in the Pacific (Chapter 7), the perseverance of indigenous cultures by a demographically devastated but persistent native population in the Caribbean (Chapter 2), the strength of West African cultures able to fend off European political subjugation for so long (Chapter 1), and creative processes of ethno-genesis in late colonial pockets of unconquered lands in the Americas (Chapter 11) offer key examples that counter a narrative of conquest and political subjugation by Europeans. And they beg the question of how much of that Spanish expansion around the globe was accidental or un-successful, leaving some areas even relatively untouched.

There are, at the same time, tentative observations that we can offer to debates in the archaeology of colonialism because of the great geographic variability captured in this volume. Here we seek to try to explain some of this variability in patterned ways that may also be applicable to other case studies of prehistoric and historic colonialism. First, we hypothesize that the intensity of contact within and between communities on the colonial landscape changed the nature of the incorporation of foreign goods and ideas. In contexts of increased frequency and intensity of interaction, such as in Spanish towns, missions, cabeceras, and so forth, we might expect to see less hybridity or syncretism in material culture because of the greater oversight potentially exercised by agents of the colonial power. For ex-ample, living just 200 m from a church likely meant that Majaltepec residents buried community members with beads and indigenous grave goods under house floors in secret (Chapter 4). On the other hand, less intense or frequent intercultural contact likely meant that foreign goods were incorporated into indigenous daily practices and worldviews in ways that included greater meaning making among indigenous peoples for themselves. In this continuum, a glass bead in a native burial is not just an object that does not belong, a chronological marker, and evidence of cultural incorporation into the colonial world. The full context is required to better understand what that hypothetical bead meant to the individual who wore it, the community that interred it with the deceased, the con-texts for its display, the value attached to it, and so on.

Second, the practices and processes of place making in colonial con-texts varied too, depending in part on the degree and direction of socio-political control of the physical and social landscape. We see examples of Spanish places in indigenous landscapes and Spanish identity cate-gories in indigenous social landscapes as much as we see examples of indigenous place making in the physical and social landscapes that the Spanish sought to remake for their own ends. These efforts at colonial place making were rarely effective replacements for pre-contact ones; as many chapters in this book (Chapters 2, 4, 5, 10, and 11) show, indigenous groups carved out or defended their own places within complex, multi-ethnic social landscapes that were variably impacted by Spanish efforts to transform them. Where colonial agents' control was perhaps greatest were the places, sometimes walled, they occupied most densely, such as missions, specific neighborhoods in Spanish towns, and administrative and church complexes. It does not follow from this, however, that the places outside such pockets of control were similarly transformed into Spanish places, even if colonists renamed them and claimed to own them on large maps. The Treaty of Tordesillas may have granted Spain and Portugal vast territories, but there remained areas well outside the control of both, such as the Dagua River region of Nueva Granada during the late eighteenth century (Chapter 11). Place making in that case was performed by people brought forcibly from West and Central Africa in a multiethnic landscape offering opportunities the likes of which did not exist in spaces more clearly under colonial domination.

In the end, this book illustrates the vast and varied nature of indigenous cultural persistence within colonies firmly, or perhaps in some cases tenuously, under Spanish rule. Across time and space, we see examples of change of indigenous cultural norms in the face of colonization as functions of preserving these traditions. In some case studies, such as Oaxaca (Chapter 4), the local culture was overrun by other colonial cultures multiple times, yet indigenous culture survived and continued. We see variations of this same theme in the creation of colonial towns (Chapter 5), within the walls of missions (Chapters 9 and 10), and in other types of restricted spaces (Chapters 1, 7, 8, 9, and 11) and other contexts. It is remarkable how in each of these varied parts of the globe, where the Spanish Empire tried so hard to be dominant, indigenous cultures persevered, albeit perhaps not in the same form as they had prior to conquest. That result is part of what Panich (2013) has referred to as the process of becoming.

ORGANIZATION OF THIS VOLUME

As "The Spanish Imperial Project" section indicates, we have elected a chronological organization for the volume. When the participants in the Society for American Archaeology / Amerind Foundation workshop that gave rise to this book gathered in the fall of 2018, it quickly became apparent that place making and cultural pluralism were themes that ran through every chapter. Thus, putting individual case studies under one heading or the other would have created artificial boundaries between groups of chapters that rightfully belonged under both themes. This chronological format instead takes the earlier date of each case study as its marker and uses that date to place the case study within the framework of the book. In this sense, the order of the chapters roughly follows the Spanish colonial enterprise itself as it spread across first one, then a second ocean in its quest for more precious metals, resources, and labor to exploit and souls to convert. Along the way, the colonists grew increasingly diverse themselves, pulling indigenous and nonindigenous individuals alike along to new places. These were the conditions under which previously unknown spaces transformed into meaningful places of colonial entanglements. Additionally, the pluralistic nature of those colonial social landscapes contributed to the unique material, sociopolitical, economic, and ideological histories that unfolded during the centuries of the global Spanish colonial enterprise. The chapters in this book, of course, capture just a small number of examples from seven world regions, but the parallels that run between them teach us much about the nature of place making and pluralism in that important period of early modern history.

ACKNOWLEDGMENTS

We thank the Amerind Foundation, Christine Szuter, and all the participants of our Amerind Seminar for the opportunity to work side by side on this chapter. The feedback from all of the participants—particularly Laura Matthew, Steve Tomka, and Kevin Lane—was extremely helpful as we revised our chapter. In addition, anonymous peer reviewers offered helpful insight and areas to expand. All told, this chapter, while written by us, is the result of collaboration with all of the seminar participants, for which we are honored and grateful.

REFERENCES

Adams, Paul C., Steven Hoelscher, and Karen E. Till. 2001. "Place in Context: Rethinking Humanist Geographies." In *Textures of Place: Exploring Humanist Geographies*, edited by Paul C. Adams, Steven Hoelscher, and Karen E. Till, xiii–xxxiii. Minneapolis: University of Minnesota Press.

Agnew, John. 1987. *Place and Politics*. Boston: Allen and Unwin.

Arkush, Brooke S. 2011. "Native Responses to European Intrusion: Cultural Persistence and Agency among Mission Neophytes in Spanish Colonial Northern California." *Historical Archaeology* 45(4): 62–90.

Bayman, James M., and John A. Peterson. 2016. "Spanish Colonial History and Archaeology in the Mariana Islands: Echoes from the Western Pacific." In *Archaeologies of Early Modern Spanish Colonialism*, edited by Sandra Montón-Subías, María Cruz Berrocal, and Apen Ruiz Martínez, 229–252. New York: Springer.

Beaule, Christine D. 2017a. "Challenging the Frontiers of Colonialism." In *Frontiers of Colonialism*, edited by Christine D. Beaule, 1–26. Gainesville: University Press of Florida.

———. 2017b. "Images of Evangelization and Archipelagos of Spanish Colonialism in Latin America and the Philippines." In *Frontiers of Colonialism*, edited by Christine D. Beaule, 325–356. Gainesville: University Press of Florida.

Berger, Stefan, and Chris Lorenz, eds. 2008. *The Contested Nation: Ethnicity, Class, Religion and Gender in National Histories*. London: Palgrave Macmillan.

Casella, Eleanor Conlin, and Chris Fowler. 2005. "Beyond Identification: An Introduction." In *The Archaeology of Plural and Changing Identities: Beyond Identification*, edited by Eleanor Conlin Cosella and Chris Fowler, 1–8. New York: Springer.

Chia, Lucille. 2006. "The Butcher, the Baker, and the Carpenter: Chinese Sojourners in the Spanish Philippines and Their Impact on Southern Fujian (Sixteenth–Eighteenth Centuries)." *Journal of the Economic and Social History of the Orient* 49(4): 509–534.

Cipolla, Craig N. 2013. "Native American Historical Archaeology and the Trope of Authenticity." *Historical Archaeology* 47(3): 12–22.

———. 2015. "Native American Diaspora and Ethnogenesis." *Oxford Handbooks Online*. January 2017. DOI: 10.1093/oxfordhb/9780199935413.013.69. Accessed February 25, 2018.

Cresswell, Tim. 2001. "Making up the Tramp: Towards a Critical Geosophy." In *Textures of Place: Exploring Humanist Geographies*, edited by Paul C. Adams, Steven Hoelscher, and Karen E. Till, 167–185. Minneapolis: University of Minnesota Press.

———. 2004. *Place: A Short Introduction*. Malden, Mass.: Blackwell Publishing.

Dietler, Michael. 2001. "Theorizing the Feast." In *Feasts: Archaeological and Ethnographic Perspectives on Food, Politics, and Power*, edited by Michael Dietler and Brian Hayden, 65–114. Washington, D.C.: Smithsonian Institution Press.

———. 2007. "Culinary Encounters: Food, Identity, and Colonialism." In *The Archaeology of Food and Identity*, edited by Katheryn C. Twiss, 218–242. Carbondale: Center for Archaeological Investigations, Southern Illinois University.

Douglass, John G., and William M. Graves, eds. 2017. "New Mexico and the Pimería Alta: A Brief Introduction to the Colonial Period in the American

Southwest." In *New Mexico and the Pimería Alta: The Colonial Period in the American Southwest*, edited by John G. Douglass and William M. Graves, 3–48. Boulder: University Press of Colorado.

Douglass, John G., Kathleen L. Hull, and Seetha N. Reddy. 2018. "The Creation of Community in the Colonial-Era Los Angeles Basin." In *The Forging of Communities in Colonial Alta California, 1769–1834*, edited by Kathleen L. Hull and John G. Douglass, 35–61. Tucson: University of Arizona Press.

Douglass, John G., and Seetha N. Reddy. 2016. "Cultural Trajectories and Ethnogenesis during Colonialism: The Mission Period in Southern California." In *Gabrielino/Tongva Origins and Development: A View from Guaspet*, edited by John G. Douglass, Seetha N. Reddy, Richard Ciolek-Torrello, and Donn R. Grenda, 353–384. Vol. 5 of *People in a Changing Land: The Archaeology and History of the Ballona in Los Angeles, California*, edited by Donn R. Grenda, Richard Ciolek-Torrello, and Jeffrey H. Altschul. Tucson: Statistical Research.

Douglass, John G., Seetha N. Reddy, Richard Ciolek-Torrello, and Donn R. Grenda, eds. 2016. *Gabrielino/Tongva Origins and Development: A View from Guaspet*. Vol. 5 of *People in a Changing Land: The Archaeology and History of the Ballona in Los Angeles, California*, edited by Donn R. Grenda, Richard Ciolek-Torrello, and Jeffrey H. Altschul. Tucson: Statistical Research.

Falk, Lisa, ed. 1991. *Historical Archaeology in Global Perspective*. Washington, D.C.: Smithsonian Institution Press.

Ferris, Neal. 2009. *Native-Lived Colonialism: Challenging History in the Great Lakes*. Tucson: University of Arizona Press.

Flint, Richard. 2009. "Without Them, Nothing Was Possible: The Coronado Expedition's Indian Allies." *New Mexican Historical Review* 84(1): 65–118.

García de los Arcos, María Fernanda. 1996. *Forzados y Reclutas: Las Criollos Novohispanos en Asia (1756–1808)*. Mexico City: Potrerillos Editores.

Gardner, Andrew, Edward Herring, and Kathryn Lomas, eds. 2013. *Creating Ethnicities and Identities in the Roman World*. London: Institute of Classical Studies.

Hackel, Steven W. 1998. "Land, Labor, and Production: The Colonial Economy of Spanish and Mexican California." In *Contested Eden: California before the Gold Rush*, edited by Ramón A. Gutiérrez and Richard J. Orsi, 111–146. Berkeley: University of California Press.

———. 2016. "Glass Beads and the Villagers of Guaspet." In *Gabrielino/Tongva Origins and Development: A View from Guaspet*, edited by John G. Douglass, Seetha N. Reddy, Richard Ciolek-Torrello, and Donn R. Grenda, 417–436. Vol. 5 of *People in a Changing Land: The Archaeology and History of the Ballona in Los Angeles, California*, edited by Donn R. Grenda, Richard Ciolek-Torrello, and Jeffrey H. Altschul. Tucson: Statistical Research.

Haley, Brian D., and Larry R. Wilcoxon. 2005. "How Spaniards Became Chumash and Other Tales of Ethnogenesis." *American Anthropologist* 107(3): 432–445.

Hordes, Stanley. 2005. *To the End of the Earth: A History of the Crypto-Jews of New Mexico.* New York: Columbia University Press.

Horning, Audrey. 2014. "Clothing and Colonialism: The Dungiven Costume and the Fashioning of Early Modern Identities." *Journal of Social Archaeology* 14(3): 296–318.

Hu, Di. 2013. "Approaches to the Archaeology of Ethnogenesis: Past and Emergent Perspectives." *Journal of Archaeological Research* 21:371–402.

Hull, Kathleen L., and John G. Douglass. 2018. "Community Formation and Integration in Colonial Contexts." In *The Forging of Communities in Colonial Alta California*, edited by Kathleen L. Hull and John G. Douglass, 3–32. Archaeology of Indigenous-Colonial Interaction in the Americas series. Tucson: University of Arizona Press.

Jamieson, Ross W. 2005. "Caste in Cuenca: Colonial Identity in the Seventeenth Century Andes." In *The Archaeology of Plural and Changing Identities: Beyond Identification*, edited by Eleanor Conlin Cosella and Chris Fowler, 211–232. New York: Springer.

Johnson, Matthew H. 2012. "Phenomenological Approaches in Landscape Archaeology." *Annual Review of Anthropology* 41:269–284.

Kelsey, Harry. 2016. *The First Circumnavigators: Unsung Heroes in the Age of Discovery.* New Haven, Conn.: Yale University Press.

Lightfoot, Kent G. 2012. "Lost in Transition: A Retrospective." In *Decolonizing Indigenous Histories: Exploring Prehistoric/Colonial Transitions in Archaeology*, edited by Maxine Oland, Siobhan M. Hart, and Liam Frink, 282–298. Tucson: University of Arizona Press.

———. 2015. "Dynamics of Change in Multiethnic Societies: An Archaeological Perspective from Colonial North America." *PNAS* 112(30): 9216–9223.

Lyons, Claire L., and John K. Papadopolous, eds. 2002. *The Archaeology of Colonialism.* Los Angeles: Getty Institute.

Mason, William M. 1998. *The Census of 1790: A Demographic History of Colonial California.* Menlo Park, Calif.: Ballena Press.

Matthew, Laura E. 2007. "Whose Conquest? Nahua, Zapoteca, and Mixteca Allies in the Conquest of Central America." In *Indian Conquistadors: Indigenous Allies in the Conquest of Mesoamerica*, edited by Laura E. Matthew and Michel R. Oudijk, 102–126. Norman: University of Oklahoma Press.

———. 2012. *Memories of Conquest: Becoming Mexicano in Colonial Guatemala.* Chapel Hill: University of North Carolina Press.

———. 2015. "Facing East from the South: Indigenous Americans in the Mostly Iberian Atlantic World." In *The Atlantic World*, edited by D'Maris Coffman, Adrian Leonard, and William O'Reilly, 79–99. New York: Routledge.

Mehl, Eva Maria. 2014. "Mexican Recruits and Vagrants in Late Eighteenth-Century Philippines: Empire, Social Order, and Bourbon Reforms in the Spanish Pacific World." *Hispanic American Historical Review* 94(4): 547–579.

Newell, Quincy D. 2009. *Constructing Lives at Mission San Francisco: Native Californians and Hispanic Colonists, 1776–1821*. Albuquerque: University of New Mexico Press.

Ostendorf, Berndt. 2003. "Is the United States Europe's Other? Is Europe the United States' Other? Yes and No." *American Ethnologist* 30(4): 493–494.

Panich, Lee M. 2013. "Archaeologies of Persistence: Reconsidering the Legacies of Colonialism in Native North America." *American Antiquity* 78:105–122.

Pillsbury, Joanne. 2002. "Inka Unku: Strategy and Design in Colonial Peru." *Cleveland Studies in the History of Art* 7:68–103.

Reddy, Seetha N., and John G. Douglass. 2018. "Native Californian Persistence and Transformation in the Colonial Los Angeles Basin, Southern California." *Journal of California and Great Basin Anthropology* 38(2): 235–259.

Restall, Matthew, and Florine Asselbergs. 2007. *Invading Guatemala: Spanish, Nahua, and Maya Accounts of the Conquest Wars*. University Park: Pennsylvania State University Press.

Rodriguez-Alegria, Enrique. 2016. "The Material Worlds of Colonizers in New Spain." In *Archaeologies of Early Modern Spanish Colonialism*, edited by Sandra Monton-Subias, Maria Cruz Berrocal, and Apen Ruiz Martinez, 39–59. Geneva: Springer International Publishing.

Rubertone, Patricia E., ed. 2009. *Archaeologies of Placemaking: Monuments, Memories, and Engagement in Native North America*. San Jose, Calif.: Left Coast Press.

———. 2012. "Archaeologies of Colonialism in Unexpected Times and Unexpected Places." In *Decolonizing Indigenous Histories: Exploring Prehistoric/Colonial Transitions in Archaeology*, edited by Maxine Oland, Siobhan M. Hart, and Liam Frink, 267–281. Tucson: University of Arizona Press.

Russell, Lynette. 2005. "'Either, or, Neither Nor': Resisting the Production of Gender, Race, and Class Dichotomies in the Pre-Colonial Period." In *The Archaeology of Plural and Changing Identities: Beyond Identification*, edited by Eleanor Conlin Cosella and Chris Fowler, 33–51. New York: Springer.

Schlanger, Sarah H. 1992. "Recognizing Persistent Places in Anasazi Settlement Systems." In *Space, Time, and Archaeological Landscapes: Interdisciplinary Contributions to Archaeology*, edited by Jacqueline Rossignol and LuAnn Wandsnider, 91–112. Boston: Springer.

Schwaller, Robert C. 2010. "Defining Difference in Early New Spain." PhD diss., Pennsylvania State University.

———. 2011. "Forging Mexican Families in the Sixteenth Century." Paper presented at the Annual Meeting of the American Society of Ethnohistory, Pasadena, California.

Seijas, Tatiana. 2014. *Asian Slaves in Colonial Mexico: From Chinos to Indians*. New York: Cambridge University Press.

Senatore, Maria Ximena, and Pedro Paolo A. Funari. 2015. "Introduction: Disrupting the Grand Narrative of Spanish and Portuguese Colonialism." In

Archaeology of Culture Contact and Colonialism in Spanish and Portuguese America, edited by Pedro Paolo A. Funari and Maria Ximena Senatore, 1–15. New York: Springer.

Silliman, Stephen W. 2005. "Culture Contact or Colonialism: Challenges in the Archaeology of Native North America." *American Antiquity* 70(1): 55–74.

———. 2009. "Change and Continuity, Practice and Memory: Native American Persistence in Colonial New England." *American Antiquity* 74(2): 211–230.

———. 2012. "Between the Longue Durée and the Short Purée: Postcolonial Archaeologies of Indigenous History in Colonial North America." In *Decolonizing Indigenous Histories: Exploring Prehistoric/Colonial Transitions in Archaeology*, edited by Maxine Oland, Siobhan M. Hart, and Liam Frink, 113–131. Tucson: University of Arizona Press.

Slack, Edward R., Jr. 2009. "The Chinos in New Spain: A Corrective Lens for a Distorted Image." *Journal of World History* 20(1): 35–67.

Stein, Gil J. 2005. "Introduction: The Comparative Archaeology of Colonial Encounters." In *The Archaeology of Colonial Encounters: Comparative Perspectives*, edited by Gil J. Stein, 3–32. Santa Fe, N.M.: School of American Research.

Stoll, Anne Q., John G. Douglass, and Richard Ciolek-Torello. 2016. "The Early Historical Period in the Ballona." In *Gabrielino/Tongva Origins and Development: A View from Guaspet*, edited by John G. Douglass, Seetha N. Reddy, Richard Ciolek-Torrello, and Donn R. Grenda, 385–416. Vol. 5 of *People in a Changing Land: The Archaeology and History of the Ballona in Los Angeles, California*, edited by Donn R. Grenda, Richard Ciolek-Torrello, and Jeffrey H. Altschul. Tucson: Statistical Research.

Tremml, Birgit M. 2012. "The Global and the Local: Problematic Dynamics of the Triangular Trade in Early Modern Manila." *Journal of World History* 23(3): 555–586.

Van Buren, Mary. 2010. "The Archaeological Study of Spanish Colonialism in the Americas." *Journal of Archaeological Research* 18:151–201.

Voss, Barbara L. 2005. "From *Casta* to *Californio*: Social Identity and the Archaeology of Culture Contact." *American Anthropologist* 107(3): 461–474.

———. 2008a. *The Archaeology of Ethnogenesis: Race and Sexuality in Colonial San Francisco*. Berkeley: University of California Press.

———. 2008b. "'Poor People in Silk Shirts': Dress and Ethnogenesis in Spanish-Colonial San Francisco." *Journal of Social Archaeology* 8(3): 404–432.

———. 2015. "What's New? Rethinking Ethnogenesis in the Archaeology of Colonialism." *American Antiquity* 80(4): 655–670.

Weik, T. M. 2014. "The Archaeology of Ethnogenesis." *Annual Review of Anthropology* 43:291–305.

1

Contact, Colonialism, and the Fragments of Empire

Portugal, Spain, and the Iberian Moment in West Africa

Christopher R. DeCorse

This chapter examines early Iberian contacts, cultural intersections, and imperial aspirations in West Africa, with particular focus on the period of initial African-European encounters between the mid-fifteenth and the seventeenth centuries. Iberian expansion is placed within the wider sociopolitical landscape of which it was a part. Yet while inescapably nested in an increasingly Eurocentric global economy and nationalist agendas, the intersections of Spain and Portugal with the non-Western world were characterized more by variability than by unitary sociocultural, economic, and political templates. Portugal maintained African colonies longer than most European powers, only granting independence to Cabo Verde, Guinea-Bissau, Angola, Mozambique, and São Tomé and Príncipe in the mid-1970s, and these countries evince an array of enduring Portuguese linguistic, social, and cultural influences. Yet these regions only represent a subset of early Portuguese intersections with Africa at the nascence of the Atlantic world. In many instances, Portugal's primary role in initial African-European entanglements in a trading network that spanned the entirety of the West African coast has been largely overwritten by the commercial dealings, sociocultural exchanges, and colonial imbroglios of other European powers, as well as the emergence of postcolonial African states. Drawing on archaeological and historical data, this chapter considers the varied African-European interactions that unfolded, Portugal's ultimate failure to retain many of its imperial outposts in West Africa, and the materialities of these encounters. I begin by reviewing early Iberian expansion and the varied nature of African-European interactions. I then review archaeological work undertaken at Elmina, Ghana, and the archaeological perception of these entanglements.

ATLANTIC CONTOURS AND NATIONAL HISTORIES

It is remarkable how quickly the contours of the modern world were defined. The era of European expansion between the mid-fifteenth and early seventeenth centuries was indeed the Iberian moment. In this Iberian world, the treaties of Alcáçovas and Tordesillas and the related papal bulls divided newly discovered lands into Spanish and Portuguese zones of influence that delineated trading rights and laid the foundation for future colonial claims. Iberian expansion framed the contours of the early modern world, witnessing the extension of Spanish dominion throughout much of the Americas and the establishment of Spanish and Portuguese outposts, trading enclaves, and colonies across Africa, Asia, Brazil, and the Atlantic islands. Yet this Iberian world was not uniform in its imperial policies and colonial projects. Although Portugal and Spain share centuries of culture history, religion, and governance and were united under the Iberian Union between 1580 and 1640, the policies enacted and the cultural intersections that unfolded were distinct. During the Iberian Union, the Habsburg monarchy ruled kingdoms that remained largely independent administratively (Elliot 2002:249–284; Goodman 2015:202–203; Oliveira Marques 1972:295–322; Valladares Ramírez 2000:14–35). While substantial administrative reforms were undertaken during this period, the management of the outposts of Cabo Verde, São Tomé, Príncipe, and the Guinea coast remained to all effects Portuguese.[1]

Iberian maritime expansion in the fifteenth century was the nascence of the Atlantic system. Islamic North Africa was considered both a threat and an economic opportunity, and the last energies of the Reconquista were diverted there. Portuguese fortified trading settlements were established in Ceuta in 1415, Qsares Seghir in 1458, and Tangiers in 1471, while Castile captured Melilla in 1497 (Newitt 2005; Oliveira Marques 1972; Payne 1973; Redman 1986; Russel-Wood 1998). In the course of the fifteenth century, the Canary Islands were colonized by Spain, and the Azores and Madeira were claimed by Portugal. Beginning in the second half of the fifteenth century, Portuguese traders sailed southward along the West African coast, hoping to bypass the Muslim monopoly of the trans-Saharan trade (Map 1.1).[2] The Portuguese settlement of Ribeira Grande on Cabo Verde was established in 1462. The coast of Central Africa was explored in the 1480s, Bartolomeu Dias rounded the Cape

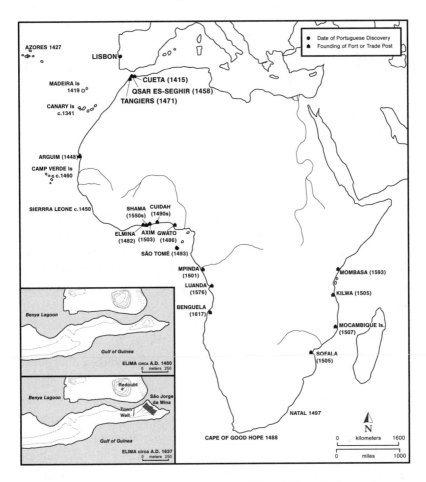

Map 1.1 Map of early Iberian expansion in West Africa; the inset plans show Elmina Castle and town in coastal Ghana ca. 1480 and 1637.

of Good Hope in 1488, western India was reached in 1498, and contact with Asia was established in the first decades of the sixteenth century. A century of consolidation and attempt at monopoly followed. These early zones of Iberian influence would be redrawn again and again, overshadowed by the designs of other European powers. However, the margins of an increasingly Eurocentric maritime world had been sketched (Braudel 1972; Wallerstein 1974).

Within decades of their arrival, Portuguese and Luso-African traders were living on the West African coast, and watering stations, lodges, and trading enclaves had been established (Brooks 2003:49–63; Green 2012:84–94; Hawthorne 2003:55–62). The contact settings represented in the early Portuguese-African intersections contrast with many of the better-known Spanish colonial projects in the Americas (Jerónimo 2018; cf. Funari and Senatori 2015; Montón-Subías et al. 2016). Many of the Portuguese-indigene encounters in continental West Africa between the mid-fifteenth and the mid-seventeenth centuries were more akin to the marginal zones and outliers of Spanish colonialism, such as the brief Basque settlements on the Canadian coast (Escribano-Ruiz and Azkarate 2015), the Spanish enclaves of Patagonia (Senatore 2015), and Spain's fleeting territorial forays in the Solomon Islands (Gibbs 2017). These endeavors were, however, equally distinct in their temporalities, objectives, and ramifications. Early Portuguese-African intersections were both foundational to the opening of the cultural intersections of the early modern world and central to the shaping socioeconomic templates that would characterize the Atlantic trade (Brooks 2003:59–63; Wheat 2016:20–67). Particularly important was the Portuguese settlement of Cabo Verde in the late fifteenth century. The Portuguese and Luso-African traders of Cabo Verde played a primary role in the initial development of European-African trade relations, while the islands' plantations, reliant on enslaved African labor, provided precedence for the later colonial projects and plantation economies of the Americas (Hawthorne 2010; Wheat 2010, 2016:104–108). Yet this insular colony, unsettled prior to the arrival of the Portuguese, contrasts dramatically with the cultural encounters on the African mainland, where European settlement was limited and European activities were circumscribed by African polities and African cultural norms.[3]

In continental West Africa, the earliest and most sustained areas of European interactions were the Portuguese trading enclaves in the Senegambia and the areas of the Upper Guinea coast to the south, areas that were already being exploited as sources of slaves for the Mediterranean and Cabo Verde before 1500 (Green 2012:88–105). These same areas were also the sites of early *lançado* settlements. The *lançados* were Caboverdians of mixed ancestry who had "thrown themselves into" African society and out of the "European orbit" (Brooks 2003:27; Green 2012:115). Notably, and in contrast to the Portuguese settlements of Cabo Verde, to a large degree these settlers operated in defiance of official sanction and to the frustration of the Crown. The Senegambia was also one of the few areas in West Africa where the Portuguese penetrated beyond the coastal zone. Several attempts were made to establish outposts in the interior, notably in Wolof territory near the mouth of the Senegal River and at Wadan and Bambuk (Wood 1967). Smaller factories and watering stations were established in Sierra Leone.

The other major focus of early Portuguese interest in continental West Africa was the region demarcated by Assine in Côte d'Ivoire and Keta in modern-day Ghana, which was the major source of African gold. This region became known as Mina, or the Mine, and in later historical sources as the Gold Coast. Portuguese ships were certainly trading at the mouth of the Pra River in modern Ghana by 1471, but visits occurred earlier (Pereira 1967:118; cf. Cortesão and Teixeira da Mota 1960:xxxi; Hair 1994:4–5). It was the potential of the gold trade that led to the founding of the Castelo São Jorge da Mina in 1482. Today known as Elmina Castle, the fort was positioned near an existing African settlement to take advantage of the trade. This was the first European fort established south of the Sahara. The Portuguese established smaller forts in Ghana at Axim in 1503 and Shama in 1526, both of which had likely been foci of trade since the fifteenth century. Smaller outposts were also established in modern-day Accra, Ghana, as well as in Benin and coastal Nigeria (Blake 1977:100–105; DeCorse 2010; Mattoso 2010:345–355; Newitt 2010).

By the middle of the sixteenth century, West Africa was part of an interconnected Iberian world. The Portuguese were maintaining an active trade along the entire West African coast and beyond, often trading goods obtained on different portions of the coast. Cotton from Senegal and iron from Sierra Leone were purchased for trade elsewhere in West Africa, and caravels brought slaves from the Bight of Benin for sale to African merchants at Elmina (Brooks 2003:75; Chouin and Lasisi 2019; Rodney 1969). Between 1485 and 1500, the Portuguese Crown also encouraged the settlement of the uninhabited island of São Tomé in the Gulf of Guinea through the granting of special trading concessions on the mainland (Blake 1977:95). The plantations on São Tomé and Príncipe were reliant on enslaved labor, and they played an important role in Portugal's engagement in West Africa down to the independence era.

The models of cultural interactions that evolved and the use of enslaved labor in West Africa subsequently provided precedent for Iberian interactions in the Americas. Christopher Columbus visited São Jorge da Mina shortly after its founding—a decade prior to his voyages of discovery—and he may well have reflected on this Portuguese fort on the African coast when he established similar outposts in the Americas (Hair 1990). The Portuguese emporia and traders of West Africa subsequently provided the primary source of enslaved Africans for the emerging Spanish colonies in the Americas. Indeed, Luso-Africans and African slaves played a major role in shaping the early Spanish colonial societies of the Americas (Wheat 2010, 2016).

With outposts, military force, and legal sanctions, Portugal attempted to maintain a monopoly on European trade in Guinea. Papal decrees were invoked to support the primacy of Portugal's claims during the war with Castile between 1474 and 1478. Spain, however, continued to make periodic efforts to infringe on Portuguese territories, including attempts to seize Cabo Verde in the 1470s (Green 2012:99–100). There were Castilian voyages to West Africa during the sixteenth and seventeenth centuries, and, when possible, the ships were captured or driven off (Hair 1994:2–5, 49–50; Newitt 2005:36–38; Vogt 1979:10–18). Political pressure from Lisbon also successfully halted preparations for both French and English voyages to Guinea (Blake 1977:60–62, 108–109). Nonetheless, the voyages of other European nations became increasingly common, and by the beginning of the sixteenth century, the trade of these interlopers surpassed that of the Portuguese. By the mid-sixteenth century, profits from Elmina were often insufficient to cover the cost of maintaining the small garrison (Ballong-Wen-Mewuda 1993; Blake 1967:49–51; Rodney 1965; Vogt 1979:170–193). In the opening years of the Iberian Union, Elmina Castle was refurbished, its defenses were modernized, yearly supply ships were sent, and the bureaucracy of the Mina trade was streamlined. However, São Jorge da Mina remained more of a liability than an asset (De Marees 1987:212–217, 221; Vogt 1979:114, 127–169). Spain's economic and political troubles at home during the last decades of the Iberian Union likely further weakened Portugal's ability to maintain control of the West African trade.

The intensity of the competition on the coast is seen in the proliferation of French, English, Brandenburger, Dutch, Swedish, and Danish forts in coastal Ghana, the region where competition was most intense (DeCorse 2001:22–28, 2010). The Dutch established a small fort at Mori, just ten miles east of Elmina, in 1612. The Dutch succeeded in capturing Elmina in August 1637, largely owing to the support lent by the African states of Kommenda and Asebu and to the incapacitated state of the Portuguese garrison (Vogt 1979:189–190). The castle subsequently remained Dutch for the next 235 years, replacing Fort Nassau at Mori as the Dutch headquarters in Guinea. The Portuguese were unable to maintain a trade post in coastal Ghana after their loss of Fort São Antonio at Axim in 1642 and their brief occupation of Christiansborg, Osu (1679–1682). However, Portugal continued an active ship trade on the coast, particularly in tobacco and slaves, through the nineteenth century (Hawthorne 2010; Vogt 1979:194–204).

AFRICAN-PORTUGUESE ENTANGLEMENTS

The Portuguese trade of the fifteenth and sixteenth centuries delineated many of the foci, margins, and systems of exchange that would characterize African-European exchange in the succeeding centuries. Yet in many respects, frustratingly little is known about fifteenth-century African customs and the nature of initial African-Portuguese interactions (see discussions in Brooks 1993:38–44; Green 2012:52–68, 70–77, 151–155; Hair 1994:13–14; Ipsen 2015:7–12; Newitt 2005:1–2). This observation is somewhat truer for the Lower Guinea coast than the Upper, George Brooks (2003) and Toby Green (2012) having provided a rich review of early African-European interactions for the latter. However, here it should be noted that some of the observations are derived from later seventeenth-, eighteenth-, and nineteenth-century sources. Aside from the locations of the principal areas of early Portuguese trade, specific details regarding the first decades of contact are left largely undescribed in contemporary accounts. While it is likely that the Portuguese traders visited much of the coast and that interactions with the African coastal polities must have been relatively common, the nature of the sociocultural intersections that unfolded is dimly perceived. Many smaller Portuguese factories, outposts, and trading sites are poorly described, and some have perhaps been left unmentioned in documentary sources. The ravages of time have largely erased them from the landscape (DeCorse 2010; DeCorse et al. 2010; Wood 1967). In many instances, no outposts were established, and trade was conducted directly from ships.

What was likely true from the onset of the first cross-cultural meetings—as it was in later centuries—is that African polities and cultural norms circumscribed Portuguese interests. Although some writers have referred to Portuguese "rule" (and European "settlement") in West Africa during the sixteenth and seventeenth centuries, these were trading enclaves, and the small European population on the coast exerted limited authority over the African populations with whom they interacted. Prior to the nineteenth century, the total number of Portuguese living on the coast from Mauritania to Angola never numbered more than a few hundred.[4] The high death rate among Europeans arriving on the African coast also limited settlement. The Portuguese and other Europeans who established outposts in Guinea were dependent on the African communities in which they were located for both provisioning and the maintenance of trade. They were at least partly subject to centuries-old African customs of exchange and reciprocity regarding the dealings of hosts and strangers. African-European interactions of the fifteenth through the eighteenth centuries can be contrasted with those that marked the onset of colonial rule in the late nineteenth century, which was characterized by much more overt European involvement in African affairs.

There are notable material traces of Portuguese cultural influences in West Africa. The Luso-African settlements at Albreda and Juffure on the Gambia River, which have been investigated archaeologically, hint at the African-Portuguese trade (Gijanto 2017:40–54). More striking is the distinctive Afro-Portuguese architecture of the Senegambia and coastal Benin (Mark 1996, 2002; Mattoso 2010). Distinctive dress, art, and architecture inscribed Luso-African identity from the first decades of settlement. However, the archaeological and architectural traces noted largely date long after the earliest period of Iberian expansion and also represent a relatively limited portion of Portuguese interests during the fifteenth and sixteenth centuries. Both Portugal and Spain would later establish colonies in continental Africa that were maintained through much of the twentieth century.[5] However, these colonial projects were quite different from those of the first centuries of Iberian expansion.

Insight into the nature of African-Portuguese interactions is provided by historical and archaeological studies of Elmina, Ghana (Ballong-Wen-Mewuda 1984, 1993; DeCorse 2001; Hair 1994; Lawrence 1963:103–130; Vogt 1979). Elmina Castle and the associated African settlement have been architecturally, historically, and archaeologically examined more thoroughly than any other early Portuguese site in West Africa. Following its founding in 1482, the castle was substantially expanded, and by the time of the Dutch capture in 1637, the fortress had largely reached its current configuration. The castle is well preserved today, and the defensive ditches, brick arches, and other architectural features dating to the Portuguese period are readily discernible.

Documentary accounts and archaeological data indicate that the original African settlement at Elmina extended along the peninsula west of the castle. It was referred to as the Aldea das Duas Partes (Village of Two Parts). This toponym likely refers to the separation of the settlement into two sections, one portion concentrated at the end of the peninsula, the other located on the landward side to the west, the two areas separated by a low saddle and depression (Map 1.1; DeCorse 2001:47–49, 2008). This division would have been striking when viewed from the sea. Although Elmina was considered to be of "considerable" size when the Portuguese arrived, the population probably only numbered a few hundred (DeCorse 2008; Vogt 1979:184). In contrast, the initial Portuguese garrison consisted of 60 soldiers, merchants, and administrators. At the time of the Dutch takeover in 1637 the Portuguese garrison consisted of 35 men, and it had often numbered even less.

A portion of the African settlement and sacred rocks at the end of the Elmina peninsula were destroyed during the castle's construction. João de Barros recounts that when the quarrymen started work on the foundations, "the blacks, seeing such destruction wrought on their sacred rocks, grieved, in as much as they saw all hope of their salvation being crushed, and, inflamed they all in great fury seized their weapons and so struck hard at the workmen" (Hair 1994:32). The Africans were subsequently appeased with gifts, and construction continued. The Portuguese accounts only hint at the conflicts and cultural missteps that undoubtedly occurred. While it is possible that the Portuguese intentionally selected the castle's site to overwrite African sacred space, it is more likely that the location was chosen for its defensive advantages and that the Portuguese were unaware of its religious significance. Sacred spaces of the Akan include natural features—rocks, streams, trees—that are largely unmarked and have only subtle indicators of their presence. Consequently, they were often unrecognized by arriving Europeans. Appeasement of the desecration through the payment of gifts is also consistent with Akan cultural practices (DeCorse 2001:181). Regardless of intentions, however, African space was made Portuguese; following the construction of Castelo de São Jorge da Mina, the African settlement concentrated in front of the castle's walls. The castle afforded a place of refuge for the town's people, as during the Dutch attack of 1606, when the women and children of the village, along with their livestock, were brought into the castle (Vogt 1979:156, 191). In time, perhaps by the middle of the sixteenth century, the Portuguese constructed a wall across the peninsula to further protect the settlement (DeCorse 2001:51).

The Portuguese both provided economic opportunity and stimulated the formation of new identities. At the time of contact, the Akan people of the Elmina settlement were likely ruled by the neighboring Eguafo state (DeCorse 2008; Hair 1994:55–56n37). However, by the first decades of the sixteenth century, the settlement was asserting its independence from the neighboring polities, and the interdependent relations that would characterize African-European interactions for the next 350 years were emerging (DeCorse 2001:38–43; Hair 1994:38–41; Vogt 1979:85–86, 124–125, 155–157, 180–182). As early as 1514, the Elmina people were acting together with the Portuguese in military engagements. Elmina warriors staffed the castle's walls and together with the Portuguese formed an effective military force. The Portuguese and other Europeans fostered rivalries between African polities and used these struggles to their advantage, a point illustrated by the role of the African state of Asebu in the successful Dutch capture of Elmina in 1637. The Portuguese reportedly brought people from Elmina to other settlements on the coast to maintain their trading interests (Feinberg 1969:24). The Portuguese were, nevertheless, tenants on the land, and they paid an annual ground rent to occupy the castle. With few exceptions, they exerted limited authority over the African settlement and adjacent hinterlands and ultimately failed in their efforts to limit African trade with other European powers. They remained dependent on the associated African community for provisioning, the landing and transport of goods, and the maintenance of trade relations with the African hinterland.

Elmina of the sixteenth and early seventeenth centuries was a place of cultural exchange and entanglement. New identities undoubtedly arose as a population of emerging African elites played an increasing role in negotiating trade and a merchant class emerged. In time, the Elmina people came to see themselves as "Elminan," distinct from the neighboring Akan population. However, Elmina seems to have remained an African town throughout the Portuguese period; it was "African" in the sense of its sociocultural and political organization, as well as its materiality. To the extent that it can be discerned, political authority within the town seems to have followed practices comparable to those of other coastal Akan towns. Portuguese sources say relatively little about the organization of early Elmina, and it is only much later in the eighteenth century that references to a single ruler (Ɔmanhen) appear, a fact that may suggest both continued subservience to the Eguafo state and Portuguese dominion (DeCorse 2001:39–43, 2008).

The Portuguese attempted to restrict the degree of interaction between the garrison and the Elmina people, particularly with regard to trade.[6] Such strictures may have limited some aspects of African-European interactions. However, given the Europeans' dependence on the local population for food and other provisions, as well as defense, it is unlikely the garrison was isolated from the town. There was no distinct European quarter, but it is possible that the average Portuguese soldier ate and lived within the settlement. Pieter de Marees (1987:220), writing in 1602, suggests that during the sixteenth century most of the members of the Portuguese garrison stayed in the town and only went to the castle to perform their duties.[7] Socioeconomic status, more than sociocultural standing, may have been more important in terms of the settlement organization. African merchants and wealthier elites lived closer to the castle, and servants and slaves may have lived and worked in the houses along with the owners. This was the case during the eighteenth and nineteenth centuries (DeCorse 2001:89–100).

A significant feature of the early Portuguese garrison at Elmina, as well as other West African fort communities, was the small number of European women (Chouin and DeCorse 2018; Hair 1994:36, 91; Vogt 1979:182). Following the founding of the castle, only three women remained with the original Portuguese garrison, and there is no evidence that Portuguese men brought European wives with them. A *regimento*, or set of regulations, set down for Elmina in 1529 listed four women who were required to cook, nurse, and, for a set fee, provide sexual services to the men (Hair 1994:36, 91; cf. Ballong-Wen-Mewuda 1984:303–304).

The regulations stipulate that the officers were not to monopolize the women, who were to be available to all members of the garrison. European men primarily relied on African women for domestic and marital relations. European men, often young and single, entered into intimate relationships with African women usually through a type of marriage referred to as *cassare*. The term is derived from the Portuguese word *cassar*, meaning "to cancel," which captures the temporary and contractual nature of a marriage that characteristically lasted only as long as the European partner worked at the emporium.[8] The offspring of these Portuguese men and African women subsequently played key roles in maintaining trade relations.

Although it is difficult to determine their numbers, mulattoes were already recognized as a distinct segment of the population during the sixteenth century, something that also characterizes many Spanish frontier-colonial populations in the Americas (De Marees 1987:36, 217; Vogt 1979:182; cf. Deagan 1983). Mulatto women were reportedly distinguished by their dress (Figure 1.1), which was influenced by European clothing.[9] Writing on the Portuguese mulatto women of Elmina in 1602, De Marees observed: "They maintain these Wives in grand style and keep them in splendid clothes, and they always dress more ostentatiously and stand out more than any other Indigenous women. They can be easily recognized, for they shave the hair on their heads very short, just as do the Men, which is not the habit of the other Women; and they also have far more ornaments on their clothes and all over their bodies, a habit which the other women do not have either" (De Marees 1987:217). The Portuguese mulatto population was of sufficient importance that special permission was obtained for them to accompany the Portuguese garrison to São Tomé following the 1637 surrender to the Dutch. It should, however, be underscored that these individuals made up a relatively small portion of the settlement's population (DeCorse 2008).

The degree to which specifically Portuguese cultural influences arose in this multiethnic setting is unclear. The Europeans' primary interest was economic, and interactions primarily unfolded within this context. Portuguese efforts to Christianize the African population of coastal Ghana met with limited success (DeCorse 2001:175–192). Beginning with the earliest Portuguese visits, there were attempts to convert the local population to Christianity. Indeed, Portuguese expansion into West Africa

Figure 1.1 Illustration from Pieter de Marees in 1602 depicting the appearance of women on the Gold Coast. The figure at the right (A) is described as "a Portuguese woman living in the Castle d'Mina, half black, half white and yellowish: such women are called *Melato* and most [Portuguese men] keep them as wives, because white women do not thrive much there. They dress very nicely and hang many Paternoster and other Beads on their bodies. They cut their hair very short, like the men, thinking that it becomes them." The other figures illustrate "Peasant Wives" who come to the coastal town from the interior (B); young girls nicely dressed in cloth and bracelets (C); and a "common woman," her body "scarred with cuts and her face smeared with paint" (D) (De Marees 1987:36, from De Marees 1602:Plate 3, reproduced courtesy of Leiden University Libraries).

was sanctioned by papal decrees, and the Crown identified their Elmina "vassals"—the townspeople—as Christian (Blake 1967:133; Pereira 1967:120–121; Vogt 1979:185). Priests served at the garrison, and several churches or chapels were built in Elmina, the earliest dating to the founding of the castle (Hair 1994:92–93n201). There were also chapels established in neighboring areas, and sources note the conversion of some Africans, among the most notable being the baptism of the people and chief of Efutu in 1503. Occasional references suggest that the majority of the Elmina population was Christian, but these were exaggerations. For Africans, conversion to Christianity in many instances was likely not viewed as antithetical to the continuation of African religious life. There were isolated instances of Christian converts who recanted their beliefs, were tried by the church, and were imprisoned in Lisbon. John Vogt (1979:55–56) discusses a female Elmina slave named Grace who had received the holy sacraments and been baptized many years before but who was accused of fetish worship. When brought before the priest at Elmina she was unable to say the Ave Maria, and a search of her house revealed a dozen fetish images. She was tried in Lisbon and condemned to "perpetual incarceration in the prison of the Holy Office" (Vogt 1979:56).

The retention of traditional beliefs and the selective acceptance of some aspects of Christianity are commonly referred to in early European descriptions of the Ghanaian coast (DeCorse 2001:179–191; Hair 1994:7–8; Vogt 1979:51–57). Indeed, the continuation of African beliefs and maintenance of religious strictures, often incomprehensible to European viewers, was seen as characteristic. The lack of success in converting the Africans was explained by the African temperament and an innate tendency to return to their traditional beliefs. This situation can be dramatically contrasted with the large number of converts and the more ready acceptance of Christianity in some parts of the West and Central African coasts (Clist et al. 2018; Thornton 2012:397–419).

MATERIALITIES OF ENTANGLEMENT

The early African-Portuguese interactions at Elmina during the fifteenth and sixteenth centuries are arguably iconic of the varied and complex entanglements of the early modern world. Cultural and social interactions were reformed, producing new identities that were "transformative beyond the normal fluctuations and adaptations typical of ethnic identity maintenance" (Voss 2015:658). Reference to their distinctive dress and to the preeminent roles that Luso-Africans played in trade relations is indicative of new practices and new identities. But how ephemeral are the traces of these early formulations? Although Elmina Castle is a monument to coastal Ghana's intersection with the emerging Atlantic world, Portuguese Elmina and the consequences of early African-Portuguese interactions are poorly perceived both historically and archaeologically. Notably, throughout the Portuguese period dwellings within the African settlement continued to be built using traditional African timber and clay construction and within African notions of spatial organization. The stone and multistory building that Elmina would come to be known for only appeared much later, during the Dutch period (DeCorse 2001:89–100).[10] The small Portuguese chapel located within the Elmina settlement seems to have played little role in Elminan life, and it was forgotten, obliterated by later house construction, and only traces remain.

Archaeologically, artifacts of Portuguese origin from the fifteenth to the sixteenth century in West Africa are almost solely represented by finds from Elmina. Despite the expanse of early Portuguese trade documented historically, the majority of this exchange—brasswares, iron, textiles, and slaves—has poor archaeological visibility (DeCorse 2001:145–149). The artifacts associated with the Portuguese garrison were recovered adjacent to the castle from what were likely refuse deposits from the late fifteenth to the early seventeenth century. The material consists almost entirely of imported ceramics, the exceptions being a shard from an etched glass tumbler, occasional pipes of the early seventeenth century, and handfuls of faunal and shellfish remains. The Iberian wares include plates in Iberian faience, as well as fragments of cups, jugs, and bowls in unglazed and lead-glazed earthenwares (Figure 1.2). The assemblage as a whole is a small subset of the wares and forms seen in Portuguese ceramic assemblages from European, Cabo Verdean, and Moroccan contexts from the fifteenth to the seventeenth century. Portuguese ceramics also occur within the African settlement of Elmina beneath seventeenth- and eighteenth-century structures (Figure 1.2). They are comparable to those associated with the Portuguese garrison. However, collectively, these few hundred artifacts represent only a minor percentage of the ceramic inventory, the majority of material being locally produced pottery.

The limited amount of European artifacts speaks to both the archaeological (in)visibility of the European trade and the resilience of African cultural traditions. The meager European trade materials from Elmina and other African sites of the mid-second millennium AD contrast dramatically with those found in later periods. Eighteenth- and nineteenth-century Dutch period contexts within Elmina town are marked by the appearance of a myriad of European ceramics, glass, and other trade

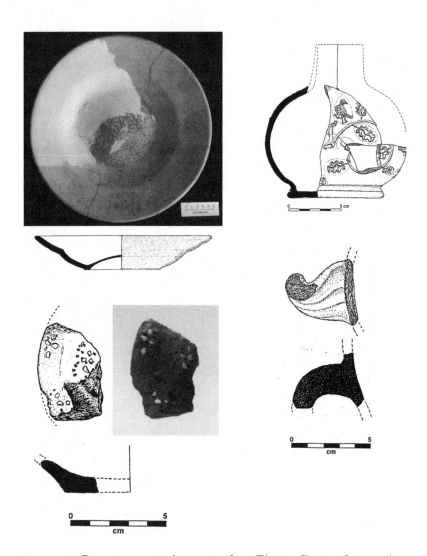

Figure 1.2 Portuguese period ceramics from Elmina: Iberian faience plate and profile (*upper left*); Rhenish stoneware jug ca. 1500–1550 (*upper right*); Portuguese earthenware with quartz inlaid decoration; Iberian redware vessel handle. Photos and illustrations by the author.

materials, as well as dramatic changes in house construction. Yet, even considering these later periods, we can query the degree to which these changes are indicative of sociocultural transformations in African society. The presence of imported trade items alone does not provide de facto markers of cultural transformation and ethnogenesis. As noted, there is substantial documentary evidence that efforts at transforming Elmina belief systems met with limited success. Rather, European ideas, customs, and practices—and their material expressions—were used, adapted, and reinvented locally in ways that were new and likely unenvisaged by Europeans.

CONCLUSION

Two things are striking about early Iberian intersections in West Africa. The first is the centrality of Portugal in early European expansion. The second is the degree to which this opening phase of European hegemony and so many of the cultural encounters that it engendered has been so thoroughly overwritten. This is not to say that Portugal's intersections in Africa are unremembered. In both Africa and Portugal, the end of the colonial era remains a visceral episode, a brutal struggle that ended in the mid-1970s and that was marked by both African independence and the overthrow of Portugal's Second Republic. However, the map of Portuguese colonial enterprises of the late nineteenth and twentieth centuries does not neatly overlie the areas of early Portuguese trade, settlement, and entanglement in Africa between the mid-fifteenth and mid-seventeenth centuries. Although both Portugal and Spain would claim colonies in Africa into the twentieth century, these did not fully reflect the areas of early Portuguese expansion and were quite different in their contours, imperial projects, and results. The scramble for spheres of influence and the colonization of Africa at the end of the nineteenth century took place when economic incentives and technological capabilities converged. This period saw a flood of trade materials mass-produced for the African market, the widespread use of quinine as a malaria prophylactic, European territorial claims, and direct rule. With the colonial partition of Africa in the last decades of the nineteenth century, many of the areas of early Portuguese enterprise in continental West Africa were incorporated into French, British, and German colonies.

There are soupçons of the Portuguese presence across the early margins of Iberian expansion. In portions of West Africa, all Europeans, regardless of nationality, are sometimes referred to as "Portuguese" (*oporto* in Temne), and any premodern structure or ruin is frequently said to be Portuguese regardless of its age or origin. At Elmina, names like "de Costa" can still be found, though the etymology is uncertain. Perhaps the most pervasive and enduring impact of the early Portuguese encounter was the introduction of a variety of American and Asian cultigens of lasting importance in West Africa, including the sweet potato, pineapple, sugarcane, orange, tobacco, and corn (DeCorse 2001:109–115). There is no question that en masse these introductions had tremendous impact on the West African diet, especially corn, which became widespread in areas such as coastal Ghana by the early seventeenth century. Here it should be underscored that the uses of these crops were transformed and shaped to local tastes; *kenke*, *banku*, and *tuo zaafi*, dishes made from fermented cornmeal eaten in Ghana, are unlike their culinary predecessors in the Americas. Archaeologically, the spread of maize cultivation in Ghana may be marked by distinctive stone mortars and pestles that are similar to the manos and metates of the Americas. Examples such as this underscore the fact that the exchanges of the Atlantic world were not unidirectional (see Chapter 11).

Considering the advent of European trade in Ghana, Paul Ozanne (1963) posed the question "indigenes or invaders?" He queried how we would assess archaeological manifestations of the early Atlantic world in the absence of documentary source material. How would it be visible? A half century later we are scarcely closer to answering this question. African-European encounters at Elmina and their materialities are not exemplars of African-Portuguese interactions. They can be contrasted with the early *lançado* settlements of the Senegambia and Portuguese missionization in the Congo. Elmina affords one example of a continuum of interactions shaped by local conditions: disparate constellations of culture, society, economy, demography, technology, biology, and historical context that shaped the nature and consequences of individual contact settings. The impacts of the early Atlantic world in many portions of West Africa are not seen in the adoption of Portuguese customs, European religion, trade materials, and the dramatic transformation of African cultural traditions. The real impacts of European expansion are instead marked by the dramatic changes in settlement patterns and the appearance of fortified towns associated with the advent of the Atlantic slave trade (DeCorse 2016; Monroe and Ogundiran 2012).

The African-European cultural imbroglios of the early modern world were largely African in their structuring and their outcomes. In contrast to many of the studies of European-indigene interactions in the Americas, in much of African archaeology cultural continuity and persistence rather than transformation have generally been accepted as givens in viewing Africa's intersections with the early modern world (Chouin and DeCorse 2010; DeCorse 1992, 2001:175–192, 2014; Ogundiran 2005:1–2; Stahl 2001:20–25). Methodologically, this perspective is expressed in the long-standing recognition by African and Africanist researchers of the importance of the direct historical approach, the use of oral traditions, and ethnoarchaeology in providing indigenous voices in the interpretation of the deep past. Interpretive frames such as these underscore the need to see "contact" and "colonialism" as conceptual boxes that only crudely capture the diversity of sociocultural processes represented. The ephemeral expression and overwriting of early Portuguese encounters in West Africa are representative of the diverse continuum of phenomena found within the social and cultural entanglements of the past and present, encounters and their material expressions that may be overwritten multiple times (see Chapter 5; Lyons and Papadopoulos 2002; Paterson 2011; Stein 2005; Stoler et al. 2007). In this respect, early Iberian intersections in West Africa resonate with this volume's push away from dichotomies such as colonizer/colonized and boundaries of core/periphery relationships to afford a more nuanced and comparative exploration of the cultural intersections of the early modern world.

NOTES

1. The term "Guinea" was historically used in European sources to refer to sub-Saharan, coastal West Africa. The Upper Guinea coast generally referred to the region from Liberia to the Senegambia, while the Lower Guinea coast ranged from Côte d'Ivoire to the Bight of Benin. The historical review presented here benefits from both recent historical scholarship that has treated Portuguese and Spanish expansion within the context of Atlantic studies and English translations of contemporary Portuguese sources. The review cannot begin to treat the extensive primary and secondary source material in Portuguese.

2. The early West African outposts are referred to throughout this discussion as Portuguese, though it is recognized that the Spanish and Portuguese Crowns were united between 1580 and 1640. For review of early Portuguese expansion along the African coast, see Blake (1967, 1977); Brooks (2003); Cortesão and Texeira da Mota (1960); Green (2012); Mattoso (2010); Morgan (2009); Newitt (2005, 2010); Parry (1990:40–46); Pereira (1967); Teixeira Mota and Hair (1989); Thornton (2012:60–99).

3. See Brooks (2003); Chouin and DeCorse (2019); Green (2012:95–119). The early Portuguese settlements on São Tomé, Príncipe, and Saint Helena were also colonies with no indigenous populations and so also distinct from the trading enclaves on the West African mainland.

4. Boxer (1972:20) estimates that the total number of Portuguese serving in overseas posts during the sixteenth century was fewer than 10,000 individuals, a small number, considering there were forts scattered across Africa, South America, India, and Asia.

5. These later colonies include Spanish Morocco and Equatorial Guinea and the Portuguese colonies of Guinea Bissau, Angola, and Mozambique.

6. For example, Vogt (1979:34) states: "Sale of personal clothing by crew members was permitted on a limited scale and all such transactions had to be made through the intermediary of the factor of the post. Direct bartering between the crews and the Africans was strictly forbidden." Ordinary members of the garrison were also to buy hens only from traders calling at the fort or from "specially entrusted individuals," who were searched on their return (Hair 1994:71n97).

7. De Maree was Dutch, and it is unlikely that he visited Elmina himself. However, he was well informed on many aspects of the coast and society.

8. Ipsen (2015); Chouin and DeCorse (2019). On the Upper Guinea coast, women entering into such arrangements were referred to as *nharas* in Crioulo and *signares* in later French sources (Brooks 2003:124–129; Wheat 2010).

9. Brooks (2003:127–128) indicates that in the *lançado* settlements of the Upper Guinea coast, *nharas* were also distinguished by their dress, which was a mixture of cloth from Cabo Verde and Europe.

10. The continuity in African construction methods is indicated by both archaeological and historical data, the former consisting of postholes and the concurrent lack of evidence for stone construction. This contrasts with documentary accounts of the Upper Guinea coast, concerning which Brooks (2003:127) notes Luso-African women living in "distinctive, rectangular-shaped dwellings furnished with European articles." These practices may have also emerged at Elmina, but there is no evidence for them.

REFERENCES

Ballong-Wen-Mewuda, J. Bato'ora. 1984. "São Jorge da Mina (Elmina) et son contexte socio-historique pendant l'occupation portugaise (1482–1637)." PhD diss., Centre de Recherches Africaines, Université de Paris.

——. 1993. *La vie d'un comptoir portugais en Afrique occidentale*. Lisbon: École des Hautes Études en Sciences Sociales, Centre d'Études Portugaises: Fondation Calouste Gulbenkian, Commission Nationale por les Commémorations des Découvertes Portugaises.

Blake, John William. 1967. *Europeans in West Africa, 1450–1560*. London: Hakluyt Society.

——. 1977. *West Africa: Quest for God and Gold, 1454–1578*. London: Curzon Press.

Boxer, C. R. 1972. *Four Centuries of Portuguese Expansion, 1415–1825*. Berkeley: University of California Press.

Braudel, Fernand. 1972. *The Mediterranean and the Mediterranean World in the Age of Philip II*, vol. 1. Translated by Seân Reynolds. New York: Harper and Row.

Brooks, George E. 1993. *Landlords and Strangers: Ecology, Society, and Trade in Western Africa, 1000–1630*. Boulder, Colo.: Westview.

——. 2003. *Euroafricans in Western Africa*. Athens: University of Ohio Press.

Chouin, Gérard, and Christopher R. DeCorse. 2010. "Prelude to the Atlantic Trade: New Perspectives on Southern Ghana's Pre-Atlantic History (800–1500)." *Journal of African History* 51(2): 123–145.

——. 2018. "Atlantic Intersections: African-European Emporia in Early Modern West Africa." In *Trade and Colonization in the Ancient Western Mediterranean: The Emporion, from the Archaic to the Hellenistic Period*, edited by Éric Gailledrat, Michael Dietler, and Rosa Plana-Mallart, 253–265. Montpellier, France: Presses Universitaires de la Méditerranée.

Chouin, Gérard L., and Olanrewaju Blessing Lassisi. 2019. "Crisis and Transformation in the 'Slave Rivers' at the Dawn of the Atlantic Trade." In *Power, Political Economy, and Historical Landscapes of the Modern World: Interdisciplinary Perspectives*, edited by Christopher R. DeCorse, 285–306. Albany: SUNY Press.

Clist, Bernard, Pierre de Maret, and Koen A. G. Bostoen, eds. 2018. *Une archéologie des provinces septentrionales du royaume kongo*. Oxford: Archaeopress Publishing.

Cortesão, Armando, and Avelino Teixeira da Mota. 1960. *Portugaliae Monumenta Cartographica*. 6 vols. Lisbon: Comemoracoes do V Centenario da Morte do Infante d. Henrique.

Deagan, Kathleen. 1983. *Spanish in St. Augustine: The Archaeology of a Colonial Creole Community*. New York: Academic Press.

DeCorse, Christopher R. 1992. "Culture Contact, Continuity and Change on the Gold Coast, 1400–1900 A.D." *African Archaeological Review* 10(1): 163–196.

——. 2001. *An Archaeology of Elmina: Africans and Europeans on the Gold Coast, 1400–1900*. Washington, D.C.: Smithsonian Institution Press.

——. 2008. "Varied Pasts: History, Oral Tradition, and Archaeology on the Mina Coast." In *Place, Event, and Narrative Craft: Method and Meaning in Microhistory*, edited by James Brooks, Christopher R. DeCorse, and John Walton, 77–93. Santa Fe, N.M.: School of American Research Press.

———. 2010. "Early Trade Posts and Forts of West Africa." In *First Forts: Essays on the Archaeology of Proto-colonial Fortifications*, edited by Eric Klingelhofer, 209–233. Leiden: Brill.

———. 2014. "Postcolonial or Not? West Africa in the Pre-Atlantic and Atlantic Worlds." Keynote address, fiftieth anniversary of the African Studies Center, University of Ibadan, Nigeria.

———, ed. 2016. *West Africa during the Atlantic Slave Trade: Archaeological Perspectives*. New York: Bloomsbury.

DeCorse, Christopher R., Liza Gijanto, William Roberts, and Bakary Sanyang. 2010. "An Archaeological Appraisal of Early European Settlement in the Gambia." *Nyame Akuma* 73:55–64.

De Marees, Pieter. 1987. *Description and Historical Account of the Gold Kingdom of Guinea*. Translated and annotated by Albert Van Dantzig and Adam Jones. Oxford: Oxford University Press.

Elliot, J. H. 2002. *Imperial Spain 1469–1716*. New York: Penguin Books.

Escribano-Ruiz, Sergio, and Agustín Azkarate. 2015. "Basque Fisheries in Early Canada, a Special Case of Cultural Encounter in Colonizing North America." In *Archaeology of Culture Contact and Colonialism in Spanish and Portuguese America*, edited by Pedro A. Funari and Maria Ximena Senatore, 239–256. New York: Springer.

Feinberg, Harvey Michael. 1969. "Elmina, Ghana: A History of Its Development and Relationship with the Dutch in the Eighteenth Century." PhD diss., Boston University.

Funari, Pedro Paulo A., and Maria Ximena Senatori, eds. 2015. *Archaeology of Culture Contact and Colonialism in Spanish and Portuguese America*. New York: Springer.

Gibbs, Martin. 2016. "The Failed Sixteenth Century Spanish Colonizing Expeditions to the Solomon Islands, Southwest Pacific: The Archaeologies of Settlement Process and Indigenous Agency." In *Archaeologies of Early Modern Spanish Colonialism*, edited by Sandra Montón-Subías, María Cruz Berrocal, and Apen Ruiz Martínez, 253–280. New York: Springer.

Gijanto, Liza. 2017. *The Life of Trade: Events and Happenings in Nuimi's Atlantic Center*. New York: Routledge.

Goodman, Robert. 2015. *Spain: The Centre of the World 1519–1682*. New York: Bloomsbury.

Green, Toby. 2012. *The Rise of the Trans-Atlantic Slave Trade in Western Africa, 1300–1589*. New York: Cambridge University Press.

Hair, Paul E. H. 1990. "Columbus from Guinea to America." *History in Africa* 17:113–129.

———. 1994. *The Founding of the Castelo de São Jorge da Mina: An Analysis of the Sources*. Madison: University of Wisconsin Press.

Hawthorne, Walter. 2003. *Planting Rice and Harvesting Slaves: Transformations along the Guinea-Bissau Coast, 1400–1900*. Portsmouth, N.H.: Heinemann.

———. 2010. *From Africa to Brazil: Culture, Identity, and an Atlantic Slave Trade 1600–1830*. New York: Cambridge University Press.

Ipsen, Pernille. 2015. *Atlantic Slavers and Interracial Marriage on the Gold Coast*. Philadelphia: University of Pennsylvania Press.

Jerónimo, Miguel Bandeira. 2018. "Portuguese Colonialism in Africa." Portuguese Colonialism in Africa. Oxford Research Encyclopedia of African History. October 2019. https://oxfordre.com/africanhistory/view/10.1093/acrefore/9780190277734.001.0001/acrefore-9780190277734-e-183. Accessed October 1, 2019.

Lawrence, A. W. 1963. *Trade Castles and Forts of West Africa*. London: Jonathan Cape.

Lyons, Claire L., and John K. Papadopoulos, eds. 2002. *The Archaeology of Colonialism*. Los Angeles: Getty Research Institute.

Mark, Peter. 1996. "'Portuguese' Architecture and Luso-African Identity in Senegambia and Guinea, 1730–1890." *History in Africa* 23:179–196.

———. 2002. *"Portuguese" Style and Luso-African Identity: Precolonial Senegambia, Sixteenth–Nineteenth Centuries*. Bloomington: Indiana University Press.

Mattoso, José. 2010. *Património de origem portuguesa no mundo: África, Mar Vermelho, Golfo Pérsico; Arquitectura e urbanismo*. Lisbon: Fundação Calouste Gulbenkian.

Monroe, Cameron, and Akin Ogundiran, eds. 2012. *Landscapes of Power: Regional Perspectives on West African Polities in the Atlantic Era*. New York: Cambridge University Press.

Montón-Subías, Sandra, María Cruz Berrocal, and Apen Ruiz Martínez, eds. 2016. *Archaeologies of Early Modern Spanish Colonialism*. New York: Springer.

Morgan, Philip. 2009. "Africa and the Atlantic, c. 1450 to c. 1820." In *Atlantic History: A Critical Appraisal*, edited by Jack P. Greene and Philip D. Morgan, 223–248. New York: Oxford University Press.

Newitt, Malyn. 2005. *A History of Portuguese Overseas Expansion 1400–1668*. New York: Routledge.

———. 2010. *The Portuguese in West Africa, 1415–1670: A Documentary History*. New York: Cambridge.

Ogundiran, Akin, ed. 2005. *Precolonial Nigeria: Essays in Honor of Toyin Falola*. Trenton: Africa World Press.

Oliveira Marques, António Henrique Rodrigo de. 1972. *History of Portugal (Volume 1): From Lusitania to Empire*. New York: Columbia University Press.

Ozanne, Paul. 1963. "Indigenes or Invaders?" *Antiquity* 37(147): 229–231.

Parry, J. H. 1990. *The Spanish Seaborne Empire*. Berkeley: University of California Press.

Paterson, Alistair. 2011. *A Millennium of Cultural Contact*. Walnut Creek, Calif.: Left Coast Press.

Payne, Stanley G. 1973. *A History of Spain and Portugal*. Madison: University of Wisconsin Press.

Pereira, Duarte Pacheco. 1967. *Esmerado de Situ Orbis*. Translated by George H. Kimble. Liechtenstein: Kraus Reprint, Nendeln.

Redman, Charles. 1986. *Qsares-Seghir: An Archaeological View of Medieval Life*. New York: Academic Press.

Rodney, Walter. 1965. "Portuguese Attempts at Monopoly on the Upper Guinea Coast, 1580–1650." *Journal of African History* 6(3): 307–322.

———. 1969. "Gold and Slaves on the Gold Coast." *Transactions of the Historical Society of Ghana* 10:13–28.

Russel-Wood, A. J. R. 1998. *The Portuguese Empire, 1415–1808: A World on the Move*. Baltimore: Johns Hopkins University Press.

Senatore, Maria Ximena. 2015. "Modernity at the Edges of the Spanish Enlightenment: Novelty and Material Culture in Floridablanca Colony (Patagonia, Eighteenth Century)." In *Archaeology of Culture Contact and Colonialism in Spanish and Portuguese America*, edited by Pedro A. Funari and Maria Ximena Senatore, 219–238. New York: Springer.

Stein, Gil, ed. 2005. *The Archaeology of Colonial Encounters: Comparative Perspectives*. Santa Fe, N.M.: School of American Research.

Stoler, Ann Laura, Carole McGranahan, and Peter C. Perdue, eds. 2007. *Imperial Formations*. Santa Fe, N.M.: School of American Research.

Teixeira Mota, A., and P. E. H. Hair. 1989. *East of Mina: Afro-European Relations on the Gold Coast in the 1550s and 1560s*. Studies in African Sources 3. Madison: University of Wisconsin Press.

Thornton, John K. 2012. *A Cultural History of the Atlantic World, 1250–1820*. New York: Cambridge University Press.

Valladares Ramírez, Rafael. 2000. *Portugal y la monarquía hispánica, 1580–1668*. Madrid: Arco Libros.

Vogt, John. 1979. *Portuguese Rule on the Gold Coast 1469–1682*. Athens: University of Georgia Press.

Voss, Barbara L. 2015. "What's New? Rethinking Ethnogenesis in the Archaeology of Colonialism." *American Antiquity* 80(4): 655–670.

Wallerstein, Immanuel. 1974. *The Modern World-System, vol. I: Capitalist Agriculture and the Origins of the European World-Economy in the Sixteenth Century*. New York: Academic Press.

Wheat, David. 2010. "Nharas and Morenas Horras: A Luso-African Model for the Social History of the Spanish Caribbean, c. 1570–1640." *Journal of Early Modern History* 14(1): 119–150.

———. 2016. *Atlantic Africa and the Spanish Caribbean, 1570–1640*. Chapel Hill: University of North Carolina Press.

Wood, Raymond. 1967. "An Archaeological Appraisal of Early European Settlement in the Senegambia." *Journal of African History* 8(1): 39–64.

2

Colonization, Transformations, and Indigenous Cultural Persistence in the Caribbean

Corinne L. Hofman, Roberto Valcárcel Rojas, and Jorge Ulloa Hung

The colonization of the Americas is one of the most transformative and notorious episodes in world history. The Caribbean was the initial space in the Americas the Spanish invaded and the first place where Amerindian-European-African intercultural dynamics played out (Map 2.1). The Caribbean, particularly Hispaniola, was where the Spanish experimented with strategies of conquest that would eventually be essential for expanding control into American continental mainland(s). The Caribbean was the port of entry to a universe of wealth that enabled the construction of the largest colonial empire of the sixteenth century. It was the key chapter of early modern Spanish colonialism (Montón-Subías et al. 2016), and as such it contributed to the establishment of Europe as the center of an increasingly connected global world (Beaule 2017). Yet while the indigenous Caribbean was at the center of the first contacts between Europe and the Americas, it eventually became largely invisible in colonial narratives. These narratives shifted to focus on conflict between colonial powers, the plantation universe, and the African slave trade (Valcárcel Rojas and Ulloa Hung 2018).

But there was more at play during this invasion than colonial narratives represent. With Christopher Columbus's landfall in 1492, the Spanish encountered a Caribbean islandscape with a plurality of island societies whose ancestors had migrated 8,000 to 6,000 years earlier from the South and possibly Central American coastal regions (Hofman et al. 2011; Keegan and Hofman 2017; Wilson 2007). The Spanish found a highly complex sociopolitical landscape with tendencies toward political centralization on Hispaniola and Puerto Rico. This area could be called a frontier or border. It was a space of interaction and confrontation between communities of the Greater and Lesser Antilles. At the time of European incursions, the Caribbean Sea was an arena of intricate networks

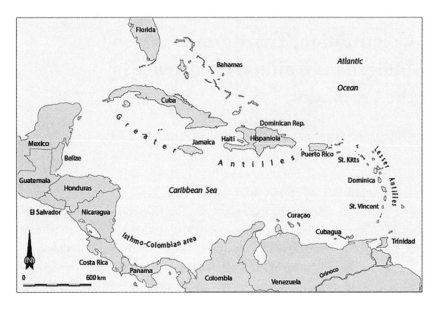

Map 2.1 Map of the Caribbean (by Corinne Hofman and Menno Hoogland).

echoing the overarching patterns of migration, mobility, and interaction among insular inhabitants and with individuals on the mainland (Hofman et al. 2014). These networks were flexible, robust, inclusive, and outward-looking systems that crossed local, regional, and pan-Caribbean boundaries (Hofman 2019; Hofman and Bright 2010; Hofman et al. 2011; Hofman et al. 2007; Hofman et al. 2014; Mol 2014; Oliver 2009). They comprised the movement of peoples and a diversity of elements, objects, ideas, and beliefs. However, the intention of these movements began to change, deliberately or through colonial action, under the newly imposed colonial sociopolitical regime. European colonizers used, manipulated, extended, changed, reinforced, interrupted, and incorporated these ancient networks for their own purposes (Amodio 1991; Hofman 2019; Hofman et al. 2014).

The first transfers of peoples, objects, and material goods between Amerindians and Europeans took place in an environment that united existing and preexisting natural and human-constructed landscapes. In essence, it reflected the construction of identities, scenarios, and places marked by plurality (Lightfoot et al. 1998), which it is essential to understand.

The neglect of the Caribbean region in historical narratives as the first port of entry to the Americas is to a great extent a direct consequence of

European colonial expansion to the mainland, the colonial quest for new resources, and the massive loss of indigenous life due to forced labor, slavery, imported diseases, and war (Valcárcel Rojas 2016b). The Caribbean islands provided testing grounds for Spanish domination and many of the economic, human, and logistic resources for the colonization of the mainland (Del Río Moreno 2012a, 2012b). Caribbean indigenous peoples participated in the colonization process as guides, translators, and laborers. They assumed multiple functions and identities in favor of the Spanish interests but also of their own living conditions and subsistence needs.

During the colonization of the islands and the continental expansion, the Antillean indigenous peoples were either no longer allowed to be "indigenous," or, in some cases, they themselves wished to no longer be perceived as "indigenous" by the colonizers. They were generalized as *indio* or Carib and were assigned naturalized cultural features, such as a peaceful or violent attitude, that the Spanish used to justify their actions toward them: they were either evangelized (the friendly *indios*) as part of a civilizing action that included intensive labor exploitation, or they were enslaved (the warring and cannibal Carib) in order to take advantage of their forced labor. Generally, the Spanish rewrote the Greater Antilles as a home to the *indios*, both free and enslaved indigenous populations that formed a homogenized "Other" and negated their likely diverse original ethnic identities. The *indio*, diverse in their indigeneity but homogenized under the new social order, survived in many places across the region. They did so in reduced numbers, adapting to the norms of life of the colonial world and often mixing with other ethnicities: *indios* and mestizos were another colonial product squeezed from ancient Caribbean indigenous societies (Valcárcel Rojas 2016b; Valcárcel Rojas and Ulloa Hung 2018).

THE MULTIPLE SETTINGS OF EARLY EUROPEAN COLONIZATION OF THE CARIBBEAN

European settlement and colonization of the Caribbean were a series of processes within and between islands. The Spanish settled most of the areas around the Caribbean Sea during the sixteenth century, but their lack of interest and subsequent failed ventures at settlement in the Lesser Antilles left these islands to the Island Carib, or Kalinago, and thus outside of their control (Hofman 2019; Hofman et al. 2019; Wilson 2007).

The island of Saint Christopher was the first to be settled by the French and British in 1623–1625. Other islands in the Lesser Antilles, such as Dominica and Saint Vincent, remained beyond European domination until the 1800s.

Early on, due to poor resources, the Bahamas and part of the Lesser Antilles were regarded as labor suppliers and were considered *islas inútiles* (useless islands) by Royal Decree (Real Cédula 1503) (Deive 1995:90–91). Their populations were transported and put to work as slaves in the gold mines on Hispaniola, Cuba, and Puerto Rico, as well as in the pearl fisheries on Cubagua (Antczak et al. 2019; Hofman 2019; Valcárcel Rojas et al. 2019).

These differential timings of interest in particular areas of colonization were influenced and sometimes determined by European geopolitics, the flows of conquest and colonization toward North, Central, and South America, how indigenous populations responded to colonization, and the presence of exploitable resources on a particular island.

Using these varied colonial and indigenous histories as a background, in this chapter we focus on three scenarios that illustrate the transformations experienced by indigenous Caribbean communities in the early years of the European invasion of their territories. First, we will examine one of the most significant transformations. This occurred in the north of Hispaniola in the region where the first Spanish incursions into the interior of the American continent were made. There, diverse relations, interactions, and exchange of material culture occurred and were created between indigenous peoples, and Europeans began to transform the lives and worldview of native populations. It was during this initial period that the first Spanish forts were built and indigenous peoples, through either relocation by or flight from the Spanish, became increasingly mobile (Hofman et al. 2018).

The second important episode of indigenous transformation we explore is the massive translocation of indigenous communities across the Caribbean Sea as they increasingly became enslaved by the Spanish. The massive forced movement of indigenous peoples started with Columbus's second voyage and expanded during his third voyage. The initial exploitation of the gold mines in the center of Hispaniola, the construction of the settlement of Concepción de la Vega on that island, and later the exploitation of the pearl fisheries on the island of Cubagua, located off the coast of what is now Venezuela, motivated this transfer of indigenous peoples as slaves, or *naborias*, across the Caribbean Sea (Hofman 2019; Valcárcel Rojas et al. 2019).

Third, we discuss the transformation experienced by indigenous peoples under new colonial conditions in the encomienda system (Arranz Márquez 1991; Deive 1995; Mira Caballos 2000; Valcárcel Rojas and Ulloa Hung 2018; Yeager 1995). The village and cemetery of El Chorro de Maíta, an early sixteenth-century encomienda in northeastern Cuba, illustrates this deeply destructive forced labor system and how the imposition of a Christian belief system changed daily life and transformed funeral practices and their associated material culture (Valcárcel Rojas 2016a). This case study and other Cuban archaeological contexts also show the adjustments and changes in the Spanish colonization strategy and in the processes of interaction with indigenous peoples.

To conclude, we present several cases that highlight the persistence of indigenous knowledge and practices in contemporary culture and daily life in Cuba and Hispaniola. These cases demonstrate that, despite colonial strategies to erase indigenous peoples and their culture, these strategies added a new dimension and sociohistorical significance to indigenous people in the structuring of the current local cultures of the Caribbean region (Hofman et al. 2018; Reyes Cardero 2018; Pesoutova 2019; Ulloa Hung and Valcárcel Rojas 2016; Valcárcel Rojas and Ulloa Hung 2018; Vega 1981).

FROM THE INDIGENOUS UNIVERSE TO A COLONIAL WORLD

According to European historic information, indigenous Hispaniola was divided into several *cacicazgos* (chiefdoms), whose number, structure, and extension have not yet been defined (Herrera Malatesta 2018; Oliver 2009; Vega 1990; Wilson 1990). *Cacicazgos* were likely a hierarchical sociopolitical organization headed by a number of leading individuals, or caciques (Redmond and Spencer 1994).

Northern Hispaniola was the first area in the Americas, following Columbus's landing on one of the Lucayan islands and his incursions into Cuba in 1492, where extensive interactions and confrontations between Amerindians and Europeans occurred (Hofman et al. 2018). It was from northern Hispaniola that the Spanish first entered the interior of the island in 1494, taking advantage of indigenous networks, knowledge, and, likely, trails. It was in this area that the Spanish acquired new information about local food, the environment, and the functioning of indigenous societies that would be key to their expansion throughout the rest of the Antillean archipelago. Hispaniola is also where their political justification for subjugating indigenous peoples for labor and slavery emerged on their quest to conquer the American continent.

Following Columbus's second voyage, the Spanish promoted and intensified the exchange of goods with the interior of the island (Guerrero and Veloz Maggiolo 1988; Hofman et al. 2018; Keehnen 2019). Such exchanges helped the Spanish establish alliances with local caciques and gain information on the location of gold. These relationships simultaneously generated prestige for the indigenous communities, or at least the caciques with whom the Spanish were interacting. On April 9, 1494, Alonso de Ojeda illustrated the importance of these exchanges in the colonization of Hispaniola in the march to the fort of Santo Tomás, where he intended to learn about and "pacify" the island. In Ojeda's account of this event, Columbus referred to sending "bells and beads" in order to exchange them for supplies with indigenous peoples. They were also used to placate these groups, as well as obtain gold from them (Keehnen 2011). This practice was so important for colonial purposes that specific people were appointed to organize and supervise the exchanges (Romeu de Armas 1991:478).

For indigenous peoples this trade was sometimes a way not only to obtain exotic items and Spanish political support but also to increase their status among other indigenous groups in the region. More than 300 indigenous sites, ranging from the precolonial to early colonial period, were recently recorded in northern Hispaniola (Hofman et al. 2018). This represents only a small portion of the settlements that may have existed at the time of Spanish incursion because of the huge land transformations created by that process (Castilla-Beltrán et al. 2018; Hooghiemstra et al. 2018). Archaeological studies around the Ruta de Colón, the first colonial route running from the initial Spanish town of La Isabela on Hispaniola's north coast to the Cibao Valley, the "Valley of Gold" in the center of the island, show a landscape characterized by rockshelters or caves used as refuges or gathering places near the sea, as well as settlements in open spaces located on top of mountains and plateaus of important mountain systems, such as the Northern and Central Cordillera (Hofman et al. 2018; Ortega 1988; Ulloa Hung and Herrera Malatesta 2015).

Settlement patterns, the management of regional and local space, and the mixture of ceramic styles within the alluvial valleys of prominent rivers within the broader Cibao Valley suggest a far greater social and cultural diversity in the region at the time of contact than demonstrated by Spanish documents. These writings, often used to legitimize Spanish misbehavior and later reinforced by nineteenth-century anthropologists, reduced the peoples of Hispaniola and the Greater Antilles in general to a mere single Taíno culture (Curet 2014; Keegan and Hofman 2017).

Characteristic villages of northern Hispaniola had a pattern of mounds and earthworks surrounding leveled areas where houses were constructed (Hofman and Hoogland 2015; Hofman et al. 2018; Sonnemann et al. 2016; Ulloa Hung 2014; Veloz Maggiolo et al. 1981). The size and location of some of the villages suggest that they were important nodes in a social and political network that connected several landscapes and places. As such, the northern Hispaniola landscape appears to reflect an interactive environment that formed the basis for a Spanish route of colonial domination. The colonial narratives about the first expeditions into the interior of Hispaniola mention a system of social relations between indigenous communities that was widely exploited by the Spanish in their explorations from La Isabela to the Cibao Valley (León Guerrero 2000). The colonizers, led by indigenous guides, moved from one indigenous village to another (Las Casas 1875:29–30). These early contacts between vastly different worlds likely created a network of places that from then on were imbued with new meanings. These meanings would become part of the mechanisms of domination of other regions, locations, resources, and populations on Hispaniola. The imagined gold and richness of the indigenous landscape were constructed by colonial ambition, and it intercepted and mixed with the economic, social, and symbolic meanings attributed to these same places by indigenous peoples long before Spanish arrival. This created landscapes where meaning and place were variably assigned and created by different groups and where the meaning embedded in these places often clashed.

CHANGING MATERIAL CULTURAL REPERTOIRES

The exchange and intercultural dynamics in the early years of colonization created novel social identities and material cultural repertoires

(Deagan 2004; Hofman and Keehnen 2019; Hofman et al. 2018; Samson et al. 2016). Gold ornaments, foodstuffs, cotton, and exotic birds were reported to be the first items exchanged for European glass beads, bells, broken bowls, objects and fragments of metal, canvas shirts, and colored cloths (Keehnen 2011, 2019). European objects, which were present in very low quantities, have been recovered from indigenous sites, sometimes in clearly segregated areas with local paraphernalia, alluding to their integration into local assemblages as prestige items (Ernst and Hofman 2015; Keehnen 2011; Lopez Belando 2013; Samson 2010). Ethnohistoric information also suggests that these early exchanges comprised intangible features, such as names, that were key to the creation of alliances (Guaitiao status/friends) and provided critical information about resources, places, rivers, mountains, and the location of gold (Mira Caballos 2004).[1]

The few European items found in Amerindian sites were apparently integrated and dispersed through the indigenous networks. Yet European pig and rat bones have also been found in fair amounts (Deagan 2004), probably indicating that some domesticates, particularly pig, were rapidly becoming part of local indigenous cuisine (Hofman et al. 2018; Van der Veen 2006). These European domesticates became an important economic and commercial medium that sustained part of the indigenous population in the later encomiendas during the period historians have called the "gold economy" (Del Río Moreno 1996, 2012a; Moya Pons 2016).[2] On the other hand, together with indigenous products, these European foods became the means of logistical support for the new expeditions to conquer other Caribbean islands and the adjacent American continent (Sued Badillo 2011).

THE FORGOTTEN ENSLAVED INDIGENOUS PEOPLE

During Columbus's third and fourth voyages (1498 and 1502), the first expeditions to the Pearl Coast of northern Venezuela were made. In need of labor to exploit the gold mines on Hispaniola and the pearl fisheries on Cubagua, as well as making the slaves a commercial product in themselves, the Spanish began to enslave indigenous people in massive numbers across the Caribbean and neighboring mainland(s) (Valcárcel Rojas et al. 2019). This enslavement was regularly coupled with long-distance movement of enslaved individuals.

This enslavement of indigenous people augmented and became more visible with the increase of the gold economy under the government of Nicolás de Ovando on Hispaniola Island. After the royal decree of December 20, 1503, the distribution of enslaved *indios* was legalized. In that same year, the forced labor of indigenous peoples was also authorized, which encouraged the enslavement of indigenous people and the arming of expeditions to capture them. The Higüey Wars (1502–1503) were also linked to this episode and provided a large number of enslaved people for the mines and the movement of caciques from Higüey to Santo Domingo (Arranz Márquez 1991).

Portuguese slavery practices developed and implemented in the Iberian Peninsula and various kingdoms that would later form Spain (DeCorse 2001; Lobo Cabrera 1990) created experiences that influenced the new and early slave trade. These experiences would eventually result in capturing and selling indigenous people within the Caribbean and later exporting them to Europe. Other European powers would eventually repeat the same processes in their respective colonial spaces. In the circum-Caribbean area, from 1493 to 1552, between ca. 250,000 and 500,000 indigenous people were enslaved (Woodruff Stone 2014). It is argued that in the Western Hemisphere this slavery involved between two and five million victims (Bialuschewski and Fisher 2017). This practice preceded and influenced the one that would be established with Africans through the transatlantic trade (Anderson-Córdova 2017; Deive 1995; Sued Badillo 1995; Valcárcel Rojas 2016a; Valcárcel Rojas et al. 2019; Yaremko 2016).

Although there has been mention of the enslavement of Lucayan and Carib in historical documents, the slavery activities carried out by rich landowners, royal officials, shipowners, and entrepreneurs were not focused on a specific ethnic group or territory but included the Greater Antilles, the Bahamas, the Lesser Antilles, and much of Venezuela, Colombia, Central America, and New Spain. Enslaved indigenous people were often young, between 10 and 25 years old, although sometimes an entire population was captured, resulting in a wider age range. Groups of enslaved individuals could be from several towns of very different origin and cultures because of the variable nature of how and why the individuals were captured. The involuntary mobility of these populations and the process of enslavement also fundamentally forced the interaction of individuals from different places. In *estancias* (ranches), mines, or pearl fisheries, free indigenous people lived with enslaved indigenous and African peoples of diverse origins. To a lesser extent they were servants in the Spanish houses, at least in the early days. It was a multicultural scenario marked by the demands that the colonial order imposed on each of these labor and social groups and in which each group had to take advantage of their previous acquired knowledge and that of others to find their own ways of survival (Altman 2013; Eugenio 2002; Valcárcel Rojas and Velázquez 2016). It is also in these spaces that the mestizos were born and many rebellions were generated. These multicultural spaces of enslaved and free folk not only brought wealth to the Spaniards but also grouped the constructed meanings of how the different colonized peoples handled and confronted their domination. These spaces laid the foundations for a process that created new social and cultural identities through the interaction of indigenous peoples with peoples from Africa and Europe.

GOLD, PEARLS, AND THE TRANSFORMATION OF SOCIAL AND CULTURAL IDENTITIES

The early centers of enslaved Amerindian labor were the Spanish towns of Nueva Cádiz de Cubagua, Venezuela, a hub of pearl extraction, and La Concepción de la Vega and Cotuí, in the Cibao Valley of Hispaniola, sites of the gold-mining industry (Antczak et al. 2019; Deive 1995; Olsen Bogaert et al. 2011). The architectural monumentality of La Vega and Nueva Cádiz demonstrates the economic power achieved in these settlements through the intensive exploitation of enslaved indigenous and African labor with a goal of organizing and intensifying mining work. This is particularly visible at Cotuí, one of the first goldmines exploited by the Spanish in Hispaniola (Olsen Bogaert et al. 2016). The mixed-material cultural repertoire and production techniques at these three sites reflect Amerindian, African, and Spanish intercultural dynamics (Antczak et al. 2019; Deagan 2004; Ernst and Hofman 2019; Ortega and Fondeur 1978; Ting et al. 2018), which are also recognizable in Puerto Real, in present-day Haiti (Deagan 1995).

Indigenous pottery continued to be produced, but in a simplified way. Vessel forms, decorative patterns, surface treatment, and vessel function changed considerably. For example, on Hispaniola the richly decorated indigenous vessels, adorned with elaborate anthropozoomorphic features, were reduced to simple handles and knobs (Ernst and Hofman 2019; Hofman 2019). New vessel shapes influenced by indigenous Central or South American, African, and Spanish prototypes emerged (Figure 2.1; Ernst forthcoming; Ernst and Hofman 2019). Spanish vessel shapes were produced with local techniques, indicating the intention of maintaining the Iberian lifestyle in the colonies (Ernst and Hofman 2019; García Arévalo 1991; Ting et al. 2018). In addition to the traditional hand-built coiling techniques, the European potter's wheel was sometimes used.

THE ENCOMIENDA SYSTEM

The encomienda system is a prime example of the transformations happening during the early sixteenth century, when local Amerindian settlements were dominated by the Spanish and their populations were supplemented by nonlocal enslaved Amerindians and Africans. Under the control of the European colonizers, they were forced to accept Christian customs and traditions and provide labor for Spanish colonial enterprises (Hofman et al. 2014; Valcárcel Rojas 2016a; Valcárcel Rojas et al. 2013). With the encomienda system, Caribbean societies and cultures radically changed, yet indigenous peoples were able to (re)negotiate certain aspects of their precontact identities and material cultural practices (Hofman et al. 2014). This is one of the settings and one of the colonial structures where the *indio* began to emerge as a colonial category and identity (Valcárcel Rojas et al. 2014).

The ways in which the indigenous peoples acquired, used, and valued European materiality were extremely diverse throughout the Caribbean, and they depended on the place, time, and characteristics of their interaction with the Europeans (Beck et al. 2016; Gassón 1996; Smith 1988). Archaeological sites in Cuba show, with respect to Hispaniola, certain changes in how indigenous communities incorporated European materials. This seems to be typical of the Cuban case and perhaps of the other Antillean colonization processes (Jamaica, Puerto Rico) where the period of initial contact and negotiation, under indigenous autonomy, does not reach the extent and force seen in Hispaniola (Valcárcel Rojas 2016a, 2019).

In indigenous communities under the encomienda system, such as El Chorro de Maíta, El Porvenir, Barajagua, and Alcala, gift kit components (brass sheets, glass beads, or hawkbells) that were characteristic

a b

c

e f

d

g h

0   10 cm

Figure 2.1 Indigenous and transcultural ceramics from early colonial contexts at Cotuí and Concepción de la Vega (Dominican Republic) (identification by Marlieke Ernst in Ernst forthcoming; Ernst and Hofman 2019): (a, b) red slipped vessel necks with excised motifs from La Vega, probably Middle or South American indigenous influence; (c) shallow bowl with red, white, and black painting, probably Middle or South American indigenous influence; (d) indigenous (Chicoid) white clay effigy vessel; (e) vessel spout with zoomorphic modeled application; (f) sherd with incised decoration and quartz inlays, probably African influence; (g) sherd with comb-dragged decoration, probably African influence; (h) African olla with indigenous applications (knobs) from the mining camp of Cotuí. (Photos by Jorge Ulloa Hung, Corinne Hofman, and Menno Hoogland.)

of the act of *rescate* (trade) at the beginning of the Spanish invasion decreased, and tools and weapons became more common (Valárcel Rojas 2019). The fact that the historical and ethnohistorical data of the Greater Antilles do not mention weapons and tools as a typical part of the artifacts for trade or gift or that the *rescate* was developed in negotiation contexts that were more common in Hispaniola than in the other islands suggests a change in the strategies of interaction and transfer of objects. This reveals a process where trade lost relevance and European objects, as referred to in certain historical sources (Marte 1981:115–120), were instead given as payment for work or services provided. At the same time, the encomienda system changed the indigenous perspective of the Spaniards and their material culture. Indigenous groups were now more geared to take advantage of Spanish technology and other resources rather than to value the exoticism of Spanish materiality (Figure 2.2; Valcárcel Rojas 2019).

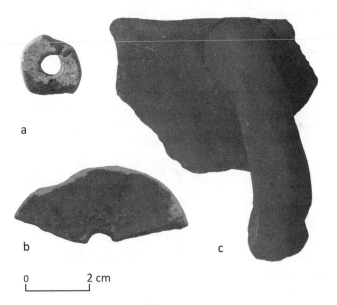

Figure 2.2 Intercultural early colonial ceramic assemblages from El Chorro de Maíta (Cuba): (a, b) modified European ceramic sherds; (c) copy of a Spanish vessel using coiling technique, El Chorro de Maíta, Cuba. (Photos by Roberto Valcárcel Rojas.)

CHANGING ATTITUDES TOWARD THE COLONIZER: TRANSFORMATIONS OF IDENTITY AND PERSISTENCE OF CULTURAL PRACTICES

El Chorro de Maíta was an indigenous village in the northeast of Cuba under colonial control in the early sixteenth century. Details on the demography and cultural behavior of the population considered to be native to the region near the site, as well as historical data on encomiendas in this part of northeastern Cuba, allow us to confirm that the indigenous population of El Chorro de Maíta lived under the encomienda system (Valcárcel Rojas 2016a). Although European objects and food such as pork (Pérez Iglesias and Valcárcel Rojas 2014) were incorporated into the life of the community, the funerary context, with more than 130 inhumed individuals, provides the greatest evidence of change. Amerindians, an individual of African descent, possible mestizos, and one immigrant from the Yucatán peninsula were buried in a confined space in the center of the village (Laffoon 2012; Valcárcel Rojas 2016a; Valcárcel Rojas et al. 2011; Weston and Valcárcel Rojas 2016). The demographic profile of the population and the structure of the cemetery indicate that infectious diseases, possibly associated with European contact, affected the El Chorro population and caused an increase in mortality (Weston and Valcárcel Rojas 2016). A decline in cranial modification was noted in the non-adult individuals, likely reflecting significant changes in indigenous identity in the early colonial period as well (Duijvenbode 2017; Valcárcel Rojas 2016a; Weston and Valcárcel Rojas 2016). The mortuary practices revealed a mix of Amerindian and European burial traditions; the flexed burials typical of precolonial practices were mixed with the European way of burying the deceased in a stretched position with the arms crossing the chest, as the Christian belief system demanded (Valcárcel Rojas 2016a). The latter practice is found in nearly 10 percent of the buried individuals, including those of indigenous origin.

European brass aglets were found with several burials, indicating, along with certain taphonomic evidence, that deceased individuals were probably dressed in European clothing. For example, in one burial a fragment of European linen was found. Other individuals were interred with a mix of *guanín* (gold and copper alloy), gold ornaments from Colombia, and European brass items. Archaeometric analysis and (ethno)historical information suggest that the indigenous peoples received all these objects from the Spanish (Martinón Torres et al. 2012; Valcárcel Rojas 2016a; Valcárcel Rojas and Martinón-Torres 2013).

There were precolonial indigenous identities, as well as identities built by the adjustment to the colonial environment, like the *indios* (people who abandon or are forced to abandon their symbols of identity and develop ways of life of colonial character) in El Chorro de Maíta. There were also other identities gestated from ethnic and cultural mix (mestizos). This is the result of a process of ethnogenesis from which new human and cultural products emerge. Some of these individuals can be considered criollos (people of Spanish descent born in the Americas) by their local birth (Valcárcel Rojas et al. 2014). It is a scenario where diverse cultural traditions interacted and coexisted. At El Chorro de Maíta, there is an ethnic intermingling that likely foreshadows a future Cuban identity. This complex mixture denies the idea of an immediate and total collapse of the indigenous world and reveals continuity beyond the moments of conquest. It reveals the indigenous and *indios* as protagonists with strength and a capacity for resistance and adjustment that traditional historiography does not perceive (Sued Badillo 1992; Valcárcel Rojas and Ulloa Hung 2018). Here, identities coexisted (indigenous, *indios*, Africans, *encomendados*, and slaves) and new identities were created, imposing a plurality that, despite being marked by domination, brought different meanings together to the place where these forgotten actors lived or died.

PERSISTENCE AND CONTINUITY IN THE CONTEMPORARY CARIBBEAN

The substitution, displacement, and/or disappearance of indigenous cultural traditions, knowledge, and peoples as suggested by traditional historical narratives (Córdova 1968; Mira Caballos 2009; Moya Pons and Flores Paz 2013) are strongly countered by their presence in modern Caribbean society. Here, persistence, understood through its multiple connotations (Panich 2013), is regarded as a phenomenon that is largely hidden by miscegenation and by the way in which the indigenous legacy was connected to or was superimposed by other cultural traditions (Pesoutova 2019; Ulloa Hung and Valcárcel Rojas 2016; Valcárcel Rojas and Ulloa Hung 2018). The ways in which colonial identities were organized and recorded in different parts of the Americas (Reyes Cardero 2018), including in the Caribbean, served to modify and hide the presence of indigenous peoples and eventually their descendants.

As part of these processes, it is possible to observe a constant formation and superposition of identities that was generated not only by colonial domination but also by indigenous resistance and adaptation. This phenomenon occurred in spaces rearranged and transformed by the Europeans, who fostered both urban and rural population centers, as well as multiple spaces of economic exploitation. The indigenous peoples participated not only in the construction of those places loaded with European colonial meanings but also in their effort to adjust and survive. It is necessary to take into consideration the indigenous nature of the many places of resettlement, refuge, and resistance where the indigenous peoples and their descendants connected their natural and symbolic environment with the new universe created and, eventually, controlled by the Europeans.

Indigenous features persist in the spiritual and material culture of the Caribbean and constitute an important part of everyday life. These elements are evident in the Dominican Republic and Cuba, where the physical presence of indigenous descendants is still maintained (Barreiro and Hartman 2018). The indigenous legacy is visible in toponyms, cuisine, crops, storage artifacts, kitchen and labor utensils, the extensive use of forms of traditional agriculture (slash-and-burn, *conucos*), house building, an array of cultural traditions, stories, and ritual practices, as well as in the intensive use of indigenous plant species for economic and curative purposes (Figure 2.3).

For example, in Cuba and the Dominican Republic the use of native materials combined with the way houses are constructed, the decisions to settle at particular elevations, good visibility, good access to fresh water sources, and protection from floods are important elements of contemporary settlement activity. Sometimes, places formerly inhabited and used by indigenous peoples are reused, and some of the precolonial techniques aimed at landscape transformation continue into the present. The production of ceramics by indigenous peoples in colonial contexts during the sixteenth century resulted in a ceramic tradition that was observed in Cuba until the eighteenth century and in the Dominican Republic until the present.

Figure 2.3 Examples of the persistence of indigenous cultural traditions recorded in Cuba and the Dominican Republic: (a) a house built with traditional techniques and materials, Amina, Dominican Republic; (b) a potter in Higüerito, Dominican Republic; (c) a sieve made of vegetable fibers used in the production of cassava, Fray Benito, Holguín, Cuba; (d) gold washing in San José de las Matas, Dominican Republic. (Photos by Jorge Ulloa Hung and Roberto Valcárcel Rojas.)

All of these aspects constitute an important part of everyday life in the Caribbean today, and this persistence of indigenous ways of doing and being is most visible in a sense of belonging and human resilience and persistence, as well as in the genetic composition of the contemporary populations (García Molina et al. 2007; Hofman et al. 2018; Martínez-Cruzado et al. 2001; Pesoutova and Hofman 2016; Rodríguez Ramos and Pagán-Jiménez 2016; Schroeder et al. 2018; Ulloa Hung 2005; Ulloa Hung and Valcárcel Rojas 2016; Valcárcel Rojas and Ulloa Hung 2018;

Vega 1981). This is of great importance in various aspects of the rural and urban world of these countries and demonstrates the various ways in which this legacy survived and is inserted into the new material universe (Ulloa Hung 2018; Valcárcel Rojas 2016b; Valcárcel Rojas et al. 2018).

In Hispaniola, the indigenous cultural legacies were also picked up by black and free mulattoes within a larger economy of cattle ranches and subsistence or domestic agriculture developed in an environment of rurality and isolation on the periphery of a large colonial village (Gonzáles 2011). For years this population maintained traditional forms of cultivation and food habits and part of the material culture originating in and transformed from precolonial indigenous cultures. In the rural portions of the island, the use of hammocks, cassava, and *conucos* (small plots for cultivation), the manufacture of pottery, and a wide variety of objects made of wood that include canoes and *santos de palo* (images of Christian saints carved in wood) were kept as important elements. *Macutos, cerones, arganas* (containers made of vegetable fibers), trays, and wooden rafts, among other things, are the basis of the rich utilitarian artisanal variety that still exists to this day (De La Cruz and Durán Núñez 2012).

CONCLUSIONS

Our research reveals a complex and diverse Caribbean sociocultural landscape on the eve of the colonial incursions. The enmeshed spheres and lines of social interaction among the indigenous communities, from precolonial moments onward, cemented a regional history marked by coexistence, interaction, and transculturation. Social networks were shaped by expanding and contracting group territories, fission and fusion of local communities, variable degrees of sociopolitical integration, and differential responses to colonization, all of which were fundamental in the formation of the modern globalized society both in the Caribbean and across the world.

The cases presented in this chapter show the variability and multiple outcomes of a universe of intercultural dynamics and contacts that is still not fully recognized or even understood today. In many ways, these contest the historical data that regularly exclude the indigenous voice and their living and working contexts. Archaeological research and discussions with contemporary island inhabitants enable us to uncover some of these subaltern strata. Archaeological data combined with historical information also show us the plurality of identities that have emerged in the colonial universe and the way they have unfolded in the most diverse spaces and places, constructing and transforming them. The ability to reach the present or provide a legacy that reaches us is a key aspect of the cultural and human nature of this region.

From the resistance and persistence of the indigenous people within their relationship to Europeans and Africans, a diverse mestizo Caribbean was born. This emergence cannot be separated from the precolonial world. This Caribbean is marked by colonial action and the destruction of indigenous societies, but it is also marked by the ability of these individuals to survive and to find ways to connect with other ethnic and cultural groups. Recovering the history of the construction of a multiethnic and multicultural Caribbean, in which the indigenous peoples are protagonists, can help overcome the Eurocentric vision that imposes a homogeneous history and a future without space for anything that is non-Western. It also connects us with a history that from its beginning is much more diverse and complex than that offered by traditional narratives based on early colonial documents.

ACKNOWLEDGMENTS

The research leading to these results has received funding from the European Research Council under the European Union's Seventh Framework Programme (FP7/2007–2013) / ERC-NEXUS1492 grant agreement number 319209. We thank the NEXUS1492 team members for their contributions, which led to many of the publications cited in this text. Foremost we would like to acknowledge the indigenous and local communities in the various islands for participating in our projects and knowledge exchange. Finally, we thank Menno Hoogland, Marlieke Ernst, Emma de Mooij, and Lewis Borck for their support with the figures and editing the English text.

NOTES

1. Guaitiao was the traditional pact of brotherhood or friendship that was made between the indigenous chiefs and that could include the exchange of names, gifts, and wives. After the arrival of the Europeans, it was used to formalize the alliances of the indigenous leaders with the Europeans.

2. The period between 1502 and 1510 on Hispaniola is known as the gold economy. This was the height of gold extraction on the island using indigenous labor through the encomienda system and slavery. During that period, cattle husbandry and other activities constituted a complementary economy to mining extraction.

REFERENCES

Altman, Ida. 2013. "Marriage, Family, and Ethnicity in the Early Spanish Caribbean." *William and Mary Quarterly* 70(2): 225–250.

Amodio, Emanuele. 1991. "Relaciones interétnicas en el Caribe indígena: Una reconstrucción a partir de los primeros testimoni os europeos." *Revista de Indias* 51(193): 51–193.

Anderson-Córdova, Karen F. 2017. *Surviving Spanish Conquest: Indian Fight, Flight, and Cultural Transformation in Hispaniola and Puerto Rico.* Tuscaloosa: University of Alabama Press.

Antczak Andrzej T., Ma. Magdalena Antczak, and Oliver Antczak. 2019. "*Rancherías*: Historical Archaeology of Early Colonial Campsites on Margarita and Coche Islands, Venezuela." In *Material Encounters and Indigenous Transformations in the Early Colonial Americas: Archaeological Case Studies*, edited by Corinne L. Hofman and Floris W. M. Keehnen, 144–172. Leiden: Brill.

Arranz Márquez, Luis. 1991. *Repartimientos y encomiendas en la isla Española (el repartimiento de Alburquerque de 1514).* Madrid: Fundación García Arévalo.

Barreiro, José, and Alejandro Hartman. 2018. "Conciencia e intencionalidad: El gens indocubano de los Rojas-Ramírez." In *De la desaparición a la permanencia: Indígenas e Indios en la reinvención del Caribe*, vol. 2, edited by Roberto Valcárcel Rojas and Jorge Ulloa Hung, 281–329. Santo Domingo: Instituto Tecnológico de Santo Domingo—Fundación García Árevalo.

Beaule, Christine D. 2017. "Challenging the Frontiers of Colonialism." In *Frontiers of Colonialism*, edited by Christine D. Beaule, 1–25. Gainesville: University Press of Florida.

Beck, Robin A., David G. Moore, and Christopher B. Rodning. 2016. Introduction to *Fort San Juan and the Limits of Empire: Colonialism and Household Practice at the Berry Site*, edited by Robin A. Beck, Christopher B. Rodning, and David G. Moore, 5–26. Gainesville: University Press of Florida.

Bialuschewski, Arne and Linford D. Fisher. 2017. "Guest Editor's Introduction: New Directions in the History of Native American Slavery Studies." *Ethnohistory* 64(1): 1–17.

Castilla-Beltrán, Álvaro, Henry Hooghiemstra, Menno L. P. Hoogland, Jaime R. Pagán-Jiménez, Bas van Geel, Michael H. Field, Maarten Prins, Timme Donders, Eduardo Herrera Malatesta, Jorge Ulloa Hung, Crystal McMichael, Will Gosling, and Corinne L. Hofman. 2018. "Columbus' Footprint in Hispaniola: A Paleoenvironmental Record of Indigenous and Colonial Impacts on the Landscape of the Central Cibao Valley, Northern Dominican Republic." *Anthropocene* 22:66–80.

Córdova, Efrén. 1968. "La encomienda y la desaparición de los indios en las Antillas Mayores." *Caribbean Studies* 8(3): 23–49.

Curet, L. Antonio. 2014. "The Taíno: Phenomena, Concepts, and Terms." *Ethnohistory* 61(3): 467–495.

Deagan, Kathleen A., ed. 1995. *Puerto Real: The Archaeology of a Sixteenth-Century Spanish Town in Hispaniola*. Gainesville: University Press of Florida.

———. 2004. "Reconsidering Taino Social Dynamics after Spanish Conquest: Gender and Class in Culture Contact Studies." *American Antiquity* 69(4): 597–626.

DeCorse, Christopher R. 2001. *An Archaeology of Elmina: Africans and Europeans on the Gold Coast, 1400–1900*. Washington, D.C.: Smithsonian Institution Press.

Deive, Carlos Esteban. 1995. *La Española y la esclavitud del indio*. Santo Domingo: Fundación García Arévalo.

De la Cruz, Manuel, and V. Durán Núñez. 2012. *Artesanía dominicana, un arte popular*. Santo Domingo: Banco Popular de la República Dominicana.

Del Río Moreno, Justo L. 1996. "El cerdo: Historia de un elemento esencial de la cultura castellana en la conquista y colonización de América (siglo XVI)." *Anuario de Estudios Americanos* 53(1): 13–35.

———. 2012a. *Ganadería, plantaciones y comercio azucarero antillano, siglos XVI y XVIII*. Santo Domingo: Academia Dominicana de la Historia.

———. 2012b. *Los inicios de la agricultura europea en el Nuevo Mundo 1492–1542*. Santo Domingo: Academia Dominicana de la Historia.

Duijvenbode, Anne van. 2017. "Facing Society: A Study of Identity through Head Shaping Practices among the Indigenous Peoples of the Caribbean in the Ceramic Age and Colonial Period." PhD diss., Leiden University.

Ernst, Marlieke. Forthcoming. "Early Colonial Mosaics, Transculturation within Ceramic Repertoires in the Spanish Colonial Caribbean, 1495–1562" (working title). PhD diss., Leiden University.

Ernst, Marlieke, and Corinne L. Hofman. 2015. "Shifting Values: A Study of Early European Trade Wares in the Amerindian Site of El Cabo, Eastern Dominican Republic." In *Global Pottery 1: Historical Archaeology and Archaeometry for Societies in Contact*, edited by Jaume Buxeda, Marisol M. I. Fernández, and Javier G. Iñañez, 195–204. Oxford: BAR Publishing.

———. 2019. "Breaking and Making Identities: Transformations of Ceramic Repertoires in Early Colonial Hispaniola." In *Material Encounters and Indigenous Transformations in the Early Colonial Americas: Archaeological Case Studies*, edited by Corinne L. Hofman and Floris W. M. Keehnen, 124–145. Leiden: Brill.

Eugenio, María Ángeles. 2002. "Situación de la mujer en las rancherías de perlas del Cabo de la Vela." *Anuario de Hojas de Warmi* 13:95–111.

García Arévalo, Manuel A. 1991. "Influencias hispánicas en la alfarería Taína." In *Proceedings of the 13th International Congress for Caribbean Archaeology*, vol. 1, edited by Edwin N. Ayubi and Jay B. Haviser, 363–383. Curaçao: Reports of the Archaeological-Anthropological Institute of the Netherlands Antilles.

García Molina, José Antonio, Mercedes Mazorra Garrido, and Daisy Fariñas. 2007. *Huellas vivas del indocubano*. Havana: Editorial Ciencias Sociales.

Gassón, Rafael A. 1996. "La evolución del intercambio a larga distancia en el nororiente de Suramérica: Bienes de intercambio y poder político en una perspectiva diacrónica." In *Chieftains, Power and Trade: Regional Interaction in the Intermediate Area of the Americas*, edited by Carl H. Langebaek and Felipe C. Arroyo, 133–154. Bogotá: Universidad de los Andes.

Gonzáles, Raymundo. 2011. *De esclavos a campesinos: Vida rural en Santo Domingo colonial*. Santo Domingo: Archivo General de la Nación.

Guerrero, José G., and Marcio Veloz Maggiolo. 1988. *Los inicios de la colonización en América*. San Pedro de Macorís: Ediciones de la UCE.

Herrera Malatesta, Eduardo. 2018. *Una isla, dos mundos: Estudio arqueológico sobre el paisaje indígena de Haytí y su transformación al paisaje colonial de la Española (1200–1550)*. Leiden: Sidestone Press.

Hofman, Corinne L. 2019. "Indigenous Caribbean Networks in a Globalizing World." In *Power, Political Economy, and Historical Landscapes of the Modern World: Interdisciplinary Perspectives*, edited by Christopher R. de Corse, 55–80. Fernand Braudel Center Studies in Social Science. Albany: SUNY Press.

Hofman, Corinne L., Arie Boomert, Alistair J. Bright, Menno L. P. Hoogland, Sebastiaan Knippenberg, and Alice V. M. Samson. 2011. "Ties with the Homelands: Archipelagic Interaction and the Enduring Role of the South and Central American Mainlands in the Pre-Columbian Lesser Antilles." In *Islands at the Crossroads: Migration, Seafaring and Interaction in the Caribbean*, edited by Luis A. Curet and Mark W. Hauser, 73–86. Tuscaloosa: University of Alabama Press.

Hofman, Corinne L., and Alistair J. Bright. 2010. "Towards a Pan-Caribbean Perspective of Pre-colonial Mobility and Exchange: Preface to a Special Volume of the *Journal of Caribbean Archaeology*." *Journal of Caribbean Archaeology*, Special Publication (3): 1–3.

Hofman, Corinne L., Alistair J. Bright, Arie Boomert, and Sebastiaan Knippenberg. 2007. "Island Rhythms: The Web of Social Relationships and Interaction Networks in the Lesser Antillean Archipelago between 400 B.C. and A.D. 1492." *Latin American Antiquity* 18(3): 243–268.

Hofman, Corinne L., and Menno L. P. Hoogland. 2015. "Investigaciones arqueológicas en los sitios El Flaco (Loma de Guayacanes) y La Luperona (Unijica): Informe preliminar." *Boletín del Museo del Hombre Dominicano* 46 (42): 61–74.

Hofman, Corinne L., Menno L. P. Hoogland, Arie Boomert, and John A. Martin. 2019. "Colonial Encounters in the Southern Lesser Antilles: Indigenous

Resistance, Material Transformations, and Diversity in an Ever-Globalizing World." In *Material Encounters and Indigenous Transformations in the Early Colonial Americas: Archaeological Case Studies*, edited by Corinne L. Hofman and Floris W. M. Keehnen, 359–384. Early Americas: History and Culture no. 9. Leiden: Brill.

Hofman, Corinne L., and Floris W. M. Keehnen, eds. 2019. *Material Encounters and Indigenous Transformations in the Early Colonial Americas: Archaeological Case Studies*. Early Americas: History and Culture no. 9. Leiden: Brill.

Hofman, Corinne L., Angus A. A. Mol, Menno L. P. Hoogland, and Roberto Valcárcel Rojas. 2014. "Stage of Encounters: Migration, Mobility and Interaction in the Pre-colonial and Early Colonial Caribbean." *World Archaeology* 46(4): 590–609.

Hofman, Corinne L., Jorge Ulloa Hung, Eduardo Herrera Malatesta, Joseph S. Jean, and Menno L. P. Hoogland. 2018. "Indigenous Caribbean Perspectives: Archaeologies and Legacies of the First Colonized Region in the New World." *Antiquity* 92(361): 200–216.

Hooghiemstra Henry, Thomas Olijhoek, Menno L. P. Hoogland, Maarten Prins, Bas van Geel, Timme Donders, William Gosling, and Corinne L. Hofman. 2018. "Columbus' Environmental Impact in the New World: Land Use Change in the Yaque River Valley, Dominican Republic." *Holocene* 28(11): 1818–1835.

Keegan, William F., and Corinne L. Hofman. 2017. *The Caribbean before Columbus*. New York: Oxford University Press.

Keehnen, Floris W. M. 2011. "Conflicting Cosmologies: The Exchange of Brilliant Objects between the Taíno of Hispaniola and the Spanish." In *Communities in Contact: Essays in Archaeology, Ethnohistory and Ethnography of the Amerindian Circum-Caribbean*, edited by Corinne L. Hofman and Anne van Duijvenbode, 253–268. Leiden: Sidestone Press.

———. 2019. "Treating 'Trifles': The Indigenous Adoption of European Material Goods in Early Colonial Hispaniola (1492–1550)." In *Material Encounters and Indigenous Transformations in the Early Colonial Americas: Archaeological Case Studies*, edited by Corinne L. Hofman and Floris W. M. Keehnen, 58–83. Leiden: Brill.

Laffoon, Jason E. 2012. "Patterns of Paleomobility in the Ancient Antilles: An Isotopic Approach." PhD diss., Leiden University.

Las Casas, Bartolomé de. 1875. *Historia de las Indias*. Vol. 2. Madrid: Imprenta de Miguel Ginesta.

León Guerrero, Montserrat. 2000. "El segundo viaje colombino." PhD diss., Universidad de Valladolid.

Lightfoot, Kent G., Antoinette Martinez, and Ann M. Schiff. 1998. "Daily Practice and Material Culture in Pluralistic Social Settings: An Archaeological Study of Culture Change and Persistence from Fort Ross, California." *American Antiquity* 63(2): 199–222.

Lobo Cabrera, Manuel. 1990. "La esclavitud en España en la edad moderna: Su investigación en los últimos cincuenta años." *Hispania* 176:1091–1104.

López Belando, Adolfo J. 2013. "Excavaciones arqueológicas en el poblado taíno de Playa Grande, República Dominicana." *Proceedings of the 25th International Congress for Caribbean Archaeology*, 254–279. Puerto Rico: Instituto de Cultura Puertorriqueña, Centro de Estudios Avanzados de Puerto Rico y el Caribe, y Universidad de Puerto Rico.

Marte, Roberto. 1981. *Santo Domingo en los manuscritos de Juan Bautista Muñoz.* Santo Domingo: Fundación García Arévalo.

Martínez-Cruzado, Juan C., G. Toro-Labrador, V. Ho-Fung, M. A. Estévez-Montero, A. Lobaina-Manzanet, D. A. Padovani-Claudio, et al. 2001. "Mitochondrial DNA Analysis Reveals Substantial Native American Ancestry in Puerto Rico." *Human Biology* 73: 491–511.

Martínon-Torres, Marcos, Roberto Valcárcel Rojas, Juanita Sáenz Samper, and María Filomena Guerra. 2012. "Metallic Encounters in Cuba: The Technology, Exchange and Meaning of Metals before and after Columbus." *Journal of Anthropological Archaeology* 31(4): 439–454.

Mira Caballos, Esteban. 2000. *Las Antillas mayores 1492–1550.* Ensayos y documentos, Iberoamericana, Madrid, and Vervuert, Frankfurt.

———. 2004. "Caciques guatiaos en los inicios de la colonización: El caso del indio Diego Colón." *Iberoamericana* 4(16): 7–16.

———. 2009. *Conquista y destrucción de las Indias (1492–1573).* Madrid: Muñoz Moya Editores.

Mol, Angus A. A. 2014. *The Connected Caribbean: A Socio-material Network Approach to Patterns of Homogeneity and Diversity in the Pre-colonial Period.* Leiden: Sidestone Press.

Montón-Subías, Sandra, Maria Cruz Berrocal, and Apen Ruiz. 2016. "Towards a Comparative Approach to Archaeologies of Early Modern Spanish Colonialism." In *Archaeologies of Early Modern Spanish Colonialism*, edited by Sandra Montón-Subías, Maria C. Berrocal, and Apen R. Martínez, 1–9. Heidelberg: Springer.

Moya Pons, Frank. 2016. *El o ro en la historia dominicana.* Santo Domingo: Academia Dominicana de la Historia.

Moya Pons, Frank, and Rosario Flores Paz. 2013. *Los Taínos en 1492: El debate demo gráfico.* Santo Domingo: Academia Dominicana de la Historia.

Oliver, José R. 2009. *Caciques and Cemí Idols: The Web Spun by Taíno Rulers between Hispaniola and Puerto Rico.* Tuscaloosa: University of Alabama Press.

Olsen Bogaert, Harold, Santiago Duval, and Frank Coste. 2011. *Sitio arqueol ógico no. 11: Investigación estructuras coloniales; Reporte de investigación.* Santo Domingo: Pueblo Viejo Dominicana Corporation, Proyecto Pueblo Viejo.

———. 2016. "Investigaciones arqueológicas en el primer campamento minero colonial de América, pueblo Viejo de Cotuí." *Boletín del Museo del Hombre Dominicano* 47:311–331.

Ortega, Elpidio José. 1988. *La Isabela y la arqueología de la Ruta de Colón*. San Pedro de Macorís: Universidad Central del Este.

Ortega, Elpidio José, and Carmen Fondeur. 1978. *Estudio de la cerámica del período indo-hispánico de la antigua concepción de La Vega*. Santo Domingo: Taller.

Panich, Lee M. 2013. "Archaeologies of Persistence: Reconsidering the Legacies of Colonialism in Native North America." *American Antiquity* 78(1): 105–122.

Pérez Iglesias, Lourdes, and Roberto Valcárcel Rojas. 2014. "Restos de cerdo en los contextos arqueológicos de El Chorro de Maíta, Holguín, Cuba." *Etnobiología* 12(2): 39–49.

Pesoutova, Jana. 2019. "Indigenous Ancestors and Healing Landscapes: Cultural Memory and Intercultural Communication in the Dominican Republic and Cuba." PhD diss., Leiden University.

Pesoutova, Jana, and Corinne L. Hofman. 2016. "La contribución indígena a la biografía del paisaje cultural de la República Dominicana: Una revisión preliminar." In *Indígenas e indios en el Caribe presencia, legado y studio*, edited by Jorge Ulloa Hung and Roberto Valcárcel Rojas, 115–150. Santo Domingo: Instituto Tecnológico de Santo Domingo.

Redmond, Elsa, and Charles Spencer. 1994. "The Cacicazgo: An Indigenous Design." In *Caciques and Their People: A Volume in Honor of Ronald Spores*, edited by J. Marcus and J. F. Zeitlin, 189–225. Ann Arbor: Museum of Anthropology, University of Michigan.

Reyes Cardero, Juan M. 2018. "Supervivencia e impronta de indios y sus descendientes en el Santiago de Cuba colonial (Siglo XVI al XIX)." In *De la desaparición a la permanencia: Indígenas e indios en la reinvención del Caribe*, edited by Roberto Valcárcel Rojas and Jorge Ulloa Hung, 83–120. Santo Domingo: Instituto Tecnológico de Santo Domingo—Fundación García Arévalo.

Rodríguez Ramos, Reniel, and Jaime R. Pagán Jiménez. 2016. "Sobre nuestras indigenidades boricuas." In *Indígenas e indios en el Caribe: Presencia, legado y estudio*, vol. 1, edited by Jorge Ulloa Hung and Roberto Valcárcel Rojas, 97–114. Santo Domingo: Instituto Tecnológico de Santo Domingo.

Romeu de Armas, Antonio. 1991. "Carta relación del segundo viaje." In *Libro copiador de Cristobal Colón*. Madrid: Testimonio Compañía Editorial.

Samson, Alice V. M. 2010. *Renewing the House: Trajectories of Social Life in the Yucayeque (Community) of El Cabo, Higüey, Dominican Republic, AD 800 to 1504*. Leiden: Sidestone Press.

Samson, Alice V. M., Jago Cooper, and Josué Caamaño-Dones. 2016. "European Visitors in Native Spaces: Using Palaeography to Investigate Religious Dynamics in the New World." *Latin American Antiquity* 27(4): 443–461.

Schroeder, Hannes, Martin Sikora, Shyam Gopalakrishnan, Lara M. Cassidy, Pierpaolo Maisano Desler, Marcela Sandoval Velasco, Joshua G. Schraiber, Simon Rasmussen, Julian R. Homburger, María C. Ávila-Arcos, Morten E. Allentoft, J. Victor Moreno-Mayar, Gabriel Renaud, Alberto Gómez-Carballa, Jason E. Laffoon, Rachel J. A. Hopkins, Thomas F. G. Higham,

Robert S. Carr, William C. Schaffer, Jane S. Day, Menno L. P. Hoogland, Antonio Salas, Carlos D. Bustamante, Rasmus Nielsen, Daniel G. Bradley, Corinne L. Hofman, and Eske Willerslev. 2018. "Origins and Genetic Legacies of the Caribbean Taino." *Proceedings of the National Academy of Sciences of the United States of America* 115(10): 2341–2346.

Smith, Marvin T. 1988. "Depopulation and Culture Change in the Early Historic Period Interior Southeast." PhD diss., University of Florida.

Sonnemann, Till F., Jorge Ulloa Hung, and Corinne L. Hofman. 2016. "Mapping Indigenous Settlement Topography in the Caribbean Using Drones." *Remote Sensing* 8(10): 791.

Sued Badillo, Jalil. 1992. "Facing Up to Caribbean History." *American Antiquity* 57(4): 599–607.

———. 1995. "The Island Caribs: New Approaches to the Questions of Ethnicity in the Early Colonial Caribbean." In *Wolves from the Sea: Readings in the Anthropology of the Native Caribbean*, edited by Neil L. Whitehead, 61–89. Leiden: KITLV-Caribbean Series 14, Brill.

———. 2011. "From Taínos to Africans in the Caribbean: Labor, Migration, and Resistance." In *The Caribbean: A History of the Region and Its People*, edited by Stephan Palmié and Francisco A. Scarano, 97–114. Chicago: University of Chicago Press.

Ting, Carmen, Jorge Ulloa Hung, Corinne L. Hofman, and Patrick Degryse. 2018. "Indigenous Technologies and the Production of Early Colonial Ceramics in Dominican Republic." *Journal of Archaeological Science: Reports* 17:47–57.

Ulloa Hung, Jorge. 2005. "Arqueología y rescate de la presencia aborigen en el Caribe." In *Una mirada al Caribe precolombino*, 30–35. Santo Domingo: Instituto Tecnológico de Santo Domingo.

———. 2014. *Arqueología en la línea noroeste de La Española: Paisajes, cerámicas e interacciones*. Santo Domingo: Instituto Tecnológico de Santo Domingo.

———. 2018. "Legado indígena: Cerámica y artesanía en la República Dominicana." In *De la desaparición a la permanencia: Indígenas e indios en la reinvención del Caribe*, vol. 2, edited by Roberto Valcárcel Rojas and Jorge Ulloa Hung, 369–423. Santo Domingo: Instituto Tecnológico de Santo Domingo—Fundación García Árevalo.

Ulloa Hung, Jorge, and Eduardo Herrera Malatesta. 2015. "Investigaciones arqueológicas en el norte de La Española, entre viejos esquemas y nuevos datos." *Boletín del Museo del Hombre Dominicano* 46:75–107.

Ulloa Hung, Jorge, and Roberto Valcárcel Rojas, eds. 2016. *Indígenas e indios en el Caribe: Presencia, legado y estudio*. Santo Domingo: Instituto Tecnológico de Santo Domingo.

Valcárcel Rojas, Roberto. 2016a. *Archaeology of Early Colonial Interaction at El Chorro de Maita, Cuba*. Gainesville: University Press of Florida.

———. 2016b. "Cuba: Indios después de Colón." In *Indígenas e indios en el Caribe: Presencia, legado y estudio*, edited by Jorge Ulloa Hung and Roberto Valcárcel Rojas, 7–48. Santo Domingo: Instituto Tecnológico de Santo Domingo.

———. 2019. "European Material Culture in Indigenous Sites in Northeastern Cuba." In *Material Encounters and Indigenous Transformations in the Early Colonial Americas: Archaeological Case Studies*, edited by Corinne L. Hofman and Floris W. M. Keehnen, 102–123. Leiden: Brill.

Valcárcel Rojas, Roberto, A. Campos Suárez, Y. Rodríguez Bruzón, and J. E. Jardines Macías. 2018. "Arqueología en Managuaco: Presencia de indios en una hacienda colonial cubana." In *De la desaparición a la permanencia: Indígenas e indios en la reinvención del Caribe*, vol. 2, edited by R. Valcárcel Rojas and J. Ulloa Hung, 247–277. Santo Domingo: Instituto Tecnológico de Santo Domingo—Fundación García Árevalo.

Valcárcel Rojas, Roberto, Menno L. P. Hoogland, and Corinne L. Hofman. 2014. "Indios: Arqueología de una nueva identidad." In *Indios en Holguín*, edited by Roberto Valcárcel Rojas and Hiram Perez, 20–42. Holguín: Editorial La Mezquita.

Valcárcel Rojas, Roberto, Jason E. Laffoon, Darlene A. Weston, Menno L. P. Hoogland, and Corinne L. Hofman. 2019. "Slavery of Indigenous People in the Caribbean Islands: An Archaeological Perspective." *International Journal of Historical Archaeology*, doi: https://doi.org/10.1007/s10761-019-00522-x.

Valcárcel Rojas, Roberto, and Marcos Martinón-Torres. 2013. "Metals in the Indigenous Societies of the Insular Caribbean." In *The Oxford Handbook of Caribbean Archaeology*, edited by William F. Keegan, Corinne L. Hofman, and Reniel Rodríguez Ramos, 504–522. New York: Oxford University Press.

Valcárcel Rojas, R., A. Samson, and M. Hoogland. 2013. "Indo-Hispanic Dynamics: From Contact to Colonial Interaction in the Greater Antilles." *International Journal of Historical Archaeology* 17:18–39.

Valcárcel Rojas, Roberto, and Jorge Ulloa Hung, eds. 2018. "Introducción: La desaparición del indígena y la permanencia del indio." In *De la desaparición a la permanencia: Indígenas e indios en la reinvención del Caribe*, vol. 2, edited by Roberto Valcárcel Rojas and Jorge Ulloa Hung, 5–39. Santo Domingo: Instituto Tecnológico de Santo Domingo—Fundación García Árevalo.

Valcárcel Rojas, Roberto, and M. E. Velázquez. 2016. "Indios en Cuba: Una nueva lectura de un documento histórico del siglo XVI." *Gabinete de Arqueología* 12:15–21.

Valcárcel Rojas, Roberto, Darlene A. Weston, Hayley L. Mickleburgh, and Jason E. Laffoon. 2011. "El Chorro de Maíta: A Diverse Approach to a Context of Diversity." In *Communities in Contact: Essays in Archaeology, Ethnohistory and Ethnography of the Amerindian Circum-Caribbean*, edited by Corinne L. Hofman and Anne van Duijvenbode, 225–252. Leiden: Sidestone Press.

Van der Veen, James M. 2006. "Subsistence Patterns as Markers of Cultural Exchange: European and Taíno Interactions in the Dominican Republic." PhD diss., Indiana University.

Vega, Bernardo. 1981. "La herencia indígena en la cultura dominicana de hoy." In *Ensayos sobre cultura dominicana*, edited by Bernardo Vega, 11–53. Santo Domingo: Museo del Hombre Dominicano.

———. 1990. *Los cacicazgos de la Española*. Santo Domingo: Fundación Cultural Dominicana.

Veloz Maggiolo, Marcio, Elpidio José Ortega, and Angel Caba Fuentes. 1981. *Los modos de vida meillacoides y sus posibles orígenes*. Santo Domingo: Taller.

Weston, Darlene A., and Roberto Valcárcel Rojas. 2016. "Communities in Contact: Health and Paleodemography at El Chorro de Maíta, Cuba." In *Cuban Archaeology in the Caribbean*, edited by Ivan Roksandic, 83–105. Gainesville: University Press of Florida.

Wilson, Samuel M. 1990. *Hispaniola: Caribbean Chiefdoms in the Age of Columbus*. Tuscaloosa: University of Alabama Press.

———. 2007. *The Archaeology of the Caribbean*. Cambridge: Cambridge University Press.

Woodruff Stone, Erin. 2014. "Indian Harvest: The Rise of the Indigenous Slave Trade and Diaspora from Española to the Circum-Caribbean, 1492–1542." PhD diss., Vanderbilt University.

Yeager, Timothy J. 1995. "Encomienda or Slavery? The Spanish Crown's Choice of Labor Organization in the Sixteenth-Century Spanish America." *Journal of Economic History* 55(4): 842–859.

Yaremko, Jason M. 2016. *Indigenous Passages to Cuba, 1515–1900*. Gainesville: University Press of Florida.

3

Native American Responses to Spanish Contact and Colonialism in the American South

Christopher B. Rodning, Michelle M. Pigott, and Hannah G. Hoover

At the point of Spanish contact in southeastern North America, there were many Native American chiefdoms throughout the American South in what Spaniards came to claim as the colonial province of La Florida (Beck 2013; Ethridge 2017; Ethridge and Mitchem 2013; Hoffman 1990, 2014; Lyon 1976; Scarry 1994b, 1996a, 1996b). The pluralistic geopolitical landscape of the Native American South encompassed many different chiefly provinces and, correspondingly, many different mound centers, which formed the towns at which chiefs resided and at which events associated with chiefly leadership took place (Map 3.1). Although these mound centers and associated chiefdoms were all associated with the broader Mississippian cultural tradition, each chiefdom had its own history, and these histories shaped the course of early encounters and entanglements with Spanish conquistadors and colonists. During the sixteenth century, indigenous groups of the Native American South conceptualized Spanish expeditions as potential enemies but also as potential allies, and chiefs and chiefdoms pursued their own interests and agendas through diplomacy, warfare, exchange, acquisition of gifts and prestige goods, and other strategies and activities. During the seventeenth century, the establishment and entrenchment of missions and mission settlements altered the cultural landscape of the Native American South, but there were aspects of Mississippian culture, chiefly leadership, and place making that persisted. This chapter considers archaeological and ethnohistoric evidence for patterns of cultural persistence, place making, pluralism, and the diverse histories of Mississippian societies that shaped the course of Spanish colonial history in the Native American South. These episodes of culture contact began not long after early Spanish exploration and settlement in the Caribbean (Deagan 1985, 1988), and several Spanish entradas in La Florida took place simultaneously with or soon after early

Map 3.1 Locations of selected Native American chiefly provinces in La Florida.

Spanish encounters with indigenous peoples of the American Southwest, Mesoamerica, the Andes, and Amazonia (Van Buren 2010). Differences between the cultural landscapes of the Mississippian South and those in other world areas contributed to different outcomes of the Spanish colonial enterprise and responses by indigenous groups to it.

PERSISTENCE

Of course, many aspects of Native American life in the American South changed after Spanish contact, but many characteristics of Mississippian culture endured and in some cases manifested themselves in new variations on traditional themes. The availability and acquisition of metal items created new sources of prestige goods, but those goods circulated in networks of exchange and interaction that predated Spanish contact (Smith 1987, 1994, 2002, 2006; Waselkov 1989). Some chiefdoms collapsed or were diminished in status relative to others (Smith 2000), but other chiefdoms emerged (Ethridge 2010), and many aspects of chiefly leadership persisted (King 2006), although in some cases chiefly status became manifested in part through diplomatic relations with Spanish colonists and access to Spanish goods (Worth 2002). Some mound centers that were powerful and prosperous towns before Spanish contact either were abandoned or were less powerful and less prosperous than they had been (King 1999; Regnier 2015; Smith 2000; Williams 1994; Williams and Shapiro 1996), but in many cases, the provinces of powerful chiefdoms from the early sixteenth century endured as major geopolitical centers in the late 1500s and 1600s (Beck 2013; Ewen 1996; Ewen and Hann 1998; Hann and McEwan 1998; Scarry 1994a, 1996c). There were major realignments of geopolitical relationships in the Native American South after early Spanish contact for sure, but aspects of chiefly leadership endured, and they shaped indigenous responses to contact and colonialism and its outcomes.

One manifestation of persistence is the case of the Apalachee province and chiefdom in northern Florida (Hann 1988, 1994; McEwan 1991, 2001; Scarry 1992, 1994a, 1996c). One of the major Mississippian mound centers along the Florida Gulf Coast was the Lake Jackson mound site (Scarry 1990; Seinfeld et al. 2015). The Lake Jackson chiefdom may have been the point of origin for marine shell that was the raw material for the circular (and sometimes square) pendants known as gorgets. These pendants were "platforms" for elaborate engraved iconography and are found in elite burials at major mound centers in northern Georgia and eastern Tennessee. Some of the elite burials in Lake Jackson mounds are associated with copper plates that have embossed iconography comparable to that seen on Mississippian gorgets and on copper plates found at Etowah and at prehistoric Mississippian mound sites like Cahokia (Illinois) and Spiro (Oklahoma). When the expedition led by Juan Pánfilo de Narváez marched northward from Tampa Bay and approached the Apalachee province in 1528, they were met with stiff resistance by Apalachee warriors, presumably motivated in part by conflicts that had arisen between the Narváez expedition and other native groups in Florida and that were probably motivated as well as by opportunities for Apalachee chiefs and warriors to accumulate power and prestige through encounter and engagement with Spanish conquistadors (Hoffman 1994a, 1994b). Several years later, the Hernando de Soto expedition was likewise met by hostility from Apalachee chiefs and warriors probably motivated in part by the memory of encounters with the Narváez expedition and the continuing interests of Apalachee chiefs and warriors in demonstrating prowess and success in warfare and diplomacy (Hudson 1994, 1997).

At the point of the Narváez and Soto expeditions, the Lake Jackson mounds were no longer the major geopolitical center in the Apalachee province; instead, the nearby settlement of Anhaica may have been the regional political center. The Soto expedition established its first winter encampment at Anhaica (Ewen 1996). The people of Anhaica abandoned the town in advance of Soto's arrival in 1539, and they burned many of the structures in the town. During the winter, Apalachee warriors harassed Soto's encampment and expedition with periodic attacks, and the Soto expedition eventually decamped and marched northward toward Ocute and Cofitachequi in 1540, after which point the Apalachee reclaimed and resettled the site. The Apalachee chiefdom endured those early Spanish entradas, and it was still present during the spread of the network of Catholic missions and Spanish colonial outposts in the Florida panhandle during the seventeenth century.

The major centers within the Apalachee chiefdom for much of the seventeenth century were Anhaica and the nearby settlement of San Luis, the latter of which was the site of both the Apalachee capital and the Spanish colonial capital of the Apalachee province from 1656 to 1704 (Hann 1994). The built environment of San Luis differed in many respects from those of Mississippian mound centers from the period before Spanish contact—most notably in the presence of the Spanish fort and town and the Catholic church and friary—but the plaza beside the church was analogous in some respects to plazas at Mississippian mound centers.

The plaza formed a middle ground of sorts—in both literal and figurative senses—in that the church was situated on one side and a monumental Apalachee council house and the house of the Apalachee chief were on the other side. The plaza was the setting for traditional Apalachee stickball games—an indigenous practice discouraged by Catholic priests but continued anyway by the Apalachee community—and it was the setting for the emplacement both of wooden crosses as Christian symbols and of large wooden posts that were landmarks for Mississippian towns and targets for stickball games. The Apalachee council house at San Luis was not built on an earthen mound, but it is one of the largest examples of the council houses present at several Mississippian sites in Florida and coastal Georgia (Thompson 2009), and it was an architectural symbol of the vitality of the Apalachee chiefdom and a monument of sorts to the persistence of the Apalachee chiefdom within the geopolitical landscape of the Native American South during the period of Spanish entradas and the mission period of the seventeenth century.

Other cases of persistence in Mississippian chiefdoms are those of the Taensa chiefdom in northeastern Louisiana (Ethridge 2010:136–138) and the Natchez chiefdom in southwestern Mississippi (Barnett 2007). The Soto expedition encountered powerful chiefdoms in northern Mississippi such as Quizquiz and Quigualtam, and they participated in warfare between the rival chiefdoms of Casqui and Pacaha in Arkansas. After Native American warriors from Quigualtam and other chiefdoms in neighboring areas drove surviving members of the Soto expedition—by that point led by Luis Moscoso—down to the mouth of the Mississippi and out of the American South in 1543, there were no recorded contacts between Native Americans and Europeans in the Lower Mississippi Valley until the French expedition led by Jacques Marquette and Louis Joliet in 1673. The geopolitical landscape had changed dramatically, but there were still vibrant and powerful chiefdoms centered at the Grand Village of the Natchez, known to archaeologists as the Fatherland site (Brown 1990; Brown and Steponaitis 2017; Lorenz 1997; Mehta 2013; Milne 2009), and in the Taensa province of northeastern Louisiana, where settlements were situated around the edges of oxbow lakes (Swanton 1911, 1946). The Taensa lived in areas close to many sites with large platform mounds that predate the point of Spanish contact in the Southeast, and there is evidence for moundbuilding at the Jordan

site between 1540 and 1685 (Kidder 1992). During the period between
Spanish and French contact in the Lower Mississippi Valley, many people moved to this area of northern Louisiana, probably in part because of
the social and political upheavals associated with early Spanish contact
in Arkansas and Mississippi and perhaps as far away as Alabama. This
part of the Southeast was a setting for the persistence of Mississippian
culture, even though specific chiefdoms collapsed and groups coalesced
into new chiefdoms, like those of the Taensa and Natchez themselves.

The persistence of Mississippian chiefdoms—altered in some ways,
resilient in others—is evident as well in the continuing significance of
prestige goods as symbols of chiefly status. Before Spanish contact, manifestations of such statuses included copper plates, copper armbands, marine shell pins and pendants, and undoubtedly perishable materials and
markings that are not preserved at archaeological sites. After Spanish
contact, metal goods such as axes, knives, chisels, and celts became material symbols of status as well. Such items have been found in burials at
several sites within the territory of the powerful paramount chiefdom of
Coosa, encompassing much of northern Georgia and adjacent areas of
eastern Alabama and eastern Tennessee (Smith 1987, 2000) and including the mid-sixteenth-century town at the King site (Hally 2004, 2008).
The acquisition of such material wealth and the prospect of alliances with
Spanish conquistadors such as Hernando de Soto (1539–1543; Hudson
1997) and Juan Pardo (1566–1568; Hudson 2005) were probably significant motivations for Mississippian chiefs in pursuing trade relations or
warfare or both with Spanish explorers and colonists.

From the macroscalar perspective of the Mississippian Southeast as a
whole, the Mississippian world was indeed dramatically altered in the aftermath of Spanish contact (Ethridge 2006, 2009, 2010), and some areas
were abandoned (Williams 1994), but some aspects of chiefly leadership
and landscape persisted or were re-created. Before Spanish contact, there
were cycles in the emergence and collapse of Mississippian chiefdoms
and shifts of the focal points of Mississippian chiefdoms across the landscape (Anderson 1994, 1996a, 1996b; Beck 2013; King 2003). These patterns in the history of Mississippian chiefdoms differed in some respects
from those set in motion by Spanish contact (Hally 2006), but there had
long been some instability in the Mississippian geopolitical landscape.
Eventually, the Mississippian world did collapse, leading to the dramatic

transformations and coalescences of communities that took shape during periods of French and English colonialism in the South during the late 1600s and 1700s, but there were aspects of Mississippian culture that endured, and there were echoes of Mississippian culture in the postcontact Native American South. Meanwhile, the course of Spanish colonialism led to diverse outcomes within different areas of the Southeast, and those differences were related in part to local histories and the strategies adopted by different communities to respond to the events and developments of the contact period.

PLURALISM

Spanish contact had diverse impacts on indigenous groups across the American South, and, similarly, different groups engaged with Spanish expeditions in different ways. After prolonged interactions with the Soto expedition in 1540 and the geopolitical instability created by it, the paramount chiefdom of Coosa was greatly diminished, and it was not as powerful or prosperous in 1560, when a contingent of men from the Tristán de Luna expedition made a foray from its colony in Pensacola inland toward Coosa in search of food (Hally 1994; Hudson et al. 1989; Hudson et al. 1985). Contact with the Soto expedition had similar effects on the chiefdom of Cofitachequi, in central South Carolina, although it was still significant in the geopolitical landscape of the Native American South in the seventeenth century (Beck 2013; DePratter 1989, 1994; Hudson et al. 2008). On the other hand, in the northern borderlands of La Florida, the people of Joara and other provinces of eastern Tennessee and the western Carolinas resisted attempts at Spanish colonization and erased several Spanish colonial towns and forts established during the period of the Juan Pardo expeditions from 1566 to 1568 (Beck and Moore 2002; Beck et al. 2016; Beck et al. 2017; Beck et al. 2010; Beck, Rodning, and Moore 2016; Moore 2002; Rodning et al. 2013). At the southern edge of La Florida, the Calusa of southwestern Florida were resistant to Spanish colonialism and attempts at converting them to Christianity for much of the 1500s and 1600s (Marquardt 2001, 2014; Widmer 1988).

The case of the Calusa is interesting in part because southern Florida is the point of first contact between Spanish colonists and indigenous peoples of the Native American South (Bushnell 2006, 2014;

Fowler Williams 1991; MacMahon and Marquardt 2004; Milanich 2014; Thompson, Marquardt, Walker, et al. 2018; Worth 2013, 2014). The first recorded encounters took place during the voyage led by Juan Ponce de León in 1513, although the hostile reception that Ponce de León received when he periodically landed to take on food and water hints at the possibility of violent encounters before that point, and he and his men took several Calusa captives when skirmishes arose near the mouth of the Caloosahatchee River along the Florida Gulf Coast. The Calusa attacked an expedition by Francisco Hernández de Córdoba in 1517, they attacked Ponce de León during his effort to colonize Florida in 1521, they resisted Dominican attempts to establish a mission in 1547, and they periodically mobilized large numbers of warriors in seaworthy canoes in response to the approach of Spanish ships. The Narváez and Soto expeditions bypassed Calusa territory, but in 1566 the aspiring colonial governor of La Florida, Pedro Menéndez de Avilés, established a garrison and Jesuit mission at the Calusa capital of Calos, on an anthropogenic island known as Mound Key (Thompson, Marquardt, Cherkinsky, et al. 2016). Calos was the residence of the most powerful Calusa chief (known as Carlos), and Menéndez married the sister of the chief as part of his effort at making an enduring alliance with the Calusa. Violent encounters between 1566 and 1569 led to the abandonment of the Spanish outpost at Calos. During the seventeenth century, several efforts by Spaniards to conquer the Calusa or negotiate with them proved unsuccessful, and so also did an effort by Franciscans to missionize the Calusa.

Despite intermittent direct contacts between Spanish colonists and the Calusa during the 1500s and 1600s, indirect contacts and the circulation of Spanish goods within southern Florida had important impacts on the Calusa chiefdom. Throughout this period, native people salvaged material items—including gold and silver—from Spanish shipwrecks along the eastern and western coasts of Florida (McGuire 2014). Like metal goods introduced directly from Spanish entradas farther north, items salvaged from Spanish shipwrecks—and in some cases shipwreck survivors—became material symbols of wealth and status within the Calusa chiefdom.

The Calusa did not really seek out interactions with Spanish colonists, but they did respond strategically to the Spanish colonial presence in Florida, and so did the community of Joara, in western North Carolina.

Soto traversed the province of Xuala in 1540 en route between the province of Cofitachequi and eastern Tennessee (Beck 1997; Hudson 1997). Pardo and his men marched inland from the Spanish colonial capital of Santa Elena in 1566, they founded Fort San Juan and the colonial town of Cuenca adjacent to the main town of Joara, and they established five other outposts in the Carolinas and eastern Tennessee in 1567 and early 1568 (Beck 2009; Hudson 2005). Pardo often asked Native American community leaders to build houses for him and his men and to set aside stores of food for them, and he inserted himself into diplomatic relations and tributary networks encompassing diverse communities and speakers of diverse languages (Booker et al. 1992). Documentary sources and archaeological evidence from the Berry site in western North Carolina, the location of Joara, Cuenca, and Fort San Juan, illustrate outcomes of these forms of interaction and engagement (Beck et al. 2016; Beck et al. 2017; Beck, Rodning, and Moore 2016). Relations between Pardo and the people of Joara began favorably, but during the spring of 1568, news reached Santa Elena that Fort San Juan had been attacked and abandoned, as had Pardo's five other outposts (Beck et al. 2018). The alliance that formed at the outset contributed to the ascendancy of Joara relative to other chiefdoms such as Cofitachequi and Coosa (Beck et al. 2010), and the conquest of Fort San Juan probably also enhanced Joara's geopolitical status (Rodning et al. 2013).

The cases of Joara and the Calusa demonstrate different outcomes from the effects of Spanish contact on other groups in the Native American South, including the chiefdoms of Coosa and Cofitachequi, which were greatly altered by contacts with the Soto expedition. For the Calusa, managing and containing the Spanish colonial presence and access to Spanish goods became closely associated with chiefly leadership. In the case of Joara, an alliance with Pardo was favorable at first, and both that alliance and the successful attack on Fort San Juan had implications for the relative statuses of Joara and other polities and communities.

PLACE MAKING

During the 1500s and for much of the 1600s, most Spanish encampments or towns in the American South were relatively ephemeral, with the significant exceptions of more enduring settlements at coastal towns like

Santa Elena, in South Carolina (South 1988), and St. Augustine, Florida (Deagan 1982, 1983, 2010a, 2010b). The Soto expedition wintered at abandoned indigenous settlements in the provinces of Apalachee and Chicaza. The Pardo expedition established colonial towns at Native American settlements. By contrast, aboriginal settlements were relatively permanent, and many had long histories, especially those sites with earthen mounds and plazas that were political capitals and ceremonial centers.

One architectural manifestation of Spanish contact in the Southeast is the emplacement of crosses at Mississippian sites. For example, written accounts refer to crosses emplaced around the plaza at San Luis during the seventeenth century (Hann and McEwan 1998). During the sixteenth century, Soto and his men placed a wooden cross on the summit of a platform mound in the capital town of Casqui, which is associated with the Parkin site in Arkansas (Ethridge 2017:xviii; Mitchem 1996). It is hard to know precisely how indigenous people interpreted these symbols, although they probably did so differently from the Spaniards, and, notably, crosses and cross-in-circle motifs were present in Mississippian iconography before and after Spanish contact (Saunders 2000). It is not hard to imagine that crosses emplaced on mounds and plazas added layers of religious and political significance to those places in the Mississippian landscape.

Other architectural manifestations of the Spanish colonial presence in the Southeast are the forts the Spaniards built (Deagan 2016), including those at Santa Elena (Thompson, DePratter, and Roberts Thompson 2016; Thompson, Marquardt, Walker, et al. 2018) and at the town of Joara (Beck et al. 2006; Beck et al. 2018). Of course, these forts were built as places of refuge and as settings for military activity, but they were also monuments of sorts to Spanish colonial hegemony and landmarks of the Spanish colonial presence in the Southeast. The visibility of these landmarks may have made them targets as well, as in the case of Native American attacks on Fort San Juan. In some ways, log stockades enclosing Spanish forts may have resembled, in a very general sense, the log stockades that enclosed major Mississippian towns (Steinen 1992) as described for the case of Mabila, the site of an epic battle between members of the Soto expedition and Native American warriors in Alabama (Knight 2009), and as known archaeologically from sites like Parkin, in Arkansas (Mitchem 2011), and the King site, in Georgia (Hally 2008).

Within the Mississippian Southeast, log stockades enclosed settlements with earthen mounds and plazas, residential neighborhoods, and the dwellings of chiefs, and although Spanish colonial forts were not residential spaces in the same sense, they were enclosures for important geopolitical centers in the colonial landscape of La Florida.

Spanish forts created divisions between Spanish colonial spaces and native settlements nearby both in the literal sense that log stockades formed the edges of them and in the more metaphorical sense that they created distance between newcomers and natives in the landscape. On the other hand, forts (and, later, missions) were places that drew in diverse groups and created settings for pluralistic colonial encounters. Leaders from diverse and in some cases distant communities traveled to Fort San Juan to meet with Juan Pardo, for example; the mission and fort at San Luis became a focal point for the main Apalachee town within the Apalachee province of Florida, and several different groups came to live in proximity to Spanish mission settlements along the Atlantic coast of Florida and Georgia (McEwan 1993; Milanich 1994, 2006; Stojanowski 2005, 2010; Thomas 1988).

These and other manifestations of the Spanish colonial presence in the Southeast, including ephemeral and seasonal encampments and colonial towns and forts, formed new layers within an aboriginal landscape of large towns, earthen mounds, and farmlands surrounding large towns and rural farmsteads. The colonial town at Santa Elena lasted for 21 years, although it was renovated and rebuilt considerably during that period (Thompson, DePratter, and Roberts Thompson 2016; Thompson, Marquardt, Walker, et al. 2018), and while of course St. Augustine has persisted as a major town and city since 1565, it too was rebuilt and even moved periodically in its early history. By the mid- to late seventeenth century, Spanish mission settlements like San Luis and others had become relatively permanent, but before that point, Spanish settlements were relatively impermanent and in many cases were short-lived.

CONCLUSIONS

Thinking about Spanish colonialisms in global and comparative perspective, the Spanish colonial enterprise in La Florida was never complete and never decisive, and while the imprints of Spanish colonialism on the

American South were profound, the Spanish colonial presence itself was not very permanent in the landscape in most areas, at least in terms of permanent settlements, during the 1500s and much of the 1600s. The Spanish colonial presence at any particular place did have effects that reverberated across the Native American South as a whole (Rodning et al. 2018), but the local outcomes of Spanish colonialism were shaped by local conditions and local community history. There were many different chiefdoms and chiefly provinces in the Native American South at the point of Spanish contact, and while many communities moved or coalesced with other groups (Ethridge 2009) and many regional polities collapsed (Hally 2006), there were elements of Mississippian culture and Mississippian chiefdoms that endured Spanish entradas and early stages in the Spanish mission system in the 1500s and 1600s.

Some places in the landscape persisted as important political centers, even as the nature of those political centers changed. Within the Apalachee province, major towns from the Mississippi period, the sixteenth century, and the seventeenth century were all located in close proximity to each other. Even the setting for the town of Cofitachequi, which did diminish in significance between the eras of the Soto and Pardo entradas, was still an important place in the landscape in the late seventeenth century.

Some new settlements and perhaps even some new mound centers were founded, often reflecting major principles of Mississippian architecture and settlement plans. One example is the Jordan site in Louisiana, where there is evidence of moundbuilding during the interval between Spanish and French contact in the Lower Mississippi Valley (Kidder 1992). Another example is the King site, in Georgia, where a Mississippian town reflecting major principles of Mississippian town layout, including a log stockade, a zone of residential structures around a plaza, and a community structure, was built soon after encounters between towns within the Coosa chiefdom and the members of either the Soto or Luna expedition (Hally 2008).

New forms of prestige goods and material wealth were introduced to the Native American South, but they were circulated and managed within networks that predated Spanish contact. Developing and maintaining access to such goods, and the alliances manifested in them, became important considerations for community leaders and community leadership. So also did opportunities to advance community interests and agendas through warfare, as evident in the attack in 1568 on Fort San Juan by warriors from Joara (Hudson 2005) and the epic battle in 1540 between members of the Soto expedition and Mississippian warriors at the town of Mabila, in southern Alabama (Knight 2009). Spanish colonialism posed new challenges and created new conditions different from those that had been present before, but native peoples of the Southeast responded to them following cultural practices and geopolitical strategies that had deep roots in the Mississippian world. Those strategies and responses sometimes favored accommodation and alliance and sometimes favored warfare and avoidance.

Archaeology has taught and can teach us much about the history of Spanish colonialism in the Native American South. One important direction for us to take is to consider further the effects of long-term patterns of environmental changes and Native American cultural history on the relatively abrupt and short-term effects of early encounters and entanglements with Spanish colonists on indigenous peoples of La Florida. Documentary evidence is rich, but there were long-term diachronic processes and historical forces that must have shaped the ways in which colonial encounters were conceptualized, experienced, negotiated, and remembered. Another important direction for us to take is to develop interpretive frameworks that emphasize indigenous viewpoints rather than those of European explorers and colonists. From an indigenous perspective, Spaniards were another group in an already pluralistic cultural landscape, and native groups adopted and adapted traditional cultural practices to engage with them through diplomacy, warfare, trade, and other forms of interaction.

ACKNOWLEDGMENTS

Many thanks to Christine Beaule, John Douglass, and the Amerind Foundation, and thanks to other seminar participants and contributors to this book. Thanks to support from several sources at Tulane University, including Howard-Tilton Memorial Library, the Stone Center for Latin American Studies, the New Orleans Center for the Gulf South, the Carol Lavin Bernick Faculty Grant program, the ByWater Institute and A Studio in the Woods, Newcomb-Tulane College, and the School of Liberal Arts.

REFERENCES

Anderson, David G. 1990. "Stability and Change in Chiefdom-Level Societies." In *Lamar Archaeology: Mississippian Chiefdoms of the Deep South*, edited by Mark Williams and Gary Shapiro, 187–213. Tuscaloosa: University of Alabama Press.

———. 1994a. "Factional Competition and the Political Evolution of Mississippian Chiefdoms in the Southeastern United States." In *Factional Competition and Political Development in the New World*, edited by Elizabeth M. Brumfiel and John W. Fox, 61–76. Cambridge: Cambridge University Press.

———. 1994b. *The Savannah River Chiefdoms: Political Change in the Late Prehistoric Southeast*. Tuscaloosa: University of Alabama Press.

———. 1996a. "Chiefly Cycling and Large-Scale Abandonments as Viewed from the Savannah River Basin." In *Political Structure and Change in the Late Prehistoric Southeastern United States*, edited by John F. Scarry, 150–191. Gainesville: University Press of Florida.

———. 1996b. "Fluctuations between Simple and Complex Chiefdoms: Cycling in the Late Prehistoric Southeast." In *Political Structure and Change in the Late Prehistoric Southeastern United States*, edited by John F. Scarry, 231–252. Gainesville: University Press of Florida.

Beck, Robin A., Jr. 1997. "From Joara to Chiaha: Spanish Exploration of the Appalachian Summit Area, 1540–1568." *Southeastern Archaeology* 16:162–169.

———. 2009. "Catawba Coalescence and the Shattering of the Carolina Piedmont, 1540–1675." In *Mapping the Mississippian Shatter Zone: The Colonial Indian Slave Trade and Regional Instability in the American South*, edited by Robbie F. Ethridge and Sheri M. Shuck-Hall, 115–141. Lincoln: University of Nebraska Press.

———. 2013. *Chiefdoms, Collapse, and Coalescence in the Early American South*. Cambridge: Cambridge University Press.

Beck, Robin A., Gayle J. Fritz, Heather A. Lapham, David G. Moore, and Christopher B. Rodning. 2016. "The Politics of Provisioning: Food and Gender at Fort San Juan de Joara, 1566–1568." *American Antiquity* 81(1): 3–26.

Beck, Robin A., Jr., and David G. Moore. 2002. "The Burke Phase: A Mississippian Frontier in the North Carolina Foothills." *Southeastern Archaeology* 21:192–205.

Beck, Robin A., Jr., David G. Moore, and Christopher B. Rodning. 2006. "Identifying Fort San Juan: A Sixteenth-Century Spanish Occupation at the Berry Site, North Carolina." *Southeastern Archaeology* 25:65–77.

Beck, Robin A., David G. Moore, Christopher B. Rodning, Timothy Horsley, and Sarah C. Sherwood. 2018. "A Road to Zacatecas: Fort San Juan and the Defenses of Spanish *La Florida*." *American Antiquity* 83:577–597.

Beck, Robin A., Lee A. Newsom, Christopher B. Rodning, and David G. Moore. 2017. "Spaces of Entanglement: Labor and Construction Practice at Fort San Juan de Joara." *Historical Archaeology* 51(2): 167–193.

Beck, Robin A., Jr., Christopher B. Rodning, and David G. Moore. 2010. "Limiting Resistance: Juan Pardo and the Shrinking of Spanish La Florida, 1566–1568." In *Enduring Conquests: Rethinking the Archaeology of Resistance to Spanish Colonialism in the Americas*, edited by Matthew Liebmann and Melissa S. Murphy, 19–39. Santa Fe, N.Mex.: School for Advanced Research Press.

———, eds. 2016. *Joara and Fort San Juan: Colonialism and Household Practice at the Berry Site*. Gainesville: University Press of Florida.

Booker, Karen M., Charles M. Hudson, and Robert L. Rankin. 1992. "Place Name Identification and Multilingualism in the Sixteenth Century Southeast." *Ethnohistory* 39:399–451.

Brown, Ian W., and Vincas P. Steponaitis. 2017. "The Grand Village of the Natchez Indians Was Indeed Grand: A Reconsideration of the Fatherland Site Landscape." In *Forging Southeastern Identities: Social Archaeology, Ethnohistory, and Folklore of the Mississippian to Early Historic South*, edited by Gregory A. Waselkov and Marvin T. Smith, 182–204. Tuscaloosa: University of Alabama Press.

Brown, James A. 1990. "Mystery Confronts History at the Natchez Temple." *Southeastern Archaeology* 9:1–9.

Bushnell, Amy Turner. 2006. "Ruling 'the Republic of Indians' in Seventeenth-Century Florida." In *Powhatan's Mantle: Indians in the Colonial Southeast*, edited by Gregory A. Waselkov, Peter H. Wood, and Tom Hatley, 195–213. Rev. and expanded ed. Lincoln: University of Nebraska Press.

———. 2014. "A Land Renowned for War: Florida as a Maritime Marchland." In *La Florida: Five Hundred Years of Hispanic Presence*, edited by Viviana Díaz Balsera and Rachel A. May, 103–116. Gainesville: University Press of Florida.

Deagan, Kathleen. 1973. "Mestizaje in Colonial St. Augustine." *Ethnohistory* 20:55–65.

———. 1982. "St. Augustine: First Urban Enclave in the United States." *North American Archaeologist* 3:182–205.

———. 1983. *Spanish St. Augustine: The Archaeology of a Colonial Creole Community*. New York: Academic Press.

———. 1985. "Spanish-Indian Interaction in Sixteenth-Century Florida and Hispaniola." In *Cultures in Contact: The European Impact on Native Cultural Institutions in Eastern North America, A.D. 1000–1800*, edited by William W. Fitzhugh, 281–318. Washington, D.C.: Smithsonian Institution Press.

———. 1988. "Archaeology of the Spanish Contact Period in the Caribbean." *Journal of World Prehistory* 2:187–233.

———. 2008. "Fifty Years of Archaeology at the Fountain of Youth Park Site (8-SJ-31), St. Augustine." Gainesville: Florida Museum of Natural History, University of Florida.

———. 2010a. "Native American Resistance to Spanish Presence in Hispaniola and *La Florida*, ca. 1492–1600." In *Enduring Conquests: Rethinking the Archaeology of Resistance to Spanish Colonialism in the Americas*, edited by Matthew Liebmann and Melissa S. Murphy, 41–56. Santa Fe, N.Mex.: School for Advanced Research Press.

———. 2010b. "Strategies of Adjustment: Spanish Defense of the Circum-Caribbean Colonies 1493–1600." In *First Forts: Essays on the Archaeology of Proto-Colonial Fortifications*, edited by Eric Klingelhofer, 17–39. Leiden: Brill.

———. 2016. "Investigating the 1565 Menéndez Defense: Field Report on the 2011–2015 Excavations at the Fountain of Youth Park Site, St. Augustine." Gainesville: Florida Museum of Natural History, University of Florida.

DePratter, Chester B. 1989. "Cofitachequi: Ethnohistorical and Archaeological Evidence." *Anthropological Studies* 9:133–156. Columbia, South Carolina, Institute of Archaeology and Anthropology.

———. 1994. "The Chiefdom of Cofitachequi." In *The Forgotten Centuries: Indians and Europeans in the American South, 1521–1704*, edited by Charles Hudson and Carmen Chaves Tesser, 197–226. Athens: University of Georgia Press.

Ethridge, Robbie. 2006. "Creating the Shatter Zone: The Indian Slave Traders and the Collapse of Mississippian Chiefdoms." In *Light on the Path: The Anthropology and History of the Southeastern Indians*, edited by Thomas J. Pluckhahn and Robbie Ethridge, 207–218. Tuscaloosa: University of Alabama Press.

———. 2009. "Introduction: Mapping the Mississippian Shatter Zone." In *Mapping the Mississippian Shatter Zone: The Colonial Indian Slave Trade and Regional Instability in the American South*, edited by Robbie F. Ethridge and Sheri M. Shuck-Hall, 1–62. Lincoln: University of Nebraska Press.

———. 2010. *From Chicaza to Chickasaw: The European Invasion of the Mississippian World, 1540–1715*. Chapel Hill: University of North Carolina Press.

———. 2017. "Navigating the Mississippian World: Infrastructure in the Sixteenth-Century Native South." In *Forging Southeastern Identities: Social Archaeology, Ethnohistory, and Folklore of the Mississippian to Early Historic South*, edited by Gregory A. Waselkov and Marvin T. Smith, 62–84. Tuscaloosa: University of Alabama Press.

———. 2018. "Foreword to Twentieth Anniversary Edition." In *Knights of Spain, Warriors of the Sun: Hernando de Soto and the South's Ancient Chiefdoms*, by Charles Hudson, xv–xxviii. Athens: University of Georgia Press.

Ethridge, Robbie, and Jeffrey M. Mitchem. 2013. "The Interior South at the Time of Spanish Exploration." In *Native and Spanish New Worlds: Sixteenth-Century Entradas in the American Southwest and Southeast*, edited by Clay Mathers, Jeffrey M. Mitchem, and Charles M. Haecker, 170–188. Tucson: University of Arizona Press.

Ewen, Charles. 1996. "Continuity and Change: De Soto and the Apalachee." *Historical Archaeology* 30(2): 41–53.

———. 2013. "History, Prehistory, and the Contact Experience." In *Native and Spanish New Worlds: Sixteenth-Century Entradas in the American Southwest and Southeast*, edited by Clay Mathers, Jeffrey M. Mitchem, and Charles M. Haecker, 274–283. Tucson: University of Arizona Press.

Ewen, Charles, and John H. Hann. 1998. *Hernando de Soto among the Apalachee: The Archaeology of the First Winter Encampment.* Gainesville: University Press of Florida.

Fowler Williams, Lucy. 1991. "The Calusa Indians: Maritime Peoples of Florida in the Age of Columbus." *Expedition Magazine* 33(2). http://www.penn.museum/sites/expedition/?p=3977.

Hally, David J. 1994. "The Chiefdom of Coosa." In *The Forgotten Centuries: Indians and Europeans in the American South, 1521–1704*, edited by Charles Hudson and Carmen Chaves Tesser, 227–253. Athens: University of Georgia Press.

———. 1996. "Platform-Mound Construction and the Instability of Mississippian Chiefdoms." In *Political Structure and Change in the Prehistoric Southeastern United States*, edited by John F. Scarry, 92–127. Gainesville: University Press of Florida.

———. 2006. "The Nature of Mississippian Regional Systems." In *Light on the Path: The Anthropology and History of the Southeastern Indians*, edited by Thomas J. Pluckhahn and Robbie Ethridge, 26–42. Tuscaloosa: University of Alabama Press.

———. 2008. *King: The Social Archaeology of a Late Mississippian Town in Northwestern Georgia.* Tuscaloosa: University of Alabama Press.

Hann, John H. 1988. *Apalachee: The Land between the Rivers.* Gainesville: University Press of Florida.

———. 1994. "The Apalachee of the Historic Era." In *The Forgotten Centuries: Indians and Europeans in the American South, 1521–1704*, edited by Carmen Chaves Tesser and Charles Hudson, 327–354. Athens: University of Georgia Press.

Hann, John H., and Bonnie G. McEwan. 1998. *The Apalachee Indians and Mission San Luis.* Gainesville: University Press of Florida.

Hoffman, Paul E. 1990. *A New Andalucia and a Way to the Orient: The American Southeast during the Sixteenth Century.* Baton Rouge: Louisiana State University Press.

———. 1994a. "Lucas Vázquez de Ayllón's Discovery and Colony." In *The Forgotten Centuries: Indians and Europeans in the American South, 1521–1704*, edited by Charles Hudson and Carmen Chaves Tesser, 36–49. Athens: University of Georgia Press.

———. 1994b. "Narváez and Cabeza de Vaca in Florida." In *The Forgotten Centuries: Indians and Europeans in the American South, 1521–1704*, edited by Charles Hudson and Carmen Chaves Tesser, 50–73. Athens: University of Georgia Press.

———. 2014. "'Until the Land Was Understood': Spaniards Confront *La Florida*, 1500–1600." In *La Florida: Five Hundred Years of Hispanic Presence*, edited by Viviana Díaz Balsera and Rachel A. May, 69–82. Gainesville: University Press of Florida.

Hudson, Charles M. 1976. *The Southeastern Indians*. Knoxville: University of Tennessee Press.

———. 1994. "The Hernando de Soto Expedition, 1539–1543." In *The Forgotten Centuries: Indians and Europeans in the American South, 1521–1704*, edited by Charles Hudson and Carmen Chaves Tesser, 74–103. Athens: University of Georgia Press.

———. 1997. *Knights of Spain, Warriors of the Sun: Hernando de Soto and the South's Ancient Chiefdoms*. Athens: University of Georgia Press.

———. 2002. Introduction to *The Transformation of the Southeastern Indians, 1540–1760*, edited by Robbie Ethridge and Charles Hudson, xi–xxxix. Jackson: University Press of Mississippi.

———. 2005. *The Juan Pardo Expeditions: Explorations of the Carolinas and Tennessee, 1566–1568*. Tuscaloosa: University of Alabama Press.

Hudson, Charles M., Robin A. Beck Jr., Chester B. DePratter, Robbie Ethridge, and John E. Worth. 2008. "On Interpreting Cofitachequi." *Ethnohistory* 55:465–490.

Hudson, Charles M., Chester B. DePratter, Emilia Kelley, and Marvin T. Smith. 1989. "The Tristán de Luna Expedition, 1559–1561." *Southeastern Archaeology* 8:31–45.

Hudson, Charles M., Marvin T. Smith, David J. Hally, Richard Polhemus, and Chester B. DePratter. 1985. "Coosa: A Chiefdom in the Sixteenth-Century Southeastern United States." *American Antiquity* 50:723–737.

King, Adam. 1999. "De Soto's Itaba and the Nature of Sixteenth Century Paramount Chiefdoms." *Southeastern Archaeology* 18:110–123.

———. 2003. *Etowah: The Political History of a Chiefdom Capital*. Tuscaloosa: University of Alabama Press.

———. 2006. "The Historic Period Transformation of Mississippian Societies." In *Light on the Path: The Anthropology and History of the Southeastern Indians*, edited by Thomas J. Pluckhahn and Robbie Ethridge, 179–195. Tuscaloosa: University of Alabama.

Knight, Vernon J., Jr., ed. 2009. *The Search for Mabila: The Decisive Battle between Hernando de Soto and Chief Tascalusa*. Tuscaloosa: University of Alabama Press.

Lorenz, Karl G. 1997. "Re-examination of Natchez Sociopolitical Complexity: A View from the Grand Village and Beyond." *Southeastern Archaeology* 16:97–112.

Lyon, Eugene. 1976. *The Enterprise of Florida: Pedro Menéndez de Avilés and the Spanish Conquest of 1565–1568*. Gainesville: University Press of Florida.

MacMahon, Darcie, and William H. Marquardt. 2004. *The Calusa and Their Legacy: South Florida People and Their Environments*. Gainesville: University Press of Florida.

Marquardt, William H. 2001. "The Emergence and Demise of the Calusa." In *Societies in Eclipse: Archaeology of the Eastern Woodland Indians, A.D. 1400–1700*, edited by David S. Brose, C. Wesley Cowan, and Robert C. Mainfort Jr., 157–171. Washington, D.C.: Smithsonian Institution Press.

———. 2014. "Tracking the Calusa: A Retrospective." *Southeastern Archaeology* 33:1–24.

McEwan, Bonnie G. 1991. "San Luis de Talimali: The Archaeology of Spanish-Indian Relations at a Florida Mission." *Historical Archaeology* 25(3):36–60.

———, ed. 1993. *The Spanish Missions of* La Florida. Gainesville: University Press of Florida.

———. 2001. "The Spiritual Conquest of *La Florida*." *American Anthropologist* 103:633–644.

Mehta, Jayur M. 2013. "Spanish Conquistadores, French Explorers, and Natchez Great Suns in Southwestern Mississippi, 1542–1729." *Native South* 6:33–69.

Milanich, Jerald T. 1994. "Franciscan Missions and Native Peoples in Spanish Florida." In *The Forgotten Centuries: Indians and Europeans in the American South, 1521–1704*, edited by Charles Hudson and Carmen Chaves Tesser, 276–303. Athens: University of Georgia Press.

———. 2006. *Laboring in the Fields of the Lord: Spanish Missions and Southeastern Indians*. Gainesville: University Press of Florida.

———. 2014. "Charting Juan Ponce de León's 1512 Voyage to Florida: The Calusa Indians amid Latitudes of Controversy." In *La Florida: Five Hundred Years of Hispanic Presence*, edited by Viviana Díaz Balsera and Rachel A. May, 49–68. Gainesville: University Press of Florida.

Milanich, Jerald T., and Charles Hudson. 1993. *Hernando de Soto and the Indians of Florida*. Gainesville: University Press of Florida.

Milne, Gregory Edward. 2009. "Picking Up the Pieces: Natchez Coalescence in the Shatter Zone." In *Mapping the Mississippian Shatter Zone: The Colonial Indian Slave Trade and Regional Instability in the American South*, edited by Robbie F. Ethridge and Sheri M. Shuck-Hall, 388–417. Lincoln: University of Nebraska Press.

Mitchem, Jeffrey M. 2006. "Investigations of the Possible Remains of de Soto's Cross at Parkin." *Arkansas Archeologist* 35:87–95.

———. 2011. *The Parkin Site: Hernando de Soto in Cross County, Arkansas*. Fayetteville: Arkansas Archeological Survey.

Moore, David G. 2002. *Catawba Valley Mississippian: Ceramics, Chronology, and Catawba Indians*. Tuscaloosa: University of Alabama Press.

Moore, David G., Robin A. Beck, and Christopher B. Rodning. 2005. "Pardo, Joara, and Fort San Juan Revisited." In *The Juan Pardo Expeditions: Explorations of the Carolinas and Tennessee, 1566–1568*, edited by Charles M. Hudson, 343–349. Tuscaloosa: University of Alabama Press.

Moore, David G., Christopher B. Rodning, and Robin A. Beck. 2017. "Joara, Cuenca, and Fort San Juan: The Construction of Colonial Identities at the Berry Site." In *Forging Southeastern Identities: Social Archaeology, Ethnohistory, and Folklore of the Mississippian to Early Historic South*, edited by Gregory A. Waselkov and Marvin T. Smith, 99–116. Tuscaloosa: University of Alabama Press.

Regnier, Amanda L. 2015. *Reconstructing Tascalusa's Chiefdom: Pottery Styles and the Social Composition of Late Mississippian Communities along the Alabama River*. Tuscaloosa: University of Alabama Press.

Rodning, Christopher B., Robin A. Beck, and David G. Moore. 2013. "Conflict, Violence, and Warfare in *La Florida*." In *Native and Spanish New Worlds: Sixteenth-Century Entradas in the American Southwest and Southeast*, edited by Clay Mathers, Jeffrey M. Mitchem, and Charles M. Haecker, 231–247. Tucson: University of Arizona Press.

Rodning, Christopher B., Jayur M. Mehta, Bryan S. Haley, and David J. Watt. 2018. "Chaos Theory and the Contact Period in the American South." In *Investigating the Ordinary: Everyday Matters in Southeast Archaeology*, edited by Sarah E. Price and Philip J. Carr, 24–38. Gainesville: University Press of Florida.

Saunders, Rebecca. 2000. *Stability and Change in Guale Indian Pottery, A.D. 1300–1702*. Tuscaloosa: University of Alabama Press.

Scarry, John F. 1990. "Mississippian Emergence in the Fort Walton Area: The Evolution of the Cayson and Lake Jackson Phases." In *The Mississippian Emergence*, edited by Bruce D. Smith, 227–250. Washington, D.C.: Smithsonian Institution Press.

———. 1992. "Political Offices and Political Structure: Ethnohistoric and Archaeological Perspectives on the Native Lords of Apalachee." In *Lords of the Southeast: Social Inequality and the Native Elites of Southeastern North America*, edited by Alex Barker, 163–183. Archeological Papers of the American Anthropological Association 3, Washington, D.C.

———. 1994a. "The Apalachee Chiefdom: A Mississippian Society on the Fringe of the Mississippian World." In *The Forgotten Centuries: Indians and Europeans in the American South, 1521–1704*, edited by Carmen Chaves Tesser and Charles Hudson, 156–178. Athens: University of Georgia Press.

———. 1994b. "The Late Prehistoric Southeast." In *The Forgotten Centuries: Indians and Europeans in the American South, 1521–1704*, edited by Carmen Chaves Tesser and Charles Hudson, 17–35. Athens: University of Georgia Press.

———. 1996a. "Looking for and at Mississippian Political Change." In *Political Structure and Change in the Prehistoric Southeastern United States*, edited by John F. Scarry, 3–11. Gainesville: University Press of Florida.

———. 1996b. "The Nature of Mississippian Societies." In *Political Structure and Change in the Prehistoric Southeastern United States*, edited by John F. Scarry, 12–22. Gainesville: University Press of Florida.

———. 1996c. "Stability and Change in the Apalachee Chiefdom." In *Political Structure and Change in the Prehistoric Southeastern United States*, edited by John F. Scarry, 192–228. Gainesville: University Press of Florida.

Seinfeld, Daniel, Daniel Bigman, John Grant Stauffer, and Jesse Nowak. 2015. "Mound Building at Lake Jackson (8LE1), Tallahassee, Florida: New Insights from Ground Penetrating Radar." *Southeastern Archaeology* 34:220–236.

Smith, Marvin T. 1987. *Archaeology of Aboriginal Culture Change in the Interior Southeast: Depopulation during the Early Historic Period.* Gainesville: University Press of Florida.

———. 2000. *Coosa: The Rise and Fall of a Mississippian Chiefdom.* Gainesville: University Press of Florida.

———. 2001. "The Rise and Fall of Coosa, A.D. 1350–1700." In *Societies in Eclipse: Archaeology of the Eastern Woodlands Indians, A.D. 1000–1700*, edited by David S. Brose, C. Wesley Cowan, and Robert C. Mainfort Jr., 143–155. Washington, D.C.: Smithsonian Institution Press.

———. 2017. "Marine Shell Trade in the Post-Mississippian Southeast." In *Forging Southeastern Identities: Social Archaeology, Ethnohistory, and Folklore of the Mississippian to Early Historic South*, edited by Gregory A. Waselkov and Marvin T. Smith, 85–98. Tuscaloosa: University of Alabama Press.

Smith, Marvin T., and David J. Hally. 1992. "Chiefly Behavior: Evidence from Sixteenth Century Spanish Accounts." In *Lords of the Southeast: Social Inequality and the Native Elites of Southeastern North America*, edited by Alex Barker, 99–109. Archeological Papers of the American Anthropological Association 3, Washington, D.C.

South, Stanley. 1988. "Santa Elena: Threshold of Conquest." In *The Recovery of Meaning: Historical Archaeology in the Eastern United States*, edited by Mark P. Leone and Parker B. Potter Jr., 27–71. Washington, D.C.: Smithsonian Institution Press.

Steinen, Karl T. 1992. "Ambushes, Raids, and Palisades: Mississippian Warfare in the Interior Southeast." *Southeastern Archaeology* 11:132–139.

Stojanowski, Christopher M. 2005. "The Bioarchaeology of Identity in Spanish Colonial Florida: Social and Evolutionary Transformation before, during, and after Demographic Collapse." *American Anthropologist* 107:411–431.

———. 2010. *Bioarchaeology of Ethnogenesis in the Colonial Southeast.* Gainesville: University Press of Florida.

Swanton, John R. 1911. *Indian Tribes of the Lower Mississippi Valley and Adjacent Coast of the Gulf of Mexico.* Bulletin 43, Bureau of American Ethnology. Washington, D.C.: Smithsonian Institution.

———. 1946. *The Indians of the Southeastern United States.* Bulletin 137, Bureau of American Ethnology. Washington, D.C.: Smithsonian Institution.

Thomas, David Hurst. 1988. "Saints and Soldiers at Santa Catalina: Hispanic Designs for Colonial America." In *The Recovery of Meaning: Historical Archaeology in the Eastern United States*, edited by Mark P. Leone and Parker B. Potter Jr., 73–140. Washington, D.C.: Smithsonian Institution Press.

Thompson, Victor D. 2009. "The Mississippian Production of Space through Earthen Pyramids and Public Buildings on the Georgia Coast, USA." *World Archaeology* 41:445–470.

Thompson, Victor D., Chester B. DePratter, Jacob Lulewicz, Isabelle H. Lulewicz, Amanda D. Roberts Thompson, Justin Cramb, Brandon T. Ritchison, and Matthew H. Colvin. 2018. "The Archaeology and Remote Sensing of Santa Elena's Four Millennia of Occupation." *Remote Sensing* 10(248), doi:10.3390/rs10020248.

Thompson, Victor D., Chester B. DePratter, and Amanda D. Roberts Thompson. 2016. "A Preliminary Exploration of Santa Elena's Sixteenth Century Colonial Landscape Through Shallow Geophysics." *Journal of Archaeological Science: Reports* 9:178–190.

Thompson, Victor D., William H. Marquardt, Alexander Cherkinsky, Amanda D. Roberts Thompson, Karen J. Walker, Lee A. Newsom, and Michael Savarese. 2016. "From Shell Midden to Midden-Mound: The Geoarchaeology of Mound Key, an Anthropogenic Island in Southwest Florida, USA." *PLoS ONE* 11(4): e0154611. https://doi.org/10.1371/journal.pone.0154611.

Thompson, Victor D., William H. Marquardt, Karen J. Walker, Amanda D. Roberts Thompson, and Lee A. Newsom. 2018. "Collective Action, State Building, and the Rise of the Calusa, Southwest Florida, USA." *Journal of Anthropological Archaeology* 51:28–44.

Van Buren, Mary. 2010. "The Archaeological Study of Spanish Colonialism in the Americas." *Journal of Archaeological Research* 18:151–201.

Waselkov, Gregory A. 1989. "Seventeenth-Century Trade in the Colonial Southeast." *Southeastern Archaeology* 8:119–133.

Widmer, Randolph J. 1988. *The Evolution of the Calusa: A Nonagricultural Chiefdom on the Southwest Florida Coast.* Tuscaloosa: University of Alabama Press.

Williams, Mark. 1994. "Growth and Decline of the Oconee Province." In *The Forgotten Centuries: Indians and Europeans in the American South, 1521–1704*, edited by Carmen Chaves Tesser and Charles Hudson, 179–196. Athens: University of Georgia Press.

Worth, John E. 1994. "Late Spanish Military Expeditions in the Interior Southeast, 1597–1628." In *The Forgotten Centuries: Indians and Europeans in the American South, 1521–1704*, edited by Carmen Chaves Tesser and Charles Hudson, 104–122. Athens: University of Georgia Press.

———. 2002. "Spanish Missions and the Persistence of Chiefly Power." In *The Transformation of the Southeastern Indians, 1540–1760*, edited by Robbie Ethridge and Charles Hudson, 39–64. Jackson: University Press of Mississippi.

———. 2013. "Inventing Florida: Constructing a Colonial Society in an Indigenous Landscape." In *Native and Spanish New Worlds: Sixteenth-Century Entradas in the American Southwest and Southeast*, edited by Clay Mathers, Jeffrey M. Mitchem, and Charles M. Haecker, 189–201. Tucson: University of Arizona Press.

———, ed. 2014. *Discovering Florida: First-Contact Narratives from Spanish Expeditions along the Lower Gulf Coast.* Gainesville: University Press of Florida.

4

Pluralism and Persistence in the Colonial Sierra Sur of Oaxaca, Mexico

Stacie M. King

Bringing together ethnohistoric accounts and archaeological data in Postclassic (A.D. 800–1521) and early colonial (A.D. 1521–1650) Nejapa, this chapter explores the interactions and intersections between multiple, diverse groups of people in the Sierra Sur region of Nejapa, Oaxaca, Mexico. In Nejapa, migration, conquest, and interregional trade relied upon and created a complex, multiethnic landscape before, during, and after Spanish colonial efforts. Between 1450 and 1650, three different colonial regimes, the Zapotec, Aztec, and Spanish, moved through, conquered, and settled Nejapa, claiming it within their newly acquired territories. As such, Nejapa's multiethnic residents were already well accustomed to making strategic choices about how to engage with foreign militaries, migrants, and merchants by the time the Spanish arrived. The archaeological evidence shows that people made various choices when confronted with colonial regimes. Some residents relocated to high mountain peaks and constructed fortified settlements to protect themselves, while others chose to seek out new opportunities for trade and exchange and claim political power, as they had always done. Various individuals used the Spanish legal system to try to solidify their social and economic standing in the newly configured political landscape, while indigenous peoples simultaneously continued to visit long-standing sacred sites in the mountains to meet their needs for spiritual and physical sustenance within exploitative colonial systems.

PLURALISM AND PERSISTENCE

At the time of the Spanish conquest, Nejapa was a diverse, multiethnic region that included Mixe, Chontal, and Zapotec language speakers. People also likely understood or spoke Nahua, given their long history in facilitating interregional trade between the highlands and the coast. The three colonizing regimes that entered the Sierra Sur were equally pluralistic. Among the Spanish colonizers were indigenous allies from across highland Mexico, enslaved Africans, European-born and criollo colonial administrators, and Dominican clergy. The Zapotecs and Aztecs also conscripted large, multiethnic militaries from among their allies, who provided soldiers in exchange for promises of land and loot.

Internal dynamics and external processes work together to shape the impact and success of colonial programs (Silliman 2005; Stein 2005). What local populations bring to the table based on their own long-term histories, alongside the experiences of heterogeneous colonizing populations, produces unpredictable "novelty, diversity, and creativity" in resultant colonial realities (Funari and Senatore 2015:22; Senatore 2015; see also chapter 3). For these reasons, Claire Lyons and John Papado-poulos (2002:7–8) argue that colonial relations are best characterized as hybrid and ambiguous. In colonial spaces, people from distinct regions and cultures must adjust to new social, economic, and political inequalities. Those in power often make concerted efforts to mark and categorize people as a way to clarify roles and relationships in colonial hierarchies (Voss 2005, 2008). While hierarchies might have been rigid on paper, people living in frontiers and rural areas likely had more flexibility and opportunities to penetrate colonial power structures.

Archaeologists should be able to assess the impact, rigidity, and complexity of colonial experiences through the study of material remains. Since material culture often mitigates social differences in colonial systems, patterns in material culture serve as evidence of the variable strategies that people employ (González-Ruibal 2015:viii; Gosden 2004; Lyons and Papadopoulos 2002:44). For example, continuities in material culture might be evidence of resilience, resistance, and/or maintenance, whereas changes might signal conscious efforts to engage and manipulate colonial systems. Variability in material culture, however, need not always accompany transformations in identity, and continuities do not always mean that people resisted or remained unchanged.

In a place like Nejapa, where residents were always culturally plural, we should expect hybrid, ambiguous, and variable signatures in material culture before, during, and after Zapotec, Aztec, and Spanish conquests and colonialisms. Living along a heavily traveled trade route meant that

Nejapa residents were accustomed to interactions with outsiders. Openness and flexibility gave Nejapa residents choices in how they could position themselves and claim rights and privileges under colonial rule. In the sections that follow, I explore colonial relations in Nejapa between 1450 and 1650 to show how the social, political, and economic circumstances of Nejapa residents changed and how Nejapa residents made sense of their transforming world. In places like Nejapa, cultural pluralism had long been the tradition; in short, what was persistent through conquests and colonialisms was pluralism.

CONQUESTS AND COLONIALISMS IN NEJAPA

The region of Nejapa, a wide, lush valley nestled in the mountainous Sierra Sur of Oaxaca, lies at the midway point on a 2,500-year-old trade route between the highland Central Valleys of Oaxaca and the coastal Isthmus of Tehuantepec (Map 4.1). Migrants and merchants had long used Nejapa as an economic crossroads and point of resupply, and Nejapa's diverse peoples, which included Mixe, Chontal, and Zapotec speakers, helped to facilitate this trade (King 2012).

Based on ethnohistoric accounts, sometime around 1450, a faction of the Zapotec ruling party headquartered in Zaachila in the Valley of Oaxaca led an army to the southern Isthmus of Tehuantepec (Burgoa 1989 [1674]; Oudijk 2008; Oudijk and Restall 2007; Wallrath 1967; Zeitlin 2005). Once in the isthmus, they conquered and displaced the multiethnic indigenous peoples who had been living there for centuries. The Dominican priest and historian Francisco de Burgoa wrote in 1674 that they did so by "*fuego y sangre*" (fire and blood) (1989 [1674]:339). The conquest may have been inspired by growing internal tensions over succession and souring relations with neighboring Mixtec polities in the Central Valleys of Oaxaca (Oudijk 2000, 2008; Sousa and Terraciano 2003; Wallrath 1967:1313; Zeitlin 2005). However, the Zapotec also likely chose the isthmus because it was an obligatory stop in interregional exchange between Central Mexico and the Pacific coast of Soconusco (Oudijk 2008; Zeitlin 2005). Gaining control in the isthmus meant controlling the trade of highly prized coastal luxury goods such as salt, chocolate, feathers, and jaguar skins (Gasco and Voorhies 1989; Oudijk 2008). They also likely anticipated the advance of the Aztec regime, which was set on controlling

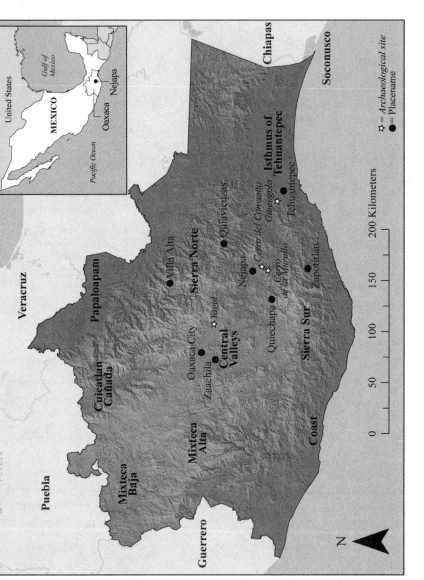

Map 4.1 Map of Oaxaca, showing the location of regions, places, and archaeological sites mentioned in the text, including Nejapa. Map prepared by Alex Elvis Badillo and Stacie M. King.

the highland–coastal trade route. Further, the Zapotec might have taken advantage of a political vacuum in the southern isthmus (Montiel Ánge-les et al. 2014); the opportunity was thus right for the Zapotec to make a strategic move.

Once conquered, the Zapotec population in the southern isthmus grew exponentially, with Zapotec settler colonists pushing out and subjugating local indigenous peoples from their headquarters in Tehuantepec, including Huave, Mixe, and Chontal speakers. Zapotec control of the southern isthmus was strong, and from their fortress at Guiengola, the Zapotecs fended off multiple Aztec conquest attempts in the late 1400s during the reign of Ahuitzotl (Burgoa 1989 [1674]:342–345; Durán 1994 [1581]:352–353, 374–379). Around 1520, after a shaky peace accord with the Aztecs, the isthmus Zapotec leaders quickly changed allegiance and established close ties with the Spanish (Chance 1981:16), helping them with their conquest designs in Guatemala and El Salvador (detailed in chapter 5). For several decades, until at least the 1550s, the Zapotec were able to maintain sovereignty in their relatively young political empire in Tehuantepec (Zeitlin 2005).

MULTIPLE MOUNTAIN FORTRESSES

According to Burgoa, the Zapotecs, in their conquest of the isthmus, built multiple fortresses across a wide area of land from Quiavicuzas in the north to Quiechapa in the south (see Map 4.1) and left behind Zapotec troops in each of them (1989 [1670]:242, 1989 [1674]:235–236). These strongholds, he contends, served multiple purposes. They (1) secured the trade route to the isthmus, (2) divided the Mixes (who lived north of the route) from the Chontales (who lived south of the route) so that they could not unite in opposition, (3) left behind troops in anticipation of an Aztec entrada, and (4) provided a place for Zapotec troops to convalesce and resupply.

Our Nejapa/Tavela Archaeological Project (PANT) survey team has documented several large archaeological sites and numerous smaller fortified sites throughout the mountains, on the highest peaks and as-sociated hilltop extensions, that could be associated with such an incur-sion (Map 4.2). The high-elevation sites take advantage of natural cliff faces and have excellent views, providing strategic points from which to monitor movement through the region. Constructed features include

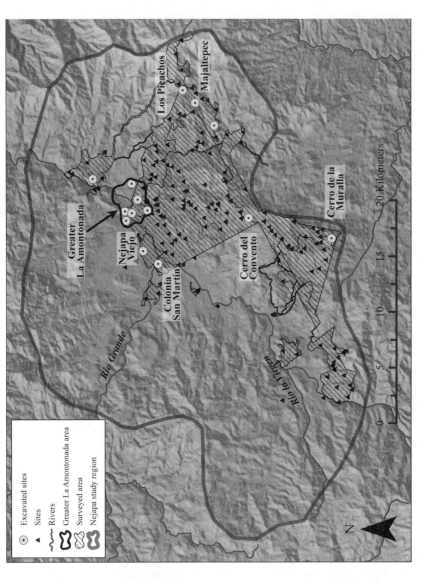

Map 4.2 Topographic map of the Nejapa/Tavela study region, showing the location of sites discussed in the text. Archaeological sites are marked with solid triangles. The circled, labeled sites are sites where we conducted excavations. Map prepared by Alex Elvis Badillo and Stacie M. King.

multicoursed stone defensive walls with hidden entrances, stones added to craggy bedrock outcrops that further restrict access, and multiple large stone walls running perpendicular to more exposed approaches. Ceramic artifacts from excavations and surface collections indicate that a majority of the construction associated with these mountaintop sites date to 1100 and thereafter.

While it is tempting to associate these sites with the above-mentioned 1450 Zapotec conquest, the archaeological evidence is equivocal (King et al. 2014; King et al. 2019). In general, the sites were built before 1450 according to long-standing local Nejapa construction methods, and the artifacts include ceramics made with local pastes and forms that are common across the entire Nejapa region. Locals, not Zapotec conquerors, likely built and occupied most of the sites (King et al. 2014). The shift to hilltop sites may have been in part a local response to increased insecurity and threat from the outside. It is also possible that Zapotecs hired (or conscripted) local residents to provide labor and goods to build garrisons/ fortresses. If these sites were Zapotec fortresses, then the material culture and construction styles should look novel, indicating a clear break from earlier traditions. Our work shows that this is not the case (King et al. 2014).

Los Picachos, for example, is a mountain fortress built by local Nejapa residents. The site extends along a 2 km long stretch of ridgeline, containing over 75 residential terraces, and a ceremonial complex with a temple at the highest point (2,150 m above sea level) (King et al. 2012). The ceramic assemblage consists of fine gray ware serving vessels and coarse ware jars, which fit well in the Postclassic Nejapa sequence. While Los Picachos is farther away from the likely camino real connecting the highland Valley of Oaxaca and the isthmus, residents of Los Picachos enjoyed relatively easy access to widely circulating ceramic styles, including gray ware tripod bowls with serpent-head supports and Pachuca obsidian, objects heavily used by highland Postclassic Zapotecs. Ceramic pastes and construction styles, however, are local and continuous, and obsidian is relatively rare (Workinger and King 2017). The site also falls within the territory that early Spanish chroniclers described as being inhabited by Mixes in the sixteenth century (King 2011; King and Konwest 2019). Further, the spatial layout of the site, with contiguous terraces climbing up and over the top of the mountain along the ridgeline, is more similar to that of other mountain-dwelling people throughout the Sierra Sur, including the Chontal-occupied zone of Zapotitlán (King and Zbor-over 2015). Although it might be tempting to identify Los Picachos as a Zapotec fortress, the preponderance of evidence indicates that it was not.

Cerro de la Muralla is a better candidate for being a Zapotec fortress (King et al. 2014). Here, the largest architectural complex, which locals call the *palacio*, consists of eight contiguous patios, with 33 rooms built around them. The whole construction sits on top of a large platform connected to a temple-patio-altar complex. The palace complex is built similarly to the Palace of Six Patios at the Zapotec site of Yagul, in the Central Valleys of Oaxaca (Bernal and Gamio 1974), and an exposed tomb jamb just outside the palace at Muralla suggests some potential affinity with highland Zapotec elite funerary practices. At Muralla, nearly all of the obsidian is from Pachuca (Workinger and King 2017), a source that was heavily quarried and distributed throughout Oaxaca via networks to which highland Zapotecs were closely linked (Levine et al. 2011; Parry 1990; Workinger and King 2017; Zeitlin 1982).

At Muralla, we found evidence of widespread use of plain tripod gray ware bowls with serpent-head supports, often associated with Late Postclassic (A.D. 1200–1521) Zapotec sites in highland Oaxaca. A massive 1 km long, 3 m high defensive wall (the *muralla* for which the site is named) encircles the elite civic-ceremonial core and some residential architecture downslope (King et al. 2012). However, different sections of the wall appear to have been built in different styles, suggesting that teams of people with different knowledge and practices contributed to its construction. Archaeological excavations inside the wall confirm a Late Postclassic occupation (A.D. 1261–1641, calibrated 2-sigma range AMS), but dated deposits from a residential complex outside the walls show that local Nejapa residents occupied the area before and during the Late Postclassic (King et al. 2019). Thus, it is unclear based on archaeological evidence alone that Zapotec conquerors and soldiers built and occupied the site in whole or in part, and there is incredible variation between these high-elevation fortified sites.

VALLEY FLOOR DIVERSITY

Colonial sources state that the native peoples who lived on the valley floor within what was to become the Spanish villa of Santiago Nexapa (now Nejapa de Madero) in 1560 were Zapotec speakers who themselves had only recently forced out the Mixes, who had been living on the valley floor for centuries (Burgoa 1989 [1674]:235). Therefore, we might look to the valley floor instead to find evidence of the Zapotec conquest. David Peterson and Thomas MacDougall (1974:59) hypothesize that mountain fortresses were likely only necessary during the initial years of Zapotec conquest. As soon as locals were "pacified" and the route was secure, migrant conquerors would have likely abandoned the fortresses and settled in permanent homes nearer to valley floor agricultural lands, such as those in the Nejapa valley. Thus, Peterson and MacDougall argue that we should be able to see a successive and sequential abandonment of fortresses along the route and a possible movement to lower-elevation valleys, which would indicate the pace and timing of the conquest itself. If Peterson and MacDougall's hypothesis is correct, and the early Spanish chroniclers are correct in their ethnic identifiers, then the Zapotecs had already secured the route to the isthmus and relocated to the valley floor prior to the arrival of the Spanish.

However, even in the valley, archaeological signatures are enigmatic. The site of Colonia San Martín lies atop a small rise at the confluence of two rivers on the valley floor and appears to have been occupied by elites with extensive knowledge of Zapotec elite material culture (King 2010; King et al. 2019). Here, at least one large multiroomed adobe building was constructed and frequently renovated with layers of red-painted stuccoed floors and walls. In some areas, only the lower half of the walls was painted red, while the interior rooms were left their natural white. Residents seemed to have been concerned about signaling to outsiders their wealth and knowledge of foreign practices by investing in red-painted stucco on public corridors and exterior public facades of the building. Colonia San Martín is also the only site that we have yet located with a large number of polychrome ceramics mimicking Postclassic International Style ceramics documented throughout Late Postclassic Oaxaca and Puebla (especially Cholula) (Forde 2016; Lind 1987, 1994; Nicholson 1982; Nicholson and Quiñones Keber 1994) (Figure 4.1). Ceramic sourcing and stylistic comparisons show that these Postclassic Nejapa polychromes are local interpretations of this widely shared elite style. Likewise, the obsidian assemblage at Colonia San Martín includes material from a wider variety of sources than are present at Los Picachos

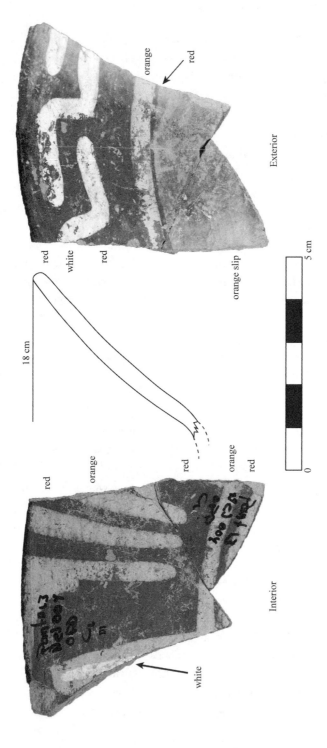

Figure 4.1 A locally made polychrome Postclassic International Style ceramic vessel fragment from Colonia San Martín. The vessel is a fine gray ware conical bowl decorated with red, orange, and white paint on the interior and exterior. Figure prepared by Elizabeth Konwest, Juan Jarquín, and Stacie M. King.

and Muralla (Workinger and King 2017), which is perhaps an indication of access to a wider network of trade goods.

The architecture and artifact assemblage at Colonia San Martín, however, contrasts sharply with assemblages from other Late Postclassic sites in Nejapa. One of these is Greater La Amontonada, a similarly situated valley floor community 2 km farther downstream whose large population was divided into various neighborhoods, each with its own smaller neighborhood ceremonial center. Greater La Amontonada's ceramic assemblage is more closely linked with wider Nejapa styles, demonstrating continuity through time with the Early Postclassic (A.D. 800–1200) in particular (Konwest 2017). One neighborhood at Greater La Amontonada, El Órgano, was involved in its own specialized craft industry of stone bead manufacture, which allowed residents to acquire rare exotic luxury goods, including polychrome ceramics, sculptures, and copper (King and Konwest 2019). Thus, the archaeological evidence across the valley floor is as varied as the evidence between fortified mountaintop sites. Despite proximity and contemporaneity, communities living on the valley floor had multiple ways of living and interacting with each other, and they experienced increased opportunities for interregional exchange with outsiders (King and Konwest 2019; Konwest 2017; Workinger and King 2017). Further, each community—and perhaps even each neighborhood—managed access to trade goods and elite wares independently. The picture that emerges from both the mountain and valley floor sites is one of pluralism, diversity, and decentralization rather than uniformity.

RITUAL PRACTICES IN A TRANSFORMING WORLD

The Dominicans were perhaps the most powerful agents of the Spanish conquest in Nejapa. After a few Spanish conquistadors entered Nejapa on early campaigns, in 1533 the Spanish tried to establish a Spanish villa on the valley floor, which quickly failed (Gerhard 1993:197). Instead, the Dominican order was the first to make a permanent entrance, setting up a local Nejapa *doctrina* (base) in 1553, which preceded the first successful permanent villa by seven years (Gerhard 1993:197). From Nejapa, the largely Portuguese- and Spanish-born Dominican clergy served rural communities across the Nejapa region, including Chontal, Mixe, and Zapotec speakers (Burgoa 1989 [1674]; Gerhard 1993; Paso y Troncoso

1905a). Many of the earliest colonial documents from Nejapa pertain to the workings of the Dominican *doctrina*. They include complaints by clergy about having to travel to mountain villages, rulings to determine who was required to provide goods and labor to the church, and indigenous complaints about abuses and nonpayment for such labor. The Dominicans supported indigenous claims of mistreatment by secular colonial authorities, clearly demonstrating the complexity, vagaries, and tensions within the colonial system. Two Nejapa archaeological sites figure prominently in this era of conquest and colonialism: Majaltepec and Cerro del Convento.

Although now abandoned, Majaltepec was one of two cabeceras (head towns) within the territory of Nejapa mentioned in the *Suma de visitas* prepared between the 1530s and 1550s (Paso y Troncoso 1905b:165) and is recorded in the *Relaciones geográficas* of 1579 as having 182 tribute-paying citizens (Paso y Troncoso 1905a:29–44). Sixteenth-century documents refer to Majaltepec as a Mixe town that was too far away for the Spanish and Dominicans to easily control. In the early decades of Spanish colonial control, elites and traders from Majaltepec requested rights and privileges in Spanish courts, including rights to land, to keep animals, to carry arms, to receive fair wages, and to travel and trade independently with towns as far away as the Central Valleys of Oaxaca (King 2011). In the first decade of the seventeenth century, the Crown ordered a series of *congregaciones* around Majaltepec, which appear to have been largely unsuccessful in depopulating the townsite. Based on archival evidence, Majaltepec was inhabited until at least 1768, when residents were party to a series of formal complaints about repartimiento abuses by corrupt *alcaldes mayores* (Baskes 2000). After this, Majaltepec is no longer mentioned in formal records.

Yet the archaeological evidence from Majaltepec indicates that interactions between indigenous inhabitants and church officials were dynamic and intimate. Not surprisingly, excavations at the abandoned townsite of Majaltepec show that the church was the most formal building at the site, with multiple rooms and thick stuccoed adobe walls with multicoursed stone bases and a formal staired entrance (King and Konwest 2019; King et al. 2012). Additionally, the church had a plaza enclosed by stone walls in front of the building, which served as an unroofed public meeting space (King et al. 2019). Although the Dominicans complained about the arduous journey to Majaltepec, the accommodations appear to have been maintained well and were intricately designed, far surpassing any other structure at the site in both size and formality.

In an adobe-walled residence about 200 m from the church, we uncovered a series of burials beneath the building's earthen floor. In an excavation unit of only 3 square meters, we uncovered the remains of eight individuals, among them women, subadults, and children buried in a manner that would not likely have been condoned by the church: beneath a house floor with offerings (King and Higelin Ponce de León 2017; King and Konwest 2019). Burial offerings included fragments of a metal blade and hundreds of glass trade beads, which residents presumably obtained through their interactions with the Dominican officials (King and Konwest 2019). Glass beads are common in Spanish colonial period sites in the Americas more broadly and were widely used and distributed by religious authorities (including Dominicans) in their proselytization efforts. Beads often show up in early colonial period cemeteries in Spanish colonies, including in indigenous graves. The Majaltepec beads are unique in Mexico and are most similar to the assemblage excavated at St. Catherines Island in the southeastern United States (Georgia), with examples that were likely produced in Spain and Italy (Blair et al. 2009). According to Elliot Blair and colleagues' (2009) typology, some of the diagnostic bead types in the Majaltepec collection date to between 1560 and 1630, providing a narrower date than radiocarbon dating does for this time frame. Based on these data, Elizabeth Konwest and I (King and Konwest 2019) argue that indigenous peoples in Nejapa selectively adopted and used introduced materials but did so within their own cultural logics, subtly subverting the imposed colonial social order.

Majaltepec was still occupied into the late 1700s despite multiple attempts to relocate residents, which shows that indigenous residents were relatively successful in maintaining some amount of independence and autonomy. If Majaltepec indeed housed Mixe language speakers throughout its history, then it seems that at least some Mixe speakers achieved distance from the Spanish colonial system while at the same time being part of it and manipulating it. As such, indigenous residents were able to leverage and strategically perform different identities when required to do so—as dutiful Catholics, as subservient or rebellious Indians, as Mixes, and as indigenous traders and entrepreneurs across wider

Oaxaca. The native community at Majaltepec was thus able to benefit from ambiguities in identity, and residents mobilized particular identities in different contexts as needed.

The site of Cerro del Convento demonstrates yet another kind of local indigenous response to religious conquest and colonialism. Cerro del Convento sits on a mesa top with a 360-degree view of the surrounding Nejapa valley. Located in modern San Juan Lajarcia, the site is positioned closest to what we believe was the primary mountain pass along the camino real between the highlands and the isthmus as one exits Nejapa toward the isthmus. Cerro del Convento has been identified in later sources as one of the Zapotec fortresses mentioned by Burgoa in 1674 (Gay 1982; Martínez Gracida 1910; Ramírez 1892). However, the archaeological data show that the site was not only used or may never have been used in the way that Burgoa described. Prehispanic architecture on the mesa top includes a rather simple ballcourt by local standards, a few stone foundations associated with humble buildings (presumably residences), and a temple built with stone and earthen fill. We excavated a Classic period hearth that dates to between 430 and 643 (calibrated 2-sigma range AMS) directly below the center of the Postclassic period ballcourt playing field (King et al. 2019). The positioning of a Postclassic ballcourt immediately on top of the earlier hearth likely means that this location was recognized and important for locals and thus was deserving of commemoration (King et al. 2017). The ceramic assemblage shows similarities with local Nejapa wares, including highly eroded, plain utilitarian serving bowls made with fine and coarse pastes (King et al. 2019; King et al. 2014). Residents used obsidian tools imported from a variety of sources from both highland Mexico and highland Guatemala, the two major source regions for obsidian on either end of the highland–coastal trade route, but in very small quantities (Workinger and King 2017).

The large cliffs that form the edge of the mesa also contain numerous rockshelters and caves, which people used periodically as far back as the Late Formative (500 B.C.–A.D. 100). We have found evidence that people modified the caves and rockshelters on the cliff face into storage areas for agricultural products during the Late Postclassic and early colonial periods (King et al. 2012; King et al. 2019). They did so by carving out the soft seams and constructing small contiguous rooms divided by stone and mud walls (King et al. 2017). People regularly visited Cerro del

Convento as part of ritual pilgrimages, leaving behind small campfires and offerings in front of the rockshelters at the base of the cliff. We have located ceramic incense burner fragments, an unfired ceramic plate (with leaf impressions), and tied fiber bundles in various intricate forms, all of which were likely placed as offerings. Based on the evidence of plant remains (over 120 different species in only 1 liter of sediment) in storage rooms built within the caves and the offerings, Shanti Morell-Hart and I (King and Morell-Hart 2019) have argued that one of the rooms at Convento was used as a seed bank to provide security during times of crisis. All of the species are native to Mexico, which means that the storage rooms most likely date to the Late Postclassic, even though the rooms yielded multiple calibrated radiocarbon dates ranging between A.D. 1027 and 1635.

Cerro del Convento was the target of Dominican *vicario* (vicar) Juan Ruiz's campaign to extirpate idolatry in the late 1500s (Barabas and Bartolomé 1984:15–16; Burgoa 1989 [1674]:242–247; Gay 1982:365–366). Ruiz had heard about the ongoing idolatry at Cerro del Convento and decided to intervene directly by hiking up the mountain with native acolytes to visit the site. Ruiz had himself lowered by rope into the cave in the upper seam, and he removed a greenstone idol, ceramics, and other offerings. That night, he lit a bonfire on top of the mountain and burned all of the remains. He also destroyed the contents of a tomb on the mesa top. According to Burgoa, the deceased was a venerated Zapotec warrior who was buried with a feathered headdress and various ceramic vessels and other goods (1989 [1674]:246). Unfortunately, we have found no evidence of this tomb at the site, and the ethnic identifier that Burgoa applies remains uncorroborated and problematic. Further, Ruiz's interventions apparently did not stop visits to the site. We located the remains of offerings and fragments of modern incense burners and braziers that date to after 1591 and are evidence of later visits.

Rather than a Zapotec fortress, Cerro del Convento appears to have been an important ritual pilgrimage site that served as a ceremonial space for ballgames and feasting, a sacred place for ritual petitions and offerings, and, later, a zone of refuge for various indigenous residents. During the early colonial period, penitents and pilgrims may have received physical sustenance in the form of seeds and foodstuffs, as well as spiritual strength and rejuvenation from their ongoing ritual visits (King et al.

2017). The generic, poor quality of the ceramics, the small number of stone tools, and the expedient nature of the remaining offerings suggest that all sorts of people visited and used the site and did so occasionally, regularly, and at times clandestinely throughout its history. Here, conquest and colonialism did little to change the meaning of the site—it was and still is an important sacred place for a variety of peoples from various places across Nejapa.

ECONOMIC OPPORTUNITIES AND CHANGE

The Spanish conquest in Nejapa took many forms and impacted the region differently over time. At the time of the first Spanish entrada, Nejapa was apparently considered to be part of the isthmus Zapotec *cacicazgo* (kingdom) under the leadership of Cosijoeza II / Don Juan Cortés (Chance 1989) and was among the lands that were granted to Cortés within the domain of his *mayorazgo* (entailed estate) in 1528 (Gay 1982:225). This suggests that Zapotecs ceded land to the Spanish when they allied with them in the 1520s. Cortés proceeded to distribute the land throughout his *mayorazgo* in encomiendas, including parcels in Nejapa (Gerhard 1993:195). These encomiendas supplied cochineal, vanilla, cacao, cotton, indigo, and corn.

The conquistadors who led the first Spanish entradas into Nejapa include Pedro de Alvarado in 1522–1523 (Matthew 2007:106; Wallrath 1967:16), Diego de Figueroa and Gaspar Pacheco in 1526–1527 (Chance 1989:17), and Francisco Maldonado in 1533 (Gerhard 1993:195). The Spanish *vecinos* of Villa Alta attempted to establish a villa in Nejapa in 1533, but it soon failed (Gerhard 1993:196). In the 1540s, Cortés's landholdings were greatly reduced, and the encomienda of Nejapa fell into the hands of property owners who lived in Antequera (later Oaxaca City) (Taylor 1972). In the *Suma de visitas* (Paso y Troncoso 1905b:165), Nejapa had three *señorios* (polities) divided into five estancias with over 200 *vecinos*, who gave tribute in the form of corn, beans, and chili. One of these, Majaltepec (Maxaltepeque), had 182 tributaries who were required to give gold and corn and later provide service in the mines. Soon after, in 1560, the Spanish "*villa de Nexapa*" was established with 16 subject communities, most of them Mixe, according to early colonial period documents (Gerhard 1993:197).

During the latter half of the sixteenth century, the economic landscape of Nejapa transformed. With the arrival of Spanish *vecinos* in Nejapa in 1560, sheep and goat ranches were established. The Dominicans ran a large sheep and goat ranch, from which the mendicant friars produced milk, cheese, and wool for their own consumption (Chance 1989:156). Due to labor requirements and church relocation policies, many indigenous people reluctantly moved to the valley floor, where most succumbed to epidemic disease between 1560 and 1580 (Paso y Troncoso 1905a:35). Fray Bernardo de Santamaría, vicar of the Dominican *doctrina*, wrote in the 1579 *Relación de Nexapa* that by then local populations had declined to the point that there were now deserted plains and fields across Nejapa where sugarcane and wheat haciendas could be established (Paso y Troncoso 1905a:38). This information likely encouraged more immigration and foreign investment.

Zapotecs in the Isthmus of Tehuantepec, Sierra Sur, and Sierra Norte were adept in using the Spanish court system as a method of securing their place in this newly reconfigured political and economic landscape (Gay 1982:190). At times, Zapotecs were able to acquire lands that were in dispute or had never been theirs in the first place (Barros van Hövell tot Westerflier 2007:25, 29–30; Oudijk 2008; Yannakakis 2007). Using this tactic, Zapotecs were able to expand their landholdings across the Nejapa region and in general fared much better than Mixes and Chontales, who often lacked both literacy and access. Between 1570 and 1600, the Zapotecs' raw population numbers grew slightly in private encomiendas, while Mixe and Chontal populations sharply declined (Gerhard 1993:198). At the same time, especially in contested places where population had thinned, Crown relocation policies (e.g., *reducciones*, *congregaciones*, and *mercedes*) aided and abetted the land grab (Owensby 2008:22). At the turn of the sixteenth century, Indian elites in Nejapa were requesting their own estancias in an effort to compete in the new economy, and Zapotec elites in the greater isthmus became significant players in the courts and in the colonial market economy (Zeitlin 1989:54, 2015).

The colonial economic landscape was highly varied and complex and was always changing. Some colonial residents—clergy, Spanish, Zapotecs, and native elites especially—enjoyed privileged positions and requested access to land and special rights, but no position was permanent or guaranteed success. Some native communities were left alone, while others filed formal complaints to manage their own economic affairs. Over the course of the early colonial period, some native communities and colonizers benefited from this system and were able to do quite well, while others had to work harder and struggled to turn a profit and survive.

DISCUSSION AND CONCLUSION

By delving into the details and complexity of multiethnic Nejapa during these centuries of colonialism, I demonstrate that pluralism was always present in Nejapa communities. People living in Nejapa, whether immigrant agents of settler colonialism or natives of the region, used diversity and multiplicity in ethnic, political, and social identities to their own benefit as needed. This created a highly diverse archaeological landscape. Neighboring communities had very different material assemblages and architectural styles, indicating that each community had independent access to merchants, stylistic ideas, and interregional networks of trade. People learned quickly how to move within various changing colonial political landscapes. Nejapa residents had long been accustomed to changing economic and political situations. Thus, when faced with multiple conquests and colonialisms, they knew how and when to engage, navigate, and withdraw. There is so much variation across Nejapa that even places that one would imagine were homogeneous, such as Zapotec fortresses, Mixe villages, and valley floor towns, produce varied and complex documentary and archaeological signatures.

Colonialism(s) placed some people in positions to take advantage of others, as is the case of native elite, religious authorities, and Spanish colonial administrators. Zapotecs, who themselves were likely relatively new settler colonists, used the Spanish legal system and their proximity to and alliance with the Dominican church to their advantage. Different valley floor communities in Nejapa were able to take advantage of the changing economic and political landscape. Residents of Late Postclassic Colonia San Martín, for example, were able to carve out a unique way of life in Nejapa using distinct styles of ceramics and architecture that linked them more broadly with Postclassic settlements outside of Nejapa. At the same time, residents of the El Órgano barrio in Greater La Amontonada had their own trade contacts and independent access to imported goods, supported by their export industry of locally made stone beads. Indigenous peoples from across Nejapa continued to visit Cerro del Convento, which was a destination for ritual pilgrimages, despite Spanish attempts to shut it down. While Zapotec soldiers may have occupied and expanded construction at Cerro de la Muralla, local Nejapa native peoples lived there before and during its occupation, perhaps providing labor for later renovations. The artifact assemblage present at Muralla indicates that occupants had access to both local and interregional economic networks.

Conquests and colonialisms also left some people vulnerable, in the position of having to hide themselves, their religious practices, and/or important foodstuffs, as is made clear by the fortified site of Los Picachos, the burial practices at Majaltepec, and the caves at Cerro del Convento, respectively. Others suffered abuses or were forced to provide labor in mines and the church, for which they were grossly undercompensated. The indigenous residents of Majaltepec had frequent interactions with the local Dominican church and the Spanish legal system in spite of their rural location in the high mountains, and residents benefited economically from these relationships. Yet at the same time, they were also able to take advantage of the distance and lack of everyday oversight to use new technologies and materials in novel ways that Catholic doctrine prohibited. People living in fortified settlements in the mountains, such as Los Picachos, selectively engaged with or retreated from economic and political networks as needed, but always acted from a position that ensured they were in control of the terms of engagement. Ultimately, it was epidemic disease that caused the most profound changes in Nejapa. By 1623, native tributaries were reduced to 60 percent of what they had been sixty years earlier. This reduction in population placed even larger tracts of land in Spanish hands and encouraged the increased in-migration of enslaved Africans and Nahua-speaking indigenous populations from Central Mexico (Escalona Lüttig 2015:40-41).

At no point in time between 1450 and 1650 did a single, unifying identity emerge out of the centuries of colonialisms in Nejapa. Nejapa was persistently pluralistic and complex. Residents had likely always spoken more than one language and moved in various circles simultaneously in order to facilitate their economic and political pursuits. Long-standing pluralism ensured that people in Nejapa, both indigenous residents and settler colonists, had various identities and networks on which to draw, which they mobilized strategically and opportunistically before, during, and after multiple conquests and colonialisms.

ACKNOWLEDGMENTS

This work would not have been possible without the generous funding provided by the National Science Foundation (Grant #BCS-1015392), National Geographic (Waitt Institute Grant #WI55-11), and Indiana University's New Frontiers in the Arts and Humanities grant program and the Office of the Vice Provost for Research. Likewise, I would like to thank the Consejo de Arqueología of the Instituto Nacional de Antropología e Historia and the Centro INAH Oaxaca for their permission and administrative assistance. The intrepid members of the Proyecto Arqueológico Nejapa / Tavela research team, Eli Konwest, Andrew Workinger, Alex Elvis Badillo, Marijke Stoll, Ricardo Higelin Ponce de León, and Shanti Morell-Hart, each played key roles. I thank John Douglass and Christine Beaule for inviting me to participate in the SAA electronic symposium that helped us to find our way to Amerind. There, John, Christine, and Amerind CEO Christine Szuter facilitated an engaging and productive conversation that streamlined the text of this chapter and helped to bring the volume together. Most importantly, I would like to thank the residents and authorities of Nejapa de Madero, Santa Ana Tavela, San Juan Lajarcia, San Carlos Yautepec, and San Bartolo Yautepec for their generous permission and continued support and collaboration.

REFERENCES

Barabas, Alicia M., and Miguel A. Bartolomé. 1984. *El rey Cong hoy: Tradición mesiánica y privación social entre los Mixes de Oaxaca*. Oaxaca: Colección de Investigaciones Sociales I. Centro INAH Oaxaca.

Barros van Hövell tot Westerflier, Alonso. 2007. "Cien años de guerras Mixes: Territorialidades prehispánicas, expansión burocrática y zapotequización en el Istmo de Tehuantepec durante el siglo XVI." *Historia Mexicana* 57(2): 325–403.

Baskes, Jeremy. 2000. *Indians, Merchants, and Markets: A Reinterpretation of the Repartimiento and Spanish–Indian Economic Relations in Colonial Oaxaca*. Stanford: Stanford University Press.

Bernal, Ignacio, and Lorenzo Gamio. 1974. *Yagul: El palacio de los seis patios*. Mexico City: Instituto de Investigaciones Antropológicas, Universidad Nacional Autónoma de México.

Blair, Elliot H., Lorann S. A. Pendleton, and Peter J. Francis Jr. 2009. *The Beads of St. Catherines Island.* American Museum of Natural History Anthropological Papers, Number 89. New York: American Museum of Natural History.

Burgoa, Francisco de. 1989 [1670]. *Palestral historial de virtudes y ejemplares apostólicos fundada del celo de insignes héroes de la sagrada orden de predicadores en este nuevo mundo de la América en las Indias Occidentales.* Mexico City: Editorial Porrua, S.A.

———. 1989 [1674]. *Geográfica descripción de la parte septentrional del polo ártico de la América y, nueva iglesia de las Indias Occidentales, y sitio astronómico de esta provincia de predicadores de antequera Valle de Oaxaca.* Mexico City: Editorial Porrúa, S.A.

Chance, John K. 1981. "Colonial Ethnohistory of Oaxaca." In *Supplement to the Handbook of Middle American Indians, Vol. 4: Ethnohistory,* edited by Ronald Spores, 165–189. Austin: University of Texas Press.

———. 1989. *Conquest of the Sierra: Spaniards and Indians in Colonial Oaxaca.* Norman: University of Oklahoma Press.

Durán, Fray Diego. 1994 [1581]. *History of the Indies of New Spain.* Norman: University of Oklahoma Press.

Escalona Lüttig, Huemac. 2015. "Rojo profundo: Grana cochinilla y conflicto en la jurisdicción de Nejapa, Nueva España, siglo XVIII." PhD diss., Universidad Pablo de Olavide.

Forde, Jaime E. 2016. "The Polychrome Ceramics of Tututepec (Yucu Dzaa), Oaxaca, Mexico: Iconography and Ideology." *Ancient Mesoamerica* 27:389–404.

Funari, Pedro Paulo A., and Maria Ximena Senatore. 2015. "Introduction: Disrupting the Grand Narrative of Spanish and Portuguese Colonialism." In *Archaeology of Culture Contact and Colonialism in Spanish and Portuguese America,* edited by Pedro Paulo A. Funari and Maria Ximena Senatore, 1–15. New York: Springer.

Gasco, Janine L., and Barbara Voorhies. 1989. "The Ultimate Tribute: The Role of the Soconusco as an Aztec Tributary." In *Ancient Trade and Tribute: Economies of the Soconusco Region of Mesoamerica,* edited by Barbara Voorhies, 48–94. Salt Lake City: University of Utah Press.

Gay, José Antonio. 1982. *Historia de Oaxaca.* Mexico City: Porrúa.

Gerhard, Peter. 1993. *A Guide to the Historical Geography of New Spain.* Rev. ed. Norman: University of Oklahoma Press.

González-Ruibal, Alfredo. 2015. Foreword to *Archaeology of Culture Contact and Colonialism in Spanish and Portuguese America,* edited by Pedro Paulo A. Funari and Maria Ximena Senatore, vii–ix. New York: Springer.

Gosden, Chris. 2004. *Archaeology and Colonialism: Culture Contact from 5000 B.C. to the Present.* Cambridge: Cambridge University Press.

King, Stacie M. 2010. *Informe final: Proyecto arqueológico Nejapa/Tavela 2009.* Final report submitted to the Consejo de Arqueología and the Centro INAH Oaxaca of the Instituto Nacional de Antropología e Historia.

————. 2011. "Rediscovering Majaltepec (Maxaltepeque), Oaxaca: The Challenges of Bridging Archaeology, Ethnohistory, and Oral History." Paper presented at the annual meeting of the American Society of Ethnohistory, Pasadena, Calif.

————. 2012. "Hidden Transcripts, Contested Landscapes, and Long-Term Indigenous History in Oaxaca, Mexico." In *Decolonizing Indigenous Histories: Exploring Prehistoric/Colonial Transitions in Archaeology*, edited by Maxine Oland, Siobhan M. Hart, and Liam Frink, 230–263. Tucson: University of Arizona Press.

King, Stacie M., and Ricardo Higelin Ponce de León. 2017. "Postclassic and Early Colonial Mortuary Practices in the Nejapa Region of Oaxaca, Southern Mexico." *Journal of Archaeological Science: Reports* 13:773–782.

King, Stacie M., and Elizabeth Konwest. 2019. "New Materials—New Technologies? Postclassic and Early Colonial Technological Transitions in the Nejapa Region of Oaxaca, Mexico." In *Technology and Tradition in Mesoamerica after the Spanish Invasion*, edited by Rani T. Alexander, 73–92. Albuquerque: University of New Mexico Press.

King, Stacie M., Elizabeth Konwest, and Alex Elvis Badillo. 2012. *Informe final: Proyecto arqueológico Nejapa/Tavela, temporada II, 2011.* Final report submitted to the Consejo de Arqueología and the Centro INAH Oaxaca of the Instituto Nacional de Antropología e Historia.

King, Stacie M., Elizabeth Konwest, Alex Elvis Badillo, Andrew Workinger, Ricardo Higelin Ponce de León, and Marijke M. Stoll. 2019. *Informe final: Proyecto arqueológico Nejapa/Tavela, temporada III, 2013.* Final report submitted to the Consejo de Arqueología and the Centro INAH Oaxaca of the Instituto Nacional de Antropología e Historia.

King, Stacie M., and Shanti Morell-Hart. 2019. "Preserving Oaxacan Foodways in the Face of Conquest: The Seed Bank at Cerro del Convento." Paper presented at the 82nd Annual Meeting of the Society for American Archaeology, Albuquerque, N.M.

King, Stacie M., Shanti Morell-Hart, and Éloi Berubé. 2017. "Sacred Worlds and Pragmatic Science in the Aftermath of Conquest: The Hidden Caves of Cerro del Convento." Paper presented at the 80th Annual Meeting of the Society for American Archaeology, Vancouver, B.C.

King, Stacie M., Andrew Workinger, Elizabeth Konwest, Alex Elvis Badillo, and Juan Jarquín Enríquez. 2014. "Un cuento de dos fortalezas en la región de Nejapa." *Cuadernos del Sur* 19(36): 21–41.

King, Stacie M., and Danny A. Zborover. 2015. "Beyond Ethnonyms: Interdisciplinary Research on Mountain Identity in the Sierra Sur of Oaxaca, Mexico." In *Engineering Mountain Landscapes: An Anthropology of Social Investment*, edited by Laura L. Scheiber and Maria Nieves Zedeño, 131–146. Salt Lake City: University of Utah Press.

Konwest, Elizabeth. 2017. "Material Markers of Community Identity in Post-classic Nejapa, Oaxaca, Mexico." PhD diss., Indiana University.

Levine, Marc, Arthur A. Joyce, and Michael D. Glascock. 2011. "Shifting Patterns of Obsidian Exchange in Postclassic Oaxaca, Mexico." *Ancient Mesoamerica* 22:123–133.

Lind, Michael D. 1987. *The Sociocultural Dimensions of Mixtec Ceramics.* Vanderbilt University Publications in Anthropology, No. 33. Nashville.

———. 1994. "Cholula and Mixteca Polychromes: Two Mixteca-Puebla Regional Substyles." In *Mixteca-Puebla: Discoveries and Research in Mesoamerican Art and Archaeology*, edited by H. B. Nicholson and Eloise Quiñones Keber, 79–99. Culver City: Labyrinthos.

Lyons, Claire L., and John K. Papadopoulos. 2002. "Archaeology and Colonialism." In *The Archaeology of Colonialism*, edited by Claire L. Lyons and John K. Papadopoulos, 1–23. Los Angeles: Getty Research Institute.

Martínez Gracida, Manuel. 1910. *Los indios oaxaqueños y sus monumentos arqueológicos.* Civilización Mixteco-Zapoteca. Unpublished report in five volumes, Biblioteca Pública Central del Estado de Oaxaca, Mexico.

Matthew, Laura E. 2007. "Whose Conquest? Nahua, Zapotec, and Mixteca Allies in the Conquest of Central America." In *Indian Conquistadors: Indigenous Allies in the Conquest of Mesoamerica*, edited by Laura E. Matthew and Michel R. Oudijk, 102–126. Norman: University of Oklahoma Press.

Montiel Ángeles, Alma Z., Victor M. Zapien López, and Marcus Winter. 2014. "La arqueología del Istmo oaxaqueño: Patrones de asentamiento, comunidades, y residencias." In *Panorama arqueológico: Dos Oaxacas*, edited by Marcus Winter and Gonzalo A. Sánchez Santiago. Arqueología Oaxaqueña 4. Oaxaca: Centro INAH Oaxaca.

Nicholson, H. B. 1982. "Mixteca-Puebla Style in the Valley of Oaxaca." In *Aspects of the Mixteca-Puebla Style and Mixtec and Central American Culture in Southern Mesoamerica*, edited by Doris Stone, 3–6. Middle American Research Institute, Occasional Paper No. 4. Tulane University, New Orleans.

Nicholson, H. B., and Eloise Quiñones Keber, eds. 1994. *Mixteca-Puebla: Discoveries and Research in Mesoamerican Art and Archaeology.* Culver City: Labyrinthos.

Oudijk, Michel R. 2000. *Historiography of the Bènizàa: The Postclassic and Early Colonial Periods (1000–1600 A.D.).* Leiden: Research School of Asian, African, and Amerindian Studies (CNWS), Universiteit Leiden.

———. 2008. "The Postclassic Period in the Valley of Oaxaca: The Archaeological and Ethnohistorical Records." In *After Monte Albán: Transformation and Negotiation in Oaxaca, Mexico*, edited by Jeffrey P. Blomster, 95–118. Boulder: University Press of Colorado.

Oudijk, Michel R., and Matthew Restall. 2007. "Mesoamerican Conquistadors in the Sixteenth Century." In *Indian Conquistadors: Indigenous Allies in the*

Conquest of Mesoamerica, edited by Laura E. Matthew and Michel R. Oudijk, 28–63. Norman: University of Oklahoma Press.

Owensby, Brian P. 2008. *Empire of Law and Indian Justice in Colonial Mexico*. Stanford: Stanford University Press.

Parry, William J. 1990. "Postclassic Chipped Stone Tools from the Valley of Oaxaca, Mexico: Indications of Differential Access to Obsidian." In *Nuevos enfoques en el estudio de la lítica*, edited by Maria de los Dolores Soto de Arechavaleta, 331–345. Mexico City: Universidad Autonoma de México.

Paso y Troncoso, Francisco del. 1905a. *Relaciones geográficas de la diócesis de Oaxaca*. Papeles de Nueva España, Geografía y Estadística, Vol. 4. Madrid: Est. Tipográfico Sucesores de Rivadeneyra.

———. 1905b. *Suma de visitas de pueblos por orden alfabético*. Papeles de Nueva España, Geografía y Estadística, Vol. 1. Madrid: Est. Tipográfico Sucesores de Rivadeneyra.

Peterson, David A., and Thomas B. MacDougall. 1974. *Guiengola: A Fortified Site in the Isthmus of Tehuantepec*. Vanderbilt University Publications in Anthropology, No. 10. Nashville: Vanderbilt University Press.

Ramírez, Rafael Isaac. 1892. *Descripción del Cerro de la Muralla, Peña del Convento, Cerro del Jabalí, y Horno de los Zapotecos*. Documentos inéditos de Manuel Martínez Gracida, Book 55. Unpublished manuscript on file in the Biblioteca Central del Estado de Oaxaca, Oaxaca.

Senatore, Maria Ximena. 2015. "Modernity at the Edges of the Spanish Enlightenment: Novelty and Material Culture in Floridablanca Colony (Patagonia, Eighteenth Century)." In *Archaeology of Culture Contact and Colonialism in Spanish and Portuguese America*, edited by Pedro Paulo A. Funari and Maria Ximena Senatore, 219–235. New York: Springer.

Silliman, Stephen W. 2005. "Culture Contact or Colonialism? Challenges in the Archaeology of native North America." *American Antiquity* 70(1): 55–74.

Sousa, Lisa Mary, and Kevin Terraciano. 2003. "The 'Original Conquest' of Oaxaca: Nahua and Mixtec Accounts of the Spanish Conquest." *Ethnohistory* 50(2): 349–400.

Stein, Gil J., ed. 2005. *The Archaeology of Colonial Encounters: Comparative Perspectives*. School of American Research Advanced Seminar Series. Santa Fe, N.Mex.: School of American Research Press.

Taylor, William B. 1972. *Landlord and Peasant in Colonial Oaxaca*. Stanford: Stanford University Press.

Voss, Barbara L. 2005. "From *Casta* to *Californio*: Social Identity and the Archaeology of Culture Contact." *American Anthropologist* 107(3): 461–474.

———. 2008. *The Archaeology of Ethnogenesis: Race and Sexuality in Colonial San Francisco*. Berkeley: University of California Press.

Wallrath, Matthew. 1967. *Excavations in the Tehuantepec Region, Mexico*. Transactions of the American Philosophical Society. Philadelphia: American Philosophical Society.

Workinger, Andrew, and Stacie M. King. 2017. "Obsidian Blade Production and Husbandry in the Nejapa/Tavela Region of Oaxaca, Mexico." Paper presented at the 80th Annual Meeting of the Society for American Archaeology, Vancouver, B.C.

Yannakakis, Yanna P. 2007. "The Indios Conquistadores of Oaxaca's Sierra Norte." In *Indian Conquistadors: Indigenous Allies in the Conquest of Mesoamerica*, edited by Laura E. Matthew and Michel R. Oudijk, 227–253. Norman: University of Oklahoma Press.

Zeitlin, Judith Francis. 1989. "Ranchers and Indians on the Southern Isthmus of Tehuantepec: Economic Change and Indigenous Survival in Colonial Mexico." *Hispanic American Historical Review* 69(1): 23–60.

——. 2005. *Cultural Politics in Colonial Tehuantepec: Community and State among the Isthmus Zapotecs, 1500–1750*. Palo Alto: Stanford University Press.

——. 2015. "Locating the Hidden Transcripts of Colonialism: Archaeological and Historical Evidence from the Isthmus of Tehuantepec." In *Bridging the Gaps: Integrating Archaeology and History in Oaxaca, Mexico: A Volume in Memory of Bruce E. Byland*, edited by Danny Zborover and Peter C. Kroefges, 363–390. Boulder: University Press of Colorado.

Zeitlin, Robert N. 1982. "Toward a More Comprehensive Model of Interregional Commodity Distribution: Political Variables and Prehistoric Obsidian Procurement in Mesoamerica." *American Antiquity* 47(2): 260–275.

5

A Tense *Convivencia*

Place Making, Pluralism, and Violence in
Early Spanish Central America

Laura Matthew and William R. Fowler

The earliest Spanish American cities—especially those founded where no prior settlement existed—provide a unique opportunity to interrogate the initial encounters and nascent structures of Spanish colonialism. Once invasion and war had created the conditions for settlement, what must it have been like to confront such a plurality of peoples, weapons, clothes, languages, animals, landscapes, foods, and other items, often in the midst of extreme violence but without knowing the full extent of the transformations under way? What did this unprecedented *convivencia* (living together) look like? We consider the question by comparing the rich archaeological and documentary records of the first successful Spanish urban foundations in Central America, Santiago en Almolonga in Guatemala and the *villa* of San Salvador in El Salvador, founded nearly simultaneously in 1527–1528.

Santiago in Almolonga lies under the modern-day towns of San Miguel Escobar and Ciudad Vieja, Sacatepéquez, Guatemala. Continuous settlement from its foundation to the present day problematizes archaeological excavation (Szecsy 1953). The city's already significant documentary record, however, was greatly augmented by the identification in the late 1990s of the Nahua *Lienzo de Quauhquechollan*—a cloth painting that depicts the invasion of Guatemala led by Santiago's founder, Jorge de Alvarado—and the rediscovery in 2011 of the city's 1530–1541 Spanish city council (cabildo) books at the Hispanic Society of America in New York City (Kramer et al. 2014).[1] The *villa* of San Salvador near Suchitoto, El Salvador, on the other hand, is the best-preserved Spanish conquest town on the American mainland. The site is completely accessible and exposed, with very light vegetation cover and no modern occupation to obscure surface features. It has suffered very little damage due to agricultural disturbances, and it has not been prone to illicit digging by looters. Built on a grid plan with a core area covering 45 ha, virtually all of the town was artificially leveled and filled with various types of densely packed constructions, making it an urban landscape of truly impressive proportions.

Santiago and San Salvador were founded by the same people around the same time, with the intention of establishing a strong Spanish foothold within Maya, Nahuat Pipil, and Xinka territory. They staked a visible claim on the landscape and turned conquistadors into colonists. Military and residential aspects of the city manifested themselves in tandem in a process fraught with danger, violence, and fear. Europeans and Africans were the minority by a large margin and had to negotiate simultaneously their position with each other, their native allies, and those whose territory they had successfully invaded. Taken together, Santiago in Almolonga and San Salvador reveal how Hispanic idealizations of conquered, urbanized space were tempered by the military and multiethnic realities of their founding.

FOUNDATION BY FORCE

The conquest of Guatemala and El Salvador was an extension of the conquest of Mexico. After the fall of the imperial capital, Tenochtitlan, in 1521, Hernán Cortés dispatched Pedro de Alvarado to conquer lands to the south. Several thousand central Mexican Nahua conquistadors led by Tlaxcalan, Cholulan, and Mexica nobility, Zapotec forces from Oaxaca, and a small contingent of Spanish conquistadors led by Alvarado invaded Guatemala in early 1524 and formed an alliance with the Kaqchikel Maya kingdom of Iximché. These combined forces—in which the Spanish were dramatically outnumbered—subdued the K'iche' Maya in the spring of 1524 and continued into western and central El Salvador by June (Matthew 2012:77–81). In El Salvador, however, the invaders met fierce resistance from the native Nahuat-speaking Pipil of the region, who, after two major battles, forced the Spaniards to return to Iximché.

Meanwhile, many Nahua in Guatemala had returned to Mexico. This left the remaining conquistadors vulnerable when the Kaqchikel Maya broke their alliance and drove the Nahua and Spaniards from Iximché in the fall of 1524. From a military camp in the formerly K'iche' highlands, Pedro de Alvarado's cousin Diego de Alvarado led the second invasion into El Salvador and founded the first truly Spanish city in Central America in the spring of 1525: the *villa* of San Salvador, probably on the same site as the later 1528 settlement, now known as Ciudad Vieja (Barón Castro 1996:41–42). The town was built in a small valley known as La Bermuda to the north of Cuscatlán Nahuat Pipil territory, which had little or no indigenous settlement at the time of the conquest but was still subject to attack (Fowler and Earnest 1985). By 1526 the local Nahuat Pipil had once again forced the invaders to retreat to Guatemala.

Fighting in Guatemala intensified in the spring of 1527 with the arrival from Mexico of thousands of Nahua reinforcements and several hundred more Spaniards under the leadership of Pedro de Alvarado's brother Jorge. This massive invasion struck at the heart of Kaqchikel territory. The Nahua and Spanish first occupied the major market town of Chimaltenango, then relocated to the nearby valley of Almolonga, where on 22 November 1527 Jorge de Alvarado founded Santiago de Guatemala. From there Diego de Alvarado and his troops left to reestablish San Salvador, which they officially founded on 1 April 1528 (Barón Castro 1996:87–91, 197–202). If the invasion of Central America was an extension of the conquest of México-Tenochtitlan, Santiago and San Salvador were extensions of each other.

The act of foundation constituted not only a legal claim to territory but also a seminal moment of urban planning in which a self-designated city council began to imagine systematically what an orderly, protective, and, above all, European space would look like in a foreign and hostile landscape. The famous Spanish American grid layout, or *traza*, descended from medieval *bastide* towns of southern France and northern Spain, as well as military settlements such as Santa Fe and Puerto Real established in Andalucía during the siege of Granada (Lauret et al. 1988; Navarro Segura 2006). It was replicated in the Caribbean by Hispaniola's military governor, Nicolás de Ovando, who supervised the founding of 15 towns across the island between 1502 and 1511 (Brewer-Carías 2006:285; Castillero Calvo 2006:11–17; Mira Caballos 2000:60–61). By 1515 the model had spread to 27 towns founded across Puerto Rico, Cuba, and Jamaica (McAlister 1984:138).

These Caribbean island cities did follow a grid pattern, but often with off-center plazas, irregularly sized blocks, and nonparallel streets. The earliest surviving example of a more stereotypically orthogonal Spanish

American *traza* is found in modern-day Panama at the site of Natá de los Caballeros, founded in 1522 during the governorship of Pedrarias Dávila (Tejeira-Davis 1996). The surveyor who worked with Dávila from 1513 to 1520, Alonso García Bravo, presumably influenced this more rigid design, which he later replicated in the Spanish *traza* of México-Tenochtitlan atop the ruins of the former ceremonial center of the Aztec city in 1523–1524 (Kagan 2000:58; Rodríguez-Alegría 2017; Tejeira-Davis 1996:54). In any case, the Spanish American *traza* did not develop through specific orders from above; the Crown issued no directives for any of these urban plans beyond their being orderly. Rather, the *traza* emerged through the application of prior experience and the development of new patterns on the ground. The city council of Santiago in Guatemala drew explicitly on this emerging New World pattern of Spanish settlement, noting on 22 November 1527 that Santiago's *traza* would be laid out "in the manner that has been done in other cities, *villas*, and places that in this New Spain are populated by Spaniards" (Sociedad de Geografía e Historia de Guatemala 1934:29–30).

On the day of Santiago's foundation the council designated a central plaza of four *solares*, or lots, for their meeting house, a prison, a church dedicated to Santiago, and two public buildings. They also made plans for a military lookout point, a chapel to Nuestra Señora de los Remedios, and a hospital and designated several dozen *vecinos*, or resident citizens (Sociedad de Geografía e Historia de Guatemala 1934:29–30). Notably, however, four months separated the act of Santiago's foundation and the council's next official meeting, at which more *vecinos* were named and the first house lots distributed. By contrast, immediately after San Salvador's official foundation, its newly appointed city council spent 15 days laying out the streets, the plaza, and the church and building a few residences. After completing this layout, each Spanish resident was assigned a house lot within the town. If the Dominican chronicler Antonio de Remesal, who apparently consulted the now-lost cabildo books of San Salvador 75 years later, was not compressing time in his brief account (Remesal and Sáenz de Santa María 1964–1966, vol. 2, bk. 9, chap. 3:201), this process appears to have been more rapid in San Salvador than in Guatemala. Despite nine months of prior fighting and significant gains made against the Kaqchikel Maya by renewed Nahua and Spanish forces under Jorge de Alvarado's leadership, one suspects that taking possession of land for a Spanish city between November 1527 and March 1528 was as militarily difficult in Guatemala as it was during the same period against the Nahuat Pipil in El Salvador. Foundation initiated place making but did not end the violence of war.

The defensive nature of both urban plans is indeed one of their most outstanding features in common. In Guatemala, Kaqchikel warfare led by the lords Kaji' Imox and B'eleje' K'at remained a threat that impeded urban development (Polo Sifontes 1986:96–98). Santiago's vulnerable western edge, where invaders could approach undetected between the volcanoes Fuego and Agua, was protected by a deep perimeter of indigenous allies from Mexico. In 1532 the council worried that the removal of rock for construction from areas around the river and the entrances and exits of the city was creating uneven surfaces on which Spaniards and their horses could stumble during an attack (Kramer and Luján Muñoz 2018:72). By 1533 the only government building that had been built in the city of Santiago was the council house (*casa del cabildo*), which doubled as the church. (The church was later shifted to an adjacent house.) Amid news of battles on the coast, sword makers and bit makers got special tax relief (Kramer and Luján Muñoz 2018:130–131, 164–165). The *Lienzo de Quauhquechollan*, painted by Nahua allies, makes the ongoing warfare patently clear, depicting clashes and sabotage on the city's very outskirts (Figure 5.1). In 1540 Kaji' Imox and B'eleje' K'at were captured, imprisoned in the city jail, and subsequently hanged (Maxwell and Hill 2006:287). Still, the city council openly expressed fear of a Maya insurrection, as Pedro de Alvarado prepared to leave town soon thereafter (Kramer and Luján Muñoz 2018:316).

San Salvador, meanwhile, was built on a small mesa formed by an extrusive basalt outcrop rising above a small natural basin south of the middle reaches of the Lempa River known as the Paraíso Basin (Fowler and Earnest 1985). The south and east sides of the town were protected by a steep, rocky slope and a sentry station or observation post on the south, just outside the *traza*. The west side was comparatively level and open, but archaeological research shows that, like Santiago, the residences of the Nahua and other indigenous allies in San Salvador were concentrated on this side of the town to form a kind of human shield. The north side also appears to have been relatively open and level (Map 5.1). Having chosen a previously unoccupied and geographically defensive site for

Figure 5.1 The *Lienzo de Quauhquechollan*. Santiago with the indigenous market (*circle*) and the Lago de Quilinizapa (*circle with bird*) to the northwest of the Volcán de Agua. © 2007 Universidad Francisco Marroquín, Guatemala. Images are available under the Creative Commons license. Attribution–Noncommercial–Share Alike.

their city, the residents of San Salvador were obviously more concerned about attacks from the south and the east, in which direction lay a number of densely indigenous Nahuat Pipil towns and a possible attack by the forces of rival Spanish conquistador Pedrarias Dávila in Nicaragua.

In both San Salvador and Santiago, indigenous laborers played a major role in the city's construction, and the demands on both people and land were significant. San Salvador was founded on top of an unoccupied mesa that required extensive leveling and terracing. The dominant natural features of the surrounding landscape are Cerro Tecomatepe, a small remnant volcanic cone to the southwest, and the extinct Guazapa Volcano to the west. The area was probably very thickly wooded at the time of the conquest, and while some labor for clearing and leveling and for construction of the town may have come in part from allied and enslaved

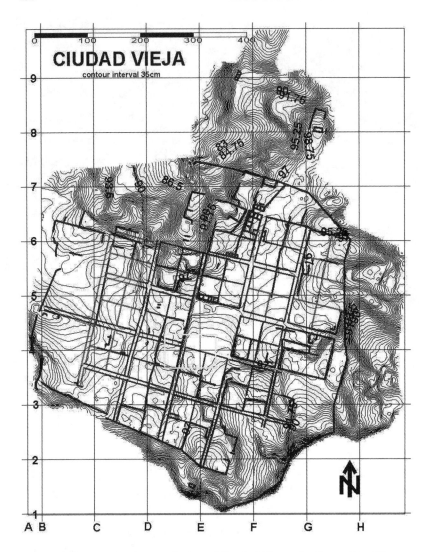

Map 5.1 Projected urban grid plan of Ciudad Vieja, the first *villa* of San Salvador. Map by Conard C. Hamilton, by permission.

Mesoamericans from other regions, it almost certainly was also provided by Nahuat Pipil commoners from towns in the preconquest Cuscatlán polity. Agricultural tribute commodities from the same local communities supplied the town with food. In Santiago, meanwhile, even the Nahua allies were asked to contribute to public works by the Santiago cabildo

(Kramer and Luján Muñoz 2018:112, 116). In 1540 Pedro de Alvarado pledged the labor and supplies of Maya from distant Tecpan Atitlán and Rabinal to construct a fountain in the raised central plaza (Kramer and Luján Muñoz 2018:136v), and indigenous merchants provided the Spanish with food staples, wax, clothes, cacao, and other goods.

The point is obvious but bears repeating: the first successful instances of Spanish place making in Guatemala and El Salvador were made possible first by the Spaniards' alliance with highly trained Nahua warriors, then by the violent displacement, both permanent and temporary, of tens of thousands of Maya, Xinka, and Nahuat Pipil peoples. The place making that occurred in both cases represented hybrid creations drawing on the spatial traditions and habitus of both Mesoamerican and European societies.

THE MESOAMERICAN MAJORITY

In this unstable atmosphere, Europeans and Africans, for whom the idealized *traza* represented a safe, familiar haven, constituted an extreme minority. Some 200 European men received the status of *vecino* in Santiago between 1527 and 1530 (Sáenz de Santa María 1991:205–210). An unknown number of other Europeans and Africans are not included in such lists but appear elsewhere in the cabildo books as property owners and officeholders. The free African Pedro de Barrera, for instance, held the office of town crier between 1536 and 1537 and owned his own house (Kramer and Luján Muñoz 2018:162, 207, 216). These Old World settlers were surrounded not only by partially subjugated but still hostile Kaqchikel Maya whose lands they had invaded but also by many hundreds if not thousands of indigenous allies from Mexico, Oaxaca, and the Soconusco. Known collectively as Mexicanos, the non-Maya indigenous allies lived on the immediate outskirts of the Spanish *traza* close to the springs that gave Almolonga its Nahuatl name. Significantly, this placed a major water source beyond the Spaniards' and Africans' direct control, although nearby rivers were also accessible. A cross at the intersection of two roadways indicated the Mexicano-Spanish boundary and the Spanish city's entrance. Boundary markers further delimited and protected the Mexicanos' lands (Kramer and Luján Muñoz 2018:14, 54–55; see also Matthew 2012:174).

In addition to its close proximity to and frequent contact with the Mexicano population, Santiago was also surrounded by mostly Maya refugees, migrants, and slaves from other regions (Kramer and Luján Muñoz 2018:146, 203–204, 210). The city council attempted to resettle this heterogeneous and fluid indigenous population into towns corresponding to royal encomienda grants of native labor and tribute obligations (Kramer and Luján Muñoz 2018:110, 139–140, 217–218), but with only partial success. Mesoamericans lived where they liked; planted milpas; killed Spanish colts, cattle, and sheep that disturbed their fields; and demonstrated their indifference to Catholic evangelization by working on Sundays (Kramer and Luján Muñoz 2018:123, 203–204, 246). Mesoamericans also entered the *traza* itself as transient laborers, servants living in Spanish households, and even residents in their own private homes (Kramer and Luján Muñoz 2018:123, 163, 299).

A large, possibly pre-Columbian indigenous market at the city's southern edge anchored the Spanish city and became a central site of multicultural contact, attracting buyers and sellers from across the region. Spaniards, Africans, Nahua, Maya, and others converged to buy and sell indigenous products such as fresh fish and salt from the Pacific coast, cacao, corn, chiles, beans, cloth, and clothing, as well as new products like cheese, wine, wool, wax, and wheat-flour cookies. Spanish peddlers and encomenderos sold local items privately from their homes in competition with indigenous sellers (Kramer and Luján Muñoz 2018:197–198, 200, 236–238, 312). The Spanish market supervisor, Diego López Gordillo, appears to have been removed from his post in part for demanding remuneration from indigenous sellers beyond the basic supplies such as firewood and food that they were obligated to provide him (Kramer and Luján Muñoz 2018:279). Spaniards also inserted themselves into the cacao trade (Kramer and Luján Muñoz 2018:160–161, 210, 344)—at this early date, a testament to cacao's intraregional rather than export value.

The material record of San Salvador makes even clearer that although the Spanish architecturally created a "little Europe" within the *traza*, these early cities were simultaneously very Mesoamerican. An indigenous population of significant proportions was concentrated on the west and south sides of San Salvador, within and just outside the boundaries of the *traza*. Nahuat Pipil servants forced into service from nearby encomienda towns also rotated in and out of the city, apparently without substantial living quarters. While San Salvador is within Nahuat Pipil territory, as there was no immediate precontact settlement on the site, all inhabitants would have been newcomers to the site by choice or by force. San Salvador's 73 Spanish *vecinos* (Lardé y Larín 2000:108–110), meanwhile, built their residences near the center of the *traza*. The foundations here are predominantly in Spanish style, with rectangular layouts, carved stone column bases, adobe ovens, blacksmiths' and smelters' workshops, and sometimes tiled floors and roofs. Aside from a very small number of Spanish imports (2.6 percent), however, the ceramic complex of San Salvador is overwhelmingly indigenous, displaying many forms and decorative modes representing continuities with Late Postclassic materials, as well as hybrid forms and motifs developed during the conquest period.

In addition to the highly visible concentrations of ceramics, obsidian artifacts occur in great numbers on the surface and have been recovered from all excavated loci. Manos and metates (grinding stones) for maize processing occur in domestic contexts and on the surface. Ceramic spindle whorls for spinning thread, found in association with indigenous residences, speak to gendered production practices. Significantly, the highest concentration of Spanish ceramics and glass in San Salvador has been found in the commercial complex across the plaza from the city council building in the very center of the *traza*. This same urban plan is replicated in Santiago, though perhaps on a smaller scale; the council books only mention four shops commissioned to be built adjacent to the city council building on the plaza rather late, in 1537–1538.

The excavations at San Salvador thus offer a window into something the Guatemalan council books rarely discuss: the maintenance or construction of indigenous identity in and around these early colonial cities. Polished ceramic ear flares and jade objects (indicating elite bodily adornment) are significant in the inventory of indigenous-associated items at San Salvador. The ceramic record from eight excavated contexts and structures and from an extensive surface collection of the site shows evidence of a mixing and matching of indigenous styles, as well as the appearance of pottery normally associated with Oaxaca. Most strikingly, Jeb Card (2007) identified a class of earthenware serving plates with wide, outflaring rims produced with native Mesoamerican technology and painted designs but with brimmed forms copied from Italian majolica. Card (2007, 2013) refers to these vessels as "hybrid plates." Unlike the situation at most other Spanish colonial settlements, this new class of vessel is more associated with indigenous use than with Spanish use, and it is especially rare in the wealthiest Spanish households. Significantly, this pattern of hybridized vessel manufacture and use is known only in other cases of forced indigenous displacement in early colonial Spanish America (Card 2007:276–299, 2013:120).

A TENSE *CONVIVENCIA*

The Guatemalan council books remind us of the delicate political and social circumstances in which such hybridization took place. In 1535 the Santiago city council complained that local Kaqchikel were selling the lands they had possessed before the invasion, to which by Spanish logic they should no longer have had any rights. Worse yet, the Kaqchikel were selling their old lands to Spaniards, further evidence of the economic relationships that were developing between the Spanish and Maya, as well as the city council's lack of control over not only the indigenous population but also its own citizens. The Maya also played the Spanish and Nahua allies against each other, for instance, in 1538, when Maya lords arrived at the city council house requesting permission to create a new town—something the Spaniards had repeatedly tried to force them to do—in lands that were occupied by the Mexicanos (Kramer and Luján Muñoz 2018:150r). The stock phrase in the council books ordering Spaniards to build outside the *traza* "sin perjuizio de los yndios" (without prejudice to the Indians) conformed to imperial expectations, but it may also have responded to the need not to provoke unduly the thousands of Mesoamericans who lived there.

Local indigenous people were also, however, vulnerable to the violence that both Nahua and Spaniards were willing to unleash against them. Complaining that the Maya were not remaining in the towns that had been created for them around nearby Lake Quilinizapa, the Spanish "gave many orders for men to go round them up, but these men treated the Indian lords badly, and this caused much scandal to both the Indians and the Spaniards" (Kramer and Luján Muñoz 2018:139–140). These men were Mexicano *calpisques*, a Nahuatl word for the Aztec adminis- trators of conquered towns; the Spanish council sometimes called them *mayordomos* and identified them by name (Kramer and Luján Muñoz

2018:208). The Spanish council decided to negotiate this potentially explosive situation themselves.

Maya and other refugee, encomienda, and migrant populations around Santiago also suffered from private slave-raiding. In 1536 the council prohibited Spaniards from rounding up feral horses to abduct Mesoamerican slaves and commoners and rapidly transport them to boats waiting on the Pacific coast (Kramer and Luján Muñoz 2018:190) and ships' captains from taking free Mesoamericans out of the city as slaves (Kramer and Luján Muñoz 2018:213). Indeed, the business of slaving constituted a major connecting thread between Santiago and San Salvador, and one wonders how much of San Salvador's *traza* was built by these Maya, Xinka, or other slaves rather than by local Nahuat Pipil populations (Kramer and Luján Muñoz 2018:84, 87, 91, 139–140, 163, 167, 191, 319).

The Santiago city council books provide valuable information about another group that thus far has remained invisible in the material record of San Salvador: Africans. As was true elsewhere in the nascent Spanish Empire, free and enslaved Africans played important, specific roles both as colonists and as enforcers of colonialism, against whom indigenous Americans often chafed (Aguirre Beltrán 1946; Restall 2000, 2005; Vinson and Restall 2009; Wheat 2016; Zabala Aguirre 2013). In Santiago, as we have already seen, Africans were artisans such as barbers and bakers, town criers, supervisors of Mesoamerican labor, and guardsmen, as well as slaves (Kramer and Luján Muñoz 2018:162, 243, 280, 311). Often, the city council books provide the names, salaries, and negotiations of these crucial urban actors. However, they also evince concern with the independence some Africans were showing, echoing problems even at the heart of empire in México-Tenochtitlan, where the leaders of an African uprising were publicly hanged in 1537 (Quiñones Keber 1995:93). Africans in Santiago were repeatedly forbidden from carrying arms unless accompanied by their masters (Kramer and Luján Muñoz 2018:62, 189), suggesting they were doing exactly that. A runaway slave was ordered to have one foot broken the first time he escaped and cut off the second time; after the third time the slave would be hanged (Kramer and Luján Muñoz 2018:218). Africans were also threatened with lashes, jail time, and a heavy fine if they entered the indigenous marketplace at the edge of the Spanish *traza*, which, unusually, was guarded by a Spaniard. African women were specifically and repeatedly prohibited from the market "for the trouble [*daño*] they cause" (Kramer and Luján Muñoz 2018:213, 235, 282).

Similarly, the council books speak volumes about the tensions between the Spanish and their Nahua and Zapotec allies. In 1532 the cabildo created a buffer zone between the Mexicanos' houses and the river to guard against conflicts with Spaniards collecting mud for making adobe bricks (Kramer and Luján Muñoz 2018:55). By 1535 some Spaniards were urging that the Mexicanos be thrown off the site they occupied ("hechen los yndios de Mexico del sytio") (Kramer and Luján Muñoz 2018:132). In 1538 and again in 1541 the Spanish unsuccessfully attempted to forcefully relocate the Mexicanos and appropriate their land (Kramer and Luján Muñoz 2018:239, 250, 260, 263, 330, 331). Mesoamerican women of all ethnicities were vulnerable to sexual assault, especially around the river and springs, where both Spaniards and Africans were forbidden to linger when women were washing or gathering water under threat of the unusually explicit punishment of four days in prison and a fine of four gold pesos for Spaniards or one hundred lashes for Africans (Kramer and Luján Muñoz 2018:85–86).[2]

Despite the tensions, construction in Santiago continued apace. Houses and the city council building were made of adobe or rammed-earth *tapia*, with planked walls and thatched roofs. In 1536 the city had a tannery and two blacksmiths; they were ordered to move outside the *traza* when sparks from their workshops caused a major fire "because the buildings of this city have coverings of straw" (Kramer and Luján Muñoz 2018:162, 188). By the end of the 1530s, most *solares* in Santiago had been distributed, and *vecinos* were constructing vineyards; successfully growing wheat, which helped stock a bakery and required a second mill for grinding flour; visiting the local tavern; and expanding roads within the city toward gold-mining areas in Honduras and to both Pacific and Atlantic ports (Kramer and Luján Muñoz 2018:234, 237, 243, 252, 254, 257, 270, 286). The church was finally approved for construction in 1536, and the Franciscans, Dominicans, and Mercedarians were planning monasteries in 1538. In the same year that Kají Imox and B'eleje' Kat were hanged, the city council building finally replaced its straw roof with ceramic tile.

If for Santiago we have a fine-grained sense of the process and timing of urbanization, in San Salvador we can more easily see its architectural and structural features. Excavations of residential and nonresidential structures and activity loci in San Salvador were conducted in the 1996, 1998, 1999, 2000, 2001, 2002, 2003, 2005, 2013, 2014, and 2015 field seasons. A total of 20 structures or activity areas have been identified and excavated. These include a large Spanish residence, several indigenous residences, a kitchen structure, two blacksmith's workshops, a commercial structure with a tavern, a church in the style of an open chapel (*capilla abierta*), an observation post, and several special-function structures. With very few exceptions, the orientations of the buildings follow the general site grid of 12 degrees. The multicourse stone wall foundations are usually 80–85 cm in width, or approximately one Spanish *vara* of 83 cm, although some foundations were thicker, in the range of 100–120 cm. The foundations run very deep, usually to at least 1 m below the top row of stones. The width and depth of foundations were correlated with the width and height of the walls supported. The basalt building stones were carefully cut, with at least one dressed face, and were laid carefully to form noticeably straight foundations. Here, too, walls were generally constructed of rammed earth *tapia*, but in some cases adobe bricks were used. Floors were either earthen or covered with *baldosas* (brick floor tiles); occasionally, cobblestones arranged in decorative patterns were used. Roofs were thatched or covered with *tejas* (ceramic roof tiles), laid over a wooden framework.

In both Santiago and San Salvador, all humans had to manage the uncontrolled, even explosive increase in the population of invasive species such as horses, sheep, cattle, and pigs, which also cleared land for new seeds and grasses such as wheat. According to the *Relación Marroquín*, which describes El Salvador in 1532, several encomenderos raised pigs in their encomienda towns. Pedro de Puelles noted that his Indians in the encomienda town of Cojutepeque kept a herd of 50 swine "para su necesidad" (for their needs) (Gall 1968:209). Sancho de Figueroa also stated that his Indians in Cojutepeque kept pigs (Gall 1968:210; Lardé y Larín 2000:159). Pedro de Liano mentioned that his Indians in Perulapa raise maize-fed pigs (Gall 1968:220). Very early we see an adoption of these animals for food; for instance, a domestic midden excavated at San Salvador yielded remains of pig or javalí, dog, rabbit, frog, catfish, freshwater snail, oyster, a crustacean, and possibly deer, cattle, chicken, and turkey, indicating a varied protein diet for the residents of the house associated with this deposit (Scott 2011). Significantly, this was a Spanish residence with a Mesoamerican kitchen, indicating perhaps that the woman of the house was of indigenous heritage and quite possibly of high status (Herrera 2007; Matthew 2012:216–224).

In Santiago the Spanish cabildo openly appreciated the place making that the growing cattle population helped them accomplish, "break[ing] up the pastures and rid[ding] it of the bad insects and animals . . . and this makes the land open and you can ride it all on horseback" (Kramer and Luján Muñoz 2018:57). In 1538 the council called for new measurements of land allotments outside the city because "now the valley is clean," revealing differences between the parcels' sizes (Kramer and Luján Muñoz 2018:225). European animals thus aided the colonizing process in unanticipated ways, but their rapid increase also caused problems even within the *traza*. Repeatedly, the city council ordered *vecinos* to limit the number of pigs they kept in pens adjacent to their houses, to build fences, and to remove their cattle and sheep to the outskirts of the city. Colts and fillies running wild in the common pastures, through people's gardens, and within the *traza* seems to have been a particular problem throughout the entire decade, mentioned no fewer than 30 times and on a regular basis. By the end of the 1530s the grass in common pastures was starting to run short (Kramer and Luján Muñoz 2018:288). In 1541 it was reported that the cattle "almost don't fit in the valley," and no one was bothering to plant wheat or Castilian trees anymore (Kramer and Luján Muñoz 2018:348). The animals brought by the Spanish and Africans committed their own kinds of violence. Along with pathogens that would kill several million indigenous people throughout Central America by the end of the sixteenth century, the animals reshaped the landscape itself (Lovell 1992; Melville 1994).

CONCLUSION

Several points emerge from this comparative exercise between two sixteenth-century Spanish American cities, Santiago and San Salvador, and two disciplines, history and archaeology. First, the precariousness of the initial Spanish foothold in Central America delayed place making. Surrounded and vastly outnumbered by Mesoamericans and often actively engaged in war, Spaniards and Africans concentrated their initial energies on defense and depended heavily on their Nahua allies (who themselves constituted a potential threat). In Santiago, a more urbanized and recognizably Castilian city that included churches, Spanish markets, and Catholic processions came a full decade after the acts of foundation. Given the clear concern with defensive lookouts and allied settlements on the city's most vulnerable sides in San Salvador, one suspects that there, too, the Spanish tiendas, tile roofs and floors, and commercial center were later developments. So far, in neither place does it appear that a Spanish church was fully constructed before each city's abandonment in the 1540s.

Second, historical archaeology should be alert to emerging networks of trade and political power between Spanish colonial sites. The two Ciudad Viejas were founded in tandem between November 1527 and April 1528 as part of an extended military campaign. Their layouts are almost identical. San Salvador was the subordinate sibling: smaller and in need of the administrative functions and contact with Spain that Santiago provided (Kramer and Luján Muñoz 2018:181, 183, 268–269). But San Salvador was also the older site of the two and its own center of economic gravity, oriented toward the developing port of Acajutla, while Santiago put resources into developing a port at Istapa. Sugar plantations were attempted near Izalco and Nahuizalco by 1536 (Kramer and Luján Muñoz 2018:186–187), and while Santiago depended on San Salvador for coastal products like salt and fish, San Salvador competed with Santiago for slaves, cacao, textiles, and other valuable market goods (Kramer and Luján Muñoz 2018:25–26, 252, 270). Although both were abandoned and reestablished within a short twenty years, these earliest Spanish cities established patterns of competition and collaboration that would persist for centuries to come (Dym 2006).

Finally, we are struck both by the dogged determination of the Spanish to re-create the world as they knew it in the Americas and by the fragility of that endeavor. Survival depended on maintaining equilibrium between the minority but aggressive invading force, on the one hand, and a majority population fractured by war, on the other. This was not only a matter of forcing Mesoamericans to build roads, supply food, and provide water and other necessities—though Mesoamericans clearly did these things. It was also a matter of the Spanish learning the limits of their power, engaging in diplomacy, and knowing when to back down. In San Salvador the archaeological record demonstrates some of the mutual influences that resulted. In Santiago the city council's inability to enforce its will and the slow pace of construction indicate the challenges it faced, while Spanish participation in the indigenous marketplace reveals a hybrid economy taking shape. Santiago's council books remind us that Africans—including African women—were visible and important contributors to this intense cultural encounter.

The violence inherent in early colonial Spanish place making manifested itself in spectacular and quotidian ways. It was embedded in the very fabric of social relations as Spaniards sought order and security through both punishment and appeasement. It was multidirectional; Nahua attacked Maya on behalf of Spaniards and Africans, Spaniards protected Nahua and Maya from Africans, Africans threatened to rebel against Spaniards, Maya manipulated Spaniards against Nahua. This violence not only was conquering and colonial but also constituted part of the crucible of urban foundations. As historian David Nirenberg has put it for another place and time (2015:viii), the Spanish *trazas* of Santiago and San Salvador were a "co-production of community and violence" in search of a "pluralist equilibrium" that was necessary for the city's very survival.

NOTES

1. We are grateful to Wendy Kramer and Jorge Luján Muñoz for sharing their transcription of the second *libro de cabildo* as it went to press. Many thanks also to Christine Beaule, John Douglass, and the rest of the volume's contributors for their careful reading and probing comments and to the Amerind Foundation for its generous support.

2. We thank Wendy Kramer for calling our attention to this point and passage.

REFERENCES

Aguirre Beltrán, Gonzalo. 1946. *La población negra de México, 1519–1810: Estudio etnohistórico*. Mexico City: Ediciones Fuente Cultural.

Asselbergs, Florine G. L. 2004. *Conquered Conquistadors*. Leiden: CNWS Publications.

Brewer-Carías, Alan R. 2006. *La ciudad ordenada*. Caracas: Criteria Editorial.

Card, Jeb J. 2007. "The Ceramics of Colonial Ciudad Vieja, El Salvador: Culture Contact and Social Change in Mesoamerica." PhD diss., Tulane University.

———, ed. 2013. *The Archaeology of Hybrid Material Culture*. Carbondale: Southern Illinois University at Carbondale, Center for Archaeological Investigations.

Castillero Calvo, Alfredo. 2006. *Sociedad, economía y cultura material: Historia urbana de Panamá La Vieja.* Patronato de Panamá Viejo. Buenos Aires: Editorial Alloni.

Castro, Rodolfo Baron. 1996. *Reseña histórica de la villa de San Salvador.* 2nd ed. San Salvador: Consejo Nacional para la Cultura y el Arte.

Dym, Jordana. 2006. *From Sovereign Villages to Nation States: City, State, and Federation in Central America, 1759–1839.* Albuquerque: University of New Mexico Press.

Fowler, William R., and Howard H. Earnest. 1985. "Settlement Patterns and Prehistory of the Paraíso Basin of El Salvador." *Journal of Field Archaeology* 12:19–32.

———. 2012. *Ciudad Vieja: Excavaciones, arquitectura y paisaje cultural de la primera villa de San Salvador.* San Salvador: Secretaría de Cultura de la Presidencia / Editorial Universitaria, Universidad de El Salvador.

Gall, Francis. 1968. "El licenciado Francisco Marroquín y una descripción de El Salvador, año de 1532." *Anales de la Sociedad de Geografía e Historia de Guatemala* 41:199–232.

Herrera, Robinson A. 2007. "Concubines and Wives: Reinterpreting Native-Spanish Intimate Unions in Sixteenth-Century Guatemala." In *Indian Conquistadors: Indigenous Allies in the Conquest of Mesoamerica,* edited by Laura E. Matthew and Michel Oudijk, 127–144. Norman: University of Oklahoma Press.

Kagan, Richard L. 2000. *Urban Images of the Hispanic World, 1493–1793.* New Haven, Conn.: Yale University Press.

Kramer, Wendy, W. George Lovell, and Christopher Lutz. 2014. *Saqueo en el archivo: El paradero de los tesoros documentales guatemaltecos.* Guatemala City: Centro de Investigaciones Regionales de Mesoamérica / Centro de Estudios Urbanos y Regionales de la Universidad San Carlos; and South Woodstock, Vt.: Plumsock Mesoamerican Studies.

Kramer, Wendy, and Jorge Luján Muñoz, eds. 2018. *Libro segundo del cabildo de la ciudad de Santiago de la provinçia de Guatemala començado a XXVII de mayo de MDXXX años.* Guatemala City: Centro de Investigaciones Regionales de Mesoamérica / Academia de Geografía e Historia de Guatemala / Universidad del Valle de Guatemala; South Woodstock, Vt.: Plumsock Mesoamerican Studies.

Larde y Larín, Jorge. 2000. *El Salvador: Descubrimiento, conquista y colonización.* San Salvador: Consejo Nacional para la Cultura y el Arte.

Lauret, Alain, Raymond Malebranche, and Gilles Séraphin. 1988. *Bastides: Villes nouvelles du Moyen Age.* Toulouse: Études et Communication.

Matthew, Laura E. 2012. *Memories of Conquest: Becoming Mexicano in Colonial Guatemala.* Chapel Hill: University of North Carolina Press.

Maxwell, Judith M., and Robert M. Hill. 2006. *Kaqchikel Chronicles: The Definitive Edition.* Austin: University of Texas Press.

McAlister, Lyle N. 1984. *Spain and Portugal in the New World, 1492–1700.* Minneapolis: University of Minnesota Press.

Melville, Elinor. 1994. *A Plague of Sheep: Environmental Consequences of the Conquest of Mexico.* Cambridge: Cambridge University Press.

Mira Caballos, Esteban. 2000. *Nicolás de Ovando y los orígenes del sistema colonial español, 1502–1509.* Santo Domingo, Dominican Republic: Patronato de la Ciudad Colonial de Santo Domingo, Centro de Altos Estudios Humanísticos y del Idioma Español.

Navarro Segura, María Isabel. 2006. "Las fundaciones de ciudades y el pensamiento urbanístico hispano en la era del descubrimiento." *Scripta Nova.* Revista electrónica de Geografía y Ciencias Sociales. Universidad de Barcelona, vol. 10, no. 218 (43), http://www.ub.edu/geocrit/sn/sn-218.htm.

Nirenberg, David. 2015. *Communities of Violence: Persecution of Minorities in the Middle Ages.* Princeton, N.J.: Princeton University Press.

Polo Sifontes, Francis. 1986. *Los Cakchiqueles en la conquista de Guatemala.* Guatemala City: Editorial Plus Ultra.

Quiñones Keber, Eloise, ed. 1995. *Codex Telleriano-Remensis: Ritual, Divination, and History in a Pictorial Aztec Manuscript.* Austin: University of Texas Press.

Remesal, Antonio de, and Carmelo Sáenz de Santa María, eds. 1964–1966. *Historia general de las indias occidentales y particular de la gobernación de Chiapa y Guatemala.* Madrid: Ediciones Atlas.

Restall, Matthew. 2000. "Black Conquistadors: Armed Africans in Early Spanish America." *Americas* 57(2): 171–205.

———, ed. 2005. *Beyond Black and Red: African-Native Relations in Colonial Latin America.* Albuquerque: University of New Mexico Press.

Rodríguez-Alegria, Enrique. 2017. "A City Transformed: From Tenochtitlan to Mexico City in the Sixteenth Century." In *The Oxford Handbook of the Aztecs,* edited by Deborah L. Nichols and Enrique Rodríguez-Alegría, 661–674. New York: Oxford University Press.

Sáenz de Santa María, Carmelo, and María del Carmen Deola de Girón. 1991. *Libro viejo de la fundación de Guatemala.* Guatemala City: Academia de Geografía e Historia de Guatemala; Comisión Interuniversitaria Guatemalteca de Conmemoración del Quinto Centenario del Descrubrimiento de América.

Scott, Elizabeth M. 2011. "Observaciones preliminares sobre los restos fáunicos de la operación 99-2." In *Investigaciones arqueológicas en Ciudad Vieja, El Salvador: La primigenia villa de San Salvador,* edited by William R. Fowler and Roberto Gallardo, 126–129. San Salvador: Consejo Nacional para la Cultura y el Arte / Ministerio de Educación.

Sociedad de Geografía e Historia de Guatemala. 1934. *Libro viejo de la fundación de Guatemala y papeles relativos a d. Pedro de Alvarado.* Prologue by Jorge García Granados. Biblioteca "Goathemala," vol. 12. Guatemala City: Sociedad de Geografía e Historia de Guatemala.

Szécsy, János. 1953. *Santiago de los caballeros de Goathemala, en Almolonga: Investigaciones del año 1950.* Translated by Y. de Oreamuno. Guatemala City: Editorial del Ministerio de Educación Pública.

Tejeira-Davis, Eduardo. 1996. "Pedrarias Dávila and His Cities in Panama, 1513–1522: New Facts on Early Spanish Settlements in America." *Jahrbuch für Geschichte von Staat Wirtschaft und Gesellschaft Lateinamerikas* 33:27–61.

Vinson, Ben, and Matthew Restall, eds. 2009. *Black Mexico: Race and Society from Colonial to Modern Times.* Albuquerque: University of New Mexico Press.

Wheat, David. 2016. *Atlantic Africa and the Spanish Caribbean, 1570–1640.* Chapel Hill: University of North Carolina Press.

Zabala Aguirre, Pilar. 2013. "Esclavitud, asimilación, y mestizaje de negros urbanos durante la colonia." *Arqueología Mexicana* 119:36–39.

6

When the Saints Go Marching In

Religious Place Making during the Early Spanish
Colonial Period in the Central Andes, 1532–1615

Kevin Lane

Although Christianity continued making steady inroads within Andean
communities in the former Tawantinsuyu over time, elements of indigenous religious practices endured alongside Christianity, as they do to the
present day (Andrien 2001:155).

In terms of distance, Spanish colonization of South America and the
Andes was at the limits of what sixteenth-century technology would
permit (Sheridan 1992:153). As a result, while the attraction of riches
and lands was a persistent lure to wannabe adventurers, the reality was
that during the first three-quarter century of colonization of the Andes, the number of Spaniards actually on the ground was limited (Cook
1981); indeed, the initial conquest was undertaken with a paltry 168 men
(Lockhart 1972). Nevertheless, a massive fall in the indigenous population and concomitant societal disruption (Stern 1993), coupled with
the silver-mining boom at places such as Potosí (Bakewell 2010) and
Castrovirreyna (Maldonado Pimentel and Estacio Tamayo 2012), among
others, meant that by the early seventeenth century the previous situation had been reversed, and large numbers of Spaniards with wives and
accompanying black slaves (primarily for work on the coast) had made
the central Andes their abode (Lockhart 1974).

Even so, early colonization was a patchy affair, and away from the
incipient urban centers, penetration by Spanish society and culture was
always difficult (this is a concern echoed by James Bayman et al. in chapter 9). This was even more apparent in the vast mountainous hinterland,
where the steep and varied ecology, inaccessibility, and altitude conspired
against significant European penetration. Even the large resettlement
programs, such as the late sixteenth-century and early seventeenth-
century *reducciones*—literally the concentration of indigenous rural populations in model villages—often failed, as the people returned to their

nearby ancestral lands (Mumford 2012). Absentee landlordism was also a common feature, reducing even further the Spanish footprint in the high Andes. Often the only Spanish presence was that of religious orders on an evangelizing mission in the Andean interior (MacCormack 1991), and this was also sparse and scattered. Indeed, apathy and war between the original conquistadors effectively delayed Christianization of the Andes until after 1554, with only the arrival of Viceroy Francisco de Toledo (1569–1581) providing the necessary impetus for persistent evangelization (Andrien 2001:161–168). Still, given the small numbers of priests, monks, and missionaries involved, it is not surprising that the early expansion of Christianity in the Andes was often hesitant, sporadic, and invariably involved significant compromises.

In this chapter, I concentrate on the liminal period and space between the end of autochthonous indigenous control of their lands and livelihood to the early Spanish colony (1532–1615). Martin Gibbs and David Roe (chapter 7) chart a similar indigenous-Spanish encounter, the difference being that in the Andes, the Spanish came and remained, playing out that initial meeting to its conclusion. Even so, during this period, early Spanish colonial rhetoric was not often matched by deeds. The religious sphere was one such area in which the desired Spanish ideal faced Andean reality. Concentrating on the prehispanic and Spanish colonial site of Kipia in the Ancash Highlands of north-central Peru, this chapter describes the cosmological arrangement of the site as envisaged first by the indigenous people and subsequently by the Spanish. Kipia is located on the westernmost mountain range—Cordillera Negra—before the Pacific Ocean, ca. 70 km inland from the sea. Even if close, relatively speaking, to the coast, the highlands were another world in which Spanish presence was concentrated in the verdant intervalley areas and small towns rather than in the more out-of-the-way villages and hamlets of the upper Andes. The area around Kipia is characteristic of this more remote world (Lane 2009).

Throughout this chapter, I tease out the contradictions between Spanish and Andean religious practice and how Spanish religious practice inscribed itself on the local setting. In this sense, I delve into the dichotomy between what I term a Spanish *religion of place* versus an Andean *religion of space* and how these interacted across the site and landscape. Essentially, I describe the long process of early Spanish colonial place making in the Andes, where Spanish religious expression first inscribed itself within the indigenous belief system before attempting to mold it. In particular, I examine how Christian monotheism during this early colonial period co-opted and negotiated indigenous animistic and polytheistic elements, thereby attempting to reinforce the entry and expansion of Christianity into the Andean highlands (Bravo Guerrera 1993), albeit a Christianity informed by indigenous precepts.

Some of these compromises persist even today and form part of the existing Hispano-Andean Christian tradition (Irarrazaval 1999). For instance, the Señor de los Milagros (Lord of Miracles) doubles up for the prehispanic coastal deity Pachacamac (MacCormack 1988; Rostworowski 1998), and the Corpus Christi procession in Cuzco appropriated much of the ritual symbolism associated with the Inka Inti Raymi ceremony (Cahill 1996), while the identity of local Andean deities was subsumed under that of Christian saints (Díaz Araya et al. 2012).

LANDSCAPES OF WORSHIP

Discussion of the dichotomy between, and the meaning of, place and space in landscape archaeology has been long and convoluted, yet perhaps Jerry Moore (2005:1; see also the introduction) got closest when he described it thus: "Space is indifferent to humanity, but place requires the inscription of human acknowledgement." Nevertheless, one could argue that *space* and the natural environs it describes have also been heavily colonized by human thought and emotion (Bradley 2000). This is especially true of conceptualized landscapes, in which there is a recursive mediation and social construction of landscape by people (Knapp and Ashmore 1999). Religion and how it imprints itself onto the landscape is one such type of conceptualization.

This leads me to suggest that place and space may be used to describe types of interaction within a religiously embedded landscape. In this sense, we would interpret a place-oriented religious landscape as one in which special markers, features, or buildings provide the crucial wherewithal to root a community, while a space-oriented religious landscape is one in which a community will encompass the totality of its environs to tether its identity. Therefore, we can start differentiating between a religion of place and a religion of space. Yet this is not to say that these two categories are fixed; rather, we recognize that while invariably all communities and their religious landscapes will contextually espouse a mixture of both, some cultures will tend toward one form more than the other.

We can distinguish between an early Spanish colonial religion of place and the then-existing Andean religion of space. Spain's religion of place in the Andes was more rooted around the physical structure of the church, in part because it delimited in many ways the extent of early Spanish control in a given area; therefore, it involved a religious experience that was mostly disarticulated from the surrounding landscape. Indeed, it is important to underline the fact that this religion of place works very well within the context of Spanish arrival in the Andes, where the incoming conquistadors were being introduced to and would eventually assimilate a new landscape. Moreover, it was a landscape over which for a long time they exerted little effective political and, by inference, physical control. During the early Spanish colony, the Catholic Christian god had few earthly manifestations in the Andes.

By way of contrast, Andean religion was homegrown and had already experienced millennia of accommodation to its particular landscape, an animated landscape that formed an integral component of local indigenous cosmogony (Bauer 1998; Lane 2011b; Millones 1980; Zuidema 2005). In this sense, an Andean religion of space evoked the totality of the landscape as a complex and intensely animated sacred backdrop cohabited by people, their crops, and their animals. Within the Andes, gods and ancestors (as well as evil spirits) were manifest at all times in everything from wind, boulders, lightning, lakes, rivers, and caves. New waves of conquest, such as the Inca, just added new complexity and layers to this animated landscape, such that one could describe the Andes as a cosmological complex where different animistic perceptions of landscape were interlinked and overlapped and where, most importantly, everything was animated (this has been termed *polyanimistic*).

During the early Spanish colonial period these two types of religious landscapes and adscriptions onto the environment vied for hegemony. On the one hand, indigenous societies attempted to accommodate Spanish religion while equally attempting to mostly maintain the status quo; on the other hand, the Spanish sought to create their own place within this region. Andean religion started with a distinct disadvantage. Polytheism has a tendency toward toleration, incorporation, or subversion of alien gods and deities as and when they are encountered. Note, for instance, the ever-expanding Roman Empire and its equally expansive pantheon of gods (Rüpke 2007). The Andes was no different: indigenous populations saw Christianity and its god very much as a new deity to be integrated within the already existing palimpsest of gods, ancestors, and spirits (Andrien 2001:160–161).

The indigenous people even had a term for this: *mañay*, or "compromise" (Millones 1987); *mañay* was what many local cultures had employed when the Inka conquered them during the fifteenth century and imposed their own deities. They saw the Spanish god in the same light, so much so that some early indigenous writers even sought to prove that Christianity had deep ancestral roots in the Andes (Guaman Poma de Ayala 1993 [1615]; Santa Cruz Pachacuti Yamqui 1993 [1613]), and thus the introduction of a Christian god was not so much an appropriation as a rediscovery. Indeed, this followed what earlier Spanish chroniclers had written, interpreting Andean populations as one of the Lost Tribes of Israel, fully immersed within the biblical narrative, and thereby presenting the Andes as a preexisting Christian religious landscape (González Díaz 2014; see also MacCormack [2001] for a comparison of Cuzco as a sacred, imperial capital in the same mold as classical Rome).

By way of contrast with Andean animistic polytheism, sixteenth-century Spain had a very different vision of religion, the world, and Spain's place in it. This Spain was a highly militarized, increasingly monotheistic, early modern state that had extinguished the last independent Muslim kingdom and expelled the Jews from its realms as recently as 1492, the same year in which Columbus made landfall in the Americas (Harvey 1992). This consolidation of Spain ushered in a golden age (1492–1659) in which the rapacity of conquest was accompanied by the righteousness of Christian evangelization, a righteousness founded on the belief of being God's chosen. With the rise of European Protestantism—also in the early sixteenth century—Spain increasingly saw itself as the Catholic bulwark against heresy and unfaith (Kamen 2014). Importantly, while Protestantism emphasized that communion with god was possible anywhere, Catholicism reiterated that this was only possible within the physical institution of the church and through the intercession of the priest. Spain's religious colonization of the Andes has to be seen against this stark background.

Indeed, it seems that while processional festivities had existed in Spain in some limited manner prior to the sixteenth century, the rise in Catholic processions—especially those associated with Holy Week—in western Europe came into their own as a reaction against the rise of Protestantism in northern Europe (Barnes 1988; Ortega Sagrista 1956). Prior to this, these types of festivities had been undertaken within the church or just outside, under the cover of the portico—a strong reminder that sixteenth-century Spanish Catholicism was very much a religion of place, even if via crucis pilgrimages and processions formed an integral component of overt displays of faith (Thurston 1914:20–21, 46). This emphasis on the physicality of the church to the general detriment of the wider environment was a feature that the Spanish attempted to introduce into the Andes.

Yet the reality remained that during the early Spanish colony, numbers were not on their side. Therefore, Spanish religious colonization during this early period often favored accommodation over imposition. Steve Wernke (2007) has observed the same pattern of occupation and repurposing of earlier prehispanic sacred places in the Colca Valley, south-central Andes. As such, a Spanish religion of place felt it necessary to occupy indigenous places, thereby evoking and preserving the link to a local religion of space, even if in time this indigenous religion of space was subverted and altered to fit Spanish colonial needs. This incremental change can be appreciated at the site of Kipia.

KIPIA: PHYSICAL ENVIRONMENT AND SITE

Kipia (Puk 9) is located in the Pamparomás district of the Cordillera Negra of the north-central highlands of Peru. These mountains represent the westernmost range of the Andes (Map 6.1). Kipia itself is set on the threshold between three ecozones (as defined by Pulgar Vidal 1946). The lowest, the *kichwa* (2,000–3,500 masl), is considered the last major, predominantly crop cultivation zone. Above lies the *suni* (3,500–4,000 masl), a mixed-economy transitional area between the lower *kichwa* and the herding alpine tundra grasslands (puna) above. Finally, we have the puna (4,000–5,200 masl), the highest ecozone before the snowline. The puna is considered a major pastoralist grassland area. This region of the Ancash highlands lies at the ecological boundary between the wet

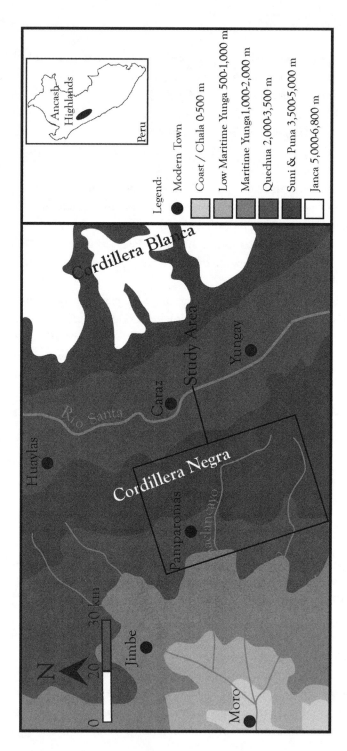

Map 6.1 Map of the study area, showing the major ecozones, geographical features, and modern towns.

puna and the wetter paramo ecozones (Custred 1977). Average rainfall is therefore high, between 500 and 1,000 mm annually (INRENA 2000). During the prehispanic period, a complex series of natural and artificial lakes captured this water for economic use (Lane 2009, 2017).

The site of Kipia is set on a ridge to the east of modern-day Pamparomás, within a bowl-shaped, midvalley area below the Cordillera Negra summits to the east. Strategically, the site dominates this area and is located on a ridge that runs west to east extending out from the eastern Shunak Massif. The Shunak Massif rises to over 4,000 m and is the natural division between an important lake zone located entirely within the upland puna and the *kichwa* and *suni* fields around and below Kipia. Situated between 3,150 and 3,400 m, Kipia is in the upper bracket of the *kichwa* ecozone, straddling the *kichwa* and *suni*, while providing an important conduit to the higher puna. The site is located at the juncture between major farming and herding zones, thereby highlighting these mainstays of the late prehispanic economy combined in its egregious South American manifestation—Andean agropastoralism.

Kipia is divided into four sectors (A to D) spread across four low hills along the ridge (Figure 6.1). Sector A comprises the westernmost area of the site and includes habitational terraces along its western, northern, and southern flanks. A banked and walled ditch physically separates A from B. I have interpreted Sector A as an Inca/Spanish colonial settlement hub (Lane 2011a).

Sector B represents the cosmological core of the site (Figure 6.1). The sector includes a large, relatively flat natural terrace interspersed with four natural rock outcrops (another one is located on the eastern extremity of Sector A). Approximately 40 m wide, this terrace is also roughly 60 m in length. The rock outcrops have been extensively modified through carving and the digging out of small niches (37) along their base. In addition, the level surfaces of these rocks were also sculpted to render channels and small pits: many of these pits contained offerings. It is probable that in the past these outcrops represented key focus points for ritual libation sessions dedicated to water worship (sensu Carrión Cachot 1955).

Among the five outcrops registered at the site, attention seems to coalesce on Rock Face 5 (RF5), which is the easternmost rock outcrop of the group. It juts out of the ground and therefore presents both ample horizontal and vertical surfaces. Furthermore, the relatively flat area

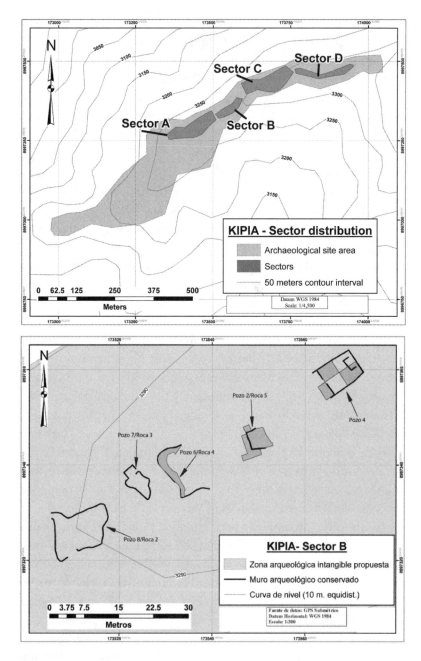

Figure 6.1 The site of Kipia, showing sectorization (*top*). Detail of Sector B, showing the *huaca-huanca* (RF5) and the Spanish church (Pit 4) (*bottom*).

behind this rock has a later, intrusive, Spanish colonial shrine/church in a classic case of sacred space appropriation. This further highlights RF5's centrality and importance within the site. It is the juxtaposition of these two features that I will consider in greater detail below.

Farther to the east is a heavily overgrown low hill, Sector C. This sector, along with Sector D, is also known locally as Corpus Rumi (body of stone). Sector C has been tentatively interpreted as a local Huaylas settlement. The last sector, D, is located at the far east of the ridge and includes a series of rock outcrops containing subterranean tombs, known as *pukullo*-type tombs (Herrera and Lane 2004).

Material culture remains from stratigraphic excavations support a Late Intermediate period (A.D. 1000–1450), Late Horizon (A.D. 1450–1532), and early Spanish Colonial occupation (A.D. 1532–1615) for the site, while objects found by locals in the area and deposited at the Pamparomás Museum indicate possible Early Intermediate period (A.D. 1–700) and Middle Horizon (A.D. 700–1000) occupations as well. This chronology is bolstered by eight radiocarbon dates (Table 6.1) that span the period in question and the prehispanic period preceding it (A.D. 1000–1615). These dates were calibrated using the SHCal curve (Hogg et al. 2013), as it better represents Southern Hemisphere dates (Ogburn 2012). Here I discuss these dates at 2-sigma (95 percent) standard variation.

Of these, MAMS15861 (A.D. 1421–1463), MAMS15865 (A.D. 1224–1285), and MAMS15867 (A.D. 1427–1464)—all three from offering pits associated with the carved rock faces in Sector B, the first two from Pit 2 (the *huanca-huaca*), and the last from Pit 6—amply straddle the late prehispanic period, including possibly early Inca occupation at the site. Following Dennis Ogburn (2012), who has argued for an earlier date for Inca imperial expansion, I propose that MAMS15861 might actually be dating an Inca offering. This would seem to be supported by a similar ranged date, MAMS15862 (A.D. 1430–1494), which dates a floor surface within which only Inca material culture items were recovered. Two further dates taken from stratigraphic deposits within the Christian chapel itself—MAMS15866 (A.D. 1498–1636) and MAMS15868 (A.D. 1497–1636)—fall mostly within the early Spanish colonial period. The final two dates, both from Sector A—MAMS15863 (A.D. 1031–1161) and MAMS15864 (A.D. 1457–1626)—date a secure Late Intermediate period and a colonial context, respectively; they complete the dates for the site.

Table 6.1 ¹⁴C Dates from the Site of Kipia (PUK9)

Lab No. MAMS	Sample No.	Sector	Pit	Stratigraphic Unit [Cut]	¹⁴C Date	δ¹³C	Cal 1-Sigma cal A.D.	Cal 2-Sigma cal A.D.
15861	Ca-8	B	2	34 [22]	489 ± 22	–21,3	1435–1454	1421–1463
15862	Ca-21	A	3	28	469 ± 23	–24,2	1440–1462	1430–1494
15863	Ca-22	A	3	28 [48]	976 ± 22	–18,7	1046–1152	1031–1161
15864	Ca-23	A	3	34	394 ± 23	–20,2	1464–1620	1457–1626
15865	Ca-25	B	2	72 [71]	802 ± 22	–19,0	1230–1280	1224–1285
15866	Ca-27	B	4	13	358 ± 18	–17,1	1506–1626	1498–1636
15867	Ca-28	B	6 (RF4)	20 [19]	482 ± 19	–27,9	1440–1455	1427–1464
15868	Ca-29	B	4	13	359 ± 20	–17,9	1506–1626	1497–1636

Note: Dates were processed at the CEZ Archäometrie gGmbH, Mannheim, Germany, and were calibrated using Oxcal v4.3.2 Bronk Ramsey (2017); r5 SHCal13 atmospheric data are from Hogg et al. (2013).

Taken in tandem, then, these dates would seem to provide a seamless occupation of Sectors A and B that spans the early eleventh century through the early seventeenth century. Indeed, the two dates from the chapel (MAMS15866 and MAMS15868) with their end date of ca. A.D. 1636 would seem to suggest a plausible *terminus ante quem* for the colonial abandonment of the site. Unfortunately, to date I have no extant archival material that would further delimit the final chronology of the site.

BETWEEN A *HUANCA* AND A CHURCH

Prehispanic and Spanish colonial devotion at Kipia centered on Sector B, specifically on the central *huanca* RF5 and the adjoining church (Figure 6.2). A *huanca* was a sacred, upright stone that doubled as an ancestor or deity-oracle (otherwise known as a *huaca*), intimately linking the people to their past and landscape (Curatola Petrocchi and Ziółkowski 2008:3). Recent research on modified or otherwise stone outcrops in the Andes has added considerable data toward understanding the pivotal cosmological importance of these features within the indigenous religious environment (Christie 2016; Dean 2010). They served as landscape referents, especially for processions that included them within a ritual setting that invoked the totality of the encompassing landscape, such as with the Inca *ceque* systems and the pilgrimages associated with them in the vicinity of Cuzco (Bauer 1998; Zuidema 1964). RF5 is a large, natural sandstone outcrop rising ca. 2 m from the ground and oriented to the northeast. The church is small (9 m long and 6 m wide), oriented on a southwest to northeast axis, and gable roofed, and an altar is set into the northeastern wall. This last fact is crucial, given that, like RF5, the church is also facing toward the northeast, thereby directly referencing the Andean landscape with which RF5 is also associated.

Both the front and the top platform of RF5 are carved. The front presents a series of lines and pitted indentations, while along the base of the rock are three sculptured niches and other additional pitting in the area immediately before the rock face. These various anthropogenic actions—the pitting, niche, and channel carving—serve to map out both a real and an idealistic plan of the nearby landscape and environs. The carved lines on the rock face appear to represent the contours of three nearby mountains, as well as a pass that can be observed from this perspective along

Figure 6.2 Detail of Sector B at Kipia, showing the *huaca–huanca* (RF5) and the Spanish church (Pit 4).

the neighboring Shunak Massif. Other features in the landscape are also referenced. The upper platform is likewise heavily modified through channeling and pitting. This is accompanied by offerings of local and river-rolled stone, ceramics, and seashells (*Spondylus*). These channels and pits could be a metaphoric representation of lakes, ponds, streams, and rivers (Lane et al. 2018).

Taken together, these elements suggest that RF5 was a feature used in water rituals, linking the local community to the nearby highland lakes and the sea as part of identity-reaffirming rituals that would have tied the local population to their *pacarina* (place of origin/emergence) (MacCormack 1991:428). Rituals enacted at the site would then cosmogonically link the *huaca-huanca* with the mountains and lakes and, through them, with extralocal bodies of water such as the Pacific Ocean and major highland lakes, including nearby Lago Conococha, and ultimately Lake Titicaca. The latter is seen as the main origin point of major highland deities, ancestors, and people, including the Inka (Urton 1999). As mentioned previously, water veneration was widespread throughout the Andes (Carrión Cachot 1955).

At a local level, this standing stone could be interpreted as a *tableau vivant* of its surrounding landscape. In a sense, Sector B was the animated theater from which local people ventured to create a profound engagement with their surroundings. In essence, the RF5 *huanca* was reimagining the physical and cosmological landscape while coincidentally reaffirming Kipia's nodal cosmogonic importance; essentially, it formed a hermeneutic circle in which projected reverence and understanding of the landscape reflected back onto the site itself. In this sense, veneration at Kipia was intrinsically externalized and linked to existing and imagined spaces, all the while centered on the structure and place of the central *huanca* (RF5). This is evidence that religions of space and place are always linked at some level. Basically, what we are discussing here is where the interrelationship between religions of space and place for Spanish colonial Kipia lies. Within the Andean context, I argue that religion of space often overshadows religion of place, but this does not correspond with early Spanish colonial imagining of the local context.

In theory, the construction of a church at this site should have served to cut local ties to the indigenous sacred landscape. Yet in practice, many of the referents of the church at Kipia maintained a direct connection to local preexisting beliefs (Figure 6.3). The church and altar were aligned along the same axis as RF5, thereby preserving the link to the mountains and lake area to the east. It is also entirely possible that given the early Spanish colony's limited understanding of Andean cosmological landscapes and their own preference for a religion of place, they viewed occupation of Kipia as the fulcrum around which their cosmological (and thereby political) control of the area would eventually pivot. Indeed, one could say that this was and continues to be an age-old practice among groups that normatively ascribe to a religion of place. In fact, at its most

Figure 6.3 Detail of Rock Face 5 at Kipia: *huanca-huaca* (A) and Santiago Chapel (B and C).

extreme, this deliberate erosion, suppression, or reinvention of a people's previous identity of place and space to reflect a new one imposed by a hegemonic or wannabe-hegemonic group has been termed "identicide" (Meharg 2001).

In this sense, one can see Christian conquest of the Iberian Peninsula and the conversion or supplanting of mosques for churches as a form of attempted identicide (see Echevarría 2003; López Guzmán 2000:132–133; Pérez Ordóñez 2005, for examples of this conversion process). Indeed, it is also Islam's—incidentally, another monotheistic religion— strong attachment to a religion of place that made it relatively easy for Christianity to sever direct architectural or place links to the supplanted religion through the repurposing of mosques and holy sites as Christian structures. Given that the conquest of the Americas was perceived by Spaniards as a continuation of the *reconquista* crusade bringing Christianity to heathens and heretics (Todorov 1984:10–13), and given Spanish Catholicism's engagement with places, it would seem that they similarly attempted to supplant and convert Andean sacred places. I argue that Spain's partial failure in repurposing the high Andes to Christianity was due to the inability to understand the indigenous connection to the totality of their cosmological landscape. Instead, the Spanish fixated on nodal places, the place making equivalent of missing the woods for the trees.

Importantly, the church itself was consecrated to Santiago (St. James the Great), patron saint of Spain. In the Hispano-Andean Christian tradition, Santiago replaced local Andean lightning deities at sites sacred to them (Hernández Lefranc 2007). The Andean lightning deity was the main godhead of water, rain, and herds, being especially sacred to pastoralists (Cardich 2000). Kipia is located within an important agropastoralist landscape, and the overt association to water of the site itself would seem to underpin its adscription to veneration of a lightning deity, resulting in the Spanish imposition of Santiago on the site.

The action of direct replacement of an Andean entity by a Christian one has been described by Wernke (2007) as a process of erasure and analogy whereby overt reference to the prehispanic past was first erased and then subverted through analogizing the Andean entity with a Christian one. In this sense, the fact that Western European Catholicism was always saint-heavy must be seen as a distinct advantage (Brown 1982), opening up myriad saintly possibilities, with accompanying attributes and feast days. So finding the "correct" saint was not random but probably an exercise of study. Therefore, saints could be co-opted to fill the role of the soon-to-be-erased local deity. If we accept as genuine Spanish and indigenous attempts to claim the Andes as a lost, previously Christian land (see above), we should not then necessarily see these substitutions as purely a cynical ploy on the part of the Spanish. There was a real sacred need by the new colonial authorities—as they saw it—to save the souls of the indigenous populations (Las Casas 1992).

Nevertheless, while the new church seems to fit into the preexisting indigenous concept of cosmology and landscape, it also constituted a definite break with the past. First, the location of the church alongside RF5 is a clear signal of sacred appropriation (see above), and second, alongside appropriation comes transformation. Therefore, veneration would increasingly have been centered on the church and its patron saint, Santiago. As elsewhere in the Andes, the intention would have been to delink indigenous belief from the wider landscape, their gods and ancestors (Gose 2003). The latter was represented at the site by the necropolis, located in Sector D. Furthermore, rather than evoking the landscape, the construction of the church and the placing of Santiago within it were clear moves toward a Spanish religion of place, with the Catholic priest as the intermediary between the Christian god and the people. Early Spanish colonial material evidence from Sector A (glass, cutlery, etc.) points to the physical presence of Spaniards at the site, possibly a priest and native attendants. While at present the area does not have a resident priest, receiving an itinerant priest from the coastal bishopric of Chimbote, it is possible that given the amount of colonial material found at the site and the importance of the area as a conduit between the coast and highlands, especially the rich inter-Andean Huaylas Valley to the east, in the early Spanish colony, religious presence in the area was more ubiquitous. That said, there were limits to what the spread and presence of this Spanish Christianity actually meant on the ground.

DISCUSSION

The imposition of the Santiago chapel on the site of Kipia was the beginning of a transformative process through which the indigenous population was meant to shed its animistic and ancestor belief system and embrace Spanish Catholicism. Even so, the process was never completed. The lack of permanent priests, coupled with ever-changing and sometimes contradictory policy guidelines from the archbishopric of Lima, as well as the viceroyalty's need for economic produce over religious conversion, meant that the evangelization of the Andean hinterland progressed in fits and starts throughout the Spanish period.

In fact, the early imposition of Christianity also met with local pushback in the form of rebellions against the Spanish and their religion, the most serious of these being the Taqui Oncoy movement (ca. 1564–1572) in the south-central Andes. The Taqui Oncoy believed that dancing, spiritual possession, and a renewed veneration of the old gods in local contexts would usher in the disappearance of the Spanish and their Christian god (Roy 2010). Yet the Taqui Oncoy's messianic ethos, while tapping long-standing Andean concepts of renewal, also harked back to Christian ideals of apocalypse and resurrection, showing how far these movements were already hybrid Hispano-Andean phenomena (Andrien 2001:171). Nevertheless, inherent to the Taqui Oncoy movement was the fact that the local *huacas*, deities materialized in place or in object, were replaced by deities materialized in persons. This was so because many of the places and objects used to symbolize *huacas* before the Spanish colony had already been destroyed (Varón Gabai 1990). This shift from places/objects to people serves to underscore that while *places* did have an importance within Andean cosmology, that importance was not necessarily transcendental; it was the relationship of the *huacas* to the local environment and its *spaces* that prevailed.

With time, the Spaniards became much more effective in their attempts at eradicating indigenous religion, whether through the destruction of idols and mummies or the proscription of native priests under the *extirpación de idolatrías* (extirpation of idolatries) pogroms beginning in the early seventeenth century. This process went hand in hand with settlement reductions (*reducciones*). While there were economic reasons for these *reducciones*, especially when faced with a collapsing native population, "most modern commentators understand *reducción* . . . as church-based settlement consolidation, . . . religious conversion and political subjugation. . . . The policy's foremost announced goal was to improve Indians' evangelization" (Gose 2016:15). It is indeed at this time, during the late sixteenth and early seventeenth centuries, that one can say that the Spanish colonists effectively started making and shaping the Andean hinterland more into their desired image, even if the emergent society was always highly syncretic. In this sense, Guaman Poma de Ayala's (1993 [1615]) panegyric to a lost, seemingly more virtuous prehispanic society would seem to date to the end of this early colony, where overt indigenous beliefs coexisted, however uneasily, with alien Spanish imperial impositions.

These externally driven processes—*reducción* and *extirpación*—led to the eventual abandonment of Kipia and its church. Our three colonial ^{14}C dates (see Table 6.1: MAMS15864, MAMS15866, and MAMS15868) and the fact that the cists within the church went unused suggest that Spanish occupation of Kipia was short, probably ending sometime in the early seventeenth century. With the site's abandonment the links between Santiago, the church, the *huaca-huanca*, and the landscape were progressively severed.

According to local history, the statue of Santiago now residing in Pamparomás was originally from Kipia (Moreno Rodríguez 1966:27, 39). Local sources interviewed during my field research (Gonzalez Rosales and Lane 2007) state that originally at the site two saints were venerated: Santiago and San Lorenzo. Sometime in the past, San Lorenzo was "exiled" to Cosma, in the adjacent northern valley, while Santiago "came down" to the *reducción* of Pampac after appearing in local people's dreams requesting this move. It now resides in Pamparomás. According to Estanislao Moreno Rodríguez's thesis (1966:27, 39) Santiago appeared to a little girl who brought him flowers, but the end result is the same. While we do not have archival and therefore chronological evidence for when the saints were split up, it is possible that this took place during or shortly after the settling of the population into the colonial towns of Cosma and Pampac. Therefore, it is likely that this occurred during the early seventeenth century. The fact that Kipia might have been holy to two saints is not surprising, given the duality at the heart of Andean religion. Effectively, this duality at Kipia most likely represented aspects of the local lightning deity (Andean deities tended to be multifaceted). With the coming of Christianity and the slow disarticulation of Andean beliefs, these various aspects became in turn different saints for different towns.

This fracturing of multifaceted deities into saints of different components of a society is not uncommon and was observed by Karsten

Paerregaard (1992) in the community of Tapay (Arequipa), where farmers increasingly venerated San Isidro (who had the power to stop the rain, bring the sun, and provide bountiful crops), while the herders maintained their devotion to St. Mary Magdalene (an aspect of the Andean earth goddess, Pachamama). Nevertheless, both communities still celebrated the Virgin of the Candelaria (another aspect of Pachamama) together. Other examples of partitioning saints into different communities exist, such as at nearby Huari, in Conchucos, where three communities subdivided themselves into the sons of Huari, each with their own particular saints and concomitant celebrations or fiestas (Venturoli 2011).

In the case of Kipia, the subsequent separation and removal of San Lorenzo and Santiago provide the strongest evidence yet for Spanish attempts to erase as many vestiges and connections as possible between the indigenous population, their religion, and the spaces and places sacred to them. This was part of late sixteenth-century state policy, as is remarked on by Gabriela Ramos (2010:89): "The concentration of often-scattered native populations into urban settlements was intended to make the teaching of the Christian doctrine easier, separate the Indians from their sacred places, and disrupt the continuity of their religious practices." In so doing, Spanish actions reveal the cosmological charge that this site of Kipia enjoyed in the local prehispanic imagination.

Even so, this delinking was never perfect, with local association with Kipia lasting well beyond its physical abandonment. Even today, Santiago is still paraded during an annual festival in his honor (July 22–24), and until recently (1970s) this parade of the modern town's patron saint included transit through Kipia. Profound changes in the religious composition of Pamparomás, essentially the rise of modern Protestant evangelization, led to the abandonment of this practice. Aside from the parading of Santiago through the town, there exists no other wider engagement with the landscape, demonstrating how far local Christianity had become a religion of place rather than one of space. Indeed, similar short processions or pilgrimages are conducted across the Central Andes, indirectly evoking prehispanic rituals, such as the Festival of the Crosses, which is celebrated in different towns during May (Mayer de Millones and Millones 2003). In an enduring reflection of the past, Santiago, like the lightning deity that preceded him, is still used as a guarantor of rains and plentiful herds.

CONCLUSION

The sixteenth century was transformational for the indigenous population of the Central Andes and its religion. Likewise, it changed the way Spanish Catholicism would henceforth imprint itself on the land. Kipia exemplifies this shift during the liminal period of the early Spanish colony (A.D. 1532–1615). Indigenous strength, coupled with sparse Spanish presence, meant that early moves toward evangelization and place making were measured and cautious. These included appropriation but also, more importantly, accommodation within the existing religious setup. This accommodation was to become a permanent feature of Hispano-Andean Catholicism.

Overt reference to the prevailing Andean religion of space belied the subtle but incremental movement to a Spanish religion of place. Subsequent political actions at the state level—*reducciones* and *extirpación de idolatrías*—cemented this changeover, leading to the abandonment of Kipia. While the move to Pampac and, subsequently, to Pamparomás of the statue of Santiago heralded the end of regular and direct veneration at Kipia, it did not end indigenous ties to the wider landscape or the imbuing of the natural with supernatural symbolism. Indeed, the emergent Hispano-Andean Christianity was always syncretic and hybrid, in turn reflecting the syncretic and hybrid identity of the locals themselves. Ironically, it is only with the rise of new evangelical churches in South America and in Peru especially since the 1970s that the original mission of the Spanish evangelizers—that of a Christian religion shorn of Andean leitmotifs—is being realized (Amat and Pérez 2008) and with that a definite hardening of a Christian religion of place.

REFERENCES

Amat, Oscar, and León Pérez. 2008. *Presencia evangélica en la sociedad peruana.* Lima: Amanecer-Perú.

Andrien, Kenneth J. 2001. *Andean Worlds: Indigenous History, Culture, and Consciousness under Spanish Rule, 1532–1825.* Albuquerque: University of New Mexico Press.

Bakewell, Peter. 2010. *Miners of the Red Mountain: Indian Labor in Potosi, 1545–1650.* Albuquerque: University of New Mexico Press.

Barnes, Andrew E. 1988. "Religious Anxiety and Devotional Change in Sixteenth Century French Penitential Confraternities." *Sixteenth Century Journal* 19(3): 389–406.

Bauer, Brian S. 1998. *The Sacred Landscape of the Inca: The Cusco Ceque System.* Austin: University of Texas Press.

Bradley, Richard. 2000. *An Archaeology of Natural Places.* New York: Routledge.

Bravo Guerrera, María Concepción. 1993. "Evangelización y sincretismo religioso en los Andes." *Revista Complutense de Historia de América* 19:11–19.

Bronk Ramsey, C. 2017. "Methods for Summarizing Radiocarbon Datasets." *Radiocarbon* 59(2): 1809–1833.

Brown, Peter. 1982. *The Cult of the Saints: Its Rise and Function in Latin Christianity.* Haskell Lectures on History of Religions. Chicago: University of Chicago Press.

Cahill, David. 1996. "Popular Religion and Appropriation: The Example of Corpus Christi in Eighteenth-Century Cuzco." *Latin American Research Review* 31(2): 67–110.

Cardich, Augusto. 2000. "Dos divinidades rel evantes del antiguo pante ón centro-andino: Yana Raman o Libiac Cancharco y Rayguana." *Investigaciones Sociales* 4(5): 69–108.

Carrión Cachot, Rebeca. 1955. "El culto al agua en el antiguo Peru: La Paccha, elemento cultural pan-andino." *Separata de la Revista del Museo Nacional de Antropologia y Arqueologia* 11(1): 1–100.

Christie, Jessica Joyce. 2016. *Memory Landscapes of the Inka Carved Outcrops.* London: Lexington Books.

Cook, N. D. 1981. *Demographic Collapse: Indian Peru, 1520–1620.* Cambridge: Cambridge University Press.

Curatola Petrocchi, Marco, and Mariusz S. Ziółkowski, eds. 2008. *Adivinación y oraculos en el mundo andino antiguo.* Colección Estudios Andinos 18. Lima: PUCP/IFEA.

Custred, G. 1977. "Las Punas de los Andes centrales." In *Pastores de Puna: Uywamichiq punarunakuna,* edited by J. A. Flores Ochoa, 55–85. Lima: Instituto de Estudios Peruanos (IEP).

Dean, Carolyn. 2010. *A Culture of Stone: Inka Perspectives on Rock.* Durham, N.C.: Duke University Press.

Díaz Araya, Alberto, Luis Galdames Rosas, and Wilson Muñoz Henríquez. 2012. "Santos patronos en los Andes: Imagen, símbolo y ritual en las fiestas religiosas del mundo andino colonial (siglos XVI–XVII)." *Alpha* 35: 23–39.

Echevarría, Ana. 2003. "La transformación del espacio islámico (siglos XI–XIII)." *Annexes des Cahiers d'Études Hispaniques Médiévales* 15:53–77.

González Díaz, Soledad. 2014. "Del génesis a los Andes: Una lectura del diluvio y las cronologías del incario a través de las crónicas (siglos XVI –XVII)." PhD diss., Universidad Autónoma de Barcelona.

Gonzalez Rosales, Dante, and Kevin Lane. 2007. *Un acercamiento antropológico al Distrito de Pamparomás: Informe preliminar.* Lima: Proyecto Arqueológico Regional Ancash—Cochayoq [ParaCo].

Gose, Peter. 2003. "Converting the Ancestors: Indirect Rule, Settlement Consolidation, and the Struggle over Burial in Colonial Peru, 1532–1614." In *In Conversion: Old Worlds and New*, edited by Kenneth Mills and Anthony Grafton, 140–174. Rochester, N.Y.: University of Rochester Press.

———. 2016. "Mountains, Kurakas and Mummies: Transformations in Indigenous Andean Sovereignty." *Población & Sociedad* 23(2): 9–34.

Guaman Poma de Ayala, Felipe. 1993 [1615]. *Nueva crónica y buen gobierno*. Translated by Franklin G. Y. Pease. Vols. 1–3. Lima: Fondo de Cultura Econ ómica.

Harvey, L. P. 1992. *Islamic Spain: 1250–1500*. Chicago: University of Chicago Press.

Hernández Lefranc, Harold. 2007. "De Santiago Matamoros a Santiago-Illapa." *Arqueología y Sociedad* 17:313–341.

Herrera, Alexander, and Kevin Lane. 2004. "Project Gallery: Issues in Andean Highland Archaeology; The Cambridge Round Table on Ancash Sierra Archaeology." *Antiquity* 78 (301), http://antiquity.ac.uk/ProjGall/herrera/index .html.

Hogg, Alan G., Quan Hua, Paul G. Blackwell, Mu Niu, Caitlin E. Buck, Thomas P. Guilderson, Timothy J. Heaton, Jonathan G. Palmer, Paula J. Reimer, Ron W. Reimer, Christian S. M. Turney, and Susan R. H. Zimmerman. 2013. "SHC al13 Southern Hemisphere Calibration, 0–50,000 Years cal BP." *Radiocarbon* 55(4): 1889–1903.

INRENA. 2000. Base de datos de recursos naturales e infrastructura: Departamento de Ancash, primera aproximaci ón. Lima: INRENA / Ministerio de Agricultura.

Irarrazaval, Diego. 1999. *Un cristianismo andino*. Quito, Ecuador: Ediciones Abya-Yala.

Kamen, Henry. 2014. *Spain, 1469–1714: A Society of Conflict*. London: Routledge.

Knapp, A. Bernard, and Wendy Ashmore. 1999. "Archaeological Landscapes: Constructed, Conceptualized, Ideational." In *Archaeologies of Landscape: Contemporary Perspectives*, edited by Wendy Ashmore and A. Bernard Knapp, 1–30. Malden, Mass.: Blackwell.

Lane, Kevin. 2009. "Engineered Highlands: The Social Organisation of Water in the Ancient North-Central Andes (AD 1000–1480)." *World Archaeology* 41(1): 169–190.

———. 2011a. "Hincapié en los Andes Nor-centrales: La presencia inca en la Cordillera Negra, Sierra de Ancash." In *Arquitectura prehispánica tardía: Construcción y poder en los Andes Centrales*, edited by Kevin Lane and Milton Luján Dávila, 123–170. Lima: Fondo Editorial UCSS / CEPAC.

———. 2011b. "Inca." In *Oxford Handbook of the Archaeology of Ritual and Religion*, edited by Tim Insoll, 571–584. Oxford: Oxford University Press.

———. 2017. "Water, Silt and Dams: Prehispanic Geological Storage in the Cordillera Negra, North-Central Andes, Peru." *Revista de Glaciares y Ecosistemas de Montaña* 2:41–50.

Lane, Kevin, Emma Pomeroy, and Milton Reynaldo Lujan Davila. 2018. "Over Rock and under Stone: Carved Rocks and Subterranean Burials at Kipia, Ancash, AD 1000–1532." *Open Archaeology* 4(1): 299–321.

Las Casas, Bartolomé de. 1992. *In Defense of the Indians.* DeKalb: Northern Illinois University Press.

Lockhart, James. 1972. *The Man of Cajamarca: A Social and Biographical Study of the First Conquerors of Peru.* Latin American Monographs Vol. 27. Austin: University of Texas Press.

———. 1974. *Spanish Peru, 1532–1560: A Colonial Society.* Madison: University of Wisconsin Press.

López Guzmán, Rafael. 2000. *Arquitectura mudéjar: Del sincretismo medieval a las alternativas hispanoamericanas.* Madrid: Cátedra.

MacCormack, Sabine. 1988. "Pachacuti: Miracles, Punishments, and Last Judgment; Visionary Past and Prophetic Future in Early Colonial Peru." *American Historical Review* 93(4): 960–1006.

———. 1991. *Religion in the Andes: Vision and Imagination in Early Colonial Peru.* Princeton, N.J.: Princeton University Press.

———. 2001. "Cuzco, Another Rome?" In *Empires: Perspectives from Archaeology and History,* edited by Susan E. Alcock, Terence N. D'Altroy, Kathleen D. Morrison, and Carla M. Sinopoli, 419–435. Cambridge: Cambridge University Press.

Maldonado Pimentel, Angel, and Venancio Alcides Estacio Tamayo. 2012. *Las primeras mitas de Apurímac al servicio de las minas de castrovirreyna 1,591–1,599.* Lima.

Mayer de Millones, Renata, and Luis Millones. 2003. *Fiestas migrantes: Calendario tradicional peruano.* Lima: Fondo Editorial del Congreso del Perú.

Meharg, Sarah Jane. 2001. "Identicide and Cultural Cannibalism: Warfare's Appetite for Symbolic Place." *Peace Research Journal* 33(3): 89–98.

Millones, Luis. 1980. "La religión indígena en la colonia." In *Historia del Peru,* edited by Fernando Silva Santisteban, 423–497. Lima: J. Mejía Baca.

———. 1987. *Historia y poder en los Andes Centrales: Desde los orígenes al siglo XVII.* Madrid: Alianza Editorial.

Moore, Jerry D. 2005. *Cultural Landscapes in the Ancient Andes: Archaeologies of Place.* Gainesville: University Press of Florida.

Moreno Rodríguez, Estanislao Guadulfo. 1966. "Estudio monográfico del distrito de Pamparomás." Thesis, Centro de Capacitaci ón y Perfeccionamiento Magisterial de Huaraz, Instituto Nacional de Perfeccionamiento Magisterial Lima-Peru.

Mumford, J. R. 2012. *Vertical Empire: The General Resettlement of Indians in the Colonial Andes.* Durham, N.C.: Duke University Press.

Ogburn, Dennis E. 2012. "Reconceiving the Chronology of the Inca Imperial Expansion." *Radiocarbon* 54(2): 219–237.

Ortega Sagrista, Rafael. 1956. "Historia de las confradías de pasión y de sus procesiones de Semana Santa en la ciu dad de Jaén (siglos XVI al XX)." *Boletín del Instituto de Estudios Giennenses* 10:9–72.

Paerregaard, Karsten. 1992. "Complementarity and Duality: Oppositions between Agriculturists and Herders in an Andean Village." *Ethnology* 31(1): 15–26.

Pérez Ordóñez, Alejandro. 2005. "Viejas mezquitas, nuevas iglesias: Materializaciones formales de la implantación del Cristianismo en la Sierra de Cádiz tras la conquista castellana (1485–1500)." *V Jornadas de Historia "Abadía. Iglesias y Fronteras" (Alcalá la Real, 2004)*:633–642.

Pulgar Vidal, Javier. 1946. *Historia y geografía del Perú*. Lima: Universidad Nacional de San Marcos.

Ramos, Gabriela. 2010. *Death and Conversion in the Andes: Lima and Cuzco, 1532–1670*. Notre Dame: University of Notre Dame Press.

Rostworowski, María. 1998. "Pachacamac and el Señor de los Milagros." In *Native Traditions in the Postconquest World: A Symposium at Dumbarton Oaks, 2nd through 4th October 1992*, edited by Elizabeth Hill Boone and Tom Cummins, 345–359. Washington, D.C.: Dumbarton Oaks.

Roy, Hélène. 2010. "En torno al Taqui Oncoy: Texto y contexto." *Revista Andina* 50:9–39.

Rüpke, Jörg, ed. 2007. *A Companion to Roman Religion*. Hoboken: Wiley-Blackwell.

Santa Cruz Pachacuti Yamqui, Joan. 1993 [1613]. *Relación de antiguedades des de reyno del Pirú*, edited by Pierre Duviols and César Itier. Travaux de l'Institut Français d'Études Andines 74: Archivos de historia andina 17. Lima/Cu zco: IFEA / CERA "Bartolomé de Las Casas."

Sheridan, Thomas E. 1992. "The Limits of Power: The Political Ecology of the Spanish Empire in the Greater Southwest." *Antiquity* 66(250): 153–171.

Stern, Steve J. 1993. *Peru's Indian Peoples and the Challenge of Spanish Conquest: Huamanga to 1640*. 2nd ed. Madison: University of Wisconsin Press.

Thurston, Herbert. 1914. *The Stations of the Cross: An Account of Their History and Devotional Purpose*. London: Burns & Oates.

Todorov, Tzvetan. 1984. *The Conquest of America: The Question of the Other*. London: Harper Collins.

Urton, Gary. 1999. *Inca Myths*. Austin: University of Texas Press.

Varón Gabai, Rafael. 1990. "El retorno de las Huacas: Estudio y documentos sobre el Taki Onqoy, Siglo XVI." In *El Taki Onqoy: Las raíces andinas de un fenómeno colonial*, edited by Luis Millones. Lima: Instituto de Estudios Peruanos / Sociedad Peruana de Psicoanálisis.

Venturoli, Sofia. 2011. *Los hijos de Huari: Etnografía y etnohistoria de tres pueblos de la Sierra de Ancash, Perú*. Lima: PUCP.

Wernke, Steven A. 2007. "Analogy or Erasure? Dialectics of Religious Transformation in the Early Doctrinas of the Colca Valley, Peru." *International Journal of Historical Archaeology* 11(2): 152–182.

Zuidema, R. Tom. 1964. *The Ceque System of Cuzco: The Social Organization of the Capital of the Inca*. Supplement to vol. 1, *International Archives of Ethnography*. Leiden: E. J. Brill.

———. 2005. "La religión inca." In *Religiones andinas*, edited by Manuel M. Marzal, 89–113. Madrid: Editorial Trotta.

7

The People of Solomon

Performance in Cross-Cultural Contacts between
Spanish and Melanesians in the Southwest Pacific,
1568 and 1595

Martin Gibbs and David Roe

In 1567 Álvaro de Mendaña led two vessels and 160 men on an expedition from Callao in Peru westward across the Pacific in search of lands of gold and dark peoples rumored in Inka legend, with the potential to claim new lands for Spain and permission to colonize if he saw fit. Two months later they made landfall at an island, which they renamed Santa Isabel. Engagement and negotiation with indigenous peoples were immediate. Over the next five months the expedition explored inland and then circumnavigated what they came to understand was an extensive archipelago, coming into contact with diverse local communities. However, as no gold was found, they decided to forgo the planned colonization and return home. In 1595, 27 years later, Mendaña set off again with a fleet of four vessels and several hundred men, women, and children with the intention of immediately establishing a colony in what were now referred to as the "Islands of Solomon." By September he had lost one of the galleons and decided to settle the nearest island (Santa Cruz) instead, far to the east of where he had intended. In less than two months, bitter interpersonal politics, violence both within the Spanish group and with indigenous islanders, and an epidemic, which claimed dozens of lives, including Mendaña's, forced a decision to abandon the enterprise and return home.

Compared to most case studies in this volume, the presence of the Mendaña expeditions in the Solomon Islands was extremely brief, while their encounters with Solomon Islanders were in many instances seemingly transitory. The question that faced us while writing this chapter was whether the themes of colonialism, pluralism, and place making were relevant in a situation where it appears that the wheels had fallen off the juggernaut of Spanish imperial expansion. In response, this chapter follows the writings of the doyen of Pacific anthropology and history, the late Greg Dening—in particular, his use of "the beach" as both physical and metaphorical meeting place between cultures and his evocation of the notion of literal and symbolic "performances" between and within groups (Dening 2004; Merwick 1994). We make no attempt in this limited space to offer a coherent and singular narrative of how colonialism was inherent within the abortive Spanish encounter with the peoples and places of the southwest Pacific. In fact, we limit ourselves to several vignettes from the expeditions of Mendaña, the first an all-male entrada, although the possibility of colonization was entertained, and the second a genuine attempt to create a new outpost of empire.

COLONIALISM AND EXPECTATION

Stephen Silliman (2005), Christine Beaule (2017), and others define colonialism as a set of physical and conceptual processes by which one group expands its territory and exerts power and control over other peoples (usually "indigenous"). Colonization is a particular and objective-driven (economic, social, religious) process of imperial expansion that implants spatially distinct (and potentially archaeologically visible) *colonies* into the territory of others. Elsewhere Martin Gibbs (2011, 2016) has written of the conceptual and practical aspects of Mendaña's acts of colonization as a means of exploring the surviving archaeological signatures of these expeditions.

People's decisions and responses were expressed in the location and nature of sites (including their abandonment) and the selection, disposition, and use of material culture. New colonists, sometimes extremely isolated from their home cultures and without any form of support or supply, could find themselves in situations very different from those originally anticipated, or in circumstances that could change suddenly and unexpectedly and, in some instances, extremely radically. What had been prepared for suddenly became irrelevant as they struggled to survive (Gibbs 2011:144).

Colonialism was also about expectations of and for oneself and one's family, group, and nation. Expectations were rarely uniform within any body of peoples and could even be wildly unmatched or inappropriate depending upon many factors, including through differential access to information (Gibbs 2016). Expectations also created particular symbolic and practical performances of role, status, and hierarchy within and

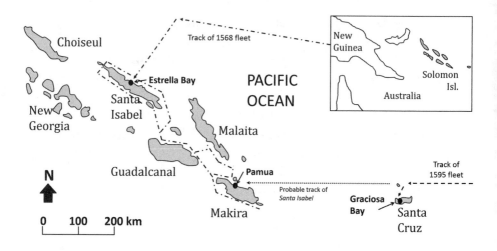

Map 7.1 The 1568 and 1595 expeditions of Álvaro de Mendaña.

beyond the group, including anticipation of secular and spiritual reward. As Kathleen Deagan has suggested, the processes of the fifteenth- and sixteenth-century Spanish colonial project were "simultaneously an invasion, a colonization effort, a social experiment, a religious crusade, and a highly structured economic enterprise" (2003:3). This certainly provided much latitude as to intention and behavior. The Spanish considered that indigenous peoples were to be incorporated into Spanish social and economic systems through the "hybrid rituals of salvation and conquest" (Jolly and Tcherkezoff 2009:4). At the most basic level, indigenous peoples were to provide food and comfort and otherwise accommodate the Spanish presence. In a more developed version, they were to be converts to Christianity and empire and a willing labor force (see also Chapter 3 for the roots of these expectations within earlier expeditions).

Spanish exploratory expeditions within the Americas and beyond were numerous throughout the sixteenth to eighteenth century, with the westward trajectory toward Asia forced upon them through the 1494 division of the globe between Spain and Portugal imposed by the Treaty of Tordesillas. Many ventures were male-only entradas to discover and claim new territories, but some expeditions were spurred on by rumors of vast wealth, most famously in the 1530s to 1540s expeditions of Francisco

Hernández de Córdoba, Hernando de Soto, and Francisco Vázquez de Coronado. In the early 1560s the noted explorer, warrior, and historian Pedro Sarmiento de Gamboa collected Inka stories of new lands and gold in the southwest Pacific, possibly even the fabled Terra Australis (Southern Land), and actively petitioned the viceroy of Peru, Lope García de Castro, to be allowed to form an expedition. By this time the viceroyalty of La Florida had also just established Spain's long-sought trade entrepôts in the Philippines and was in the throes of developing the renowned Manila galleon route. In Sarmiento's proposal, García de Castro presumably saw prospects for the expansion of empire, a new southern route into Asia under his control, riches to be discovered, colonies to be established, and populations to be converted. Faced with an opportunity for personal and familial advancement, he nominated his 25-year-old nephew, Álvaro de Mendaña, as leader of the expedition, naming him *adelantado* (governor), conquistador, and lord of the Western Isles, with rights to conquer and colonize (Jack-Hinton 1969; Spate 1979:121). The hastily organized expedition, with two ships and about 160 men, departed on November 20, 1567 (Camino 2008). We only have limited details on the composition of the company, although it included 70 soldiers, four Franciscan friars, a number of possibly African slaves, and the sailors, officers, and expedition leaders, including the disgruntled Sarmiento, now reduced to a role as pilot (Amherst and Thomson 1901:xix).

Mendaña was to be counseled by older and experienced hands, including three Franciscan friars who accompanied the expedition with a set of directives regarding considerate treatment of any indigenous peoples encountered. However, as a product of the encomienda system, with its combination of land grants and rights to the forced labor and taxation of indigenous peoples, he presumably had an expectation of duplicating this system afresh on the western side of the Pacific. The other participants had been promised incentives, including land and gold, while others were press-ganged onto the ships. In addition to the Inka stories that inspired the expedition, there was the "imagined" Pacific and its islands and peoples, which surely influenced the preparations for the voyage and the expectations for this venture (Camino 2005, 2008; Green 1973). One advantage of the short time frame of Mendaña's expeditions was that the focus was more squarely on these initial intentions and expectations.

MISTAKEN IDENTITY

After two and a half months of sailing, Mendaña's ships finally anchored in what they named Estrella (Star) Bay on the land (later realized to be an island) they called Santa Isabel. So commenced the acts of (re)naming in recognition of spiritual and secular patrons, which started the redefinition of landscape and which still marks the postindependence landscape of the sovereign nation of the Solomon Islands.

As soon as the ships entered the bay, a flotilla of canoes filled with armed but otherwise friendly men calling out "Tabriqui! Tabriqui!" approached the two ships. An exchange of small gifts, words, and gestures (see Chapter 2), which included the islanders imitating the sign of the cross, then took place. Late nineteenth-century translators noted that *tabriqui* is not within local vocabularies but suggested a cognate with the Polynesian *te ariki*, meaning "chief" (Amherst and Thomson 1901:109). This may provide a critical clue for the structure of the encounters that were occurring and the nature of subsequent events, although caution is warranted on the written Spanish sources' reliability with respect to references to vernacular terms and phrases. The Solomon Islands archipelago is well-known for its linguistic complexity, boasting some 63 distinct languages, with eight of them on Santa Isabel alone (Tryon and Hackman 1983:19, 23). Vernacular terms rendered and/or interpreted by the Spanish authors may have been facilitated with the assistance of "local" interpreters who may themselves have been unfamiliar with some of the languages that were being encountered and whose familiarity with Spanish would have been somewhat basic also. However, it is also worth noting that archaeological and ethnohistorical evidence from this area suggests this was a time of significant socioeconomic intensification that saw the emergence of larger polities and what might now be more recognizably identified as "chiefdoms" (Carter et al. 2012).

Although there is little doubt that this was the "first contact" with Europeans, these particular Pacific Islanders were enmeshed in webs of cross-cultural encounters and relationships with peoples from other islands through networks of social, economic, and religious trade and exchange (Jolly and Tcherkezoff 2009:2; Spriggs 1997). Others have already written of first contact with Europeans as a nonevent in which the foreigners were simply contextualized as "just another trader" (Torrence

2000:107). Later anthropologies of Santa Isabel would record the term *mae vaka*, or "ship people," as a catchall for outsiders, whether Polynesian or European (Bogesi 1948:355; White 1991:84). However, the term *te ariki* suggests that the dark-skinned Melanesian peoples of Santa Isabel may have thought these light-skinned strangers arriving on their large seagoing vessels with whitish-brown woven sails were Polynesian traders, with whom they had intermittent contact (Dunmore 1974). That (mis) identification may have activated a set of protocols and expectations for how the encounter should proceed. Calling for the chief was a means of establishing hierarchy and engaging the processes of trade and exchange (see also Chapter 11 for Spanish categorizations of political entities). We suggest that the failure of the Spanish to understand or meet those expectations may have underlain much of the subsequent activity and confusion for both groups.

It is also important to recognize that this was not the first encounter between the Spanish and cultural "others." Apart from the pluralistic nature of relations between the mixture of ethnicities and cultures aboard ship (see below), preceding generations had experienced cross-cultural contact in the Americas and Africa. As many of the chapters in this volume attest, there was a body of diverse experiences and perspectives even within the "Spanish" group that might have come into play in different interactions.

THE RITUALS OF POSSESSION

Soon after the vessels dropped anchor, Mendaña landed and enacted the rituals of possession, raising a cross and adoring it while the priests sang "Vexilla Regis Prodeunt" (Abroad the regal banners fly). Mendaña then claimed the island for the Spanish Crown. No doubt, on this and many other occasions, mass performed by the Spanish was closely observed by the indigenous people. The people of Gaghe (Estrella Bay) understood ritual and quite probably wondered what spirits the strangers had brought with them and sought to manage and to what ends.

Several months later, as the Spanish commenced their tour of the neighboring islands, the rite of raising and adoring the cross was repeated with each major landfall. On the island they named Guadalcanal they raised a cross on a small hill and performed a mass before retreating to their ships. That evening they observed several local men remove the cross and carry it away. The next morning they watched the cross being returned, with the local people presumably having inspected it (Amherst and Thomson 1901:39).

MANY EXCHANGES

In the opening encounters, the Spanish sailors actively made gifts of the hats, beads, and small bells that were the normal stuff of Spanish trade with indigenous groups (see Chapters 2 and 3), with a return of coconuts, root vegetables, and water. Within a day Mendaña was visited by what the Spanish describe as the local chief, named Bilé, with whom he exchanged names, a well-established process in Melanesia of creating a social and economic bond between equals. It should, however, be understood that a Melanesian "chief" was not necessarily hereditary or all-powerful, so Spanish assumptions about the role that chiefs might play in their relationships with them may have been erroneous.

The following day Mendaña made a return visit to Bilé and ordered his men to sing and play instruments, with the islanders dancing to the foreign music (Amherst and Thomson 1901:113–114, 233). Such interactions of music and dance were to be a continuing feature of cross-cultural encounters throughout the Pacific (Clendinnen 2003). These early meetings were solely with men, with Mendaña recording that after the Spanish had been on the island for several days, another "chief" arrived, with several women aboard his canoes. However, Mendaña turned them away, believing it was an attempt to entice the crew (Amherst and Thomson 1901:117). How the islanders perceived the sexuality of an outwardly all-male crew rejecting female company may have been the source of some confusion, although they would also have been familiar with vessels carrying all-male crews in voyages of trade, warfare, or other rituals during which sexual abstinence was expected or required. There are no subsequent reported incidents of sexual contacts with women, although one might presume that if these did occur, they happened away from the judgment of Mendaña or his officers.

Over the next several weeks Mendaña was at pains to explain, via sign language and a growing shared lexicon, the nature of the Christian god and that Bilé and all those in the islands were now subjects of the king of Spain. Mendaña interpreted Bilé's imitations of the sign of the cross as understanding and acquiescence, but at the same time he deflected Bilé's requests to meet the king, who Bilé presumably thought remained aboard the galleon (Amherst and Thomson 1901:174). Bilé in turn tried to explain the various groups and polities on Santa Isabel. In one incident, a group of canoes from more distant groups arrived at the ships, apparently prepared for battle. Bilé confronted them with his own canoes, and they surrendered and departed. He told Mendaña that this foiled attack had been organized by another senior chief and that the several chiefs in the canoes "had called upon him to join them against me, but that he had refused, and bade me call him if they came against me, and he would help me" (Amherst and Thomson 1901:115). Mendaña made several unsuccessful appeals to Bilé to make peace with his neighbors, presumably under their new corporate allegiance to the Spanish Crown.

EXTRAORDINARY EVENTS AND EXTRAORDINARY MEASURES

The question of whether Polynesians and Melanesians perceived early European visitors as more than human, as ghosts, returned ancestors, or some other type of spirit being, is extremely complex (Jolly 2009). The misperception about the Spaniards' identity lent a pragmatic edge to the initial engagements on Santa Isabel. However, as events proceeded, it appears possible that as the visitors continued to behave oddly, islanders' views of and responses to the Spaniards' presence may have changed. Mendaña relates how, after several weeks on the island, a new chief, named Bené, arrived in the bay:

> He sent me a quarter of human flesh which seemed to be that of a boy, with some roots of vinahu, saying to me in his language, "Naleha, naleha!" which signifies "eat it." I accepted the present, and, being greatly grieved that there should be this pernicious custom in that country, and that they should suppose that we ate it, I ordered everyone to stand aside so that the tauriqui might see what was done. Then I caused a grave to be dug at the water's edge, and had the quarter buried in his presence, and said to him in his language, "Teo naleha arra," which signifies "I do not eat it." He

regarded this very attentively, and, seeing that we set no value on the present, they all bent down over their canoes like men vexed or offended, and put off and withdrew with their heads bent down. (Amherst and Thomson 1901:169)

Based on this, the several Spanish chroniclers all concluded that cannibalism was rife among the islanders, although later ethnography suggests that only certain types of ritual cannibalism were practiced on Santa Isabel, and they were related to absorbing enemies' power (Bogesi 1948:224; Dunmore 1974; McNab 1914:256). However, human sacrifice (usually captives, including children, from other tribes) was considered appropriate on occasions of great significance, such as establishing a new canoe house (Bogesi 1948; White 1980). Whether Bené saw the Spanish as hungry spirits who required an extreme response by being offered human flesh (Bogesi 1948:328) or whether this was a sacrifice indicating the gravity of the encounter is unknown. Clearly, the refusal was cause for consternation.

A final note is an oral history collected from Estrella Bay in the 1930s that records that the Spanish were called *nguanguai*, or "ghosts carrying disease." When subsequent ships were sighted the women and children were sent into the bush to hide, while the men prayed that the disease-carrying ghosts would leave (Bogesi 1948:355). Whether this was truly oral history or a memorate (a perceived supranormal encounter) that was associated with the Spanish or a response that relates to later visitors is hard to determine, although the connection between ships and disease may be worth consideration in regard to long-term impacts on local populations.

AWAY FROM THE BEACH

Having accepted gifts and apparently expressed their willingness to become the king's newest vassals, the islanders were now expected to supply the Spanish with food and assistance. While the initial exchanges did include food, the Spaniards' diminished stores and lengthy sojourn meant that Spanish demands rapidly exceeded the islanders' subsistence economies. In particular, the Spanish craving for meat was almost insatiable. Pigs were often seen, but to the intense frustration of the Spanish the villagers were reluctant to relinquish them. There was no recognition that while the fish, roots, and coconuts previously offered were subsistence foods, pigs were wealth, status indicators, and a requirement for ceremonies and special occasions. To relinquish them was a significant loss to a family and community and a possible affront to the ancestors.

Mendaña felt that despite his efforts to befriend Bilé, the villagers' unwillingness to provide food endangered the expedition's service to God and king. He asked the friars if he could proceed inland and find provisions that would allow them to commence explorations of neighboring islands. The friars acknowledged that Mendaña had done all he could, and since the indigenes refused to supply food, despite professing friendship and fealty, he could advance inland and take what was required as long as no other property "nor their wives and children" were taken (Amherst and Thomson 1901:118). If the islanders resisted or were violent, the soldiers could defend themselves and guard secured provisions, but they were not to pursue the islanders or make war. As the soldiers marched into the mountains the islanders initially warned them off and indicated they were to return to the beach. The Spanish proceeded regardless, ransacking villages for food, burning huts, destroying shrines, and shooting to kill. They also evolved a system of taking hostages in order to force a ransom of food for their return or to use them as interpreters.

THE DANGER IN GIFTS

Following this was a period of tension and uncertainty when Bilé avoided meeting with Mendaña, although he finally came to the ship with great gravity.

> He ordered one of his brothers . . . to take off all the bracelets he wore on one arm and the plate from round his neck, and then had them well washed; when this was done, he bade me send my men aside and seat myself, for he wished to come on board. [He] came along the side to where I was, and seated himself beside me without speaking; then he made the sign of the cross with his hands, and looked up to heaven; then he raised his hands, and put the bone plate round my neck and the bracelets on my arm, and after doing this, he remained awhile without speaking. I understood that

he was making me a great present, and that they thought a great deal of it, for these things are only worn by chiefs. (Amherst and Thomson 1901:125)

The gift of status items was in itself important and symbolic, although whether the signing of the cross was truly a case of syncretism or simply an acknowledgment that the Spanish set great store by the gesture is hard to know. More interesting is the washing of the ornaments. Many Melanesian groups believed in sorcery (and still do), and bodily residues, including sweat or hair, on an object, especially one of power, could provide the means for strangers to cause harm (Jolly 2009:88).

Several attempts have been made to locate possible archaeological remains associated with the 1568 expedition's camp in Estrella Bay, but all have proved unsuccessful (Gibbs 2011). There may be several reasons, but the most likely is that Santa Isabel is on the edge of a subduction zone, and that section of the coast is sinking. Sea-level rise and tsunami damage are also readily visible, making it probable that the near-shore sites have eroded or are now submerged.

A DIVERSITY OF RESPONSES

The Spanish finally commenced their expeditions around the archipelago, intent on finding supplies and assessing resources, peoples, and geography, taking at least one man from Estrella Bay as an interpreter (Amherst and Thomson 1901:36). This maritime entrada encountered diverse populations and responses. South of Estrella Bay, the Spanish saw villages of several hundred huts and recorded fleets of several dozen large canoes coming to meet them (Amherst and Thomson 1901:35). In some locations they were treated to formal greetings, gifts of food, and various forms of trade and exchange, although rarely did they obtain substantial supplies (Amherst and Thomson 1901:27). Other populations showed limited interest in the strangers and no interest in trade. In several instances, the situation turned hostile, with the navigator Gallego estimating between 600 and 700 warriors massed to meet them, sometimes in canoes capable of carrying 50 men (Amherst and Thomson 1901:26, 28, 41). While these numbers may have been exaggerated, these were significant shows of power (compare Chapters 2 and 3).

The Spanish came prepared to shoot, sometimes to scare, but often to kill, if threatened (Amherst and Thomson 1901:27). Occasionally, they set fire to villages in retribution for killings (Amherst and Thomson 1901:52–54). They also continued trading kidnap victims and stolen canoes for food (Amherst and Thomson 1901:32, 35). It can be assumed that word of these rampages and dangerous strangers spread.

Cruising the Guadalcanal coast, Gallego reported, "When we were near the land they began throwing stones at us, saying; 'Mate! Mate!' meaning that they would kill us" (Amherst and Thomson 1901:31–32). In return the Spanish used harquebuses to shoot and kill two people before landing and raiding their villages for food. Early translators suggested a translation of the word *mate* as "kill," consistent with the Spanish suggestion that they were chanting "kill, kill" (see Amherst and Thompson 1901:xxxi). However, *mate* can also be rendered as "[the] dead" and may indicate that the light-skinned Spanish were in this instance viewed as the ghosts of the dead, possibly lost on route to Marapa, the isle of the dead, located at the southeast tip of Guadalcanal. On San Cristobal (now Makira) another encounter also seems to have occasioned a similar spiritual response (Gallego in Amherst and Thomson 1901:56; Mendaña in Amherst and Thomson 1901:178).

At each new island the act of formal possession in the name of the king occurred (Gallego in Amherst and Thomson 1901:29, 49, 56). Attempts were made to explain to any peoples encountered, particularly those identified as chiefs, the nature of the Christian god and that they were now the subjects of the king of Spain, noting their apparent obeisance (Amherst and Thomson 1901:90). How this understanding of sovereignty was communicated and what responses the islanders were actually performing in return remain questionable. The Spanish also continued to collect intelligence on peoples, populations, and resources via their own observations and interviews with people encountered or kidnapped. The possibility of gold remained prominent in their minds (Amherst and Thomson 1901:182). All of these considerations constituted a kind of place making from the Spanish perspective of exploitability.

Having cruised the islands for several months amid increasing violence ashore and tensions aboard, Mendaña called an assembly of all the company and took a vote on whether to stay or leave. While all praised the country they had seen and considered that gold was still a possibility, they were divided as to whether to settle. Concerns were raised about poor health, there being too many natives and not enough ammunition, that the ships were in poor repair, and that they were too far from Peru, the latter presumably reflecting concerns about future supply and contact. The consensus was to depart, although one writer notes that it was Mendaña's decision and that "if he had wished it, a settlement would have been formed without opposition" (Amherst and Thomson 1901:92). Following the conclusion of the expedition, whatever tenuous relationships existed between the shipboard company dissolved into two decades of legal cases, appeals, and claims for compensation (including by Sarmiento) or recognition of rights (by Mendaña), as well as enquiries by the Spanish authorities into the cost of the failed venture and the conduct of those aboard (see Kelly 1965:93–153).

SECOND EXPEDITION: COLONIZATION

Twenty-seven years of petitioning in Spain, Rome, and Peru for the right to return and take up his entitlements as *adelantado* of the Western Isles (Hill 1913:656) undoubtedly saw Mendaña become a seasoned performer, extolling the virtues of those far-off lands and enhancing the potentials of a colony. He may even have come to believe his claims himself. When he finally obtained permission for a new expedition there were several additional factors. In an empire still smarting from its losses in the armada in the battles against England, Mendaña funded the expedition through the dowry of his new wife, Isabella. In return, she and her three brothers claimed additional rights as leaders aboard the ships and then in any subsequent settlement. Colonization was to be immediate, and the four vessels included about 380 men, women, and children of Spanish, South American, mestizo, and African descent. For this expedition we have detailed lists of the names of the participants, categorized for each ship into a generic list of settlers (mostly male), followed by more specific listings of married men (*casados*), menservants (*gente de seruicio*), women (*mugeres*), children of married couples (*hijos de casados*), ship's company (*gentes de mar*), cabin boys (*grumetes*), women servants (*mugeres de seruicio*), youths (*muchachos*), servant boys (*moços de seruicio*), and soldiers (*soldados*) (Kelly 1965:399–409; see also Chapter 11 for the nature of these categorizations). Lists of menservants, cabin boys, servant boys, and women servants are annotated as being *indio/india*, *mulato/mulata*, or *negro/negra*, although for the remainder of the passengers and crew, ethnicities are only occasionally alluded to in the narrative.

Once again taking Franciscan friars for guidance, the expedition was now also subject to King Phillip II's Ordinances for Settlement, which included rules to prevent mistreatment of and war with indigenous groups (Kelly 1966:82; Nuttal 1921). Despite this, the mood of the voyage was set on route by the slaughter of an estimated 200 people on the Marquesas Islands, where the Spanish had stopped to resupply. The miscalculations of Mendaña's previous expedition's travel speeds also meant that the voyage was not the estimated three weeks but over three months, with supplies of food, wood, and water almost gone when a thick volcanic dust cloud forced the fleet to halt overnight. The galleon *Santa Isabel* presumably missed the signal to stop, and when morning came, it was gone, taking with it most of the supplies and 180 people, never to be seen again. Unsure of his location, Mendaña decided to settle the nearby Santa Cruz Islands (Nendo) as a waypoint for later expeditions to the Solomons and Terra Australis.

Much of what then happened on Santa Cruz mirrored the first expedition. On drawing into a bay the vessels were met by canoes full of islanders calling Jauriqi, once again presumably hoping to establish the processes expected of visitors (Markham 1904:41). Santa Cruz was the hub of a complex trading system that saw red feather currency, women, shell discs, food, fabric, and canoes traded and retraded through an archipelago of volcanic and coral islands and between groups whose languages are the epitome of the diversity that marks the cultural landscapes of the southeast Solomons (Davenport 1962; Tryon and Hackman 1983:25, 70ff.). This system drew together voyagers speaking unfamiliar languages and with a remarkable variety of physical and cultural characteristics. The multicultural "Spanish" with their large "canoes" may not have been immediately identified as anything other than another trading group. Two centuries later and following the wrecks of the ships in the expedition led by Jean-François de La Pérouse on nearby Vanikoro, alien French objects were easily absorbed and found new meaning in these trade systems (Clark 2003).

Mendaña met with the local "chief," an older man named Malopé, and, based on the norms learned in the previous expedition, once again exchanged names and gifts. However, the language of Estrella Bay that Mendaña so confidently attempted to use on both the Marquesas and in the far eastern part of the Solomon Islands proved to be of no use. Once again the Spanish made immediate demands for food and especially pigs, ranging around the coasts and pushing inland. However, this time theft, arson, and murder by the Spanish were nearly immediate and with almost no restraint, despite Mendaña's exhortations for peace. Malopé clearly attempted to act for amity, and after repeated clashes provoked by the Spanish there was an extraordinary scene where Malopé finally accompanied the Spanish around the bay collecting pigs, sweet potatoes, and water from each village while the villagers waited in silence, watching their food and wealth being stripped away from them (Markham 1904:75).

MARKING THE LAND

Mendaña, sick and barely able to rise from his bed aboard ship, had selected a site for settlement only to find that the camp master had changed the location and started clearing ground and constructing huts. He was, however, able to resist demands that the colonists simply take over an existing village, which many argued would save the hard labor of starting afresh (Markham 1904:46). Mendaña was eventually able to go ashore to help with the marking out of the new settlement, deciding on where key elements, including the church and burial ground, were to go, while houses were already being constructed. Analysis of the texts suggests that even in such a remote setting, far from Spain, these were in accordance with the Ordinances (Gibbs 2015; Nuttal 1921). The work of Laura Matthew and William Fowler (see Chapter 5) on the similarities between the Ciudad Viejas of Guatemala and El Salvador also speaks to the drive toward some levels of standardization in the physicality of Spanish settlement patterns, even in the decades prior to the formal Ordinances being instituted.

Since this was obviously not the promised destination, tensions within the colonizing group were immediate. Many wanted to go home or keep looking either for Terra Australis or for the lost *Santa Isabel*, which was believed to have continued on to the Solomon Islands (Markham 1904:54). When they were rebuffed by Mendaña, those wanting to depart engaged in a program of murder of islanders in an attempt to incite a violent response and force a withdrawal. Compelled into action by the increasing threat to his authority, Mendaña and his followers went ashore and engaged in an extreme performance of his power by executing the camp master, who was believed to be the ringleader, as well as several others (Markham 1904:78). Their heads were then placed on spikes at the entry to the camp, primarily as a sign to other dissenters against Mendaña's rule. Despite this, violence against the islanders continued, and within a day a party of soldiers had slain Malopé. The excuse was that although Malopé had given all that he had, his refusal to give more was an act of treason (Markham 1904:81).

There is no surviving direct oral history of the Spanish presence on Santa Cruz. However, the story of the Spanish has been taught to Solomon Islanders for nearly a century, and many take an interest in these events and performances, albeit through a very different lens. During our archaeological fieldwork, one of the senior men in the village nearest to the Spanish settlement site reflected on this incident of the heads being placed outside the camp. As he saw it, in Santa Cruz tradition, if someone is caught stealing, then the stolen item is placed in the middle of the village to show shame and remorse. The heads of the camp master and other dissenters put on poles at the front of the Spanish village were therefore to be interpreted as a demonstration of guilt and shame at their thefts of food, the destruction of property, and the murder of villagers.

There is some archaeological evidence of the 1595 colony visible as surface or near-surface pottery sherds (but no other artifact types) scattered over an area adjacent to the freshwater stream at the southeast corner of Graciosa Bay (Gibbs 2011; Green 1973). Despite intensive survey and excavation to detect any of the structures or the graveyard mentioned in the accounts of the settlement, results were ambiguous and unsatisfying, although there is also compelling evidence for storm surge and tsunami damage on the site. One conclusion reached is that while the sherds are clearly Spanish, the site where they have been recovered may not be the settlement but an indigenous village, which ^{14}C dates on material recovered suggest was abandoned at around the time of the Spanish presence. The pottery may be the remains of trade activity or some other form of cultural activity (see discussion below). The Spanish colony site is now thought to have been 100 m northeast in a valley that fits more closely with the textual record, but thanks to considerable disturbance as a result of World War II era bulldozing and filling, it now has little or no archaeological potential (Gibbs 2015).

EPIDEMIC AND DEPARTURE

In the next few weeks, an epidemic spread through the camp, and more than 40 persons died and were buried in the new graveyard, including Mendaña. His wife, Isabella, inherited the title of governor but within days decided to abandon the colony. Mendaña's body was disinterred in secret and smuggled aboard one of the ships for return to Spain. Twenty-first-century interpretations of these events are complex. We were told by several older men of the nearby villages that the violence that ensued between islanders and the Spanish was a result of the Spanish sailors interfering with local women—an undocumented but plausible situation. Second was that the epidemic and mass death of the Spanish occurred because they had made their settlement at the site of a powerful and malevolent spirit. Related to this, the absence of Mendaña's body—which, having exchanged names with Malopé, should in Santa Cruz tradition have been interred beneath Malopé's hut—happened because the spirit at the settlement site had "taken" him, and in fact Mendaña's spirit was still trapped at the site.

A LACK OF TEXT

Much of this narrative has focused on a consideration of the historical texts, but as a final note we offer an instance where the lack of text means archaeology has to provide the dominant voice (Beaule 2017:7). The galleon *Santa Isabel*, lost from Mendaña's 1595 expedition with its 180 men, women, and children and a cargo full of colonizing supplies, was never seen again. However, in 1970 and then again during our own research from 2010, extensive scatters of Spanish pottery sherds were found at Pamua on San Cristobal (Makira), 400 km west of Santa Cruz, on almost precisely the last known bearing of the galleon (Gibbs 2015; Green 1973). Typological and geochemical tests show these sherds are exact matches for those from Mendaña's Santa Cruz settlement site (Kelloway et al. 2014). Excavations show that the indigenous village site in which the ceramic sherds were found had been occupied for several hundred years but was clearly abandoned at the time of or soon after the Spanish presence, with the sherds being in the uppermost stratigraphic layer (Blake et al. 2013).

We do not know if the *Santa Isabel* landed and the people tried to settle as per the original plan, stayed a short time and left, were killed, died of an epidemic, or were absorbed into the local population. Excavations of a burial mound that is somewhat anomalous to nearby indigenous burials have uncovered half a dozen badly deteriorated east–west-oriented shallow skeletons, which have proven frustratingly resistant to DNA or isotope analyses (Blake et al. 2013). There was a single aiglet in close association to one body and a single chevron bead in the deflated mound deposit, but without a better identification it remains impossible to tell whether these scant remains represent persons from the Spanish vessels, islanders wearing Spanish clothing, or a reuse of European cultural items in indigenous ornamentation.

On closer examination, the distribution of ceramic sherds was notably focused on burial grounds and close to former shrines, both being contexts in which spiritually dangerous objects might have been managed. It may have been that after the Spanish had departed, died, or otherwise ceased to be a group defined as "foreign," the sherds and other objects were collected; here, as on Santa Isabel, both ghosts and objects can carry "disease" (Gibbs 2016). It may be that the final act of performance at the close of the Spanish encounter was to neutralize their existence and the potentially toxic spiritual charge on any objects associated with them. Do we see here perhaps the physical signature of an inexplicable event for which there were no indigenous coping strategies other than a conscious act of forgetting that required the sequestration of things and the abandonment of a place?

CONCLUSIONS

The events during and ultimate failures of both of the Mendaña expeditions were a result of clashes between expectations and realities. The "beach" as constructed by Dening (2004) was a liminal space where exchanges of goods, languages, and ideas could take place and allowances could be made for peculiarities of behavior. However, what we have tried to show in this chapter is that even within that scenario there were performances within and between groups based on their various expectations and intentions.

Although focus in these sorts of studies is often between "the Spanish" and "the indigenous," there has been less interest in the idea that the expeditions themselves and especially the shipboard spaces were also pluralistic settings. The persons aboard the Spanish vessels, whether ethnically or culturally from Spain, Peru, Africa, or elsewhere, and regardless of personal motivations or access to power, underwent a form of ethnogenesis in that the processes of sharing the shipboard culture and the necessities of the voyage re-created these diverse individuals as a single group. This new collectivity was reinforced at the point of arrival, where they were almost certainly viewed by the Solomon Islanders as a single group of outsiders. Those aboard the vessels, regardless of sex, age, race, or ethnicity, *became* "the Spanish," united into a synthetic community by their relationship to the performances of church, state, status, and roles in the context of the expeditions, and especially aboard ship, and then through their differences from the islanders they encountered. This was the foreshadowing of the "unprecedented *convivencia*" described by Matthew and Fowler (Chapter 5), potentially setting them on the trajectory for the transformation of identities and ethnogenesis described by Juliet Wiersema (Chapter 11).

Within the parameters of the shared "Spanish" system, the expeditions were laden with practical and symbolic behaviors and rites to assert or negotiate or reify status. In both expeditions, there was constant internal social and political tension, mediated via particular performances of power (and equally of resistance and disobedience) in both the religious and secular realms, including in extreme cases the execution of dissenters. In some instances, these internally directed performances co-opted the indigenous peoples, sometimes in ways that were amicable, such as through successful trade and exchange for supplies or assistance, and sometimes via brutality and murder to incite reciprocal violence and force the hands of those in charge of the expedition.

We argue that the Solomon Islanders engaged with the Spanish with the anticipation that the latter would conform to acknowledged norms of behavior for maritime visitors or at worst quickly come to understand those structures. The islanders' performances were built around a notion that social and economic relationships were to be constructed that would be of benefit to both sides but that the visit itself would be ephemeral. Modest supplies of food and access to the beach and even to nearby stands of timber to allow basic activities and repairs to boats were clearly reasonable. Political alliance and with it protection from intruders were afforded to the visitors, perhaps as much to maximize potential advantage to the host group. These instances of contact in liminal space were also interpreted as *events* in an indigenous continuum of being in, interpreting, and engaging in a world constructed in fundamentally different ways. In belief systems where nothing was a "natural event" and where cause and effect were understood partly through appeals to the "supernatural," the Spanish arrivals demanded explanation not only in their own right but also as elements of a dynamic world that was finely balanced between possibility and peril.

The Spanish interaction with the Solomon Islanders was, in contrast, built around their notions of colonial expansion and rapid incorporation of the islanders into the religious and economic imperatives of empire. The rituals performed were those of establishing the authority of church and state in this far-flung corner of the world. Having explained as best they might to those islanders they identified as "chiefs" their new position as vassals within that structure, and having received in return what they felt was adequate acknowledgment, evidenced by the islanders making the sign of the cross, the immediate expectation was that food, labor, and assistance would be provided. Failure to do so was in effect treason and justification to unleash vengeful justice. On Santa Isabel the Spanish moves from that transitory space of the beach to the inland areas in search of food and information on economic resources (such as gold) resulted in shifts from accommodation to emphatic attempts to direct the apparently wayward soldiers back to the beach, which then ended in violence on both sides. Each side clearly felt vindicated. The Spanish behavior was obviously so aberrant that responses from the islanders also embraced reactions to a more extreme and possibly spiritual "other," inadvertently raising in the Spanish visitors the specters of cannibalism and demonic worship and thus reinforcing their desire to subjugate and convert.

In the second expedition, Mendaña's enthusiasms for a new colony might also have condemned it by raising expectations to unreasonable levels. Once the colonists were on Santa Cruz the immediacy and permanency of colonization created an unbearable tension. They had landed in the wrong place, in consequence of which so many of the advantages that might have accrued from prior knowledge of language, culture, and environment, all of which had been won through the travails of the first expedition, were now irrelevant. In this new environment, the promised gold, property, malleable "natives," and potential for wealth and status were missing. Instead there were hard work, hunger, and disease. The political tensions already within the Spanish group, the more pressing urgency for food supplies, and some colonists' strategy of trying to incite a violent response from the islanders in order to force a Spanish departure all immediately skewed behaviors and actions. The courageous attempts by Malopé and Mendaña toward conciliation were futile, even as they both attempted to create the structures of relationship. It is clear that the unique situation in which both found themselves was such that the tried-and-tested behaviors of both sides were inadequate to the task of reconciliation. Should we consider, therefore, that at least some of the behaviors recorded by the Spanish—and possibly purposefully forgotten by the indigenes— were aberrant to such an extent that they defy complete understanding through appeals to well-established ethnographic parallels or historically documented norms? We can only ask whether those aboard the lost *Santa Isabel*, reaching the intended destination but waiting fruitlessly for the remainder of the expedition, were seen to have behaved in similarly aberrant ways and then paid the ultimate price through warfare or epidemic.

Even from modern perspectives, Solomon Islanders understand the Spanish as exhibiting aberrant behaviors. Through a different cosmology, those behaviors might have been caused by and certainly interacted with the spiritual. However, just as other writers have established that episodes of cross-cultural contact—or, perhaps here, cultural contacts through the cross—were not necessarily the earth-shattering or transforming events that we might imagine, we can suggest that those encounters have subsequently become benchmark events and continue to be interpreted and understood through an indigenous lens.

One of the marked contrasts between the first and second expeditions is their respective approach to place making. The 1568 voyage was exploratory, and much attention was given to moving about the newly discovered island chain, recording information on landscape, resources, and peoples. Places were named, and the rituals of raising and adoring the cross were performed, making claims for the state while also portending the transformation into a Christian landscape. While the first campsite at Estrella Bay may have been occupied for two or more months while the colonists constructed a small *bergantín* (a two-masted sailing vessel similar to a brigantine), there was no intention to create a colony at that site. Most subsequent campsites during explorations were transitory. While none of the original maps from the 1568 expedition have been located, maps created several years later depicted the islands encountered, although whether these maps were copied from the originals or were derived from a reading of the expedition's several written accounts is not known. Many of these island names and place-names were adopted by later cartographers in the late eighteenth- and early nineteenth-century European "rediscovery" of the islands.

The 1595 voyage is almost the reverse in that it immediately focused on one area for the purposes of colonization. The systematic processes of clearance, construction, and apportioning in accordance with imperial dictate and personal aspiration were foremost in the processes of engagement with place. Relatively few names are mentioned, and there is no record of mapping. However, for both expeditions there is limited physical evidence of the Spanish presence when contrasted to other examples in this volume (e.g., Chapter 5), with archaeology locating no trace of the 1568 expedition and the merest shadows of the 1595 colony (Gibbs 2011). Ironically, it is the Pamua site on Makira (San Cristobal), where we have no knowledge of the fate of the lost *Santa Isabel* and the "Spanish" aboard or how they engaged with that landscape and its peoples (if at all), that retains the most obvious physicality (Blake et al. 2013). The apparently complete absence of traditional knowledge and stories of the Spanish at all of these sites in a culture that is built upon remembrance and stories hints that the failure of the Spanish project in the Solomons was then matched by a process of minimalizing or even deliberately forgetting that presence (Gibbs 2016), in effect creating a final rejection of the colonists' attempts to create new places within that landscape.

REFERENCES

Amherst of Hackney, Lord, and Basil Thomson, eds. 1901. *The Discovery of the Solomon Islands by Alvaro de Mendaña in 1568*. London: Hakluyt Society.

Beaule, Christine D. 2017. *Frontiers of Colonialism*. Gainesville: University Press of Florida.

Blake, Natalie, Martin Gibbs, and David Roe. 2013. "Late Prehistoric Burial Structures and Evidence of Spanish Contact at Makira, Solomon Islands." *Journal of Pacific Archaeology* 4(2): 69–78.

Bogesi, George. 1948. "Santa Isabel, Solomon Islands." *Oceania* 18(3): 208–232, and (4): 328–357.

Camino, Mercedes. 2005. *Producing the Pacific: Maps and Narratives of Spanish Exploration*. New York: Rodopi.

———. 2008. *Exploring the Explorers: Spaniards in Oceania 1519–1794*. Manchester: Manchester University Press.

Carter, Melissa, David Roe, and John Keopo. 2012. "Recent Recoveries of Archaeological Ceramics on Santa Isabel, Central Solomon Islands." *Journal of Pacific Archaeology* 3(2): 119–122.

Clark, Geoffrey. 2003. "Indigenous Transfer of La Pérouse Artefacts in the Southeast Solomon Islands." *Australian Archaeology* 57:103–111.

Clendinnen, Inga. 2003. *Dancing with Strangers*. Sydney: Text Publishing House.

Davenport, William. 1962. "Red Feather Money." *Scientific American* 206:94–104.

Deagan, Kathleen. 1983. *Spanish St. Augustine: The Archaeology of a Colonial Creole Community*. New York: Academic Press.

———. 2003. "Colonial Origins and Colonial Transformations in Spanish America." *Historical Archaeology* 37(4): 3–13.

Dening, Greg. 2004. *Beach Crossings: Voyaging across Times, Cultures, and Self*. Philadelphia: University of Pennsylvania Press.

Dunmore, John. 1974. "A French Account of Port Praslin, Solomon Islands, in 1769." *Journal of Pacific History* 9:172–182.

Gibbs, Martin. 2011. "Beyond the New World: The Failed Spanish Colonies of the Solomon Islands." In *Historical Archaeology and the Importance of Material Things*, edited by Julie Schablitsky and Mark Leone, 121–142. Ann Arbor, Mich.: Society for Historical Archaeology.

———. 2016. "The Failed Sixteenth Century Spanish Colonizing Expeditions to the Solomon Islands, Southwest Pacific: The Archaeologies of Settlement Process and Indigenous Agency." In *Archaeologies of Early Spanish Colonialism*, edited by Sandra Monton-Subias, Maria Cruz-Beccoral, and Apen Ruiz Martinez, 253–279. New York: Springer-Verlag.

Green, Roger C. 1973. "The Conquest of the Conquistadors." *World Archaeology* 5(1): 14–31.

Hill, Roscoe. 1913. "The Office of Adelantado." *Political Science Quarterly* 28(4): 646–668.

Jack-Hinton, Colin. 1969. *The Search for the Islands of Solomon 1567–1838*. Oxford: Clarendon Press.

Jolly, Margaret. 2009. "The Sediment of Voyages: Re-membering Quiros, Bougainville and Cook in Vanuatu." In *Oceanic Encounters: Exchange, Desire, Violence*, edited by Margaret Jolly, Serge Tcherkezoff, and Darrell Tryon, 57–111. Canberra: ANU ePress.

Jolly, Margaret, and Serge Tcherkezoff. 2009. "Oceanic Encounters: A Prelude." In *Oceanic Encounters: Exchange, Desire, Violence*, edited by Margaret Jolly, Serge Tcherkezoff, and Darrell Tryon, 1–36. Canberra: ANU ePress.

Kelloway, Sarah, Steven Craven, Mark Pecha, William Dickinson, Martin Gibbs, Timothy Ferguson, and Michael Glascock. 2014. "Sourcing Olive Jars Using U-Pb Ages of Detrital Zircons: A Study of 16th Century Olive Jars Recovered from the Solomon Islands." *Geoarchaeology* 29:47–60.

Kelly, Celsus. 1965. *Calendar of Documents: Spanish Voyages in the South Pacific and the Franciscan Missionary Plans for Its Islanders*. Melbourne: Franciscan Historical Society.

———, ed. 1966. *La Australia del Espíritu Santo*. Cambridge: Cambridge University Press.

Markham, Clements, ed. 1904. *The Voyages of Pedro Fernandez Quiros*. London: Hakluyt Society.

McNab, Robert, ed. 1914. "Records Relating to de Surville's Voyage." *Historical Records of New Zealand* 2:230–295. Wellington: Government Printer.

Merwick, Donna, ed. 1994. *Dangerous Liaisons: Essays in Honour of Greg Dening*. Melbourne: History Department, University of Melbourne.

Nuttal, Zelia. 1921. "Royal Ordinances Concerning the Laying Out of New Towns." *Hispanic American Historical Review* 55(4): 743–753.

Silliman, Stephen. 2005. "Culture Contact or Colonialism?" *American Antiquity* 70(1): 55–74.

Spate, Oscar. 1979. *The Spanish Lake*. London: Croom Helm.

Spriggs, Matthew. 1997. *The Island Melanesians*. Oxford: Blackwell.

Torrence, Robin. 2000. "Just Another Trader?" In *The Archaeology of Difference*, edited by Robin Torrence and Annie Clarke, 101–141. London: Routledge.

Tryon, Darrell T., and Brian Hackman. 1983. *Solomon Islands Languages: An Internal Classification*. Canberra: Australian National University.

White, Geoff. 1991. *Identity through History: Living Stories in a Solomon Islands Society*. Cambridge: Cambridge University Press.

Woodford, Charles M. 1926. "Notes on the Solomon Islands." *Geographical Journal* 68(6): 481–487.

8

Places, Landscapes, and Identity

Place Making in the Colonial Period Philippines

Stephen Acabado and Grace Barretto-Tesoro

Colonialism has been thought to be disruptive to indigenous cultures, especially when the entanglements prioritize assimilation. Traditional scholarship underscores this impression, since most studies focus on the process of colonization. More recently, scholars have emphasized the way colonized peoples have responded to culture contact (Acabado 2017; Lightfoot 2005; Panich 2010, 2013; Rodríguez-Alegría 2008; Silliman 2005, 2009, 2012). These studies have also mediated the idea of continuity and persistence amid the order imposed by colonial powers. Barbara Voss (2015) argues that indigenous populations respond creatively to the unequal power relationship to perpetuate certain aspects of their culture.

The changes brought by foreign powers often result in plurality within and among conquered groups, even when colonization aims to develop a monolithic culture. This process happens "within" because of new identities that emerge out of the new power dynamics and "among" because of the colonial strategy to divide and conquer. While persistence could be argued to be a dominant theme in studies such as ours, plurality makes it a dynamic process.

These responses are demonstrated in how landscapes are constructed and conceptualized in colonial settings. Using the concept of place making (Adams et al. 2001; Cresswell 2004; Rubertone 2009), we investigate space and how it becomes a place filled with meaning and identity. The imposition of Spanish order in the Philippines appears to have transformed the landscape drastically, but these changes are not monolithic.

In the Philippines, the influence of the Spanish Empire was magnified by the rapid conversion to Catholicism among lowland indigenous groups. This also resulted in the marginalization of non-Christianized upland groups and the continued distinction and division among those who were directly colonized and those who successfully resisted Spanish conquest. The processes of conversion, accommodation, and resistance have been the basis for present-day identities of Filipinos. In this chapter, we provide two case studies that describe divergent responses to Spanish colonialism, both of which are anchored on landscape and place making (Map 8.1).

This chapter argues that culture contact provided the venue for Philippine groups to craft their identities in relation to the more powerful Spanish Empire. The Ifugao and the Tagalog marked space and place to develop their identities, which were centered on the landscape. Among the Tagalog of Pinagbayanan, San Juan, Batangas, classes of material goods were used in ways that were distinctly different from how colonial elites utilized exotic goods, which became the link of Pinagbayanan to a new form of social hierarchy. Similarly, the Ifugao rice terraces became the impetus for the intensification of social differentiation (Acabado et al. 2018), which provided the organizational prerequisite to fight off conquest. In essence, they were marking their place within the colonial Philippine society.

In the first case study, we highlight the ability of the Ifugao to successfully resist colonization by organizational shifts anchored on landscape management (Acabado 2017, 2018; Acabado et al. 2019). The Ifugao case provides a follow-up to Martin Gibbs and David Roe's work (Chapter 7) of the failure of conquest; the Ifugao were able to respond creatively to the pressures of the Spanish push to the northern Philippines. This successful resistance catalyzed the identity of the Ifugao, who are portrayed in dominant historical narratives as uncolonized. As such, Ifugao identity is based on three fundamental aspects of their history: they were uncolonized, they had a long history of using a rice-terracing system, and rice played a central role in their culture. The Ifugao inhabit the interior of the Philippine Cordillera and are known for their rice terraces.

The second case study, which focuses on the Tagalog from the town of Pinagbayanan, San Juan, Batangas, is a classic example of how the policy of *reducción* reorganized Philippine communities. *Reducción* forced and/or stimulated the development of towns and urban areas in the Philippines, where migrants' and local residents' socioeconomic, political, and religious differences were highlighted in the new settlement. This new space provided the emergence of a new social status, which is referred to as *ilustrado* (enlightened).

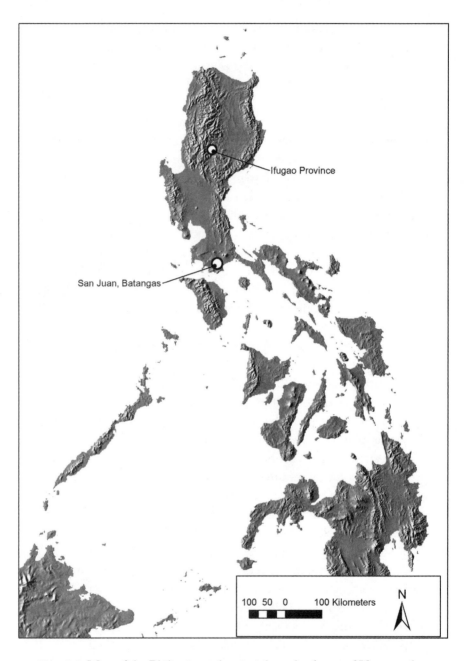

Map 8.1 Map of the Philippines, showing the upland area of Ifugao and the lowland town of San Juan, Batangas.

These two case studies emphasize the varied responses of indigenous groups to contact with hegemonic powers. In Ifugao, landscape modification for wet-rice cultivation became the fulcrum with which they resisted conquest. Thus, the later emergence of wet-rice cultivation is considered as one of the responses of the Ifugao to the arrival of the Spanish in the northern Philippines. Elsewhere, Acabado (2010, 2015, 2017, 2018) argues that the highlands become a refugium for lowland populations who were avoiding the Spanish. He further argues that the highlands are pericolonial areas that served as a venue for political and economic consolidation far from the central administration in Manila. Archaeological, ethnographic, and spatial datasets strongly support rapid subsistence, environmental, and social change in the region soon after the arrival of the Spanish in northern Luzon at ca. 1573 C.E. (Acabado 2018).

In Pinagbayanan, the development of towns was influenced by migrants through the transformation of space into a place that became their home. We argue that although the indigenous population strictly followed the European concept of settlement, their relationship with the physical space followed an emic tradition that operated on a network that revolved around the acquisition and possession of foreign objects. The foreign markers of wealth and status, which are permanent and physical in the landscape, and the indigenous notion of prestige, which is fluid and movable, make a powerful combination that secured the local elites' social position.

PLACE MAKING AND IDENTITY

A space becomes a place when the space becomes a representation of social relations that "define and create social and spatial contexts" (Adams et al. 2001:xiv). In this sense, place is both personal and political, and "place making is a product of social practices of constructing place and inscribing memories, which do not necessarily require particular skills or special sensibilities" (Rubertone 2009:13). A place, then, guides us to navigate spaces and helps us define our identity. A place is "dynamic and fluid" (Adams et al. 2001:xxi–xxii). Multiple identities can inhabit a place, and a place can create multiple identities, including dominant and nondominant groups that are subjected to an ideology or follow a different one.

Three things make a place: "its location," the "setting for social relations," and a "sense of place" (Cresswell 2004:7; see also Agnew 1987). As our case studies illustrate, rice fields and colonial towns became meaningful spaces that provided the venues for new institutions and identities to emerge in the midst of colonial imposition. In Ifugao, rice fields are thought to have anchored successful resistance to conquest; in Pinagbayanan, new identities emerged as a response to the colonial enterprise.

Thus, the place referred to in this chapter is not just the geographical and physical location; instead, it includes place or position in the society using the physical dimension of space as the background (Cresswell 2004:2; see also the introduction to this volume). In the Spanish Philippines, the place, which is the new town, is class-based and map-based (Gipouloux 2011:15), whereas indigenous settlements were usually linear, following the contour of the landscape (Javellana 2017:90). In Ifugao, where the Spanish were never able to establish a permanent presence, villages maintained local settlement patterns.

SPANISH CONQUEST AND COLONIALISM IN THE PHILIPPINES

Ferdinand Magellan, sailing under the flag of the Spanish Empire, dropped anchor along the coast of the central Philippines on March 19, 1521. His voyage to the Philippines was spurred by the objective of discovering a western route to the Spice Islands, which are located south of the Philippine archipelago. Although Magellan planted the Spanish flag in the Philippines in 1521, it was not until 1565 that Miguel Lopez de Legaspi formally established a colonial government in present-day Cebu City.

The establishment of the Spanish colonial government in the Philippines was a consequence of the discovery of a safe route between the Philippines and Mexico, the *torno viaje*, which facilitated the famous Manila–Acapulco trade. The Philippines was an afterthought in the conquest of the East Indies, as the archipelago was thought to be an expensive possession, but the islands offered the potential springboard to trade with and to colonize China (Skowronek 1998).

Legaspi moved the administration capital from Cebu to Manila in 1571 because Manila's location facilitated trade with other Asian cities; the area also has one of the best harbors in the archipelago (Pearson

2001). Within six months of his capture of Manila, his grandson, Juan de Salcedo, led an expedition to explore the western coastal region of northern Luzon in search of the famed Igorot gold (Scott 1974).

The *torno viaje* eased the Manila–Acapulco galleon trade, which introduced Philippine communities to European and American goods from 1565 to 1815 and brought Asian goods to the Old and New Worlds (Legarda 1999). After 1815, foreign trade expanded due to more new ports and shipping subsidies granted by Spain (Legarda 1999). Profits from international trade created the rise of the middle class, the *ilustrados*.

The Manila area was an economic center even prior to Spanish arrival in the sixteenth century (Kimuell-Gabriel 2013; Scott 1994) and continued to be so until the present. Manila is a "hinge," or *charnière*, a concept developed by Jean Gottman that refers to the connection between a place and a network. Manila linked the Philippines to the Southeast Asian and global networks. The influx of objects from other nations came with ideas, knowledge, languages, images, technologies, and beliefs (Gipouloux 2011:14).

These connections also facilitated the European education of the local elites, which allowed them to develop and later reinforce their nationalist views (Heidhues 2000:121). The Manila–Acapulco galleon trade promoted the movement of ideas. During this period, Manila was connected to North America, South America, Europe, and Asia (Gipouloux 2011:13). This globalizing process defied national and territorial boundaries, penetrating spaces that did not conform to the map-based knowledge of the Europeans. The plaza complex gave rise to the notion of center and periphery, which can be translated into dominant and subordinate (Gipouloux 2011:22). And in the larger scale, Manila was and still is the center, while Pinagbayanan was simultaneously Manila's periphery and San Juan's center.

As Manila increasingly became the center of commerce and politics, provinces around it were being reorganized, with new towns established or existing towns infused with new inhabitants from elsewhere. As an example, San Juan, established in the late 1840s, received migrants who were arguably members of the local elites from other towns and were considered *ilustrados*. Their family names were recorded in archival documents as political leaders. These family names are still present in San Juan. The arrival of new migrants in Pinagbayanan is apparent, since the recovered imported items from the stone-based houses (Barretto-Tesoro 2015) were interpreted to have been used by the occupants to distance themselves from the rest of the residents while simultaneously asserting their presence and strengthening their connection to the place they now called home.

The northern Philippines, including Ifugao, was affected directly by the galleon trade. As agricultural products in the Cagayan Valley were main exports of the Philippines, the Spanish colonial administration constructed infrastructure and roads that cut through the traditional territory of the Ifugao (Lim Pe 1978:196). Most present-day cities and towns that are adjacent to Ifugao started as garrison towns that were meant to secure the supply route between northern Cagayan Valley and Manila (Tejon 1982:50). This provided the Ifugao an opportunity to access the colonial economic system.

THE IFUGAO

The Ifugao of the northern Philippines are known for their magnificent rice terraces (Figure 8.1); they are also famous for successfully resisting multiple attempts by the Spanish at conquest. Resistance against the Spanish has become the foundation of Ifugao identity and how lowland Filipino groups view the Ifugao (Acabado 2017, 2018). Dominant Philippine historical narratives even describe the Ifugao as "original Filipinos" owing to presumed isolation of the groups from colonial processes. These descriptions have entered the national consciousness, since basic-education history textbooks reify the flawed premises of a pejorative model. The long-history proposition for the origins of the rice terraces (Barton 1919; Beyer 1955) also reprises the racialization and exoticization of identity formation. Recent archaeological and ethnographic information, however, actively humanizes the Ifugao.

The proposed 2,000-year origin of the rice terraces is not based on any scientific data; rather, data focus on the observations and racial assumptions of pioneer anthropologists. Current ethnographic and archaeological information suggests a recent origin of the agricultural marvels, the construction and subsequent expansion of which appear to have been responses of the Ifugao to colonialism.

Figure 8.1 The Nagacadan rice terraces in Kiangan, Ifugao.

Acabado (2017, 2018) argues that in the 1500s, the Ifugao inhabited both the highland Cordillera and lowland Magat Valley region of present-day Nueva Vizcaya (Keesing 1962). Highland Ifugao mainly cultivated taro, while the Magat Valley Ifugao were wet-rice cultivators. The arrival of the Spanish in Luzon forced migration into the uplands in the early 1600s. Archaeological data from the Old Kiyyangan Village indicate rapid population increase and a shift to wet-rice cultivation during this period.

The shift to wet-rice production provided the organizing mechanism for the Ifugao to fight off attempts by the Spanish at conquest, since wet-rice production requires a specific form of social organization (Bray 1994; Greenland 1997). Wet-rice cultivation necessitates management of water flow depending on the life cycle of rice—too much or too little water will kill the crop. This involves a complex water management system that could only be achieved with specialization. In addition, once the shift to wet-rice cultivation occurred, the land tenure system would have favored land ownership, as opposed to communal access. The agricultural shift thus signaled a culture centered on rice production, distribution, and consumption. For instance, Ifugao social status is customarily measured by the amount of a person's rice landholdings and her or his family's ability to sponsor feasts (which requires ritual animals, rice, and rice wine) (Acabado et al. 2018; Lapeña and Acabado 2017). The shift facilitated the emergence of Ifugao identity primarily based on landscape practices that are still practiced today.

RICE, IDENTITY, AND PLACE

The centrality of rice in Ifugao culture is manifested in how the Ifugao equate their rice terraces to life itself; the rice fields are considered as deified grounds sanctified by a covenant between the gods and their ancestors. As such, all sacred myths (*hu'uwa*) of the Ifugao are set in the terraces. It is fascinating that even though wet-rice cultivation was only introduced in the Ifugao agricultural suite after 1650, rice symbols have shaped Ifugao cosmology.

Furthermore, agricultural rituals anchored on the rice life cycle emphasize this aspect of Ifugao culture. Indeed, feasts of merit that elevate individuals in the social hierarchy were preconditioned on existing rice field holdings. An individual's social status was defined by rice through rituals that necessitated the invocation of numerous agricultural gods. Ritual rice fields were consecrated to set the pace of community labor and establish the sociopolitical hierarchy.

The shift to wet-rice cultivation is argued to have provided the impetus for social differentiation, since intensified agriculture requires a specific form of management (Bray 1994; Greenland 1997). As manifested by the archaeological record (Acabado et al. 2019; Lapeña and Acabado 2017; Yakal 2017), frequency of ritual fauna and exotic goods increased soon after contact with the Spanish. As argued elsewhere (Acabado 2018:2), the rice terraces became the venue where social practice and *habitus* were acted and rice production and its associated rituals became the structuring mechanism for Ifugao solidarity.

The maintenance of Ifugao agricultural practices is a testament to the power of place making. Since resistance to conquest was anchored on the shift to wet-rice production, intensified social differentiation and thus new statuses emerged. A similar pattern can be observed in the lowlands, where the Spanish had a stronger footprint.

PINAGBAYANAN: A NEW PLACE, A NEW HOME

The Spanish followed specific guidelines in establishing towns as stated in the Laws of the Indies (Barretto-Tesoro 2015). Despite its homogeneous and orderly street layout, the plaza complex, a system of settlement introduced by the Spanish in the late sixteenth century, creates alienation, segregation, and exclusion. The Spanish occupation of the Philippines ordered status based on religion and ethnicity against the backdrop of the plaza complex. The plaza is the center of the town, and on each side on a grid layout following cardinal directions are the church, administrative offices, tribunal, and houses of elites. As one moves farther from the center or from within hearing distance of the church bells, the social status decreases (Barretto-Tesoro 2015).

Two stone-based houses (Figure 8.2), dating to the late 1800s, were excavated in Pinagbayanan, San Juan, Batangas, from 2009 to 2011 (Barretto-Tesoro 2015). Constructed using volcanic tuff blocks and lime mortar, these two domestic units were part of the plaza complex. To date, excavations in Pinagbayanan indicate that no precolonial settlement

Figure 8.2 A section of Structure A, one of the two stone-based houses in Pinagbayanan, San Juan, Batangas (photo by A. Tesoro).

was established in the immediate vicinity, signifying that the town was a *reducción*. Historical accounts noted that the first migrants were from neighboring towns. In the early 1880s, due to a big flood, the parish priest requested the administrative government to relocate the town capital inland. The elites opposed the move, but the central government finally ordered the town to be transferred in 1890 (Barretto-Tesoro and Hernandez 2017). The new town exemplifies space categories that emerged in colonial Philippines, the designation of places inside the town (civilized/colonized/orderly) and localities outside the new settlements (savages/brigands/pagans/disorder) (Javellana 2017:92). A point that we emphasize in this chapter is the reverse sense of place between colonists and natives (Cresswell 2004:9). What may be a place for the indigenous population is just space for the colonists, and vice versa.

This may explain why the dichotomy between the inside (place) and outside (space) of town associated with civilized and brigands, respectively, is a view of the Spanish not shared by the locals. In the new space, people oriented themselves based on the church's location, while the indigenous relation with space was based on land and sea, *silangan* (where the sun rises) (Javellana 2017), *ilawod* (downstream), and *ilaya* (upstream) (Salazar 2013; Scott 1994). For the locals, places exist outside the settlement to which they had social, emotional, filial, cultural, religious, economic, and perhaps even political ties long before Spanish arrival. The voids were not unknown in the traditional context. If the Spanish viewed mountain dwellers or those living outside the *bayan* (town) as savages, for the indigenous population the mountains were "sacred places," "secret lair[s] and refuge" (Javellana 2017:96; Salazar 1997).

SYMBOLIC CAPITAL: OBJECTS, SOCIAL NETWORKS, AND PLACES

In Pinagbayanan, owning beautiful objects strengthened the connection of the migrants to the place, a newly established town at the time of their transfer. These everyday domestic objects were an assertion that the migrants belonged here. These objects reflected the migrants' daily lives, experiences, and ties in this town. They were reminders of a new life in this new town. Since the stone-based houses were newly constructed and durable, it was challenging for the locals to transfer

immediately inland due to flooding when they themselves just transferred to Pinagbayanan from nearby towns. They initially did not want
to move until they received orders from the governor general (Barretto-
Tesoro and Hernandez 2017). The presence of imported items suggests
that the inhabitants of the stone-based houses were wealthy and prestigious. However, these items not only were economic in nature but also
represented what Pierre Bourdieu (1984) refers to as symbolic capital.
Symbolic capital refers to "acquired tastes, knowledge, appreciation,
and consumption of aesthetically pleasing forms" (Duncan and Duncan
2001:42). These items give prestige to the people who owned and used
them, separating them from the rest of the local population. Losing
control over the physical space, which the Spanish commandeered, the
indigenous population, particularly the local elites, searched for an al-
ternate venue to exercise control over their land and settlement. Control
over international trade was one way to access prestige and status. They
acquired goods from all over the world, as free trade granted them access to a multitude of items beyond China. These imported items are
symbolic capital, representations of esoteric knowledge (Helms 1991:83)
that elite individuals want to control. For the people residing in Pinagbayanan, the possession and display of imported objects validated and
reinforced the migrants' prestige in the new town and their potency to
rule the political, economic, and social domains. Integration in the network is integration in the system that can break or make the longevity
and success of one's clan.

It may appear that the objects themselves are important, but if we
look at object-human relationships, it is the symbolic value attached to
these objects that makes them status symbols. It has been established
that imports from faraway places, objects that traveled long distances,
have higher values. We argue that the occupants of the two stone-based
houses considered the symbolic value of the items in their possession.

During this period, the emerging elites were aspiring to access European goods (and connections), since Asian, particularly Chinese, goods
were not highly valued (Diokno 1998; Hau 2017). Access to such symbolic capital, as well as the colonial economic system that emphasized
economic, social, cultural, and religious capital (Hau 2017), further wid-
ened the gap between social classes, thus enabling the rise of the *ilustrados*
against the backdrop of free trade after the end of the galleon trade.

To support our point, we integrated the imported items, such as medicine bottles, wine bottles, and porcelain sherds, recovered from the two stone-based houses in Pinagbayanan into the occupants' daily experiences. These experiences engaged the full range of human senses, which Fenella Cannell (1999) and Michael Pinches (1991) describe as tangible, sensorial, and experiential—for instance, the ingestion and smell of cod liver oil, the taste of liquor, brushing teeth using a proper toothbrush, the feel of coins minted in Spain, the application of oil or balm, the sheen and smooth touch of porcelain from Europe, the buttons from France that adorned garments, the touch of shiny furniture. They fostered intimate relationships with the objects: holding the objects, holding a part of where they came from, wearing, touching, drinking, and ingesting them. The *ilustrados* embodied European sensibilities as they metaphorically absorbed the spirit of these foreign objects to demonstrate their increasing connectedness to the global network, thereby denoting prestige and status and thus legitimizing their presence in their new place. They reinforced their differences, separating themselves from the locals by representing the body through goods while simultaneously strengthening their relationship to the new town.

The effort to acquire imported goods is also associated with the process of aestheticization (Eagleton 1990). More importantly, attachments between people and place, known as topophilia, are manifested through "aestheticization of place and landscape" (Duncan and Duncan 2001:41). Transformation and/or redecoration of the landscape make the place meaningful to its inhabitants, creating a sense of home. In Pinagbayanan, the process of aestheticization is not confined to beautifying the landscape, particularly, the Spanish practice of grid layout to beautify space by bringing visual order. It also includes the acquisition of beautiful things. For instance, the occupants observed dental hygiene with the use of a modern toothbrush issued by a German dispensary (Barretto-Tesoro 2011). They had access to modern and imported medication, such as Chamberlain's pain balm from Iowa (Cruz 2014) and Scott's emulsion of cod liver oil with lime and soda from New York (Cruz 2014) (Figure 8.3). Hauthaway shoe polish from Massachusetts was used for leather shoes (Cruz 2014) so a man could look the part of a Europeanized Filipino. The presence of Japanese Gold Paint suggests that the owners of the house had wooden furniture that needed varnishing.[1] This could be an instance

Figure 8.3 Bone toothbrush (*top*) (photo by A. Tesoro). Bottle of a pain balm (*left*) and cod liver oil (*right*) (modified after Cruz 2014).

of japanning (a European imitation of Asian lacquer work), which was a popular look in the mid-1800s. Japanese Gold Paint can also be used for gilding on porcelain.[2]

The emergence of the *ilustrado* class signifies the appearance of bourgeois ideology in the Spanish Philippines, since the imported objects have deeper meaning attached to them. They suggest that owners of these objects have knowledge and skills only available to individuals who can acquire such goods. More importantly, they denote ideas of progress that emulate European imagery of modernity and civility. These objects shape the body movement of the end users. They regulate the way the owners eat, how they handle dinnerware and wine bottles, how they apply balm, how they use a toothbrush, and how they appreciate what is beautiful. They add to the users' skills because these objects force users to act and behave in a way that separates them from the rest of the population, simultaneously highlighting their access to objects of wealth.

PLACE MAKING AND IDENTITY

The Laws of the Indies guided the Spanish in establishing towns during the colonial period in the Philippines. Many of these settlements were *reducciones*, or forced resettlements, which means that early settlers had no connection with the land. Through ordering and modifying the physical landscape as dictated in the Laws of the Indies, the Spanish gained control over the new land. For the local migrants, there is perhaps a reverse sense of place that could be considered as part of the aestheticization process. Aestheticization made space meaningful, consequently making the area a place of residence, their home (Eagleton 1990). Aestheticization was originally used to refer to the modification of physical surrounding, but in Pinagbayanan, local elites extended the idea to the acquisition of goods, which can be argued as persistence of indigenous traditions of prestige economics. This would have facilitated the transformation of space as meaningful place for both locals and new migrants. As opportunities to obtain these goods increased due to free trade, these items eventually became symbols of wealth and status. The new middle class emerged. Securing their position in the social hierarchy by residing in sturdy stone-based houses located near the church and fortifying their position in a social network that governs their connectivity to the global world, the *ilustrados* became a powerful force in Philippine society.

The *ilustrado* class differs in the source of their identity. It is neither based on ethnicity nor religion, which was prevalent during the Spanish period. Apart from historical documents that identify the occupants of the two stone-based houses as Batangueños, who are members of the ethnolinguistic Tagalog group, no archaeological materials support their ethnicity. What is visible is the *ilustrado* identity, represented by foreign items shared in many historical sites, such as those found in Manila. Being an *ilustrado* crosses ethnolinguistic boundaries. Even in historical documents, the term referred to the middle class regardless of cultural affinity. Being an *ilustrado* was one trajectory an *indio* (native) or mestizo could take during the late Spanish occupation of the Philippines in the late nineteenth century. The creation of the *ilustrado* identity was driven by socioeconomics, which later became a source of national political movements.

Similarly, prestige economics appear to have been intensified in Ifugao and catalyzed social statuses, which were based on the amount of rice landholdings an individual was able to maintain. As detailed by Acabado (2018), the shift to wet-rice cultivation and massive landscape transformations would have provided the needed sociopolitical organization required in fighting a more powerful entity. The mountainous terrain might have played a part, but it is the conscious effort of the Ifugao to consolidate political and economic resources that were vital to the resistance. This has shaped Ifugao identity and is evident even today.

CONTINUITY AND CHANGE: MEANINGFUL PLACE, SPACES OF IDENTITY

Voss (2015:686) calls for a serious examination of how archaeologists have utilized the concept of ethnogenesis. Previous iterations of the concept have focused on the idea of the loss or extinction of indigenous cultures (Panich 2013:16), but recent archaeological investigations on culture contact have highlighted the observation that conquered and/or colonized groups tend to perpetuate certain aspects of their culture.

The case studies highlighted in this chapter show just that: the effects of conquest and colonialism are more dynamic than what has been previously thought of. In Pinagbayanan, the new place was accompanied by the rise of new identities, accommodating the status quo offered by the colonial administrators. *Reducción* gathered previously distinct ethnic and/or kinship identities into a bounded place, which resulted in the emergence of new institutions. The *ilustrados*, as the new elite, transcended ethnic and linguistic identities, as their status was based on the ability to mirror the colonial state of affairs. To some extent, we still see this among present-day Christianized Filipinos.

On the other hand, the identity of contemporary Ifugao revolves around the long history of their terraces and the historical narratives that they were uncolonized—both concepts proposed by earlier scholars appear to leave Ifugao agency. Acabado (2017) has argued that these earlier models failed to identify how the indigenous group creatively responded to entanglements in the Philippine colonial period because of the inordinate focus on the exotic. Instead of humanizing the Ifugao, ideas of deep history and the uncolonized fundamentally shaped how lowland Filipinos view the former.

Archaeological evidence strongly suggests that the Ifugao were able to resist Spanish conquest by accepting the economic pressures exerted by the colonial administration. The shift to wet-rice cultivation gave them the ability to consolidate the political and economic resources they needed to solidify their ethnic identity. This pattern is observed today with the assimilation of the Ifugao into the Philippine state and the dominance of the market economy.

As a dynamic culture, the Ifugao have responded to this process with ingenuity by choosing to be part of the larger Philippine society but maintaining their identity. Following James Scott's (1985:29) argument that powerless groups contest domination by "foot dragging, dissimulation, false compliance, pilfering, feigned ignorance, slander, arson, sabotage, and so forth," we contend that the Ifugao responded to cultural domination creatively—by actively choosing options that were advantageous for their own purposes. Taken in a more positive way than how Scott illustrates how peasants around the world fight the perils of the market economy, the Ifugao chose to strengthen the power of their rice fields.

The Pinagbayanan and Ifugao examples show that colonization did not result in a homogeneous culture; on the contrary, the process encouraged regional differences that we still see today. Pinagbayanan, as a recipient of *reducción*, enhanced their Tagalog identity combined with European concepts of social elites. In Ifugao, they strengthen their cultural identity by emphasizing their distinctiveness from Christianized Filipinos. Both groups' notions of uniqueness are fundamentally based on place and landscape.

NOTES

1. The inscription on this bottle was initially read as Japanese Cold Paint (Barretto-Tesoro et al. 2009:59).
2. www.antique-bottles.net.

REFERENCES

Acabado, Stephen. 2010. "The Archaeology of the Ifugao Agricultural Terraces: Antiquity and Social Organization." PhD diss., University of Hawaii-Manoa.
———. 2015. *Antiquity, Archaeological Processes, and Highland Adaptation: The Ifugao Rice Terraces*. Manila: Ateneo de Manila University Press.
———. 2017. "The Archaeology of Pericolonialism: Responses of the 'Unconquered' to Spanish Conquest and Colonialism in Ifugao, Philippines." *International Journal of Historical Archaeology* 21(17): 1–26.
———. 2018. "Zones of Refuge: Resisting Conquest in the Northern Philippine Highlands through Environmental Practice." *Journal of Anthropological Archaeology* 52:180–195. doi.org/10.1016/j.jaa.2018.05.005.
Acabado, Stephen, Grace Barretto-Tesoro, and Noel Amano. 2018. "Status Differentiation, Agricultural Intensification, and Pottery Production in Precapitalist Kiyyangan, Ifugao, Philippines." *Archaeological Research in Asia* 15:55–69.
Acabado, Stephen, Jared Koller, Chin-hsin Liu, Adam Lauer, Alan Farahani, Grace Barretto-Tesoro, Jonathan Martin, and John A. Peterson. 2019. "The Short History of the Ifugao Rice Terraces: A Local Response to the Spanish Conquest." *Journal of Field Archaeology* 44(3): 195–214.
Adams, Paul C., Steven Hoelscher, and Karen E. Till. 2001. "Place in Context: Rethinking Humanist Geographies." In *Textures of Place: Exploring Humanist Geographies*, edited by Paul C. Adams, Steven Hoelscher, and Karen E. Till, xiii–xxxiii. Minneapolis: University of Minnesota Press.
Agnew, John. 1987. *Place and Politics*. Boston: Allen and Unwin.
Barretto-Tesoro, Grace. 2011. "Lost in and on Manila: What Do I Know about Manila? Understanding the Materiality of Manila." In *Manila: Selected Papers of the 19th Annual Manila Studies Conference, August 31–September 1, 2010*, edited by Lorelie D. C. de Viana, 1–19. Manila: Manila Studies Association and National Commission for Culture and the Arts.
———. 2015. "The Application of the Laws of the Indies in the Pacific: The Excavation of Two Old Stone-Based Houses in San Juan, Batangas, Philippines." *International Journal of Historical Archaeology* 19(3): 433–463.
Barretto-Tesoro, Grace, and Vito Hernandez. 2017. "Power and Resilience: Flooding and Occupation in a Late Nineteenth Century Philippine Town." In *Frontiers of Colonialism*, edited by Christine D. Beaule, 149–178. Gainesville: University Press of Florida.

Barretto-Tesoro, Grace, Philip Piper, Anna Pineda, Pauline Basilia, Joan Tara Reyes, Jasminda Ceron, Eleanor Lim, Kathryn Ann B. Manalo, Kristyn Maguire, Marie Louise Antoinette Sioco, and Arnelito Ramirez Jr. 2009. *An Archaeological Investigation of "Structure A" in San Juan, Batangas*. Archaeological Studies Program, University of the Philippines.

Barton, Roy F. 1919. "Ifugao Law." *University of California Publications in American Archaeology and Ethnology* 15:1–186.

Beyer, Henry O. 1955. "The Origins and History of the Philippine Rice Terraces." In *Proceedings of the Eighth Pacific Science Congress, 1953*. Quezon City: National Research Council of the Philippines.

Boivin, Nicole, Dorian Q. Fuller, and Alison Crowther. 2012. "Old World Globalization and the Columbian Exchange: Comparison and Contrast." *World Archaeology* 44(3): 452–469.

Bourdieu, Pierre. 1984. *Distinction: A Social Critique of the Judgement of Taste*. Cambridge, Mass.: Harvard University Press.

Bray, Francesca. 1994. *The Rice Economies: Technology and Development in Asian Societies*. Berkeley: University of California Press.

Cannell, Fenella. 1999. *Power and Intimacy in the Christian Philippines*. Cambridge: Cambridge University Press.

Cresswell, Tim. 2004. *Place: A Short Introduction. Short Introductions to Geography*. Maldern: Blackwell Publishing.

Cruz, Melodina Sy. 2014. "Looking through the Glass: Analysis of Glass Vessel Shards from Pinagbayanan Site, San Juan, Batangas, Philippines." *Hukay* 19:24–60.

Diokno, Maria Serena I. 1998. "The Rise of the Chinese Trader." In *Life in the Colony*, vol. 4, *Kasaysayan: The Story of the Filipino People*, edited by Maria Serena I. Diokno and Ramon N. Villegas, 47–69. Hong Kong: Asia Publishing Company Limited.

Duncan, James S., and Nancy G. Duncan. 2001. "Sense of Place as a Positional Good: Locating Bedford in Space and Time." In *Textures of Place: Exploring Humanist Geographies*, edited by Paul C. Adams, Steven Hoelscher, and Karen E. Till, 41–54. Minneapolis: University of Minnesota Press.

Eagleton, Terry. 1990. *The Ideology of the Aesthetic*. Cambridge: Basil Blackwell.

Gipouloux, François. 2011. *The Asian Mediterranean: Port Cities and Trading Networks in China, Japan and Southeast Asia, 13th–21st Century*. Translated by Jonathan Hall and Dianna Martin. Cheltenham, U.K.: Edward Elgar.

Gottman, Jean. 1983. "Capital Cities." *Ekistics* 50(2): 88–93.

Greenland, Dennis. 1997. *The Sustainability of Rice Farming*. New York: CAB International and International Rice Research Institute.

Hau, Caroline S. 2017. *Elites and Ilustrados in Philippine Culture*. Quezon City: Ateneo de Manila University Press.

Heidhues, Mary Somers. 2000. *Southeast Asia: A Concise History*. London: Thames and Hudson.

Helms, Mary W. 1991. "Esoteric Knowledge, Geographical Distance, and the Elaboration of Leadership Status Dynamics of Resource Control." In *Profiles in Cultural Evolution*, edited by Terry Rambo and Kathleen Gillogly, 333–349. Ann Arbor: University of Michigan Press.

Javellana, Rene B. 2017. *Weaving Cultures: The Invention of Colonial Art and Culture in the Philippines*. Quezon City: Ateneo de Manila University Press.

Keesing, Felix. 1962. *The Ethnohistory of Northern Luzon*. Stanford, Calif.: Stanford University Press.

Kimuell-Gabriel, Nancy. 2013. "Ang tundo sa inskripsyon sa binatbat na tanso ng Laguna (900 MK–1588)." In *Ang saysay ng inskripsyon sa binatbat na tanso ng Laguna*, edited by Carmen V. Peñalosa and Zeus A. Salazar, 113–167. Quezon City and Pila: BAKAS and Pila Historical Society Foundation, Inc.

Lapeña, Quenny G., and Stephen B. Acabado. 2017. "Resistance through Rituals: The Role of Philippine 'Native Pig' (*Sus scrofa*) in Ifugao Feasting and Sociopolitical Organization." *Journal of Archaeological Science: Reports* 13:583–594.

Legarda, Benito J. 1999. *After the Galleons: Foreign Trade, Economic Change and Entrepreneurship in the Nineteenth Century Philippines*. Quezon City: Ateneo de Manila University Press.

Lightfoot, Kent G. 2005. *Indians, Missionaries, and Merchants: The Legacy of Colonial Encounters on the California Frontiers*. Berkeley: University of California Press.

Lim Pe, Josefina. 1978. "Spanish Contacts with the Ifugaos (1736–1898)." *Philippiniana Sacra* 13(38): 193–249.

Panich, Lee M. 2010. "Missionization and the Persistence of Native Identity on the Colonial Frontier of Baja California." *Ethnohistory* 57(2): 225–262.

———. 2013. "Archaeologies of Persistence: Reconsidering the Legacies of Colonialism in Native North America." *American Antiquity* 78(1): 105–122.

Pearson, Michael. 2001. "Spanish Trade in Southeast Asia." In *The Pacific World: Lands, People and History of the Pacific, 1500–1900, Vol. 4*, series edited by Dennis O. Flynn and Arturo Giráldez, 161–182. Burlington: Ashgate Publishing.

Pinches, Michael. 1991. "The Working Class Experience of Shame, Inequality, and People Power in Tatalon, Manila." In *Marcos to Aquino: Local Perspectives on Political Transition in the Philippines*, edited by Benedict J. Tria Kerkevliet and Resil B. Mojares, 166–186. Quezon City: Ateneo de Manila University Press.

Rodríguez-Alegría, Enrique. 2008. "Narratives of Conquest, Colonialism, and Cutting-Edge Technology." *American Anthropologist* 110(1): 33–43.

Rubertone, Patricia E., ed. 2009. *Archaeologies of Placemaking: Monuments, Memories, and Engagement in Native North America*. New York: Routledge.

Salazar, Zeus A. 2013. "Tundun-pailah-binwangan: Ang sistemang ilog ilawud-ilaya ng Katagalugan, bilang halimbawa ng isang proseso ng pagkabuo ng mga sinaunang pamayanan ng Kapilipinuhan." In *Ang saysay ng inskripsyon sa binatbat na tanso ng Laguna*, edited by Carmen V. Peñalosa and Zeus A.

Salazar, 341–467. Quezon City and Pila: BAKAS and Pila Historical Society Foundation, Inc.

Scott, James C. 1985. *Weapons of the Weak: Everyday Forms of Peasant Resistance.* New Haven, Conn.: Yale University Press.

Scott, William Henry. 1974. *The Discovery of the Igorots: Spanish Contacts with the Pagans of Northern Luzon.* Quezon City: New Day Publishers.

———. 1994. *Barangay: Sixteenth-Century Philippine Culture and Society.* Quezon City: Ateneo de Manila University Press.

Silliman, Stephen W. 2005. "Culture Contact or Colonialism? Challenges in the Archaeology of Native North America." *American Antiquity* 70(1): 55–74.

———. 2009. "Change and Continuity, Practice and Memory: Native American Persistence in Colonial New England." *American Antiquity* 74(2): 211–230.

———. 2012. "Between the Longue Durée and the Short Purée: Postcolonial Archaeologies of Indigenous History in Colonial North America." In *Decolonizing Indigenous Histories: Exploring Prehistoric/Colonial Transitions in Archaeology*, edited by Maxine Oland, Siobhan Hart, and Liam Frink, 113–132. Tucson: University of Arizona Press.

Skowronek, Russell K. 1998. "The Spanish Philippines: Archaeological Perspectives on Colonial Economics and Society." *International Journal of Historical Archaeology* 2(1): 45–71.

Tejon, Guillermo. 1982. *Juan Villaverde, O.P., Missionary and Road Builder.* Manila: University of Santo Tomas Press.

Voss, Barbara L. 2015. "What's New? Rethinking Ethnogenesis in the Archaeology of Colonialism." *American Antiquity* 80(4): 655–670.

Yakal, Madeleine A. 2017. "Exotic Beads and Jar Burials: Social Status in the Old Kiyyangan Village, Ifugao, Philippines." MA thesis, UCLA.

9

Colonial Surveillance, *Lånchos*, and the Perpetuation of Intangible Cultural Heritage in Guam, Mariana Islands

James M. Bayman, Boyd M. Dixon, Sandra Montón-Subías, and Natalia Moragas Segura

The colonization of the Pacific Islands by the Spanish and other European powers was spectacular and profound in its consequences. Unfamiliar technologies, gender systems, material cultures, languages, disease pathogens, and worldviews altered the lived experience of native communities in unprecedented ways (Bayman 2008, 2107; Bayman and Peterson 2016; Cruz Berrocal and Tsang 2017; Flexner 2014; Hezel 1989; Montón-Subías 2019; Montón-Subías et al. 2018; Russell 1998:317–322; Stannard 1989). Because Guam's native Chamorro were the earliest population in the Pacific Islands to experience contact with Europeans, they provide a compelling example of resilience spanning several centuries of colonialism by Spanish and subsequent powers (i.e., American and Japanese) (Map 9.1). Documentary accounts of Guam's colonial history are abundant and richly detailed in aggregate, yet archaeology offers an underutilized resource for interpreting the materiality of its colonial history (for notable exceptions, see Dixon et al. 2013; Dixon et al. 2017; Dixon et al. 2010). We argue that archaeology in the Pacific (including the Mariana Islands) must make a sustained effort to engage in the production of knowledge about both the materiality and the intangible cultural heritage of Oceania's traditional societies. Such research is necessary so that Oceania's colonial past is featured in ongoing discussions of intangible cultural heritage elsewhere in the world. Because Guam was located on the maritime route of the Manila galleon (Chaunu 1960; Giraldez 2015; Schurz 1939; Spate 1979), it witnessed and experienced a tapestry of cultural influences from the Americas and Asia, particularly New Spain and the Philippines. Together, with the advent of the Jesuit mission in the Marianas, Guam is home to the earliest example of urbanism during the early modern period in remote Oceania.

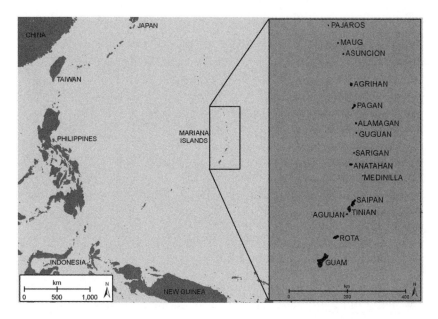

Map 9.1 Mariana Islands in the Pacific (courtesy of Mike T. Carson).

Our chapter integrates a suite of archaeological and documentary sources to interpret the consequences of the *reducción* in the late seventeenth century and its ramifications through the nineteenth century. It was during this event that Guam's native Chamorro were forcibly relocated into district villages in a colonial effort to control them following decades of strife and conflict. Although the implementation of the *reducción* introduced profound changes in Chamorro culture, land use at *lånchos* (ranch-farms) away from coastal villages ensured the persistence of particular customs and traditions beyond the reach of surveillance by Spanish authorities (Perez Hattori 2004:16). The success of native Chamorro in perpetuating vital aspects of their intangible cultural heritage (e.g., language, values, behavior, songs, stories) persisted into the twentieth century (Souder 1992:226–231; Thompson 1947:281–291) and reverberates to this day (Atienza and Coello 2012; Van Peenan 2008). Our use of the term "intangible cultural heritage" echoes dimensions of a statement by UNESCO: "Cultural heritage does not end at monuments and collections of objects. It also includes traditions or living expressions inherited from our ancestors and passed on to our descendants, such as oral traditions, performing arts, social practices, rituals, festive events, knowledge and practices concerning nature and the universe or the knowledge and skills to produce traditional crafts." Because UNESCO's use of this term is global in scope, it must be translated to local circumstances and cultural imperatives. In the Mariana Islands, we equate "intangible cultural heritage" with the concept of Kostumbren Chamorro, a term that encompasses the range of Chamorro practices, values, and customs (Perez Hattori 2004:15). To comprehend this phenomenon and the role of *länchos* in perpetuating intangible cultural heritage, we must situate Guam and the Mariana Islands in their historical context.

GUAM AND THE MARIANA ISLANDS IN HISTORICAL CONTEXT

In A.D. 1521 the fleet and crew of Fernando de Magallanes (Ferdinand Magellan in English) encountered Guam during his exploration for the Hispanic monarchy. Guam, the largest and southernmost island in the Marianas archipelago, was the first inhabited Pacific island witnessed by Europeans, and the Spanish contact period in the Mariana Islands began with Magallanes's visit. Seventeenth-century Spanish accounts of trade with the indigenous Chamorro underscore their strong desire for iron and other nonlocal goods (García 1683:112, 195; Pobre de Zamora [1598–1603], in Martínez 1997:418, 442; see also Quimby 2011). Early Spanish-Chamorro contact remained volatile, so trade was undertaken by raising and lowering baskets along ropes that connected European ships and Chamorro canoes. Spanish accounts charged that the Chamorro people were crafty traders and offered baskets with thin layers of rice atop coconut shell and sand. The theft of a small rowboat from one of Magallanes's ships also instigated a violent conflict when 40 men from the expedition landed, burned several houses and boats, and killed seven native Chamorro (Pigafetta [1525], in Riquer 1999:115–116). For these reasons, the Spanish name for the Mariana Islands was Islas de los Ladrones (Islands of the Thieves) (Russell 1998:13).

At contact, Chamorro lived in buildings atop megalithic pillars (*haligi*) and caps (*tasas*); today such structures are known as *latte*, and they were initially constructed no later than 1000 (Athens 2011; Carson 2012; Graves 1986). Unfortunately, however, detailed descriptions or drawings of them were not made by early European visitors (Russell 1998:221), yet the megalithic pillars are often preserved in the archaeological record. The construction of *latte* buildings began to wane sometime after Spain's formal claim to the Mariana Islands by Miguel López de Legazpi and the inception of the galleon trade in 1565 and especially after the establishment of a Jesuit mission in 1668 (Map 9.2).

The Manila galleons had arrived in Guam on a sporadic basis for 250 years, from 1565 to 1815, ending a few years before Mexico gained independence from Spain in 1821. The export of New World silver (from Potosí and other mines in the Americas) to China in exchange for spices, porcelains, silk, and other luxury goods was a source of great wealth for some Spanish elites. Galleon ships averaged 1,700–2,000 tons and were loaded with up to 1,000 passengers along with mail, supplies, and silver to trade for Oriental valuables once they arrived in the Philippines. Once

Map 9.2 Map of churches and villages in Guam about 1672 by Padre Alonso López (from the collection of the Richard F. Taitano Micronesian Area Research Center, University of Guam).

the galleon trade captured the attention of various world powers, such as the Dutch and the English, the Spanish constructed forts in Guam to protect their dominance of Pacific maritime trade. Guam also benefited from annual *situado payments* of silver and other goods from the Spanish Crown to its colonial governors, missionaries, and soldiers on the island.

Not all Chamorro welcomed the 1668 Jesuit mission, and violent conflict ensued for three decades until Spanish governors and their soldiers stifled indigenous opposition in 1698 (Hezel 2015; Rogers 1995:58–73; Russell 1998:300–315). Key to the success of the Spanish in dominating the native Chamorro was their forcible relocation into large villages on Guam and on the islands of Saipan and Rota. By 1730, however, most of the Mariana Islands north of Guam and Rota (e.g., Aguijan, Tinian, and Saipan) were depopulated until the nineteenth century (Rogers 1995:73). The implementation of this policy, known as the *reducción* (1697–1698), was instigated by the Spanish governor with the support of the military and Jesuit clergy. During the *reducción*, the colonial government, under the authority of Governor Quiroga y Losada, divided Guam into six administrative districts (*partidos*) (today known as Hagatña, Jinapsan, Pago, Agat, Umatac, and Inarajan) to facilitate Spanish rule. Each district centered on a *pueblo* (village) and a parish church. Governor-appointed *alcaldes* (mayors) ruled each district via a hierarchy of soldiers and converted Chamorro leaders whose families comprised the indigenous elite (Rogers 1995:64). Priests were also fundamental in the parish churches, but their policies and interests frequently conflicted with those of *alcaldes* and governors. While native Chamorro were not required to pay taxes, and an encomienda system was not "officially" installed on Guam, the natives were in practice obliged to work on the lands that belonged to the Crown, as well as those owned by the governors, the *alcaldes*, and the Jesuits. Such labor also sustained other agents of Spanish rule, including some (but not all) soldiers. Chamorro who managed to retain access to their ancestral lands worked them as *lånchos*, where they cultivated crops such as corn, sweet potatoes, rice, and fruit trees and raised pigs, chickens, cattle, and Asian water buffalo (Rogers 1995:75). As Chamorro were compelled to attend weekly religious services, many families practiced a dual-residence system whereby they worked their rural *lånchos* during the week and returned to their district village to attend weekend services and comply with civic obligations.

Spanish contact and colonialism also brought tragedy as the Chamorro population plummeted in the face of diseases that arrived with the Spanish galleons, mission clergy, and soldiers. This was especially true in Guam and the southern islands (e.g., Rota, Saipan), which experienced the earliest and most frequent contact with the Spanish. In contrast, some of the Mariana Islands to the north (e.g., Pagan and Sarigan) maintained their relatively high populations until they were relocated during implementation of the *reducción* (Athens 2011:328). An estimated 50,000–150,000 Chamorro resided in the Marianas at the onset of the Spanish mission, but their population decreased to 5,000 or less by the early eighteenth century (Underwood 1976:203). Over 50 Spanish governors ruled the Marianas during a period of 230 years, and most of those who ruled after 1744 resided on Guam in the Plaza de España, the governor's palace (Figure 9.1). Following the Spanish-American War in 1898, Spain surrendered control of Guam, and it became a colony of the United States along with the Philippines and Puerto Rico. Although Chamorro

Figure 9.1 Spanish governor's palace remnant at Plaza de España, Hagåtña, Guam (Wikimedia Commons, the free media repository).

society suffered astonishing impacts—particularly after the *reducción*—
their agency in perpetuating various traditions in the context of their
rural *lånchos* (Perez Hattori 2004:16) is a hallmark of their resilience.

PLACE MAKING, *LÅNCHOS*, AND THE MATERIALITY OF INTANGIBLE CULTURAL HERITAGE

The investigation of land use and place making in the Mariana Islands
offers an opportunity to understand the cultural imperatives that enabled
Chamorro to perpetuate their intangible cultural heritage after Spanish
contact and colonialism. The advent of *lånchos* following implementation
of the Spanish policy of the *reducción* was profoundly significant, and
their investigation through archaeology has recently intensified (Dixon
et al. 2020). Integrating documentary and archaeological perspectives
offers an approach to understanding *lånchos* that foregrounds Chamorro
agency in accommodating and resisting Spanish colonial efforts to establish religious and political hegemony between the seventeenth and
twentieth centuries.

DOCUMENTARY PERSPECTIVES

Early seventeenth-century Spanish documentary records offer insights
on the organization of land use and settlement prior to the *reducción* and
colonization of the Mariana Islands. In 1602 Juan Pobre de Zamora, a
Franciscan lay brother, spent several months on the Mariana island of
Rota, where he wrote an account of his visit (Pobre de Zamora [1598–
1603], in Martínez 1997; see also Driver 1983). His report reveals that
81 years after Magallanes's landfall on Guam, the Chamorro still practiced
their traditional lifeways (Rogers 1995:19–20). Precolonial Chamorro
subsistence included a combination of farming and foraging for marine
and terrestrial resources. Juan Pobre de Zamora observed that "they go
to the hillside or jungle to see their farm plots where every able-bodied
person goes to work" (Driver 1983:209). Farming and gardening in the
Mariana Islands included a variety of root and tree crops: various species of taro (*Colocasia* spp.), yams (*Dioscorea* spp.), breadfruit (*Artocarpus*
spp.), coconut (*Cocos nucifera*), banana (*Musa* sp.), pandanus (*Pandanus*
sp.), Federico palm (*Cycas circinalis*), sugarcane (*Saccharum officinarum*),

betel palm (*Areca catechu*), and betel pepper vines (*Piper betel*) (Russell 1998:167, Table 8). Although the scale of its production is unknown, a suite of evidence indicates that rice (*Oryza sativa*) was also cultivated in the Mariana Islands (but not elsewhere outside of Southeast Asia) before Spanish contact (Hunter-Anderson et al. 1995).

Juan Pobre's account implies that Chamorro subsistence at times included settings beyond their villages, along with a corresponding emphasis on marine resource consumption and coastal settlement during the early contact period. Documentary accounts by later visitors in the Mariana Islands, such as Louis de Freycinet (1825) in the early nineteenth century, assert that residents of coastal settlements (known as *matua*) were members of the highest class in Chamorro society, whereas inland residents (known as *mangatchang*) were in a lower class. However, Pobre's early account in 1602 fails to draw such a distinction. Consequently, documentary claims of class divisions among the Chamorro by Le Gobien, a French Jesuit who never visited Guam, might simply be a reflection of his own society (Peterson 2012:202).

In either case, it appears that most Chamorro did not practice a formal dual-residence system of land use until the *reducción* was institutionalized in the late seventeenth century. Only then, it seems, did many Chamorro use two residences, a coastal village and inland *låncho* where they could freely practice aspects of their intangible cultural heritage beyond the view of Spanish colonial authorities (see Thompson 1947:294–295). This dual-residence pattern, wherein individual families maintained parcels of property for gardening and farming, was documented again in the late eighteenth century (1771–1772) by Julien Crozet's voyage (Rochon 1891:92–93). By the late nineteenth century, land tenure on Guam had evolved as the church and elite Chamorro-Spanish mestizo (*manak'kilo*) families acquired large hacienda estates that sharply distinguished them from impoverished Chamorro (*manak'papa*), who typically lacked Spanish ancestry (Rogers 1995:75, 105). Although many Chamorro did not own property under Spanish rule and were compelled to serve as laborers, those who managed to retain or acquire their ancestral lands worked them as *lånchos*, where they engaged in subsistence farming and animal husbandry (Rogers 1995:75, 105). Moreover, Chamorro who operated *lånchos* were also well positioned to practice their intangible cultural heritage into the early twentieth century.

Following the Spanish-American War, for example, village health in-
spections by the U.S. Navy's insular patrol were thwarted by Chamorro
who hid at their inland *lånchos* (Perez Hattori 2004:30). Such locales
enabled them to perpetuate aspects of their intangible cultural heritage,
including (but not limited to) traditional herbal healing by *suruhanu*
(male healers) and *suruhana* (female healers). Other holdovers of intangible cultural heritage that persisted into the twentieth century included
betel nut chewing, stone throwing, folk tunes (Kantan Chamorrita), ceremonies (birth, death, betrothal, and marriage), some forms of social
organization, and certain attitudes and values, including respect for elders
at home and ancestral spirts at *lånchos* (Thompson 1947:281–291). Such
customs and behaviors were more freely exercised at rural *lånchos* in the
mid-twentieth century when regulations by the U.S. Navy impinged on
rights as simple as whistling or spitting in the streets (Thompson 1991:83).

ARCHAEOLOGICAL PERSPECTIVES

Archaeological evidence of land use in Guam's interior and elsewhere
in the Mariana Islands spanned several centuries, beginning by the first
millennium, through the *reducción*, and into the early nineteenth century
(Table 9.1). Resource extraction and settlement of Guam's inland settings are signaled by rockshelters, campsites, *latte* sets, charcoal-stained
mounds of soil, pottery scatters, stone and shell tools, stone piles, and
low cobble walls (Bulgrin 2006; Carson 2012; Craib 1994; Dixon et al.
2011; Dixon and Gilda 2011; Dixon and Schaefer 2014; Dixon et al. 2010;
Hunter-Anderson 2012; Moore 2005). The calibration of archaeology
and paleoenvironmental signatures of climate change, as well as episodic
events (droughts and high precipitation), hints that inland land use, resource extraction, and settlement varied across time on Guam (Hunter-
Anderson 2012:164–173) (see Table 9.1).

Latte sets are widely distributed in both inland and coastal settings
(Carson 2012; Kurashina 1991; Reinman 1977), and most of them exhibit
features and assemblages indicative of resource extraction and/or low-
intensity farming such as shifting cultivation (Table 9.2). Inland *latte*
sets rarely exhibit the evidence of long-term residential settlement that is
characteristic of coastal *latte* sites (Bayman et al. 2012; Craib 1986). The
abundance of artifact scatters throughout Guam's interior in those places

Table 9.1 Generalized model of inland settlement and land use on Guam

Time Period	Land-Use Pattern	Context	Selected Sources
Early *latte* (1000)	Early inland land use	Population growth	Moore 2005
Middle *latte* (1000–1400)	Acceleration of inland land use	Population growth	Hunter-Anderson 2012:164–166
Late *latte* to contact (1400–1521)	Contraction of inland land use	Climate change	Dixon et al. 2012:213–214; Hunter-Anderson 2012:167
Contact to the *reducción* (1521–1700)	Relocation to coastal district villages	European trade, introduced diseases, population decrease	Bayman et al. 2012
The *reducción* to the Spanish-American War (1700–1898)	Dual residence: inland *lånchos* and coastal district villages	Low population, *låncho* farming	Moore 2007; Dixon et al. 2016; Spoehr 1957:139–154

where *latte* sites are relatively scarce—such as the northern plateau—likely functioned as short-term *lånchos*. Residences at such locales were probably quite similar to the double "lean-to" structures (*sadigane*) of wood and palm fronds that were still used in rural Guam into the mid-twentieth century (Thompson 1947:282). Such structures are not easily detected in the archaeological record, yet careful fieldwork could enhance their documentation. Indeed, local cobble platforms of square and rectangular shapes have been noted on the surface at some pre–World War II *lånchos* in North Finegayan (Dixon et al. 2016; see Table 9.2); such features could have served as rough flooring for thatched structures that were temporary in nature. A correlation between such *lånchos* and deeper soil settings has also been documented (Dixon et al. 2020) at abandoned concrete water cisterns, stone or brick above-ground ovens (*hotno*), and glass, porcelain, or metal artifacts, occasionally with a metate or possible mano fragment (Dixon et al. 2016; see Table 9.2).

Although the so-called Lost River Village in inland southern Guam includes more than 33 *latte* sets (Table 9.2), evidence of long-term residential settlement is lacking (in all but one case): there are no burials, and the depth

Table 9.2 Information on selected inland archaeological sites on Guam that were occupied before, during, and/or after the *reducción*

Site Name / #	Topographic Setting	Features	Material Culture	Period and Time Span	Source
South Finegayan, 66-08-0141	Northern Plateau	Latte, rock ovens, ash and charcoal midden	Ceramics, adze fragments, marine shell, slingstone	*Latte* to postcontact, 1295–1810	Dixon et al. 2020
Lost River Village	Southern Uplands	33+ *latte*, marine shell midden	Scatters of ceramic, lithic, and ground stone	*Latte* to postcontact (?), 690–1650	Dixon and Gilda 2011
M221	Southern Uplands (Manenggon Hills)	2 *latte*, hearth, cooking and disposal mound	Ceramics, Spanish pottery, Ming porcelains, metal, ground stone, adzes, chipped stone, worked marine shell and beads	Late *latte* period to postcontact, 1400–1650 (*latte* no. 2), 1200–1400 (*latte* no. 1)	Craib 1994
M201	Southern Uplands (Manenggon Hills)	3 plant cultivation pits	Ceramic scatter, yam (*Dioscorea*) thorns, coconut shell	Early *latte* period, 986–1210	Moore 2005
66-08-1350, Feature 1	North Finegayan (Dededo)	Concrete water cistern	Porcelain, bottle glass, metal, possible stone mano	Historic, 1700–1945	Dixon et al. 2016

66-08-2303, Feature 24	North Fine-gayan (Magua)	Push pile within bamboo grove and soil-filled depression	Porcelain, stoneware, white ware, bottle glass, metal blades, stovetop lid, tin roofing, 50-gallon drum for water, handmade brick, nails, carpentry tools, toy gun, pig and deer bone, Japanese canteen lid, U.S. 50-caliber clip, *latte* period ceramics and lithics	*Latte* period to historic, 1400–1945	Dixon et al. 2016
66-08-2305, Feature 6	North Fine-gayan (Potts Junction)	"Spanish" oven (*borno*), cobble platform	Japanese beer and sake bottles on the surface, porcelain, tiles, hand-made metal ash shovel	Historic, 1700 to 1945	Dixon et al. 2016
66-09-2689, Feature 5	Talofofo (Acapulco)	*Latte* sets and late 1800 artifacts	Blue shell edge, red sponge ware, porcelain, while ware, green bottle base pontil, metal mattock head, *latte* period ceramics and lithics	Late *latte* period to historic, 1400 to 1945	Dixon et al. 2014

and density of midden are relatively limited (Dixon and Gilda 2011:76). Still, archaeological evidence that Guam's southern interior was used extensively before contact is abundant (Dye and Cleghorn 1990), even if such use may not have matched the intensity of coastal settlement with respect to the number of *latte* sets. However, it is likely that thatched houses atop wood piles were constructed at some inland locales where stone for making *latte* pillars (*haligi*) was lacking or otherwise difficult to quarry. Notably, thatched houses atop wood piles (rather than stone piles) were still used in Guam's villages as late as the 1920s (Dixon and Schaefer 2014; Flores 2011:74; Laguana et al. 2012:85, 88, 107; Montón Subías 2019: 414; Thompson 1940:462, 1947:282). Moreover, the layout and ground plan of such rural settlements sometimes duplicated certain aspects of ancient *latte* sites such as paralleling coastlines or streams (Thompson 1947:282). The construction of relatively formal streets, however, was likely a Spanish introduction.

Confirmation that inland settings were used for several centuries prior to Spanish contact and colonialism is a key finding: it underscores the potential of historical memory in perpetuating intangible cultural heritage in Chamorro society at *låncho* settlements following the *reducción* in the late eighteenth century. Inland land use is especially well-documented in northern Guam, where a *latte* residential site with cooking features and plant microfossils (pollen, phytoliths, starch residues) from well-dated contexts signals farming and resource extraction both before and during the *reducción* (Dixon et al. 2020). Economic plants that were cultivated included *pandanus*, coconut, and taro (Dixon et al. 2020). This site is a striking example of a locale where inland farming and resource extraction were practiced in proximity to a standing *latte* set that witnessed use prior to contact, was abandoned, and was later revitalized into a Chamorro *låncho* during the colonial period.

Another apparent *låncho* site on Guam is the *latte* site of Pulantat (MaGYo-1 site designation). It includes no fewer than 34 *latte* sets in the south-central part of the island along the banks of two small streams (Reinman 1977:49). Although its midden debris is relatively limited, it includes stone mortars (*lusong*) and scattered pottery and stone tools (Reinman 1977:49–51, 153–154). Radiocarbon dates on excavated charcoal yielded postcontact dates ranging from 1710 to 1770 (Reinman 1977:51). Together, these late radiocarbon dates and the recovery of two porcelain sherds hint that this *latte* site was established as a *låncho* residence following the advent of the *reducción*. Intriguingly, in the mid-twentieth century this site was regarded with "a superstitious reverence on the part of the natives . . . where a large stone is said to be growing" (Osborne 1947:34). This observation illustrates that Chamorro belief in *taotaomo'na* (ancestral spirits) in places that their families once lived or farmed persisted more than four centuries after contact with Europeans, as it does to this day in the twenty-first century. Cultural memory substantiates Chamorro claims to ancestral lands that were utilized as *lånchos* following the *reducción*.

Guam's landscape harbored many other Spanish-period *lånchos*, and they await recognition and detailed attention by archaeologists. For example, three inland sites in Geuss Valley (MaGMe-9 to MaGMe-11) (Reinman n.d.:41) with an abundance of "Spanish ware" ceramics and ground stone tools warrant intensive archaeological investigation to further ascertain the materiality of *lånchos*. *Latte* sets with similar late nineteenth-century assemblages have been identified in a locale named Acapulco in the middle of the Talofofo drainage (Dixon et al. 2014; see Table 9.2). Such places offered traditionally sanctified settings where Chamorro could practice and perpetuate vital dimensions of their intangible cultural heritage beyond the view of Spanish colonial authorities.

DISCUSSION AND CONCLUSIONS

Together, documentary sources and archaeological materials offer an integrated perspective on the ancient history of land use and how it presaged the perpetuation of intangible cultural heritage in Chamorro society. Somewhat ironically, it was the *materiality* of land use at colonial period *lånchos* that facilitated the persistence of intangible cultural heritage that first crystallized by 1000 and perhaps even earlier. Farming and resource extraction at *lånchos* and other rural locales by some (if not all) Chamorro provided a degree of isolation that freed them to more easily behave and communicate how they desired, beyond the view of their colonizers (Perez Hattori 2004:16). They could enact precolonial customs and share traditional stories that honored the spirits of their ancestors (*taotaomo'na*).

That farming and resource extraction persisted at *lånchos* after the Spanish colonial period and into the early twentieth century should not be surprising. Such practices are corroborated by José R. Palomo's

(1992) childhood recollections of resource extraction on his family's farm on the inland plateau of northern Guam. Their *låncho* offered deer and *fanihi* (fruit bat) along with plant materials and foods including *fadang* (*Cycas cirinalis*), *Hibiscus tiliaceus* bark, seeds of *Artocarpus mariannensis* (*lemmai*), and yams (*dagu*) (cited in Dixon et al. 2012:218). Census data in Guam reveal that 63 percent of Chamorro males in 1930 worked as farmers (Thompson 1947:352–353, Table 6). Again, the relative isolation of Chamorro farmers freed them to enact customary forms of behavior beyond the view of naval administrators. Perhaps ironically, this was only 13 years after the U.S. colonial governor sought to relocate Chamorro away from their clustered villages and onto their dispersed *lånchos* as a measure to improve sanitation and health conditions (Perez Hattori 2004:34).

Tragically, *lånchos* also served as refuges for Chamorro when they were colonized by the Japanese in the early 1940s (Rodgers 1995:162) and shortly thereafter when they suffered the violence of World War II. Inland (and even coastal) *lånchos* are still held by some families on Guam and elsewhere in the Mariana Islands, and such places serve as scenes for family events and activities (Bevacqua 2019). Similarly, use of plants for traditional medicine is still practiced by folk healers, *suruhanas* (female) and *suruhanus* (male). Other examples of intangible cultural heritage include various customs such as *chenchule'* (expected contribution), *ayuda* (helping and sharing), and *inafa'maolek* (being present at an event or expressing support) (Perez Hattori 2004; Na' Puti and Rohrer 2017) and would have also been practiced among neighbors in rural *lånchos*. These instances of intangible cultural heritage are only a few of many that persisted in Chamorro society during and after Spanish contact and colonialism, and ongoing research promises to further illuminate this phenomenon (see Montón-Subías et al. 2018).

Cultural memory of inland land use after the *reducción* and resettlement in coastal villages ensured the perpetuation of intangible cultural heritage at rural *lånchos* beyond the reach of surveillance by Spanish authorities and subsequent colonial powers. In so doing, Chamorro charted a path that enabled them to both accommodate and resist hegemonic control of their destiny by Spanish authorities and subsequent colonial powers. While this particular example of place making is unique in some respects, it also echoes other strategies of accommodation and resistance that were devised by native peoples elsewhere in Oceania and beyond.

REFERENCES

Athens, J. Stephen. 2011. "*Latte* Period Occupation on Pagan and Sarigan, Northern Mariana Islands." *Journal of Island and Coastal Archaeology* 6:314–330.

Atienza, David, and Alexandre Coello. 2012. "Death Rituals and Identity in Contemporary Guam (Mariana Islands)." *Journal of Pacific History* 47(4): 459–473.

Bayman, James M. 2008. "Technological Change and the Archaeology of Emergent Colonialism in the Kingdom of Hawai'i." *International Journal of Historical Archaeology* 13:127–157.

———. 2017. "'Great Powers' in the Pacific Islands: A Calibrated Comparison of Spanish and Anglo-American Colonialism." In *Historical Archaeology of Early Modern Spanish Colonialism*, edited by Maria Cruz Berrocal and Cheng-hwa Tsang, 1:123–145. Gainesville: University Press of Florida.

Bayman, James, Hiro Kurashina, Mike Carson, John Peterson, David Doig, and Jane Drengson. 2012. "Household Economy and Gendered Labor in the 17th Century A.D. on Guam." *Journal of Field Archaeology* 37(4): 259–269.

Bayman, James, and John Peterson. 2016. "Spanish Colonial History and Archaeology in the Mariana Islands: Echos from the Western Pacific." In *Archaeologies of Early Modern Spanish Colonialism*, edited by Sandra Monton-Subias, Maria Cruz Berrocal, and Apen Ruiz Martinez, 229–252. New York: Springer International Publishing.

Bevacqua, Michael L. 2019. "*Låncho*: Ranch." Guampedia.com. https://www.guampedia.com/lancho-ranch/.

Bulgrin, Lon. 2006. "'Fina'okso Antigo': Pre-contact Soil Mounds in the Interior of Rota." *Micronesian Journal of the Humanities and Social Sciences* 5(1/2): 31–41.

Carson, Mike. 2012. "An Overview of *Latte* Period Archaeology." *Micronesia* 42:1–79.

Chaunu, P. 1960. *Les Philippines et le Pacifique des Ibériques: XVIe, XVIIe, XVIIIe siècles*. Paris: S.E.V.P.E.N.

Craib, John. 1986. "Casa de los Antiguos: Social Differentiation in Protohistoric Chamorro Society." PhD diss., University of Sydney.

———. 1994. "Archaeological Investigations of an Inland Latte Site (M221) at Manenggon Hills, Yona, Guam." Report on file at Micronesian Archaeological Research Services, Mangilao.

Cruz Berrocal, Maria, and Cheng-hwa Tsang. 2017. Introduction to *Historical Archaeology of Early Modern Colonialism in Asia-Pacific: The Southwest Pacific and Oceanian Regions*, edited by Maria Cruz Berrocal and Cheng-hwa Tsang, 1–9. Gainesville: University Press of Florida.

Dixon, Boyd, Huw Bartow, James Coil, William Dickinson, Gail Murakami, and Jerome Ward. 2011. "Recognizing Inland Expansion of Latte Period Agriculture from Multi-disciplinary Data on Tinian, Commonwealth of the Northern Mariana Islands." *Journal of Island & Coastal Archaeology* 6(3): 375–397.

Dixon, Boyd, and Laura Gilda. 2011. "A Comparison of an Inland Latte Period Community to Coastal Settlement Patterns Observed on Southern Guam." *People and Culture of Oceania* 27:65–86.

Dixon, Boyd, Laura Gilda, and Tina Mangieri. 2013. "Archaeological Identification of Stone Fish Weirs Mentioned to Freycinet in 1819 on the Island of Guam." *Journal of Pacific History* 48(4): 349–368.

Dixon, Boyd, Andrea Jalandoni, and Cacilie Craft. 2017. "The Archaeological Remains of Early Modern Spanish Colonialism on Guam and Their Implications." In *Historical and Archaeological Perspectives on Early Modern Colonialism in Asia-Pacific and the Pacific*, edited by Maria Cruz Berrocal and Cheng-hwa Tsang, 1:195–218. Gainesville: University Press of Florida.

Dixon, Boyd, Andrea Jalandoni, Erik Lash, and Richard Schaefer. 2014. *Proposed Guam and CNMI Military Relocation 2012 Roadmap Adjustments SEIS. Volume I: Potential Indirect Impact Area In-Fill Cultural Resources Study Narrative.* Cardno, Guam.

Dixon, Boyd, and Richard Schaefer. 2014. "Reconstructing Cultural Landscapes for the Latte Period Settlement of Ritidian: A Hypothetical Model in Northern Guam." *British Archaeological Review International Series* 2, 663:64–73.

Dixon, Boyd, Richard Schaefer, and Todd McCurdy. 2010. "Traditional Farming Innovations during the Spanish and Philippine Contact Period on Northern Guam." *Philippine Quarterly of Culture & Society* 38(4): 291–321.

Dixon, Boyd, Samuel Walker, Mohammad Golabi, and Harley Manner. 2012. "Two Probable Latte Period Agricultural Sites in Northern Guam: Their Plants, Soils, and Interpretations." *Micronesica*, Supplement 8, 42(1/2): 216–266.

Dixon, Boyd, Danny Welch, and Lon Bulgrin. 2020. "Archaeological Roots of Traditional Land Use and Resistance to Spanish Colonial Engagement on Guam." *Asian Perspectives* (in press).

Dixon, Boyd, Danny Welch, Terry Rudolph, and Isla Nelson. 2016. *Archaeological Data Recovery in Support of the J-001B Utilities and Site Improvements at Naval Base Guam Telecommunications Site, Guam.* Cardno, Guam.

Driver, Marjorie. 1983. "Fray Juan Pobre de Zamora and His Account of the Mariana Islands." *Journal of Pacific History* 18:198–216.

Dye, Tom, and Paul Cleghorn. 1990. "Pre-contact Use of the Interior of Southern Guam: Recent Advances in Micronesian Archaeology." *Micronesica* Supplement 2:261–274.

Flexner, James L. 2014. "Historical Archaeology, Contact, and Colonialism." *Journal of Archaeological Research* 22:43–87.

Flores, J. 2011. *Estorian Inalahan: History of a Spanish-Era Village in Guam.* Hagåtña: Irensia.

Freycinet, Luis Claude de. 1825. "Voyage autour du monde, entrepris par ordre du roi: . . . Exécuté sur les corvettes . . . l'uranie et la physicienne, pendant les années 1817, 1818, 1819 et 1820; publié sous les auspices de . . . le comte Corbière." Pour la partie historique et les science, Imprimerie royale.

García, F. 1683. *Vida y martirio del venerable padre Diego Luis de San Vitores.* Madrid: Imprenta de Juan García Infanzón.

Giraldez, A. 2015. *The Age of Trade: The Manila Galleons and the Dawn of the Global Economy.* London: Rowman & Littlefield.

Graves, Michael. 1986. "Organization and Differentiation within Late Precontact Ranked Social Units, Mariana Islands, Western Pacific." *Journal of Field Archaeology* 13:139–154.

Perez Hattori, Anne. 2004. *Colonial Dis-ease: US Navy Health Policies and the Chamorros of Guam, 1898–1941.* Pacific Islands Monograph Series 19. Honolulu: University of Hawai'i Press.

Hezel, Francis. 1989. *From Conquest to Colonization: Spain in the Mariana Islands 1690 to 1740.* Saipan: Division of Historic Preservation.

———. 2015. *When Cultures Clash: Revisiting the Spanish-Chamorro Wars.* Saipan: Northern Marianas Humanities Council.

Hunter-Anderson, Rosalind L. 2012. "Running to Stay in Place: An Adaptive Escalation Model for the Latte Period." *Micronesica* 42:148–182.

Hunter-Anderson, Rosalind L., Gillian B. Thompson, and Darlene R. Moore. 1995. "Rice as a Prehistoric Valuable in the Mariana Islands, Micronesia." *Asian Perspectives* 34:68–89.

Kurashina, Hiro. 1991. "Prehistoric Settlement Patterns on Guam." *Journal of the Pacific Society* 14(2):1–18.

Laguana, Andrew, Hiro Kurashina, Mike T. Carson, John A. Peterson, James M. Bayman, Todd Ames, Rebecca A. Stephenson, John Aguon, and Ir. D. K. Harya Putra. 2012. "Estorian i Latte: A Story of Latte." *Micronesica* 42(1/2): 80–120.

Martínez Perez, Jesus. 1997. *Fray Juan Pobre de Zamora: Historia de la pérdida y descubrimiento del galeón* San Felipe. Ávila: Diputación Provincial de Ávila.

Montón-Subías, Sandra. 2019. "Gender, Missions, and Maintenance Activities in the Early Modern Globalization: Guam 1668–98." *International Journal of Historical Archaeology* 23:404–429.

Montón-Subías, Sandra, James Bayman, and Natalia Moragas. 2018. "Arqueología del colonialismo español en la Micronesia: Guam y las poblaciones Chamorras." In *Repensar el colonialismo: Iberia, de colonia a potencia colonial,* edited by Beatriz Marín-Aguilera, 303–336. Madrid: JAS.

Moore, Darlene. 2005. "Archaeological Evidence of a Pre-contact Farming Technique on Guam." *Micronesica* 38(1): 93–120.

———. 2007. "Latte Period and Spanish Period Archaeology at Old Pago Guam." Report prepared for Richard Untalan and Guam Preservation Trust. Micronesian Archaeological Research Service, Mangilao. Report on file at Guam Preservation Trust.

Na'Puti, Tiara, and Judy Rohrer. 2017. "Pacific Moves beyond Colonialism: A Conversation from Hawai'i y Guåhan." *Feminist Studies* 43(3): 537–547.

Osborne, Douglas. 1947. "Chamorro Archaeology." Manuscript on file at Hamilton Library, University of Hawai'i at Mānoa, Honolulu.

Palomo, José R. 1992. *Recollections of Olden Days*. MARC Educational Series no. 13. Mangilao: Micronesian Area Research Center, University of Guam.

Peterson, John. 2012. "Latte Villages in Guam and the Marianas: Monumentality or Monumenterity?" *Micronesica* 42:183–208.

Quimby, Frank. 2011. "The Hierro Commerce: Culture Contact, Appropriation and Colonial Entanglement." *Journal of Pacific History* 46(1): 1–26.

Reinman, Fred M. 1977. *An Archaeological Survey and Preliminary Test Excavations on the Island of Guam, Mariana Islands, 1965–1966*. Miscellaneous Publications no. 1. Mangilao: Micronesian Area Research Center, University of Guam.

———. n.d. "Notes on an Archaeological Survey of Guam, Mariana Islands, 1965–66." Preliminary report to the National Science Foundation, Grant #65-662. On file at the Hamilton Library, University of Hawai'i at Mānoa, Honolulu.

Riquer, Isabel de. 1999. *Antonio Pigafetta: El primer viaje alrededor del mundo: Relato de la expedición de Magallanes y Elcano*. Barcelona: Ediciones B.

Rochon, Abbé Alexis Marie de. 1891. *Crozet's Voyage to Tasmania, New Zealand, the Ladrone Islands, and the Philippines in the Years 1771–1772*. Translated by H. Ling Roth. London: Truslove & Shirley.

Rogers, Robert. 1995. *Destiny's Landfall: A History of Guam*. Honolulu: University of Hawai'i Press.

Russell, Scott. 1998. *Tiempon I Manomofo'ona: Ancient Chamorro Culture and History of the Northern Marianas Islands*. Micronesian Archaeological Survey Report 32. CNMI Division of Historic Preservation, Saipan.

Schurz, William L. 1939. *The Manila Galleon*. New York: E. P. Dutton & Co.

Souder, Laura M. Torres. 1992. *Daughters of the Island: Contemporary Chamorro Women Organizers on Guam*. MARC Monograph Series no. 1. Lanham: University Press of America.

Spate, O. 1979. *The Spanish Lake*. Minneapolis: University of Minnesota Press.

Spoehr, Alexander. 1957. *Marianas Prehistory: Archaeological Survey and Excavations on Saipan, Tinian, and Rota*. Fieldiana: Anthropology 48. Chicago: Field Museum of Natural History.

Stannard, David E. 1989. *Before the Horror: The Population of Hawai'i on the Eve of Western Contact*. Honolulu: Social Science Research Institute, University of Hawai'i at Mānoa.

Thompson, Laura. 1940. "The Function of Latte in the Marianas." *Journal of the Polynesian Society* 49(195): 449–465.

———. 1947. *Guam and Its People*. Rev. 3rd ed. Princeton: Princeton University Press.

———. 1991. *Beyond the Dream: A Search for Meaning.* MARC Monograph Series no. 2. Mangilao: Micronesian Area Research Center, University of Guam.

Underwood, Jane H. 1976. "The Native Origins of the Neo-Chamorros of the Mariana Islands." *Micronesica* 12(2): 203–209.

United Nations Educational, Scientific and Cultural Organization (UNESCO). 2019. *What Is Intangible Cultural Heritage?* https://ich.unesco.org/en/what-is -intangible-heritage-00003.

Van Peenan, Mavis. 2008. *Chamorro Legends on the Island of Guam.* Mangilao: Micronesian Area Research Center, University of Guam.

10

Contested Geographies

Place-Making Strategies among the Indigenous Groups of South Texas and Northeastern Mexico

Steve A. Tomka

The borderland between northeastern Mexico and Texas has been a contested place for hundreds, if not thousands, of years. This chapter describes the strategies employed by indigenous groups to gain access to contested hunting territories, seek relevance in the pluralistic social space of the missions, and claim for themselves a small corner of the symbolic world of the afterlife. During Late Prehistoric times (750–1750), interband relationships forged through exogamous and patrilocal marriage practices served to gain access to otherwise inaccessible hunting territories. These same social strategies were later used to carve out contested social spaces within the pluralistic context of the missions. In contrast, in the face of the hostility of the Catholic Church of the times toward indigenous ceremonial practices, neophytes sought to blend symbolic place-holders of their own into the religious lexicon of the church. Through these actions and by grafting elements of their daily and ceremonial lives (e.g., decorated shell) onto church-sanctioned religious items, indigenous groups sought to secure space within the symbolic realms of the church even in the afterlife. The theme of this chapter echoes patterns described by other contributors to this volume that exemplify the ingenuity of cultural practices employed by indigenous groups to shape and control their geographic (see Chapter 5), social, and spiritual landscapes (see Chapters 4 and 8).

ACCESSING HUNTING GROUNDS

Around 1300 a significant shift took place in climatic conditions across much of the northern hemisphere. This shift, which lasted until well into the 1800s, came to be known as the Little Ice Age (Foster 2012). As a result, by the mid-fifteenth century, bison populations began to increase throughout the southern plains (Bozell 1995; Dillehay 1974:184). Historic accounts (Weniger 1997) suggest that once bison herds reached the Llano Estacado they descended onto the prairies along the Red, Brazos, and Colorado River corridors (Huebner 1991). Occasionally they continued to the southern tip of the Edwards Plateau, descended the escarpment, and crossed the Rio Grande.

As early as the mid-sixteenth century, indigenous groups in Nueva Vizcaya, Coahuila, and Nuevo León systematically hunted bison without ever having to cross the Rio Grande (Turpin 1987). Not only did bison become their staple food source, but much of their material culture came to reflect their dedication to follow the buffalo, including the use of hides for housing, clothing and shoes, and even shields (Portillo 1886).

By the turn of the century, however, the number of buffalo had declined, and their migrations rarely reached the Rio Grande (Espinosa 1964:764). More common in the Spanish diaries of the period were mentions of herds being seen on the Edwards Plateau, the northern reaches of South Texas, and the Coastal Plains (Foster 1995). During the next two hundred years and continuing well into the mid-eighteenth century, bison herds were primarily distributed throughout the grasslands that spanned the area between the Trinity and San Antonio Rivers.

In response, some indigenous groups from northeastern Mexico traveled north onto the Edwards Plateau only to descend along east-flowing streams onto the Blackland Prairie, lying below the escarpment. Here, where water and grasslands were abundant, bison stretched as far as the eye could see. Systematic reviews and summaries of Spanish entradas indicate that during the eighteenth century six out of ten groups living in northeastern Mexico traveled this 200-mile distance in hopes of being rewarded with meat and hides for buffalo robes (Tomka 2016). Other groups took a more easterly route, traveling to the Coastal Prairies and Plains, where expanses of bluestem attracted large bison herds across the landscape, which was dotted with live oak motts.

However, the social landscapes of South Texas, the nearby Coastal Plains, and the Blackland Prairie were already crowded with local groups (Newcomb 1961). Five clusters of bands occupied distinct parts of these regions (Map 10.1). The first of these, the Karankawa cultural entity, consisted of the Karankawa proper, the Copane, Cuxane, Coapite, and perhaps Coco. These five groups, related by language and culture (Ricklis

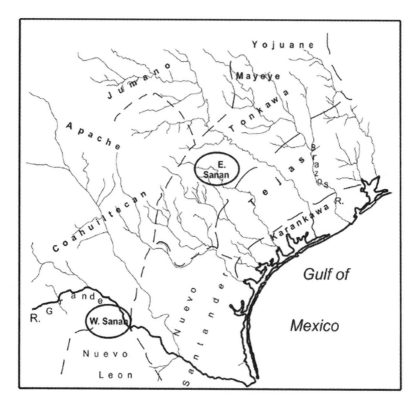

Map 10.1 Regions of Texas and northeastern Mexico mentioned in the text.

1996:4), occupied the shores and off-shore islands of the Texas Gulf Coast (Johnson and Campbell 1992:207). They occasionally traveled in-land along river valleys and engaged in bison hunting at some distance from their usual coastal adobes (Ricklis 1996:101–110). The Sanan groups consisted of western (four nations) and eastern (11 nations) branches (Johnson and Campbell 1992). The western Sanan groups occupied northeastern Coahuila, northwestern Nuevo León, and the middle Rio Grande drainage. The eastern branch controlled territories across the Central Coastal Plains between the Guadalupe and Colorado Rivers (Johnson and Campbell 1992:207). During the mid-eighteenth century, Tonkawa groups occupied portions of Central Texas between the Brazos and Trinity Rivers (Newcomb and Campbell 2001). Groups that later became affiliated with the Tonkawa (Mayeye, Yojuane, and Ervipiame

[Hierbipiame]) were in South Texas and northeastern Mexico as early as the 1670s (Bolton 1910). The Tejas social field consisted of numerous groups that were part of an extensive exchange network that fostered both social and political alliances, aggregated at times to form large communal hunting parties, and also shared a highly efficient bison procurement and processing toolkit. Groups that were members of this alliance occupied a large portion of Central Texas and extended into the Coastal Plains to the southeast (Arnn 2012) and the northern reaches of the South Texas brush country.

Given this already crowded social landscape, accessing the highly coveted bison herds presented significant logistical and social challenges to hunter-gatherers living south of the Rio Grande. This was exacerbated by the highly territorial nature of most of these groups. Entering a territory that belonged to another nation or tribe without permission was a risky proposition that typically led to intergroup conflicts and war (Arlegui 1851:138, 147–148; Portillo 1886:161–171; Salinas 2009; Wade 2003).

In 1674, after having questioned the captains of numerous Indian nations that lived south of the Rio Grande, Antonio Balcarcel Rivadeneira Sotomayor provided an *informe* to the Audiencia de Guadalajara summarizing what he learned from the proceedings. He reported that wars between groups often occurred because "it is forbidden to cross the lands of others not even to step on their trails, nor to take the tunas and roots that are found on the sides of the trails, over the bison there are big deaths." He further stated that the indigenous groups he interviewed were often engaged in bloody conflicts with local groups: "For the bison it is necessary to cross the Rio del Norte, where it is necessary to carry out battles and vengeances" (Portillo 1886:160–171).

In response to the potential for conflict in this crowded social landscape, the indigenous groups of northeastern Mexico devised a variety of approaches, each built on distinct social networks characterized by different regional interaction spheres, population movements, and settlement patterns. The first approach, direct access to distant hunting grounds, relied on sheer numbers of warriors to keep enemies at bay. One of the earliest descriptions of such a hunt comes from accounts of the Castaño de Sosa expedition of 1590 (Carter 2009; Hammond and Rey 1966; Schroeder and Matson 1965). During the trip, the expedition encountered Jumano bison hunters north of the confluence of the Pecos

River and the Rio Grande. The hunts, orchestrated in the lower Pecos and Devils River region on the southern tip of the Edwards Plateau, appeared to have taken place during the winter (Turpin 1987:425). In contrast, the Jumano and other groups from central and northwestern Coahuila, including the Bobole, Yorica, Hape, Guiquisale, Geniocane, Terocodame, Bibit, Pinanaca, Manos Prietas, Xaeser, and Bocora, also participated in summer and fall bison hunts near the headwaters of the San Marcos River (Hatcher 1932). Hunting parties returned south of the Rio Grande as the cold weather set in.

Most of these aforementioned indigenous groups were part of two of the four confederacies (Bolton 1959:304), the Guiquisale and Bobole. The Guiquisale Confederacy was composed of 24 nations, and the Bobole included 13 nations, 16 nations were part of the Catujano, and another 9 nations formed the final confederacy. Historical accounts (Griffen 1969; Hatcher 1932:59; Leutenegger 1981:50; Portillo 1886:71–72, 161–171; Steck 1932:11–12; Wade 2003:9) and Spanish entradas show that 26 (42 percent) of these 62 nations pursued bison on the Edwards Plateau and nearby (Tomka 2016).

Overall, nearly half of the nations that lived along the upper-middle section of the Rio Grande and were members of one of the four confederacies also engaged in the pursuit of bison on and off the Edwards Plateau. In effect, membership in these confederacies served multiple functions, including harassing the Spanish settlers of the region, protecting each other from Apache and Comanche raiders, and controlling access to bison-hunting territories located north of the Rio Grande (Wade 2003).

The second approach relied on hunter-gatherers from northeastern Mexico and South Texas coalescing into multination encampments that provided greater hunting opportunities and communal defense, if needed. These large multination hunting parties often consisted of indigenous groups with homelands in northeastern Mexico accompanied by groups who resided in South Texas and the Central Coastal Plains.

A hint of how these encampments may have been organized comes from the deposition provided by don Lorenzo, an Ervipiame, interviewed in 1688 in the Presidio San Fernando de Coahuila by Alonsó de León, captain and governor of the province of Coahuila and Texas. Lorenzo stated that there were only a few people left of his community at the time of León's visit because the other members of his nation were at the time (July) gathered with the Tejas; they planned to return to Coahuila during the cold weather (Portillo 1886:237–238). The Ervipiame were allies of the Tejas and were visiting them to hunt bison in the province. The presence of entire families rather than male-dominated specialized hunting parties enhanced the chances that new social bonds would be formed between friendly nations and further strengthened between old friends.

The nature and depth of these social bonds were described by the members of these groups themselves under questioning by Fray Mariano Francisco de los Dolores y Viana. In 1762, when he visited the Mayeye and Yojuane and asked the captains of those nations if they would travel and settle into a mission built for them in the upper San Antonio River basin, they replied that "they could not go far from their relatives, nor leave the lands that are in the country of the Tejas, because of the commerce they conduct with them, which is the way they acquire many necessary things, nor could they separate from the neighboring nations and allies, because they are mixed with them, and married with each other" (Arricivita 1792:323).

An extreme example of these multination encampments may be the *ranchería grande* sites noted by Spanish explorers in the province of Texas. The Spanish referred to any large multiethnic encampments of indigenous groups by this term. One such *ranchería* was located just west of the crossing of the Brazos River in east-central Texas (Foster 1995:118). It had been in existence since 1690 and continued to be used well into the 1760s (José Antonio de Alzate y Ramirez map, 1768). At the time of Domingo Ramón's visit in 1716, six nations from south of the Rio Grande (Ervipiame, Ticmamara, Mesquite, Mixcale, Xarame, and Sijame) were present, as were the local Asinai, Cantone, Pabmaya, and Payaya nations. The inhabitants were eager to trade buffalo hides with the Spaniards (Foik 1933:16). The membership of these *rancherías* varied over time. In 1718, when the Alarcón expedition encountered the *ranchería*, the Indian nations included the Sana, Emet, Toho, Mayeye, Huyugan, and Curmicai (Hoffmann 1935:69). In 1721, when Margués the Aguayo visited the *ranchería*, in addition to the aforementioned groups, the members of the Viday and Agdoca nations also were part of the encampment (Forrestal

1935:35). The residents in these encampments included not only warriors but also women and children (Foik 1933).

Over time, the nations in the *ranchería* consisted of at least three distinct language groups, including Tonkawa (Tonkawa proper), possible Tonkawa (Yojuane and Mayeye), Coahuitecan (Hierbipiame), and Bidai (Bidai proper, Orcoquisa, and Deadose) (Bolton 1914:365). The bulk of the groups were from Central and South-Central Texas groups. Joining them were several Coahuiltecan groups.

To explore the characteristics of these multination encampments, I consulted eleven entradas to extract descriptions of the multination encampments they encountered north of the Rio Grande. These entradas included (1) the Bosque de Larios expedition of 1675; (2) Governor Alonso de León's 1689 expedition; (3) Governor Alonso de León's 1690 expedition; (4) Governor Domingo Terán de los Rios's expedition between 1691 and 1692; (5) Governor Gregorio Salinas Varona's expedition of 1693; (6) the Espinosa expedition of 1707; (7) the Espinosa, Olivares, and Aguire expedition of 1709; (8) the Ramón and Espinosa expedition of 1716; (9) the Alarcón expedition of 1718; (10) the Rubi expedition of 1767; and (11) the Solís expedition of 1768. The principal reference I consulted for these accounts is William Foster (1995) and the primary references listed within.

A total of 31 multination encampments were encountered during these entradas, and 143 named indigenous bands were identified by the diarists. The smallest camps included just two groups and consisted of a couple of dozen individuals, while the largest camps included 10 ($n =$ 2 camps) and 13 groups, respectively, and were estimated to consist of between 1,000 and 3,000 individuals. Two of the three encampments with 10 or more bands included members of confederacies, independent bands, and bands that were members of the Tejas social field. Of these 143 groups, 62.2 percent were groups with homelands found south of the Rio Grande; the remaining 37.8 percent resided north of the river. Of the 31 encampments, nearly one-third ($n = 10$, 32.2 percent) were camps in which local bands outnumbered nonlocal bands. There were only three (9.7 percent) encampments where the number of local and nonlocal bands was even. In 18 of 31 camps (58.1 percent), the number of nonlocal groups outnumbered the local groups.

As indicated by the members of these encampments themselves, the shared occupation of these multination encampments was based on long-established relationships forged on the basis of intermarriages between groups. The fact that the populations that inhabited these encampments consisted of entire families rather than specialized hunting parties further enhanced opportunities to expand social networks across new ethnic and territorial boundaries. Over time, these encampments self-generated and likely enhanced the development of additional ties between members.

Among Coahuiltecan groups, marriage relationships were one of the key practices that allowed them to build and maintain economic ties. The majority of the Coahuiltecan groups followed exogamous marriage practices combined with patrilocal residential patterns (Ruecking 1953:364, 367). In addition, the low number of marriage-age women in some indigenous societies (e.g., the Karankawa; Gatschet 1891:129) encouraged the use of marriage practices to open access to new hunting territories. Band elders worked out marriage arrangements across ethnic boundaries to gain access to new hunting or gathering territories (Anderson 1999:40–42). In addition, the ties developed through marriage also lessened the likelihood of hostilities between groups. Members of the Yojuane, Mayeye, and Muruame, who came to be affiliated with the Tonkawa by the mid-eighteenth century, also intermarried among each other and with members of the neighboring Tejas social field (Arnn 2012:209–233). These ties and the institution of marriage, which was embraced by the Catholic Church, provided an ideal mechanism for hunter-gatherers during protohistoric and early historic times and likely during prehistoric times. It served them again in the pluralistic world of the missions.

THE WORLD OF THE MISSIONS

Between 1718 and 1731 five missions were established in the upper San Antonio River basin (Map 10.2). The first of these, Misión San Antonio de Valero (the Alamo), was founded with an indigenous population that followed Fray Antonio de San Buenaventura Olivares from Misión San Francisco de Solano, south of the Rio Grande, to the San Antonio River. Misión San José y San Miguel de Aguayo was established in 1720 primarily with local indigenous groups from the nearby region. In 1731 three missions from East Texas (Misión Nuestra Señora de la Purísima Concepción, Misión San Francisco de la Espada, and Misión San Juan Capistrano) were moved to the San Antonio River valley.

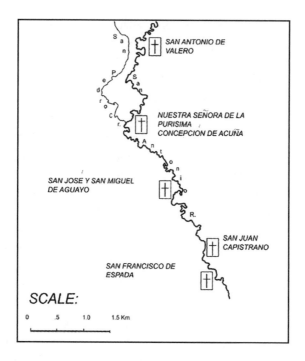

Map 10.2 Map of the location of the five missions in the upper San Antonio River basin.

As the friars set about establishing missions north of the Rio Grande and began to reduce members of dozens of groups, they dramatically altered the former social landscape. At the time of its founding, each mission relied on a "starter population" typically composed of 250–300 individuals from two or three bands (Leutenegger 1981:169). For instance, at Misión San Antonio de Valero some 75 Christianized Xarame, Siabane, and miscellaneous allied nations accompanied Fray Olivares from Solano to San Antonio (Schuetz 1979:48). By early 1719, the number of neophytes had increased to 165 individuals, and in combination with members of two other groups (Payaya and Pamaya), the population of the mission reached 499. The members of the Xarame and Payaya nations combined represented 75 percent of the mission's population. By virtue of their numeric superiority, these nations also represented the power block within the mission.

Immediately following the act of possession of each mission, the friars designated the leaders of the most numerous native groups to positions of power and responsibility. The native officials appointed by the missionary included the *mayordomo*, or superintendent, of the mission, the fiscal, the superintendent's assistant, the foreman (*caporal*), the overseer, and the head groom. The mayordomo's office was permanent, as was the foreman's position. The mission Indians in turn elected the governor and the mayor (*alcalde*), each of whom served a one-year term. Their election occurred on the Feast of the Circumcision of Our Lord following Mass. When two or more large groups were present at the possession ceremony, the positions of authority were split between them and thereafter rotated among the most numerous named groups.

As a result of these electoral practices, bands that were in the minority found themselves having little influence. In addition, new recruits brought to the missions after their founding also entered a social landscape dominated by members of the original founding bands. For instance, over the next 74 years, until secularization, as many as 67 additional groups joined Misión San Antonio de Valero. The majority (49 of 67; 73.1 percent) of these groups consisted of fewer than nine individuals. Therefore, there were many unmarried individuals from whom to choose partners.

To gain a voice in this pluralistic social landscape, groups in the minority leaned once more on marriage to access space in the social hierarchy of the missions. The mission registers of marriages for Misión San Antonio de Valero (1719–1785) and Misión Concepción (1733–1790) document the role of marriage as a mechanism through which groups in power attempted to maintain that power, while underrepresented groups sought a role in the mission social space. The marriage register of Misión San Antonio de Valero covers the period from 1703 through the 1780s. The marriage records for Misión Nuestra Señora de la Purísima Concepción include the years 1733 through 1790. Originals of these records are housed in the Catholic Archives of San Antonio, and microfilm copies are available in the archives of the Bexar County Clerk, in San Antonio, Texas.

The records of Misión Valero indicate that almost a quarter (23 percent) of the population living at the mission may have already married outside of their group before they joined the mission. In the case of the

Misión Concepción neophyte population, 9.5 percent of the men may have married outside of their named band before arriving at the missions. In each case, women who married outside of their group outnumbered males (33 women to 28 men at Valero, and 19 women and 4 men at Concepción).

Tables 10.1 and 10.2 provide breakdowns of the married indigenous populations compiled from the Alamo and Concepción marriage records, respectively. For purposes of analysis, the married male and female populations were divided into subgroups based on the number of married men and women present at the missions. In general, a small number of bands were represented by 20 to 40 married men and women. These bands were typically part of the founding populations. A slightly larger number of bands were represented by 10–19 married men and women each. The bulk of the mission population, however, consisted of bands represented by fewer than 10 married men and women.

At Misión San Antonio de Valero, nations with 20 to 40 married men included the Xarame, Sana, Coco, and Payaya. The Coco and Payaya nations also had 20 or more married women in their ranks, while the Sana and Xarame had 18 to 20 married women among their numbers. The Ypandi also had 20 married women among their members at Misión San Antonio de Valero, although the nation only included nine married men. Table 10.1 presents the data for the Misión San Antonio de Valero married population.

The table indicates that bands with 20 or more married men tended to marry women from bands that also had 20 or more married women. At the individual band level, however, there was considerable variation in this strategy. For example, of the 29 male Coco residents of Misión San Antonio de Valero, 25 (86.2 percent) married Coco women in the mission. In contrast, of the 29 Sana males, only 13 (45 percent) married Sana women, and of the 27 Xarame males, only 7 (26 percent) married Xarame women. Even more dramatically, of the 39 Payaya males, only 1 (2.5 percent) married a Payaya women. In contrast to this pattern, young women belonging to groups in power were much less likely to marry men belonging to bands that were not in power (i.e., bands with fewer than 19 men [11.1 percent] and bands with fewer than 9 men [8.7 percent]) and were least likely (1.6 percent) to marry men who had already married before arriving to the mission (Table 10.1). Women who belonged

Table 10.1 Breakdown of marriage patterns among married male and female residents of Misión San Antonio de Valero

Population Size Groups / Married Women	Bands with 20–40 Married Men (Payaya, Coco, Sana, Xarame)	Bands with 10–19 Married Men (Hierbipiame, Siaguan)	Bands with 1–9 Married Men (38 Bands)	Multiethnic Married Men (25 Bands)
Bands with 20–35 married women (Coco, Sana, Payaya, Xarame, Ypandi)	74.6	11.1	8.7	1.6
Bands with 10–19 married women (Hierbipiame, Tou)	35	40	20	5.0
Bands with 1–9 married women (38 bands)	55.2	29.9	14.9	0
Multiethnic married women (28 bands)	35.2	17.6	11.8	5.9

Table 10.2 Breakdown of marriage patterns among married male and female residents of Misión Concepción

Population Size Groups / Married Women	Bands with 20–40 Married Men (Pajalache, Tacama, Patumaco, Manos de Perro)	Bands with 10–19 Married Men (Sanipao, Siguipil, Tilpacopal)	Bands with 1–9 Married Men (11 Bands)	Multiethnic Married Men (4 Bands)
Bands with 20–35 married women (Pajalache, Tacame, and Manos de Perro)	58.5	18.9	18.9	9.4
Bands with 10–19 married women (Patumaco Sanipao, Tilpacopal, Siguipil)	45.4	31.8	18.2	4.2
Bands with 1–9 married women (19 bands)	36.4	9.1	54.5	0
Multiethnic married women (18 bands)	20.7	10.3	31.0	37.9

to small bands (i.e., between 1 and 9 women per band) that would not otherwise have a social standing within the mission had a high rate of marrying men from bands that were in positions of power (55.2 percent). Similarly, women who had married before arriving to the mission also tended (35.2 percent) to remarry men from bands that tended to hold more social status in the mission.

Table 10.2 presents the same breakdown within the married population of Misión Concepción. At Misión Concepción, the Pajalache, Tacame, Manos de Perro, and the Patumaco bands had 20 or more married men and women. The first three bands also had 20 or more married women in their ranks. A second group of nations (Sanipao, Siguipil, and Tilpacopal) each included 15 married men, and Patumaca, Sanipao, Tilpacopal, and Siguipil each had at least 10–19 married women. The remainder of the bands were each represented by fewer than 10 individuals.

The table indicates that men belonging to bands in numerically superior positions tended to marry women from the same nations (58.5 percent). At the individual band level, however, there was considerable variation in this strategy, paralleling the patterns noted among the Valero neophyte population. For example, of the 28 married Manos de Perro men, 20 (71.4 percent) married Manos de Perro women. In contrast, of the 46 Tacame males, only 18 (39.1 percent) married Tacame women in the mission, and of the 48 Pajalache males, only 12 (25 percent) married Pajalache women. Of the 46 Patumaco males, none married Patumaca women, although there were 19 Patumaca women who had married males from other bands, including those in positions of power (32 percent) while in the mission. Young women belonging to groups in power were much less likely to marry men belonging to bands that were numerically inferior (18.9 percent) and were least likely to marry men who had already married (9.4 percent) before arriving to the mission.

The marriage patterns among women from small bands (bands with 10–19 women and bands with 9 or fewer women) reflect a strong tendency to seek marriage alliances with men from bands that were represented in higher numbers (45.4 percent and 36.4 percent, respectively) than their own bands. In contrast to the Misión San Antonio de Valero population, at Misión Concepción, women who had married before arriving had a higher likelihood (37.9 percent) of remarrying men who had been married before arriving at the mission.

The data support the perspective that through marriage, the members of minority groups seemed to capture a role in social processes and were able to give voice to their desires and aspirations even if their former social/ethnic identity no longer represented the weight that it may have had in the past. Even relying on marriage as the vehicle through which a band could carve out social space within the pluralistic society of the mission, however, small groups remained at a disadvantage because more often than not they had to marry members of other small groups, thereby further eroding their identity.

MARKING SPACES IN THE SYMBOLIC REALM

Prior to entry into the missions, the Coahuiltecan and related indigenous groups had a rich cosmological lexicon expressed through the Txē complex (Ruecking 1954:332–337). The complex consisted of ceremonies that celebrated or commemorated significant events in the lives of individuals and the group. Ceremonial celebrations were elicited by various events such as good harvests, successful hunts, victories in battle, the celebration of peace, the establishment of new alliances, and significant rites of passage in the lives of band members. Some events were imbued with religious significance and were often associated with the performance of shamanistic practices and deity worship. Participants "dressed themselves in their best and married couples painted their faces with red ocher" (Ruecking 1954:334). Participants decorated their bodies with the finest beads, necklaces, and colored bird feathers and tattooed and painted their bodies for the occasion (Pérez 2016).

As some of the celebrations took place over multiple days, the nights were filled with dances (*mitotes*) that continued well into the morning hours. Coupled with the consumption of peyote and other substances, these overnight dances, shrouded in smoke and darkness, often led to various out-of-body experiences that, when witnessed by friars and other uninitiated individuals, must have been well outside of the norms of Christian behavior. Within the confines of the highly nomadic and flexible membership of small Coahuiltecan bands, the celebrations, which often also included the consumption of large amounts of food, achieved the integrative role of bringing together the family, the members of the immediate group, and even neighboring bands (Ruecking 1954). The social contract that was established between band leaders and members through the gathering and redistribution of large quantities of food to the participants also provided a validation of the powerbase of the leader and solidified his position within the group.

The beads, necklaces, arm bands, and personal items that accompanied everyone in their daily lives and connected the daily to the ceremonial also served to bridge the here and now and the hereafter. Late prehistoric (800–1750) cemetery sites and components excavated on the coast and in the Coastal Plains (Jackson et al. 2004; Perttula 2001; Tomka and Mahoney 2004) and those investigated in South Texas (Collins et al. 1969; Hester 1969; Hester and Rogers 1971; Hester and Ruecking 1969; Jackson et al. 2004; Terneny 2005) are likely to have strong parallels to the burial practices of later hunter-gatherers who roamed the same regions. These cemeteries and individual burials contain either flexed, bundled, or cremated remains associated with large amounts of grave goods (Prewitt 1974:61–62). Burial offerings ranged from shell pendants and beads, to bone awls, lithic tools, red ocher, worked oyster shell, incised bone fragments, bone beads, asphalt and circular sandstone disks, *Oliva sayana* tinklers and beads, disk-shaped beads, deer antler beam fragments, large roughly triangular conch whorls, perforated canine teeth, and incised rectangular bone pendants (Jackson et al. 2004; Wingate and Hester 1972:122). These personal items connected individuals to their daily lives and reminded them of the spiritual life, which was most vividly expressed around the *mitotes* that encircled the fires that burned through the night.

The official policy of the church toward the performance of *mitotes* was described in the instructions for the missionaries of Misión Concepción written circa 1760 (Leutenegger 1976:41). The church recognized the varied circumstances and reasons for the performance of *mitotes*. It concluded, therefore, that while their performance for superstitious reasons should be forbidden, the dances should be permitted when done as a form of celebration.

However, seen from the outside and without the benefit of translation, and combined with the use of peyote, the hallucinogenic effects of its consumption, the participation of a shaman, and the performance of rituals that implied reverence of supernatural forces, the *mitotes* were quickly targeted for eradication (Forrestal 1931:12–13; Ruecking 1954:337). Within the context of the missions, the Catholic Church was the sole guide and owner of the spiritual life of the residents. There was no space within the Catholic religion for other forms of belief or for questioning its basic tenets, least of all for the native religious view, which included multiple deities typically worshipped during peyote-fueled dances.

The friars endeavored to eradicate the practice of the *mitote* and combat its impact on the hearts and minds of the neophytes (Forrestal 1931:17, 21) by inflicting severe punishment (lashings, jail time, and shackles) on those who were found to participate in these practices and through relentless religious instruction. The goal of religious instruction was to reinforce the church's teachings through repetition. The day began with the sound of the church bells calling the neophytes to religious service at dawn (Castañeda 1938:28). The first service was followed by more religious instruction typically lasting one half to one hour. It took place in the plaza in the shadow of the church. The instructions may have been given in Spanish while interpreters tried their best to communicate the meaning of the teachings to the recent arrivals. Once the work in the fields was done, the natives again gathered in front of the church for additional religious instruction and the rosary. Each evening, the bell was rung, signaling the start of evening religious instruction in the church.

In addition, three times a week the religious instruction was led by the *fiscal* and focused on questions of catechism. The instruction culminated in the singing of the Alabado or the Bendito. Twice a week, boys and girls separately received religious instruction from the *fiscal*. The instructions began with the recital of the Our Father, followed by the listing of the Commandments, the Sacraments, and the formula for confession and concluded with the singing of the Alabado or Bendito (Leutenegger 1976:37–38). These routines were tailored to drive out the desire to continue the practice of the *mitote* among neophytes. Yet *mitotes* continued to be practiced by many indigenous groups well into the nineteenth century (Pérez 2016).

Coupled with the persistence of the *mitotes*, indigenous groups continued to incorporate into their daily lives pieces of personal gear and paraphernalia that were part of their lives during premission times. Manufacture-failed arrow points, shell beads, and bird-bone tubular beads are regularly found at the missions, indicating their continued manufacture. When finished, these items would take their place in daily and ritual performances, continuing the connections of individuals to their homelands and to practices that were part of their daily lives prior to entering the missions.

Indigenous burials from mission cemeteries often contain associated materials of Spanish manufacture symbolic of Catholic religious values (e.g., a brass crucifix, a brass medallion, a copper chain with a wooden rosary worn around the neck, a crucifix, a rosary of square-cut lignite and glass beads). In addition, however, some burials also retain items symbolic of indigenous spiritual value. For instance, excavations at the campo santo of Misión Refugio contained the remains of 165 individuals in 37 burial features (Tennis 2002:151–196). The mission was built among the Karankawa Indians and was in operation between 1795 and 1830 (Tennis et al. 2002). Fourteen of the interments had burial offerings. The offerings associated with three of the burials consisted of crucifixes and copper pendants. In contrast, eleven other interments were accompanied by personal items that no doubt had a great deal of symbolic meaning, including shell beads, shell pendants, and fragments of worked shell (n = 5), glass trade beads (n = 2), an animal-tooth pendant (n = 1), and red ocher, either smeared on the bones or found next to the remains (n = 3). Similar examples come from excavations at Misión Espíritu Santo de Zúñiga, located in Goliad, Texas. Excavations carried out at the site in 1935 uncovered 77 burials. Unpublished excavation notes indicate that fourteen individuals were interred with offerings. The majority of the offerings consisted of one or more glass trade beads. Six individuals had trade beads and additional offerings. One adult burial was accompanied by a lead disc pendant, scissors, and a comb made of rodent teeth set in an asphalt binding. A second adult had 48 glass trade beads, a copper crucifix, and a broken flint knife. A child burial was associated with a string of rosary beads, glass trade beads, and a copper pendant in the shape of an eagle. With the exception of two burials with flint bifaces as offerings and the person with the comb burial, no other individuals were accompanied by offerings that reflected their premission heritage.

However, the persistence of material culture from premission times into the mission period and its recurrence in burial contexts exemplify the desire of neophytes to carry their identity forward and to take into the afterlife elements of their own ideological expressions either as artifacts that were placeholders in such symbolic events or as artifacts that could be grafted onto otherwise Christian symbolism, sharing thereby the

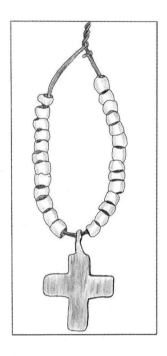

Figure 10.1 Brass crucifix strung on a necklace and surrounded by shell beads.

same symbolic space. Perhaps no burial-associated artifact is more emblematic of the multicultural world of the neophytes than the brass crucifix surrounded by 26 shell beads (Figure 10.1), recovered from one of the burials excavated in the 1960s at Misión San Juan at the San Antonio Missions Historical Park and World Heritage Site (Schuetz 1969). This artifact crystallizes the two worlds of the neophytes who became inhabitants of the missions, held on to their roots, and carved out their space in the world of the afterlife by combining the *mitote* and the ultimate symbol of Christianity in their final passage into the afterlife.

This chapter discussed three examples of place making among indigenous groups of South Texas and northeastern Mexico from the sixteenth through the eighteenth century. The examples illustrate the multidimensional nature of strategies of place making and the distinctiveness of space acquisition within the context of pluralistic social contexts. It is natural to jump to the conclusion that the interest in place making in contemporary anthropology is prompted by our multination world. After all, the scale of cross-cultural contacts, migration, and dislocation is unprecedented in our history. Each of these contexts represents fertile ground for both arriving and receiving social groups to notice differences in customs and the contexts, the places, where interactions take place. Yet just as the study of colonialism proved over time that culture contact was also a fact of life prehistorically, so too did space marking and place making seem to be general universal tendencies of the species since the first origin myths were told around the campfire and the first cairn was erected at the edge of the village marking territorial limits.

The three examples cited above show the multidimensionality of a single strategy, intergroup marriage, to provide access to both physical places and social spaces. During the sixteenth and seventeenth centuries, the return of large bison herds to the southern Great Plains prompted indigenous groups to seek access to them by building intergroup networks that spanned regional boundaries. Marriage, one of the more common tools in the social toolkit, came to be employed to bridge distant places to provide reciprocal access to new hunting grounds. In the pluralistic world of the missions, marriage came to be used to unlock doors in the social space of mission leadership. In this case, the friars, through their indigenous surrogates and veneer of unbiased electoral practices, created and controlled access to the less tangible but nonetheless critical decision-making landscape of the missions. Members of underrepresented bands used marriage to leap-frog the power structure and jump to the front of the line. Groups that had otherwise little chance of representation could rapidly insert themselves into the power structure by marrying into it. The fact that elders of these indigenous communities were actively engaged in connecting the dots to achieve certain outcomes only shows the intentionality of the practices and highlights the fact that the process had a suprahousehold dimension.

Finally, while marriage practices were highly effective strategies to access geographic places across a broad region and social spaces within the missions, they could not carve out a corner of the symbolic space within the Christian religion. To accomplish this, indigenous groups grafted onto the Christian religious lexicon elements of their traditional material culture to acquire and claim as their own a corner of the new religious space even into the afterlife. The personal items that they wore on their bodies during the *mitote* dances and other acts of the Txē ceremonial complex came to represent markers that symbolically anchored individuals to their traditional, abstract, yet highly relevant past. Yet the burial-associated artifacts also fulfilled the role of markers, literally planted in the ground but symbolizing the claim to a piece of the Catholic religious universe, which the friars were selling to the neophytes. Symbolic spaces being by definition intangible, they cannot be bought and sold, but their ownership can be demonstrated through the markers one possesses. Crucifixes and rosary beads signal a membership in the religious club that tells the initiated "I am in [the Catholic world]." Wearing a religious artifact onto which shell beads have been added signals with "a nudge and a wink" to members of one's own premission community that "I am still in [the tradition world of my forebearers]." The fact that some individuals went into the afterlife having no idea of what they would encounter there but with the intent to "hedge their bets" in both spiritual worlds is witness to the impact of the missions and the friars on the traditional symbolic space of the neophytes. From the perspective of the neophytes, the retention of their own premission personal items with strong ceremonial associations also indicates perhaps that after having spent a portion of their lives between these two worlds, the experiences left them more confused, conflicted, and stranded between two symbolic spaces.

REFERENCES

Anderson, Gary C. 1999. *The Indian Southwest 1580–1830: Ethnogenesis and Reinvention*. Norman: University of Oklahoma Press.

Arlegui, José de. 1851. *Crónica de la provincia de N.S.P.S. Francisco de Zacatecas*. Mexico City: J. B. de Hogal.

Arnn, John W., III. 2012. *Land of the Tejas: Native American Identity and Interaction in Texas, A.D. 1300 to 1700*. Austin: University of Texas Press.

Arricivita, Fray Juan Domingo. 1792. *Crónica seráfica y apostólica del colegio de propaganda fide de la Santa Cruz de Querétaro en la Nueva España, dedicada al santísimo patriarca el señor San Joseph, segunda parte. Don Felipe de Zúñiga y Ontiverso, México*. Google Books. Original from Universidad Complutense de Madrid. Accessed March 2015.

Bolton, Herbert E. 1910. "Tonkawa." In *Handbook of American Indians North of Mexico*, edited by Frederick Webb Hodge, 2:998–999. Bulletin of American Ethnology No. 30. Washington, D.C.: Smithsonian Institution.

———. 1914. "The Founding of the Missions on the San Gabriel River, 1745–1749." *Texas State Historical Association* 17(4): 323–378.

———. 1959. *Original Narratives of Early American History: Spanish Exploration in the Southwest 1542–1706*. New York: Barnes and Noble.

Bozell, John R. 1995. "Culture, Environment, and Bison Populations on the Late Prehistoric and Early Historic Central Plains." *Plains Anthropologist* 40(152): 145–163.

Carter, William B. 2009. *Indian Alliances and the Spanish in the Southwest, 750–1750*. Norman: University of Oklahoma Press.

Castañeda, Carlos E. 1938. *The Mission Era: The Missions at Work 1731–1761*. Austin, Tex.: Von Boeckmann–Jones Co.

———. 1939. *The Mission Era: The Passing of the Missions 1762–1782*. Vol. 4 of *Our Catholic Heritage in Texas 1519–1936*. Austin, Tex.: Von Boeckmann–Jones Co.

Catholic Archives, Archdiocese of San Antonio. Birth, Marriage, Death Registers of Missions San Francisco Solano and Nuestra Señora de la Purísima

Concepción. Microfilm at the Catholic Archives and the Bexar County Archives.

Collins, Michael B., Thomas R. Hester, and Frank A. Weir. 1969. "Two Prehistoric Cemetery Sites in the Lower Rio Grande Valley of Texas. Part I: The Floyd Morris Site (41CF2), a Prehistoric Cemetery Site in Cameron County, Texas." *Bulletin of the Texas Archeological Society* 40:157–166.

Dillehay, Tom D. 1974. "Late Quaternary Bison Population Changes on the Southern Plains." *Plains Anthropologist* 19(65): 180–196.

Espinosa, Isidro Felix de. 1964. *Crónica de los colegios de propaganda fide de la Nueva España*. Washington, D.C.: Academy of American Franciscan History.

Foik, Paul J. 1933. "Captain Don Domingo Ramón's Diary of His Expedition into Texas in 1716." *Preliminary Studies of the Texas Catholic Historical Society* 2(5): 3–23.

Forrestal, Peter P., trans. 1931. "The Solís Diary of 1767." *Preliminary Studies of the Texas Catholic Historical Society* 1(6): 2–42.

——, trans. 1935. "Peña's Diary of the Aguayo Expedition." *Preliminary Studies of the Texas Catholic Historical Society* 2(7): 3–68.

Foster, William C. 1995. *Spanish Expeditions into Texas 1680–1768*. Austin: University of Texas Press.

——. 2012. *Climate and Culture Change in North America AD 900–1600*. Austin: University of Texas Press.

Gatschet, Albert S. 1891. "The Karankawa Indians, the Coastal People of Texas." *Archaeological and Ethnological Papers of the Peabody Museum* 1(2): 79–84.

Griffen, William B. 1969. *Culture Change and Shifting Populations in Central Northern Mexico*. Tucson: University of Arizona Press.

Hammond, George P., and Agapito Rey. 1966. *The Rediscovery of New Mexico, 1580–1594*. Albuquerque: University of New Mexico Press.

Hatcher, Mattie A. 1932. "The Expedition of Don Domingo Terán de los Ríos into Texas." *Preliminary Studies of the Texas Catholic Historical Society* 2(1): 3–57.

Hester, Thomas R. 1969. "Part III: The Floyd Morris and Ayala Sites: A Discussion of Burial Practices in the Rio Grande Valley and the Lower Texas Coast." *Bulletin of the Texas Archeological Society* 40:157–166.

Hester, Thomas R., and R. W. Rogers. 1971. "Additional Data on the Burial Practices of the Brownsville Complex, Southern Texas." *Texas Journal of Science* 22(4): 367–371.

Hester, Thomas R., and Frederick Ruecking Jr. 1969. "Additional Materials from the Ayala Site, a Prehistoric Cemetery Site in Hidalgo County, Texas." *Bulletin of the Texas Archeological Society* 40:147–157.

Hoffmann, Fritz L., trans. 1935. *Diary of the Alarcón Expedition into Texas, 1718–1719*, by Fray Francisco Céliz. Los Angeles: Quivira Society.

Huebner, Jeffrey A. 1991. "Late Prehistoric Bison Populations in Central and Southern Texas." *Plains Anthropologist* 36(137): 343–358.

Jackson, A. T., Steve A. Tomka, Richard B. Mahoney, and Barbara A. Meissner. 2004. *The Cayo del Oso Site (41NU2). Volume I: A Historical Summary of Explorations of a Prehistoric Cemetery on the Coast of False Oso Bay, Nueces County, Texas.* Archeological Studies Program Report No. 68, Environmental Affairs Division, Texas Department of Transportation; Archaeological Survey Report No. 350, Center for Archaeological Research, University of Texas at San Antonio.

John, Elizabeth A. H. 1996. *Storms Brewed in Other Men's Worlds: The Confrontation of Indians, Spanish, and French in the Southwest, 1540–1795.* Norman: University of Oklahoma Press.

Johnson, Leroy, and Thomas N. Campbell. 1992. "Sanan: Traces of a Previously Unknown Aboriginal Language in Colonial Coahuila and Texas." *Plains Anthropologist* 37(140): 185–212.

Kress, Margaret K. 1931. "Diary of a Visit of Inspection of the Texas Missions Made by Fray Gaspar José de Solís in the Year 1767–1768." *Southwestern Historical Quarterly* 35(1): 28–76.

León, Alonso de. 1909. *Historia de Nuevo León con noticias sobre Coahuila, Tejas y Nuevo Mexico por el capitan Alonso de León, un autor anónimo y el general Fernando Sanchez de Zamora.* Documentos inéditos o muy raros para la historia de México. Publicados por Genaro Garcia, vol. 25. Libreria de la Uda., de Ch. Bouret.

Leutenegger, Fray Benedict, transcriber and trans. 1976. *Guidelines for a Texas Mission: Instructions for the Missionary of Mission Concepción in San Antonio (ca. 1760).* San Antonio: Old Spanish Missions Historical Research Library at San Jose Mission.

———, transcriber and trans. 1981. *Letters and Memorials of Father Presidente Fray Benito Fernandez de Santa Ana 1736–1754: Documents on the Missions of Texas from the Archives of the College of Querétaro.* San Antonio: Old Spanish Missions Historical Research Library at Our Lady of the Lake University.

———, transcriber and trans. 1985. *Letters and Memorials of Fray Mariano de los Dolores y Viana 1737–1762: Documents on the Missions of Texas from the Archives of the College of Querétaro.* San Antonio: Old Spanish Missions Historical Research Library at Our Lady of the Lake University.

Newcomb, W. W., Jr. 1961. *The Indians of Texas: From Prehistoric to Modern Times.* Austin: University of Texas Press.

Newcomb, William W., Jr., and Thomas N. Campbell. 2001. "Tonkawa." In *Plains Indians*, edited by Raymond J. DeMallie, pt. 2:953–964. *Handbook of North American Indians*, vol. 13. Washington, D.C.: Smithsonian Institution.

Pérez, Francisco Mendoza. 2016. "El mitote en el noreste mexicano entre el siglo XVI y el siglo XVIII." MA thesis, El Colegio de Tamaulipas, Ciudad Victoria, Tamaulipas.

Perttula, Timothy K. 2001. "Hunter-Gatherer Mortuary Practices in the Rio Grande Plains and Central Coastal Plains Archeological Regions of Texas." *La Tierra* 28(3–4): 2–83.

Portillo, Esteban L. 1886. *Apuntes para la historia antigua de Coahuila y Texas.* Edited by Amado Prado. Saltillo: Tipografía El Golfo de México.

Prewitt, E. R. 1974. "Preliminary Archeological Investigations in the Rio Grande Delta of Texas." *Bulletin of the Texas Archeological Society* 45:54–75.

Ricklis, R. A. 1996. *The Karankawa Indians of Texas: An Ecological Study of Cultural Tradition and Change.* Austin: University of Texas Press.

Ruecking, Frederick, Jr. 1953. "The Social Organization of the Coahuiltecan Indians of Southern Texas and Northeastern Mexico." *Texas Journal of Science* 5(3): 357–388.

———. 1954. "Ceremonies of the Coahuiltecan Indians of Southern Texas and Northeastern Mexico." *Texas Journal of Science* 6(5): 330–339.

———. 1955. "The Coahuiltecan Indians of Southern Texas and Northeastern Mexico." Thesis, University of Texas at Austin.

Salinas, Martín. 1990. *Indians of the Rio Grande Delta: Their Role in the History of Southern Texas and Northeastern Mexico.* Austin: University of Texas Press.

———. 2012. "Sedentarismo en las adaptaciones de los cazadores y recolectores del Bajo Río Bravo." In *People, Places, and Conflicts in Northeastern Mexico and Texas,* edited by R. E. Arboleyda Castro, J. B. Hawthorne, G. L. Cisneros, and G. A. Ramirez Casilla, pp. 79–106. Universidad Autónoma de Tamaulipas.

Schroeder, Albert H., and Dan S. Matson. 1965. *A Colony on the Move: Gaspar Castaño de Sosa's Journal 1590–1591.* Santa Fe, N.Mex.: School of American Research.

Schuetz, Mardith K. 1969. *The History and Archaeology of Mission San Juan Capistrano, San Antonio, Texas, Vol. 2: Description of the Artifacts and Ethno-history of the Coahuiltecan Indians.* Report No. 11, State Building Commission, Archaeology Program, Austin, Tex.

———. 1979. "The Indians of the San Antonio Missions 1718–1821." PhD diss., University of Texas at Austin.

Steck, Francis B. 1932. "Forerunners of Captain de León's Expedition to Texas, 1670–1675." *Preliminary Studies of the Texas Catholic Historical Society* 2(3): 5–32.

Tennis, Cynthia L., ed. 2002. *Archaeological Investigations at the Last Spanish Colonial Mission Established on the Texas Frontier: Nuestra Señora del Refugio (41RF1), Refugio County, Texas.* Vols. 1 and 2. Archeological Studies Program Report No. 39, Environmental Affairs Division, Texas Department of Transportation; Archaeological Survey Report No. 315, Center for Archaeological Research, University of Texas at San Antonio.

Terneny, Tiffany T. 2005. "A Re-evaluation of Late Prehistoric and Archaic Chronology in the Rio Grande Delta of South Texas." PhD diss., University of Texas at Austin.

Tomka, Steve A. 2016. "The Indigenous Cultures of Coahuila and Texas: Nomadic People in a Contested Land." Paper presented at the First Bexar County Heritage Symposium, San Antonio, Texas.

Tomka, Steve A., and Richard B. Mahoney. 2004. "Discussion and Summary." In *The Cayo del Oso Site (41NU2), Volume I: A Historical Summary of Explorations of a Prehistoric Cemetery on the Coast of False Oso Bay, Nueces County, Texas*, edited by A. T. Jackson, Steve A. Tomka, Richard B. Mahoney, and Barbara A. Meissner, pp. 63–80. Archeological Studies Program Report No. 68, Environmental Affairs Division, Texas Department of Transportation; Archaeological Survey Report No. 350, Center for Archaeological Research, University of Texas at San Antonio.

Turpin, Solveig A. 1987. "Ethnohistoric Observations of Bison in the Lower Pecos River Region: Implications for Environmental Change." *Plains Anthropologist* 32(118): 424–429.

Wade, Maria F. 2003. *The Native Americans of the Texas Edwards Plateau, 1582–1799.* Austin: University of Texas Press.

Weniger, Del. 1997. *Explorer's Texas: The Animals They Found.* Burnet, Tex.: Eakin Press.

Wingate, R. J., and Thomas R. Hester. 1972. "Ten Burials from Green Lake, Texas." *Florida Anthropologist* 25(3): 119–126.

11

Importing Ethnicity, Creating Culture

Currents of Opportunity and Ethnogenesis along the Dagua River in Nueva Granada, ca. 1764

Juliet Wiersema

In eighteenth-century Nueva Granada (comprising today's Colombia, Ecuador, Panama, and Venezuela), the Dagua River region was a multicultural backwater inhabited by Europeans, Indians, and Africans. The greatest majority of the region's residents, however, were African, brought against their will to extract gold along the river's shores.

In this chapter, I attempt to sketch out a very preliminary notion of what emerging ethnicity looked like in a remote corner of the Spanish Empire in the final decades of colonial rule. In this essay, I argue that people forcibly displaced from West and Central Africa came to construct new societies and identities. Africans in the Dagua River region quickly adapted to the physical and political environment, controlling terrestrial and river commerce, effectively fighting Crown monopolies, purchasing their freedom, and establishing free communities. Africans' ability to master an inhospitable landscape, together with their critical mass, the great need for their labor, the region's remoteness, and the lack of Spanish colonial oversight all worked to create opportunities for both enslaved and free. On the margins of empire, people from elsewhere engaged in ethnic intermixing, laying the foundations for an emergent multicultural Afro-Colombian population. Their descendants would remain until the early twentieth century.

This chapter looks specifically at African ethnogenesis and place making along the Dagua River in the later eighteenth century.[1] By focusing on a concrete geographic area at a specific moment in time, this study adds to the growing scholarship on emerging identities and ethnicities of frontier regions in the Spanish Empire. (For other case studies on emerging identities in this volume, see Chapters 1, 4, and 8.)

With the aim of teasing out subtle clues about ethnicity in the Dagua River region, I look to a large, hand-drawn, watercolor map with an extensive legend dating to the late Spanish colonial period (Map 11.1). This manuscript map of 1764, corresponding to today's southwestern

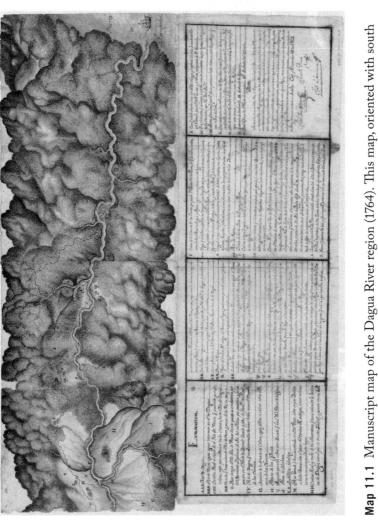

Map 11.1 Manuscript map of the Dagua River region (1764). This map, oriented with south at top and west at right, depicts an area of roughly 900 km² that begins southwest of Cali and ends in the port of Buenaventura. The Dagua River bisects the map horizontally, flowing into the Pacific Ocean at right. The largest settlement is the free town of Sombrerillo. Library of Congress, Geography and Maps Division, https://www.loc.gov/item/2001622517/.

Colombia, pictorially documents a gold-mining region and a vital corridor to the Pacific (Wiersema 2018). The map's central feature, the Dagua River, was a fluvial highway linking the interior of the country to the port of Buenaventura. In this area, where acidic, humid soils hampered local crop cultivation (Romero 2017:25), the river acted as a lifeline to miners, slaves, and its few residents. A more critical examination of this cartographic work, together with information drawn from archival documents, reveals that Africans not only adapted to the local environment but quickly became central actors in the region's economy.

Rendered in brilliant watercolor, the Dagua River map (60 × 86 cm) stretches across eight sheets of laid paper, depicting an area of approximately 900 km². Striking is the absence of towns, plazas, and churches, features that are ubiquitous on nearly every other map documenting the Spanish Americas. These omissions underscore the Dagua region's great distance from larger administrative centers in Nueva Granada such as Cartagena, Tunja, and Santa Fé de Bogotá. Even Cali, the town nearest to the Dagua River region, lay beyond the parameters of the map.

The map is oriented with south at top and west at right, and the river is framed by dramatic color-coded topography: blue represents mountain ridges, green indicates dense jungle, and brown reflects steep escarpments. Along the river, haciendas, small settlements, and mining claims are marked by tiny structures. At the map's center are the two largest settlements, the hacienda of Las Juntas and the town of Sombrerillo. Las Juntas was one of the few cultivable zones in the area and was a nexus point for the region, where goods like tobacco, meat, and aguardiente (cane brandy) were imported from Cali and other fertile parts of the Cauca Valley before they were redistributed to the mining regions of the Chocó (Martínez Capote 2005:38–39; Romero 1991:142; West 1952:112). The largest settlement on the map, Sombrerillo, was a free town whose residents worked as overland carriers (*cargueros)* and canoe polers (*bogas*), effectively linking the Cauca Valley to the port of Buenaventura (Lane and Romero 2001:35).

THE DAGUA RIVER REGION: A VITAL CORRIDOR BETWEEN CALI AND BUENAVENTURA

The Dagua is one of the few rivers that flow to the port of Buenaventura. From the beginning of the Spanish conquest, Buenaventura was identified as a strategic port controlled by Cali's elite. It was the only Pacific port that permitted access to the Andean interior (Valencia Llano 2014:235). Goods brought into Buenaventura from Spain via Panama would travel through the Dagua River region to Cali. Conversely, gold mined along the Dagua would sail out of Buenaventura, ideally to Spain. As such, the Dagua River area represented a potentially lucrative economic corridor. Getting to Cali from Buenaventura, however, was no easy task. One of the earliest documented Spanish attempts was made in 1541. Torrential downpours, rising water levels, impassable terrain, unnavigable paths, and a dwindling food supply thwarted every step of the journey. In the end, it took the party 30 days to arrive to Cali and cost the lives of 17 Spaniards and 20 horses (Arboleda 1956:1:46–47). While initially of interest to Spain, the Dagua's isolation and its challenging topography relegated it a frontier region, one largely beyond the reach of colonial authorities.

If the Dagua River region was distant from the nearest town of Cali, it was seemingly light years away from Nueva Granada's principal port, Cartagena. The journey from Cali to Las Juntas (depicted in the center of Map 11.1) could take up to a week's time. Travel from Cartagena to Las Juntas, meanwhile, required around 50 days (West 1952:125) and necessitated the navigation of steep mountains, slippery paths, dense forests, and treacherous rivers. Apart from being time-consuming, the trip was costly and dangerous. A 1776 letter to the viceroy emphasized that getting from place to place happened only at tremendous expense and great risk to one's life (AGN Militias y Marinas, tomo 126, fol. 203v [1776]).

A BRIEF OVERVIEW OF NUEVA GRANADA

To better understand the peculiarities of the Dagua River region, it is worth briefly discussing the unusual nature of Nueva Granada itself. Nueva Granada was discovered and colonized in the first quarter of the sixteenth century, with the Caribbean coastal cities of Santa Marta and Cartagena founded in 1525 and 1533, respectively. Nueva Granada was not, however, established as a viceroyalty until 1719 (McFarlane 1993:26–28). Its first iteration was short-lived. By 1723 the Crown had concluded that the cost of maintaining it outweighed any benefits (McFarlane 1993:192). Another fifteen years would pass before this viceroyalty was reinstated, in 1738 (McFarlane 1993:194–195).

Nueva Granada was less densely populated than New Spain or Peru. In 1778–1780, only 800,000 people inhabited the entire viceroyalty. Its capital, Santa Fé de Bogotá (home to just 20,000), was one-fifth the size of Mexico City in 1790 and one-third the size of Lima in 1791 (McFarlane 1993:32–34; Miño Grijalva 2002:xiv). Differing from New Spain and Peru, Nueva Granada did not have sizeable indigenous, Spanish, or criollo representation. By the mid-seventeenth century, Nueva Granada's indigenous populations had been decimated in many areas (McFarlane 1993:34). Its remoteness and its relative economic impoverishment meant there were few incentives for Spaniards to come or to stay. By 1770 nearly half of Nueva Granada was comprised of free people of mixed ethnicity (46 percent), with just over a quarter European (26 percent). Indigenous people comprised 20 percent of the population, and 8 percent were African enslaved (McFarlane 1993:34–38).

The viceroyalty's dramatic topography (including three formidable mountain chains, which divide it vertically) made travel from the interior to the coast and vice versa unusually onerous (McFarlane 1993:40). Urban centers like Santa Fé de Bogotá and Tunja were not easy to get to from ports of entry, meaning that once the month-long trip by sea from Cádiz to Cartagena was complete, another one to two months awaited the traveler before reaching the capital of Santa Fé de Bogotá (Helg 2004:49). The roads most traveled were rivers (West 1952:123). Other areas were accessed by mule train and narrow paths, which washed away in the rainy season. All modes of communication were unreliable, hazardous, and slow (Helg 2004:49). Most of Nueva Granada's population lived deep in the country's interior (McFarlane 1993:32), yet travel to these parts presented formidable challenges to imperial administrators.

IMPORTING ETHNICITY

In the early period of discovery and colonization, the Cauca Valley (including the Dagua River region) was inhabited by dozens of indigenous groups and subgroups, many of whose origins remain mysterious (Romoli 1974:376). Sixteenth-century Spaniards described these Indians as docile and good-natured (Escobar 1991 [1582]:346), a factor that decidedly worked against them. In 1536 there were approximately 30,000 indigenous people, but by 1634 populations had dropped to 420 (Escobar

1991 [1582]:345; Romoli 1974:382). Indigenous numbers in the mountains near Cali also saw precipitous decline, falling from 8,000 to 600 (Escobar 1991 [1582]:346). While native people were afflicted by epidemics and exploitation (McFarlane 1993:34), decimation of the indigenous in the Dagua River region was attributed to forced travel between Buenaventura and Cali. In *Gobierno de Popayán: Calidades de la tierra* (1582), Fray Geronimo Escobar relayed that each Indian was obligated by his *encomendero* (holder of an encomienda, or grant of native labor and tribute) to make three trips per year transporting goods from Cali to the port of Buenaventura and bringing cargo from the ships in port back to Cali. The trip of 25 leagues (140 km) took 12 days each way, in part due to the condition of the terrain but also because each Indian was required to carry over 22 kilos (2 arrobas) of weight (Escobar 1991 [1582]:346). In the later sixteenth and seventeenth centuries, unsuccessful attempts were made to repopulate the area (Romero 2017:35–36).

Gold mines had been discovered in the neighboring mountains of Raposo (to the south) by 1579, leading to mining expansion along the Pacific (Valencia Llano 2014:236). By the late seventeenth century, mines had been established along the Dagua River. Many were prosperous by 1719, leading to an increased need for labor (Arboleda 1956:2:22; Colmenares 1975:101–105; Valencia Llano 2014:237). It was enslaved Africans who comprised this labor force as work gangs, or *quadrillas* (Barona 1986:61–66). Africans quickly became the majority of the Dagua region's inhabitants.

ETHNICITIES ON MAPS

Ethnic realities are not explicitly inscribed on maps, but they can be gleaned from a careful reading of details (Leibsohn 2014). On the Dagua River map, the river and its streambeds, which were worked by African *quadrillas*, is our first clue to the African presence in this area. The roads, some of the worst in the Americas (many too narrow to accommodate mules), were traversable only by human porters, many of whom were African. The canoe depicted along the Dagua's shores at the center of the map (Map 11.2) was a primary mode of transport in this region, one controlled almost exclusively by African polers. It is worth noting that the only human figures appearing on the Dagua River map are those navigating a canoe down the river's rapids. Further evidence of African presence

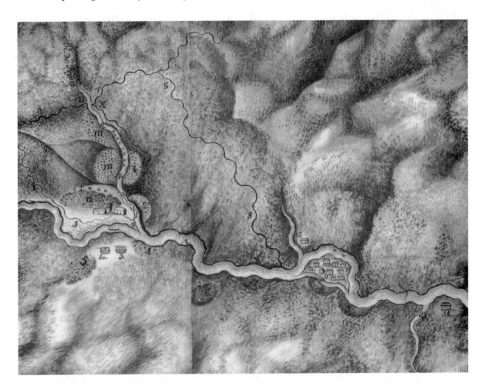

Map 11.2 Detail of the manuscript map of the Dagua River region (1764), showing the central node of Las Juntas at left (1) and the free settlement of Sombrerillo at right (2). Sombrerillo enjoyed a strategic location along the Dagua River (A) and was also the most populated place in the area.

can be found in the map's largest settlement, Sombrerillo (Map 11.2). This free community was inhabited by families of free blacks, Indians, mestizos, mulattoes, and a few white merchants (Arboleda 1956:2:102; Lane and Romero 2001:35–36). At first glance, they appear nowhere, yet a closer reading reveals that the African presence is everywhere.

ETHNOGENESIS: DEFINITION AND DISCUSSION

Where specifically in Africa did the Dagua River region's inhabitants come from, and what circumstances led to their successful adaptation to this new environment? (For case studies of successful adaptation in this volume, see Chapters 1, 4, and 8.) In the arrival and settlement of people to this area from different parts of the African continent, can we find convincing evidence of ethnogenesis?

Ethnogenesis (from the Greek *ethnos* [ἔθνος], "group of people, nation," and *genesis* [γένεσις], "beginning, coming into being") has been defined as the formation or emergence of an ethnic group (*Merriam-Webster*). Ethnos refers to those sharing a common language, ancestry, culture, and/or territory (e.g., an ancestral homeland). Through the process of ethnogenesis, a group of people becomes ethnically distinct from others.

In their essay "Mapping Ethnogenesis in the Early Modern Atlantic," James Sidbury and Jorge Cañizares-Esguerra (2011) note that enslaved Africans in the Americas were first enslaved in Africa through warfare. Most communities included enslaved people. African polities were constantly integrating ethnic outsiders before, during, and after the era of the Atlantic slave trade. Taking captives from their natal communities and forcing them to adapt to new cultures was an "endemic condition" in precolonial African polities, one that led to ongoing ethnogenesis (Sidbury and Cañizares-Esguerra 2011:185). In short, ethnogenesis was not an outcome particular to Africans displaced to the Americas because this phenomenon was happening much earlier in Africa itself. Given the histories of warfare and slaving in Africa, James H. Sweet has noted that ethnogenesis unfolded in West Africa much as it did in the Americas. Dislocated peoples, in their efforts to reconstitute social connections, often found themselves searching for the "broadest expressions of cultural sameness" (Sweet 2011:210).

IDENTIFYING ETHNOGENESIS

Given colonial realities—where local populations were annihilated and relocated and their lands repopulated through the introduction of non-native groups brought in forcibly or voluntarily—it seems reasonable to conclude that ethnogenesis took place across the Americas and in Nueva Granada specifically. Barbara Voss (2015:658) has emphasized, however, that ethnogenesis must be demonstrated, not assumed. In identifying ethnogenesis, we must determine (1) whether ethnic identities were important in a given context and (2) if ethnic identities were substantively transformed in the process.

For Nueva Granada, a primarily mixed-race society with a comparatively small percentage of Europeans and criollos, racial divisions mattered much less than they did in societies with more rigid ethnic hierarchies (McFarlane 1993:38). From the 1778–1780 census, Anthony McFarlane identified four primary socioethnic categories: whites, black slaves, Indians, and "free people of all colors." Whites, which referred to Spaniards, criollos (descendants of Spaniards born in the Americas), and Europeans (French, Italian, etc.), comprised 26 percent of the population. Indians, or those indigenous to the Americas, represented 20 percent. Slaves, or enslaved Africans, formed 8 percent of Nueva Granada's population in 1778–1780 (McFarlane 1993:32–34, 353). The overwhelming majority (46 percent) was comprised of *libres de todos colores* (free people of all colors), a catch-all term that came to encompass various subgroups, including *mestizos, negros, mulatos, zambos, pardos*, and *montañeses* (Garrido 2005:167–168).[2] As a socioethnic category, *libres de todos colores* underscored the race mixing that had transpired over generations, making it impossible to determine mixtures of ethnicity. (Nueva Granada's large number of free people [46 percent] was equivalent to indigenous populations in other parts of the Spanish Andes [Garrido 2005:167–168].) Despite these attempts at classification, these socioethnic categories served only to further obscure the geographical origin and cultural affiliation of the people referenced.

In the Dagua River region, the demographic percentages were notably different from those in the larger Viceroyalty of Nueva Granada. Along the Dagua, Europeans and criollos made up just 3 percent of the area's population, with Indians representing 9 percent and free people making up 17 percent.[3] Significantly, enslaved Africans comprised 71 percent of the Dagua River's population (McFarlane 1993:356). As the overwhelming majority (and in spite of their enslaved status), Africans were able to assert their rights and fight Crown policies that went against their interests. In the paragraphs that follow, we will examine who had migrated into the Dagua River region by the eighteenth century and from where they came. Later in the chapter, we will look at the emergent ethnicities resulting from this displacement.

AFRICANS IN NUEVA GRANADA

Africans were brought to Nueva Granada from West and Central Africa as a result of the Atlantic slave trade. The earlier trade (1570–1640) forced migration of people from Upper Guinea, Lower Guinea, and Angola

(Colmenares 1997:20–21; Mathieu 1982:160–161; Wheat 2011:12). The later trade brought individuals from a more concentrated area of the Lower Guinea Coast: the Gold Coast and the Bight of Benin, corresponding to today's Ghana and Nigeria (Borucki et al. 2015:446). Slaves in the earlier period were sent to cities to undertake domestic labor. The later trade (specifically between 1740 and 1760), however, brought slaves to remote mining areas on the Pacific coast, specifically Chocó and Raposo, where they replaced the decimated indigenous labor force (Barona 1986:61; Colmenares 1997:41, 56; McFarlane 1993:75–76; Soulodre-LaFrance 2001:89–90). Their arrival to the area coincided with the exploitation of mines from 1714 to 1736 (Colmenares 1975:62).

THE DAGUA RIVER REGION: A LOCUS OF ETHNOGENESIS?

Africans brought to the Dagua River region came via Cartagena. From this Caribbean port, they were transported by canoe along the Magdalena and Cauca Rivers (see West 1952:124). Africans undoubtedly arrived through back channels as well, coming into the port of Buenaventura (Valencia Llano 2014:240), the body of water featured prominently on the Dagua River map.

Information on the African origins of the Dagua River region's inhabitants can be gleaned from slave censuses and mining inventories, where slaves are listed by first name and ethnonym, or "nation" designation. Ethnonyms such as Mina, Araras, Popo, Chamba, Carabali, and Congo often became an enslaved individual's last name (Colmenares 1997:21–25). For example, Africans coming to Nueva Granada between 1703 and 1740—noted in sales and inventories as Mina—referenced those from the Mina coast but may have included Fante, Asante, Ga, and Akwamu, among others. Meanwhile, those noted as Popo, Araras, and Chamba corresponded roughly with the Bight of Benin, between the Volta and Niger Rivers. After 1730 Central Africa became an important source for slaves. In archival documents and inventories, those from Central Africa are noted as Congo. Some Africans arriving to Cartagena between 1740 and 1780 are described in documents as Carabalis, Ibos, and Ibibo-efik. These ethnonyms suggest an origin in the Bight of Biafra (at the mouth of the Cross River).

The challenge with ethnonyms is that they are inherently unreliable. Ethnic nomenclature, assigned by Europeans, provides only an approximation of an African's place of origin (Colmenares 1997:21–22; DeCorse 1999:135–136; Lovejoy 1989:378). Ethnonyms might refer to the West African port of embarkation rather than to an enslaved person's nation of origin (Curtin 1969:184–185; Lohse 2002:74). Underscoring the notion that port of embarkation and ethnicity could be poles apart was the observation made by a Frenchman in 1715 that only 5 percent of the slaves sold at Ouidah originated within that kingdom (Lohse 2002:80; Law 1991:184). Further complicating matters, Spanish slave masters ethnically classified and reclassified the same African-born individuals using different terms throughout their lifetimes. Meanwhile, slaves, when asked about their ethnic origins, often volunteered a different term from that used by their masters. Slaves might have seen themselves as part of a smaller, more specific ethnic group or, in other cases, part of a broader linguistic, cultural, or sociopolitical sphere (Lohse 2002:82–84). Identity and the formation of identity for Africans forcibly exported to the New World as a result of the Atlantic slave trade was shaped by many factors and often transcended ethnicity or original group identity (Hall 2005:26–54).

The ethnonyms documented for the Dagua River region suggest that Africans came from the Gold Coast, the Bight of Benin, the Bight of Biafra, Central Africa, and Senegambia. Corresponding ethnonyms include Mina, Popo, Mandinga, Nango, Arara, Chamba, Congo, Carabali, and Angola. While these ethnonyms suggest a range of ethnicities and cultural backgrounds, individuals were, in fact, associated with a relatively small number of linguistic groups. More than a third of the slaves arriving to Cartagena shared a common tongue or understood one another using a similar Bantu language (Castillo Mathieu 1982:256).

Mining inventories from this region dating to the first half of the eighteenth century reflect a preponderance of African ethnonyms (ACC Signatura 8806 Colonia Judicial 1-17 Minas [1762–1766]). This suggests that the slaves listed were recent arrivals to the Americas. By the second half of the eighteenth century, however, most African slaves inventoried were designated as "criollo/a," indicating they had been born in the Americas (Colmenares 1975:107). Given the propitious conditions along the Dagua River, there is evidence for an increasing number of *negros libres* (free blacks).

These mining inventories (embedded within wills and testaments) are an important source of information on emerging ethnicities. The 1752 mining inventory of Santa Barbara del Salto lists 26 slaves, including children. While an admittedly small sample, the majority is ascribed the ethnonym Mina (corresponding to the Gold Coast). Also represented are Carabali (Bight of Biafra) and Chamba (Bight of Benin), with one slave designated as Congo, suggesting a Central African origin. The second largest number after those from the Gold Coast (Mina) are designated as "criollo/a," indicating African heritage but American origin (ACC Signatura 8806 Colonia Judicial I-17 Minas, fols. 58–62 [1762–1766]). Two decades later (1772–1773), slaves associated with the Dagua mines of Triana de San Geronimo de las Benedicciones were inventoried. Of the 19 slaves listed (including children), criollos comprised the largest percentage, with smaller representation from Central Africa (Congo), the Bight of Benin (Chamba), the Bight of Biafra (Carabali), and the Gold Coast (Mina) (ACC Signatura 11347 Colonia Judicial I-17 Minas, fols. 4r–5r [1772–1773]).

These two mining inventories are particularly valuable because, in addition to first name and ethnonym, they document age, name of spouse, and spouse's ethnonym. Also provided are names and ages of corresponding children. Essentially, we are given a glimpse of emergent family units along the Dagua River. For example, from the 1772–1773 inventory, we have Negro Isidro, captain of the *quadrilla*, designated as Chamba. He is 40 years old and is married to Negra Rita, Caraballi, also 40 years of age. They have two children: a 14-year-old son, Tomas (designated as Zambo), and a 6-year-old daughter, Negrita Antonio. The inventory continues with another ethnically mixed couple, Negro Simon, Conga, of 40 years and his wife, Flora, Negra Criolla, 30 years.

Mixed-ethnicity family units are also found in the earlier inventory (1752) from Santa Barbara del Salto. Hipolito, Mina, captain of the *quadrilla*, and 37 years of age, is married to Juana Maria, criolla of 37 years. Meanwhile, Luis, Mina, 28, is married to Phelipa, criolla, 15. Tomas, criollo, 46, and his wife, Caterina, Mina, 36, have a daughter, Casia, who is 8 years old. Alejandro, Chamba, 28, is married to Maria, criolla, who is 17 years old. Vicente, Mina, 30, is married to Maria, Conga, 22. Their son, Alberto, is 1 year old (ACC Signatura 8806 Colonia Judicial I-17 Minas, fols. 58v–59r [1762–1766]).

Through these mining inventories we catch a glimpse of the insipient foundations of an emerging multiethnic Afro-Colombian population in the Dagua River region. Inventories chronicle the unions of Africans who may have originated in different regions, cultures, and language groups—Chamba married to Caraballi, Conga married to criolla, Mina married to criolla, Chamba married to criolla, Mina married to Conga— but who forged new identities and communities through multicultural marriage alliances and shared experiences.

To return to the question of ethnogenesis for the Dagua River region, we can revisit those conditions for ethnogenesis laid out by Voss (2015) that hold the most relevance for the Dagua River region. The first would be migration and displacement, in which place-based identities lose relevance and are supplanted by new ethnic identities. The second would be the emergence of new ethnic identities as a result of shared experiences of oppression from or resistance to a dominant group or institution (Voss 2015:658). In the Dagua River region, all first-generation Africans would have come as a result of forced migration and displacement. All would have experienced the horrendous Atlantic crossing, or Middle Passage, in the hold of a slave ship. These same individuals would have then undertaken the arduous two-month trip from Cartagena to the Dagua River region. Others may have been part of contraband expeditions coming into the port of Buenaventura, where a shorter but equally taxing overland trip to the Dagua region awaited them. Even if these journeys were not made together, these collective experiences, stories, and memories likely paved a path to unity and collective identity. Second-generation criollo slaves would have been spared the trauma of transatlantic displacement but would have shared with their parents and other first-generation slaves the same oppression imposed by Europeans and, eventually, would participate in resisting the Spanish colonial system. As a result, African place-based identities likely lost their relevance in the Dagua River region, supplanted by new identities based on experience and oppression as opposed to geographical origin or cultural heritage.

THROUGH MASTERY OF ENVIRONMENT CAME AUTONOMY

In the Dagua River region, gold mining, fluvial and overland transport, and subsistence agriculture were the primary industries. (In essence, all of these were tied to gold extraction.) Those Africans who had been forcibly imported to this region either possessed or acquired the skills

necessary to meet these local needs. Was this knowledge—placer mining, cultivation in tropical climates, and the skillful navigation of water
craft—brought from West Africa or developed in situ? Many African
slaves sent to mining areas in Nueva Granada stemmed from agrarian
cultures with rich gold-working traditions. Slaves from these regions
(the Gold Coast, the Bight of Benin) were likely sought for their native
skill sets, including gold mining and crop cultivation (Maya 1998:45–48,
2010:113). Those from the Bight of Benin, an area with early metallurgi-
cal traditions, were familiar with techniques for exploiting and extracting
gold (Maya 1998:41–42, 2010:113). A seventeenth-century source, Jean
Barbot's extensive and illustrated *Description of the Coasts of North and
South Guinea* (based in part on Barbot's observation from 1678–1682),
discussed methods used on Africa's Gold Coast to collect raw material:
"The natives either dig [the gold] out of the earth, or gather [it] from
the bottom of rivers and streams" (1732:5:145).[4] Given their familiarity
with placer mining, Africans coming to the mineral-rich Dagua River
region from the Gold Coast (Mina) and the Bight of Benin (Araras,
Popo, Chamba) would likely have understood the work they were expected to undertake. This knowledge may have enabled them to quickly
adapt to their new environment and become more autonomous (Maya
1998:45–46).

One of the significant ways Africans in the Dagua River region gained
autonomy was through the navigation of canoes. The lack of roads in
this region meant the Dagua River was the principal artery for trade
and transport. It was also the most efficient means of supplying mines
downriver with staples brought into Las Juntas (see Map 11.2). Those
possessing the skills to navigate the Dagua and move goods down its currents were in demand and well-paid. Such place-specific skills were also
developed by offspring of *cassare* unions at the early Portuguese garrison
at Elmina (see Chapter 1).

Africans may have learned to navigate dangerous river currents, including the Dagua, from indigenous inhabitants (Romero 2017:69).
Nonetheless, many Africans in the Dagua region came from lands where
river and sea navigation in small and large canoes was a way of life. Many
lines of evidence support that they had mastered the canoe (both its
construction and its navigation) in West Africa long before their arrival
to Nueva Granada (Dawson 2018).

The canoe played a significant role in West African trade and commerce (Smith 1970:521–524). Its importance for coastal, lagoon, and riparian peoples has been equated to that of the horse for the history of the savannah states (Smith 1970:532). In early accounts of the Guinea Coast, a distinction was made between canoes used in the open sea and those confined to the rivers and lagoons (Smith 1970:516). Canoes varied in size and carrying capacity, with smaller crafts carrying one to four people and larger crafts holding up to one hundred (Smith 1970:518).

Specifics about canoe navigation were recorded by nineteenth-century explorers. Mungo Park, on travels through Bamako in Mali along the Niger River, noted that canoes were moved through rapids by first tying them with ropes to the shoreline and then pushing the canoes forward with long poles (1838:51). Similar methods are described for the Dagua and Magdalena Rivers (Helg 2004:49; Pombo 1850:108–110; Saffray 1948 [1869]:312). John Duncan (1846:146), writing for the Royal Geographic Society of London in 1846, described canoe travel through lagoons near the Gulf of Guinea, between Popo and Ouidah, where crafts were propelled by long poles, with four men to one large canoe. James A. Croft (1873–1874:188–189), exploring the Volta River between Ada Foah and Kpong in 1873, wrote of canoes over 12 m long and .5 m wide, sharpened at each end and propelled by five men who paddled on occasion but found poles most useful in navigating boulders and rapids. (Croft notes that extra poles were brought along, as many got stuck between the rocks and could not be freed.) Poles were also a primary mode of propelling crafts through the Dagua (Pombo 1850:109–110), as depicted in Figure 11.1.

Barbot highlighted the skill and dexterity of "Mina blacks" who deftly paddled canoes through rough waters near Ouidah "without being sunk, overset, or split to pieces," avoiding both death and considerable loss of goods (1732:5:157). Nineteenth-century French explorer Charles Saffray observed that navigation in the upper Dagua was as difficult as it was dangerous; the life of the passenger often depended upon a shout, a gesture, a glance from the person navigating the canoe. So swift were the currents of the Dagua that Saffray lost a friend who traveled just fifteen minutes behind him (1948 [1869]:311–312). The raw nerve and shrewd ability of Afro-Colombian canoe polers made an indelible impression on Gaspard-Theodore Mollien as well. Traveling down the Dagua nearly fifty years earlier, he described the black pilots as brave and daring, able

Figure 11.1 View of Las Juntas. While likely romanticized, this image conveys the perils of travel by canoe along the Dagua River and the dramatic topography of the area. This image suggests that even in the mid-nineteenth century, Las Juntas was more of an outpost than a town. Of particular note are the men in canoes who navigate using long poles. Illustration by François Louis Niederhäusern-Koechlin, based on a sketch by Charles Saffray published in "Voyage à la Nouvelle-Grenade par M. le Docteur Saffray (1869)," in *Le tour du monde: Nouveau journal des voyages*, vol. 26 (Paris: Librairie Hachette, 1875), 92.

to skillfully avoid rapids and dodge rocks and whirlpools without fear of capsizing the canoe (Mollien 1944 [1823]:296). The accounts of Saffray and Mollien emphasize that the Dagua's torrents and currents were extreme, yet Barbot's writing leaves little doubt that West Africans' ability to navigate such waters ran in their blood.

EXERTING RIGHTS, CONTROLLING COMMERCE, PURCHASING FREEDOM, AND BUILDING FREE COMMUNITIES

Other factors paved the way to opportunity and autonomy for enslaved and free Africans living along the Dagua River. (For the economic autonomy of the Ifugao in the Philippines, see Chapter 8.) The great demand for labor enabled many slaves in the Dagua River region to rent themselves out as prospectors (*mazamorreros*), canoe polers, and porters on their days off (Romero 2017:145ff., 196; ACC Signatura 11501, Colonia Civil IV-11 gobierno, fol. 99v [1773]). A canoe poler could make four patacones, or pesos (a silver coin of eight reales [see Marzahl 1978:198]), per round trip from Las Juntas to El Salto (a short but dangerous trip), where the mines of Aguasucia were located (see Map 11.2, where the small structure at far right marked with [14] identifies the Aguasucia mines). Additionally, porters were entitled to a pound of meat and a ration of bananas for each trip. They became skilled at skimming off the top, opening up sacks of meat, filling them with rocks, then sealing them up again so that nothing appeared to be missing when the cargo was weighed (Romero 2017:176; BN Fondo Comuneros RM 370, fols. 69v–75 [1780]). Through these various modes of employment, Africans were able to earn a significant amount of money. Extrapolating from the wages of canoe polers alone—four patacones made on a given Sunday—we might hypothesize that a person could work 52 Sundays a year and earn 208 patacones, a sum that would enable him to buy his freedom or that of a family member (costing between 300 and 400 patacones) in less than two years' time.[5]

Contributing to their autonomy was the fact that Africans and their descendants comprised the majority of the Dagua River region's inhabitants. Given the frontier conditions along the Dagua River, Spanish landholders and mine owners were often in absentia, remaining in Cali while their paid administrators ran operations in the interior (Colmenares 1975:106; Lane 2000:47, 94ff.). A similar phenomenon is discussed for haciendas in Nejapa in Stacie King's case study (Chapter 4).

This lack of oversight enabled slaves and free slaves living in the greater Dagua River region to successfully fight Crown monopolies that went against their interests. For example, in 1766 a successful revolt against the *estanco de aguardiente* (Crown monopoly on the sale of cane brandy) took place in Las Juntas, Sombrerillo, and Calima, where rioters attacked, drank, and sold jugs of aguardiente without anyone to stop them (AGN Militias y Marinas, tomo 126, fol. 199–204 [1776]; McFarlane 1984:26).

Aguardiente was an especially important commodity in mining regions. The monopoly oversaw the alcohol's distillation and distribution and forbade local production (McFarlane 1984:22, 1993:199–200). The monopoly met with great resistance in both rural and urban areas. Just the year before, in 1765, the plebeian population of Cali rose up against colonial authorities, protesting the monopoly (Anonymous 1937:247; McFarlane 1984:26). Because the 50 Spaniards residing in Cali could not defend themselves against the much larger plebeian population, which exceeded 3,000, the cabildo voted to suspend the monopoly rather than face the wrath of the populace (Anonymous 1937:251–252; Arboleda 1956:2:329–331; McFarlane 1984:26).

With the recent plebeian disturbance in mind, Pedro Garcia Valdez, *teniente de la compañía de forasteros españoles de la ciudad de Popayán*, wrote desperate letters to Cali's cabildo in March 1766 and the viceroy in April 1766.[6] Because the only people in the Dagua River region on a regular basis were African slaves, he noted, a successful revolt against the monopoly had taken place, threatening the safety of the *estanquero* (the official in charge of overseeing the aguardiente monopoly), who fled to Cali for safety (AGN Militias y Marinas, tomo 126, fol. 200v [1776]). The dearth of Spaniards in the region equated to an "absence of leadership." More men were needed to defend the area than the *quadrillas de negros* who worked the mines. Fighting them would put the Spaniards in grave danger because, armed, the *quadrillas* would be pushed to extreme measures (AGN Militias y Marinas, tomo 126, fols. 200r–203v [1766]). Rather than punish the perpetrators, it was recommended that for the safety of all involved, the monopoly be abolished.

In addition to exercising their rights, resisting Crown policies, and controlling the flow of goods into and out of the area, Africans could also curtail the flow of goods when it served their interests. In the same letter to the viceroy that advocated for the abolishment of the monopoly, Garcia Valdez reported that the porters who brought supplies and staples into the region had gone on strike, leaving him without meat for five days (AGN Militias y Marinas, tomo 126, fols. 200v–201r [1776]).

Over time, Africans in the Dagua River region would purchase their freedom and establish free communities. One of the largest free towns in the area, Sombrerillo, features prominently on the Dagua River map ([11], seen in Map 11.2). Occupying a strategic location downriver from Las Juntas (Map 11.2), Sombrerillo was one of two places from which the Dagua River could be navigated. (Because of its strong currents, sudden turns, and myriad waterfalls, only 50 of the Dagua's 150 km could be traveled in the Spanish colonial period, and then only by small canoe [Martínez Capote 2005:36].)

As early as 1739, Sombrerillo was described as a hedonistic place whose residents did not participate in mass, drank to excess, committed robberies and attacks, and lived scandalously (Arboleda 1956:2:102). The canoe polers here were accused of inciting the slaves, establishing "little shops along the road where they get drunk with the slaves" (Lane and Romero 2001:36). Nevertheless, other documents reveal that little to no effort was exerted by Spanish colonial authorities to curb this activity.

Sombrerillo was home to 150 porters in addition to "indios, negros, mulatos, mestizos y aún blancos" (Arboleda 1956:2:102), all of whom came from remote regions. Some were runaway slaves, while others were white merchants, yet all lived by the transport trade linking the Pacific coast to Cali. Sombrerillo's residents, particularly canoe polers and overland carriers, were highly mobile and well-informed (Lane and Romero 2001:35–36). As a critical stop along the Dagua River, Sombrerillo was also one of the few places on the river with an *aduana* (customs stop), which charged a tax on merchandise that passed through it (Romero 2017:175).

PERSISTENCE

In a remote mining area, Africans' ability to overcome challenges of topography and Spanish colonial oppression led to their persistence in the

Dagua River region. Their physical distance from Spanish administrators and their ability to adapt to their challenging environment enabled them to control terrestrial and river commerce, resist royal aguardiente monopolies, purchase their freedom, and build free communities. Their descendants would continue to inhabit this area until the early twentieth century (Martínez Capote 2005:22, 115, 123–124; Romero 2002:182–186). The fact that displaced Africans came to comprise the largest portion of the area's population created conditions ripe for the emergence of new cultural groups. The ethnic intermixing of people from different parts of Africa (reflected in mining inventories and slave censuses) gave rise to today's Afro-Colombian population in the Dagua River region. The Dagua River map helps to document the emergence of new African-based ethnicities in this area and highlights the critical role that Africans played in the region's society and economy.

ACKNOWLEDGMENTS

I am grateful to the Amerind symposiarchs, Christine Beaule and John Douglass, for the opportunity to reflect on place making, pluralism, and persistence for Africans in the eighteenth-century Dagua River region. I owe a great debt to them and to the Amerind participants for their friendship, instrumental feedback, and insightful suggestions.

NOTES

1. A future project examines all represented ethnicities in this area—Europeans, Indians, and free people of all colors, as well as Africans. Wiersema, "The History of a Periphery: Spanish Colonial Cartography from Colombia's Pacific Lowlands, 1710–1810."

2. *Mestizos* refer to those of mixed indigenous-European parentage; *negros* refer to those of African origin; *mulattoes* refer to mixed African and European parentage; *zambos* refer to mixed indigenous and African parentage; *pardos* refer to those with brown skin, ostensibly with some African parentage; and *montañeses* refer to indigenous people living in the mountainous areas of the Cauca Valley.

3. The indigenous population was not local but had been brought from Raposo and elsewhere in the 1750s and 1760s (AGN Visitas SC.62, Raposo y Dagua: Diligencias de Visita [1761–1762]; AGN Caciques e Indios, tomo 11, fols. 633–663 [1754]).

4. For problems with this larger text, see Law (1982).

5. For manumission transactions, see sale of a female slave, 390 patacones (AHC Escribano notaria segunda, libro 4, fols. 95–98 [1773]); another female slave, 400 patacones (AHC Escribano notaria segunda, libro 4, fols. 222v–223, 400–400v [1773]); and a male slave, 290 patacones (AHC Escribano notaria segunda, libro 5, fols. 279–279v [1774]).

6. This title can be loosely translated as "lieutenant in the company of Spanish *forasteros* from the city of Popayán." This was a military regiment posted to the Americas during the viceroyalty that was composed entirely of peninsular Spaniards. In this instance, *forastero* alludes to a nonnative outlander or incomer.

REFERENCES

Anonymous. 1937. "Cali en 1765: Informe rendido al virrey sobre la supresión del estanco de aguardiente y los movimientos y subversivos que eso ocasionó." *Boletín Histórico del Valle* (43–45): 246–252.

Arboleda, Gustavo. 1956. *Historia de Cali desde los orígenes de la ciudad hasta la expiración del periodo colonial.* Vols. 1–3. Cali: Biblioteca de la Universidad del Valle.

Barbot, Jean. 1732. *Description of the Coasts of North and South Guinea in a Collection of Travels and Voyages some now Printed from Original Manuscripts others now First Published in English.* 6 vols. A. & J. Churchill.

Barona, Guido. 1986. "Problemas de la historia económica y social colonial en referencia a los grupos negros, siglo XVIII." In *La participación del negro en la formación de las sociedades latinoamericanas,* edited by Alexander Cifuentes, 61–80. Bogotá: Instituto Colombiano de Antropología.

Borucki, Alex, David Eltis, and David Wheat. 2015. "Atlantic History and the Slave Trade to Spanish America." *American Historical Review* 120(2): 433–461.

Castillo Mathieu, Nicolás del. 1982. *Esclavos negros en Cartagena: Sus aportes léxicos.* Bogotá: Instituto Caro y Cuervo.

Colmenares, German. 1975. *Cali: Terratenientes, mineros y comerciantes, siglo XVIII.* Cali: Universidad del Valle.

———. 1997. *Historia económica y social de Colombia.* Vol. 2. Popayán: Una Sociedad Esclavista 1680–1800, 2nd ed. Bogotá: Tercer Mundo Editores.

Croft, James A. 1873–1874. "Exploration of the River Volta, West Africa." *Proceedings of the Royal Geographical Society of London* 18(2): 183–194.

Curtin, Philip D. 1969. *The Atlantic Slave Trade: A Census.* Madison: University of Wisconsin Press.

Dawson, Kevin. 2018. *Undercurrents of Power: Aquatic Culture in the African Diaspora.* Philadelphia: University of Pennsylvania Press.

DeCorse, Christopher. 1999. "Oceans Apart: Africanist Perspectives of Diaspora Archaeology." In *"I Too, Am America": Archaeological Studies of African-American Life,* edited by Teresa A. Singleton, 132–155. Charlottesville: University Press of Virginia.

Duncan, John. 1846. "Notes of a Journey from Cape Coast to Whyddah, on the West Coast of Africa." *Journal of the Royal Geographical Society of London* 16:143–153.

Escobar, Fray Geronimo de. 1991 (1582). "Gobierno de Popayán: Calidades de la tierra." In *Relaciones histórico-geográficas de la Audiencia de Quito, siglos XVI–XIX*, edited by Pilar Ponce Leiva, 1:332–358. Madrid: Consejo Superior de Investigaciones Científicas, Centro de Estudios Históricos.

Garrido, Margarita. 2005. "'Free Men of All Colors' in New Granada: Identity and Obedience before Independence." In *Political Cultures in the Andes, 1750–1950,* edited by Nils Jacobsen and Cristóbal Aljovín de Losada, 165–183. Durham, N.C.: Duke University Press.

Hall, Gwendolyn Midlo. 2005. *Slavery and African Ethnicities in the Americas: Restoring the Links.* Chapel Hill: University of North Carolina Press.

Helg, Aline. 2004. *Liberty and Equality in Caribbean Colombia, 1770–1835.* Chapel Hill: University of North Carolina Press.

Lane, Kris. 2000. "The Transition from Encomienda to Slavery in Seventeenth-Century Barbacoas (Colombia)." *Slavery and Abolition* 21(1): 73–95.

Lane, Kris, and Mario Diego Romero. 2001. "Miners and Maroons: Freedom on the Pacific Coast of Colombia and Ecuador." *Cultural Survival Quarterly* 25(4): 32–37.

Law, Robin. 1982. "Jean Barbot as a Source for the Slave Coast of West Africa." *History in Africa* 9:155–173.

———. 1991. *The Slave Coast of West Africa, 1550–1750: The Impact of the Atlantic Slave Trade on an African Society.* Oxford: Clarendon Press.

Leibsohn, Dana. 2014. "Dentro y Fuera de los Muros: Manila, Ethnicity, and Colonial Cartography." *Ethnohistory* 61(2): 229–251.

Lohse, Russel. 2002. "Slave-Trade Nomenclature and African Ethnicities in the Americas: Evidence from Early Eighteenth-Century Costa Rica." *Slavery and Abolition* 23(3): 73–92.

Lovejoy, Paul. 1989. "The Impact of the Atlantic Slave Trade on Africa: A Review of the Literature." *Journal of African History* 30(3): 365–394.

Martínez Capote, Ana Beiba. 2005. *Orígenes del municipio de Dagua.* Alcaldía Municipal de Dagua.

Marzahl, Peter. 1978. *Town in the Empire: Government, Politics, and Society in Seventeenth-Century Popayán.* Austin: University of Texas Press.

Maya Restrepo, Luz Adriana. 1998. "Demografía histórica de la trata por Cartagena 1533–1810." In *Geografía humana de Colombia: Los Afrocolombianos,* 6:11–52. Instituto Colombiano de Cultura Hispánica.

———. 2010. "Malí, Benín y Kongo: Tres grandes reinos del Africa Occidental conectados con la historia de Colombia." In *Rutas de libertad: 500 años de travesía,* edited by Roberto Burgos Cantor, 107–122. Bogotá: Pontificia Universidad Javeriana.

McFarlane, Anthony. 1984. "Civil Disorders and Popular Protests in Late Colonial New Granada." *Hispanic American Historical Review* 64(1): 17–54.

———. 1993. *Colombia before Independence: Economy, Society, and Politics under Bourbon Rule.* Cambridge: Cambridge University Press.

———. 1995. "Rebellions in Late Colonial Spanish America: A Comparative Perspective." *Bulletin of Latin American Research* 14(3): 313–338.

Miño Grijalva, Manuel. 2002. *La población de la ciudad de México en 1790: Estructura social, alimentación y vivienda.* Mexico City: Instituto Nacional de Estadística, Geográfica, Informática, El Colegio de Mexico.

Mollien, Gaspard-Théodore. 1944 (1823). *El viaje de Gaspard-Théodore Mollien por la República de Colombia en 1823.* Bogotá: Biblioteca Popular de Cultura Colombiana.

Pombo, Manuel. 1936. "Bajando el Dagua, 1850." In *La niña Agueda y otros cuadros*, 105–118. Bogotá: Editorial Minerva.

Romero, Mario Diego. 1991. "Sociedades negras: Esclavos y libres en la costa Pacífica de Colombia." *América Negra* 2:137–151.

———. 2002. *Sociedades negras en la costa Pacífica del Valle de Cauca durante los siglos XIX y XX.* Cali: Gobernación del Valle de Cauca.

———. 2017. *Poblamiento y sociedad en el Pacífico colombiano, siglos XVI al XVIII.* Cali: Universidad del Valle.

Romoli, Kathleen. 1974. "Nomenclatura y población indígenas de la antigua jurisdicción de Cali a mediados del siglo XVI." *Revista Colombiana de Antropología* 16:374–478.

Saffray, Charles. 1948 (1869). *Viaje a Nueva Granada.* Bogotá: Biblioteca Popular de Cultura Colombiana.

Sidbury, James, and Jorge Cañizares-Esguerra. 2011. "Mapping Ethnogenesis in the Early Modern Atlantic." *William and Mary Quarterly* 68(2): 181–208.

Smith, Robert. 1970. "The Canoe in West African History." *Journal of African History* 11(4): 515–533.

Soulodre-La France, Renée. 2001. "Socially Not So Dead! Slave Identities in Bourbon Nueva Granada." *Colonial Latin American Review* 10(1): 87–103.

Sweet, James H. 2011. "The Quiet Violence of Ethnogenesis." *William and Mary Quarterly* 68(2): 209–214.

Valencia Llano, Alonso. 2014. "Los origenes coloniales del puerto de Buenaventura." *Historia y Memoria* 9:221–246.

Voss, Barbara. 2015. "What's New? Rethinking Ethnogenesis in the Archaeology of Colonialism." *American Antiquity* 80(4): 655–670.

West, Robert C. 1952. *Colonial Placer Mining in Colombia.* Baton Rouge: Louisiana State University Press.

Wheat, David. 2011. "The First Great Waves: African Provenance Zones for the Transatlantic Slave Trade to Cartagena de Indias, 1570–1640." *Journal of African History* 52(1): 1–22.

Wiersema, Juliet. 2018. "The Manuscript Map of the Dagua River: A Rare Look at a Remote Region in the Spanish Colonial Americas." *Artl@s Bulletin* 7(2): 71–90.

ARCHIVAL SOURCES

ABBREVIATIONS

Archivo Central de Cauca, Popayán, Colombia (ACC)
ACC Signatura 8806 Colonia Judicial I-17 Minas (1762–1766)
ACC Signatura 11347 Colonia Judicial I-17 Minas (1772–1773)
ACC Signatura 11501 Colonia Civil IV-11 gobierno (1773–1774)
ACC Signatura 11511 Colonia Civil IV-10 ea (1764–1766)
Archivo General de la Nación, Bogotá, Colombia (AGN)
AGN Caciques e Indios, tomo 11, fols. 633–663 (1754)
AGN Militias y Marinas, tomo 126, fols. 199–204 (March–April 1776)
AGN Visitas SC.62, Raposo y Dagua: Diligencias de Visita, fols. 595–715 (1761–1762)
Archivo Histórico de Cali (AHC)
AHC Escribano notaria segunda, libros 4 and 5 (1773–1774)
Biblioteca Nacional, Bogotá, Colombia (BN)
BN Fondo Comuneros RM 370 (1780)

CONTRIBUTORS

Stephen Acabado, associate professor of anthropology, UCLA. His research focuses on the archaeology of indigenous responses to colonialism, particularly in Bicol and Ifugao, Philippines.

Grace Barretto-Tesoro, associate professor of archaeology, University of the Philippines. She is interested in the changing representation of various segments of society from the late precolonial period to the early Spanish period in the Philippines.

James M. Bayman, professor of anthropology, University of Hawai'i at Mānoa. His research on Spanish and Euro-American contact and colonialism focuses on the Hawaiian Islands and the Mariana Islands.

Christine D. Beaule, associate professor of languages and literatures of Europe and the Americas and director of the General Education Office, University of Hawai'i at Mānoa. Her work focuses on Spanish colonialism in both the Philippines and the central highland Andes.

Christopher R. DeCorse, professor of anthropology, University of Syracuse. His research focuses on the archaeology, history, and ethnography of sub-Saharan Africa, particularly on how archaeology can help us understand the transformations that occurred in Africa during the period of the Atlantic trade.

Boyd M. Dixon is a senior archaeologist for the Cardno GS office in Guam and the Commonwealth of the Northern Mariana Islands. He has over 40 years of archaeological experience in North America, Latin America, Western Europe, and the Pacific Basin. His interests are equally varied and embrace prehistoric and historic patterns of settlement, subsistence, interaction, power, and conflict. He has also been a research associate at the Micronesian Area Research Center at the University of Guam.

John G. Douglass, vice president of research and standards at Statistical Research, Inc., and adjunct professor in the School of Anthropology at the University of Arizona. His research has focused on indigenous-colonial interaction, religious performance, household archaeology, and community creation in the American Southwest, California, and Mesoamerica.

William R. Fowler, associate professor of anthropology, Vanderbilt University. His research focuses on the archaeology and history of the conquest period in Mesoamerica, including Guatemala and El Salvador.

Martin Gibbs, professor of anthropology, University of New England, Australia. His research interests are in the historical and maritime archaeologies of the Australia-Pacific region, including the Spanish colonial period.

Corinne L. Hofman, professor of Caribbean archaeology, Faculty of Archaeology, Leiden University, and researcher at the Royal Netherlands Institute of Southeast Asian and Caribbean Studies. Her focus is on indigenous archaeology and heritage with special interest in the deep history of the Caribbean and indigenous-African-European interactions.

Hannah G. Hoover, doctoral student in anthropology, University of Michigan. Her interests include the archaeology of colonialism in the American South and in the Mediterranean.

Stacie M. King, associate professor of anthropology, Indiana University. Her research focuses on the long-term history of peoples of Oaxaca, Mexico, between 1500 B.C. and the present. Her publications address colonial entanglements, household social organization, identity, interregional interaction and exchange, craft production, mortuary practices, food sharing, soundscapes, and public archaeology.

Kevin Lane, CONICET researcher and faculty member, Institute of Archaeology, University of Buenos Aires, Argentina. His research in part focuses on identity during the colonial period in the Andes, studying the relationship between indigenous people's concept of space, place, and landscape and how it connected to colonial views.

Laura Matthew, associate professor of history, Marquette University. Her research focuses on the impact of indigenous history and society on Spanish conquest and colonialism, and vice versa, in southern Mesoamerica, especially Guatemala.

Sandra Montón-Subías, ICREA research professor, Universitat Pompeu Fabra. Her research includes analyzing the consequences that Spanish colonialism and Jesuit missionization had on the native Chamorro populations of Guam and the Mariana Islands in the western Pacific.

Natalia Moragas Segura, Serra Hunter Professor in the Department of History and Archeology of the University of Barcelona. Her research interests include the archaeology and history of America during the prehispanic and early colonial times.

Michelle M. Pigott, doctoral student in anthropology, Tulane University. Her interests focus on Native American experiences in the American South in the aftermath of European contact and colonialism, including the Apalachee diaspora in the Gulf South.

Christopher B. Rodning, professor of anthropology, Tulane University. His research interests include encounters and entanglements between Native Americans and European explorers and colonists in western North Carolina and elsewhere in eastern North America.

David Roe, archaeology manager at Port Arthur Historic Site Management Authority, Tasmania, Australia, and adjunct professor (archaeology) at the University of New England, Australia. His research is on the archaeologies of the Pacific and Australian convict archaeology.

Roberto Valcárcel Rojas, lecturer at the Technological Institute of Santo Domingo and researcher at the Faculty of Archaeology, Leiden University. His research interests focus on the Caribbean, specifically

Cuba and the Dominican Republic, including studies in pre-Columbian iconography and indigenous cultural regions, the investigation of early ceramic sites, early colonial interactions, and archaeological heritage management.

Steve A. Tomka, director of the Cultural Resources Program, Raba Kistner Inc. His long-term research interests include the multifaceted aspects of indigenous-colonial interactions at Spanish missions across Texas and northeastern Mexico.

Jorge Ulloa Hung, research professor, Instituto Tecnológico de Santo Domingo (INTEC), researcher at the Faculty of Archaeology, Leiden University, and manager of the archaeology department at the Museo del Hombre Dominicano. His research interests include early ceramics, the Spanish colonial period, and indigenous legacies and persistence in the Caribbean, especially in the Dominican Republic and Cuba.

Juliet Wiersema, associate professor of art history, University of Texas, San Antonio. Her research examines the visual and material culture of the prehispanic and late Spanish Colonial Andes, specifically Peru and Colombia. Her current work examines manuscript cartography from eighteenth-century Nueva Granada (Colombia).

INDEX

aestheticization, in Pinagbayanan, 213–15

Africa, 3, 7, 8, 10, 274. *See also various regions*

Africans, 7, 10, 19, 36; in Central America, 137, 146; in Dagua River region, 267, 272–73, 278–86; on Hispaniola, 64, 72; in Nueva Granada, 13, 24, 275–76; in Santiago en Almolonga, 141–42

Afro-Colombians, 267, 278–79; canoe use, 281–83

agriculture: Caribbean, 72; Dagua River region, 279, 280; Ifugao, 206–8, 209; Mariana Islands, 223, 226, 228–29, 235–36

agro pastoralism, Andean, 157

aguardiente, monopoly on, 284, 285

Aguasucia (Nueva Granada), 283

Ahuitzotl, 109

Akan, at Elmina, 39–40, 41

Alabama, 88, 92, 95

Alarcón expedition, 247

Albreda (West Africa), 38

alliances, 73n1, 131; on Hispaniola, 60, 62; Mississippian-Spanish, 88, 90, 91, 94–95; Zapotec-Spanish, 109, 120

Alvarado, Diego de, 131–32

Alvarado, Jorge de, 130, 132

Alvarado, Pedro, 13, 120, 131, 134, 137

Alvarado brothers, 12, 15

American South, 83–84; coastal towns, 91–92; Mississippian culture in, 85–89; Spanish impacts on, 93–94

Amerindians, 10, 13; enslaved, 62–64

Andes, 11, 150–51, 153, 166, 169; *reducciones* in 167–68, 170

Angola, 275, 277

Anhaica (La Florida), 86

Antequera (Oaxaca), 120

Antilles, 55, 57

Apalachee chiefdom, 92, 94; persistence of, 85–87

Araras, 276, 277, 280

Arkansas, Mississippian culture, 87, 92

Asebu, 37

Asia, 19, 20, 33. *See also* Philippines

Axim (Ghana), 35, 37

Aztecs, 105, 106, 107, 109

Bahamas, 58, 63

Balcarcel Rivadeneira Sotomayor, Antonio, 245

Bambuk (Senegambia), 35

Barajagua (Cuba), 65

Barbot, Jean, *Description of the Coasts of North and South Guinea*, 280, 281

Barrera, Pedro de, 137

Barros, João de, 39

Batangueños, 215–16

beads: glass trade, 6, 9, 14, 23, 117; in Greater La Amontonada, 122–23

B'eleje' K'at, 134, 142

belief systems: Solomon Islanders, 192, 195; West African, 44

Bené, 183, 184

Benin, Bight of, Enslaved people from, 276, 277, 278, 280

Berry site, 91

Biafra, Bight of, 276, 277, 278

Bidai speakers, 248

Bilé, 182, 183, 185–86

bison, 242–43

bison hunting, by multination groups, 245–48, 261

Bobole Confederacy, 246

Bosque de Larios expedition, 248

Bourbon Reforms, 12

Buenaventura (Colombia), 269–70 , 272, 276, 279

Burgoa, Francisco de, 107

burials, 6, 193; El Chorro de Maíta, 68–69; at Majaltepec, 23, 117, 123; Mississippian, 85, 88; Texas, 257, 259–60

cabaceras, in Oaxaca, 116

Cabo Verde, 31, 32, 34, 36

caciques, 59, 60, 63, 73n1

Cagayan Valley (Philippines), 206

Cali (Colombia), 269, 270, 272, 284

California, racial/identity transformation in, 20–21

Calima (Nueva Granada), 284

Calos (La Florida), 90

Calusa, 7, 89–90, 91

cannibalism, Solomon Islands, 183–84

canoes: African use of, 280–81; on Dagua River, 281–83

Carabalis, 276, 277, 278

Caribbean, 3, 7, 8, 9, 10, 13, 73; colonialism in, 57, 132–33; encomienda in, 65, 67, 74n2; enslavement in, 58–59, 62–64; persistence in, 69–72; sociopolitics in, 55–56

Caribs, 57, 63

Carlos, Chief, 90

Carolinas, 89, 91

Cartagena, 270, 276, 279

Casqui, 87, 92

Castaño de Sosa expedition, 245–46

caste system, 3, 19; California, 20–21

Catholicism, Catholic Church, 14, 86; in Andes, 154–55, 166–67, 170;

identity, 259–60, 261–62; saints in, 165–66; at Texas-Mexico missions, 242, 257–58

cattle ranching, 72, 74n2, 144

Catujano Confederacy, 246

Cauca Valley (Nueva Granada), 269, 271

census records, for California, 20–21

Central Africa, 7; enslaved people from, 275–76, 277, 278

ceramics, 191; Caribbean, 64–65, 66f, 67f, 70; on Hispaniola, 64–65, 66f, 67f, 71f; Nejapa Valley, 111, 112, 113, 114f; in San Salvador, 139–40

Cerro del Convento (Oaxaca), 116; as ritual pilgrimage site, 118–20, 123

Ceuta (North Africa), 32

Chamba, 276, 277, 278, 280

Chamorros, 12, 14, 222; colonialism, 226–28; at contact, 224–25; cultural heritage, 223, 230; *latte* sites, 230–35; traditional lifeways, 228–29, 235–36

Chicaza province (La Florida), 92

chiefdoms: Mississippian, 85–89; Solomon Islands, 180, 183

China, trade networks, 12, 15, 204

chinos, 20

Chocó (Nueva Granada), 269, 276

Chontal speakers, 105, 107, 109, 115, 121

Christianity, 8; and Andean religion, 154, 166–67

Christianization, 14, 43–44, 59, 65, 182; in Andes, 151, 152, 170; in Elmina, 42–43; in Nejapa Valley, 115–20; in West Africa, 42–43

Christiansborg, 37

church, 153; in Kipia, 11, 159, 161, 163, 164f 165, 166

Cibao Valley (Hispaniola), 60, 61, 64

Ciudad Vieja (Guatemala), 132, 136f

Coahuila, indigenous groups in, 243, 244, 246, 247

Coahuiltecan speakers, 248, 249; Txē complex celebrations, 256–57
Coastal Plains (Texas), indigenous groups, 243–44, 257
Coco, 243, 252
Cofitachequi chiefdom, 89, 91, 94
Cojutepeque (El Salvador), 143
Colca Valley (Peru), 155
Colombia, 63, 267–69. *See also* Dagua River region
colonialism, 3, 23, 177–78; in American South, 89, 92–94; in Caribbean, 56, 57; expectations, 177–78; Mariana Islands, 225–28; in Nejapa Valley, 105–6, 121–23; in Philippines, 200–201; responses to, 200–201; in Isthmus of Tehuantepec, 107, 109
Colonia San Martín (Oaxaca), 113, 114*f*, 115, 122
colonies, 13–14, 19; Portuguese, 31, 50n3; resources, 13–14
colonization, 57, 121, 177, 222, 250; Hispaniola, 59–60; Mendaña's expedition, 177, 188–92, 195–96; of Philippines, 204–6; of Solomon Islands, 188–92
Columbus, Christopher, 36, 55, 58, 62
Concepción de la Vega, La, 58, 64; ceramics from, 66*f*, 67*f*
Congo, enslaved people from, 276, 277, 278
conquests, of Nejapa Valley, 105, 107, 109, 113, 120–21
convivencia, 11, 130; in Santiago en Almolonga, 140–43
Coosa chiefdom, 88, 89, 94
copper, in Mississippian culture, 6, 85–86
Córdoba, Francisco Hernández de, 90
Coronado, Francisco Vázquez de, 15, 179
Corpus Christi procession, in Cuzco, 152

Corpus Rumi (Kipia), 159
Cortés. Hernán, 8, 10
Cosijoeza II (Juan Cortés), 120
cosmology: Andean, 151, 153; Coahuiltecan, 256; Ifugao, 208; Kipia, 157–58, 163
Cotuí (Hispaniola), 64, 66*f*
Croft, James A., 281
criollos, 69, 275, 277
crosses: in Mendaña's rites of possession, 181, 182, 183; at Mississippian sites, 92
Crozet, Julien, 229
Cuba, 58, 59, 65, 132; cultural persistence in, 70–71; El Chorro de Maíta, 68–69
Cubagua (Venezuela), 58, 62
Cuzco (Peru), 152, 154

Dagua River region (Nueva Granada), 13, 24, 267–69, 275; Africans in, 272–74, 276–78, 283–86; canoe travel on, 281–83; mixed-ethnicity families in, 278–79
dance, 182; *mitote*, 256–58
Dávila Pedrarías, 133, 135
deities: Andean, 152, 165, 167; as saints, 165–66, 168–69
demographics: Mariana Islands, 227; Nueva Granada, 271–72, 274–75, 286n2; Santiago en Almolonga, 137–38
Dening, Greg, 177
Descriptions of the Coasts of North and South Guinea (Barbot), 280
Dias, Bartolomeu, 32–33
diseases, 68, 192, 227
doctrinas, in Nejapa Valley, 115, 116
Dolores y Viana, Mariano Francisco de los, 247
Dominican Republic: cultural persistence in, 70–72; pottery from, 66*f*, 67*f*, 71*f*

Dominicans: in Majaltepec, 6, 116–20; in Nejapa Valley, 115–20, 121
Duncan, John, 281
Dutch: in Elmina, 37, 45, 47; Ghanaian forts, 36–37

economic landscape, of Nejapa, 121–22
ecozones, around Kipia, 155–57
Edwards Plateau (Texas), 243, 246
Efutu (West Africa), 44
Eguafo state (West Africa), 40, 41
El Chorro de Maíta (Cuba), 59, 65, 67f, 68–69
elites, 21, 226; at Elmina, 40–41; Filipino, 205, 212, 215–17; Mississippian burials, 85–86; Nejapa Valley, 121–22
Elmina (Ghana), 31, 35, 36, 37, 39, 48; Christianization efforts at, 43–44; Dutch material culture in, 45, 47; identity formation at, 44–45; Portuguese at, 41–42. 49; sacred spaces at, 39–40; social structure of, 40–41
Elmina Castle, 35, 37, 38; African sacred rocks at, 39–40; Portuguese at, 41–42, 50n6
El Porvenir (Hispaniola), 65
El Salvador, 10, 11, 15, 130, 131; European foods in, 143–44; Spanish conquest of, 131–32
encampments, multination bison hunting, 246–49
encomienda, 59, 120, 138, 143, 272; in Caribbean, 65, 67, 68, 74n2
enslaved peoples, 12, 14, 19, 271; Africans as, 274, 275–76; Caribbean islanders, 58, 62–64; places of origin, 276–77; in West Africa, 35–36. *See also* slave trade
entradas, 120, 178–79, 248; in Americas, 10–11
epidemics, 68, 192
Ervipiame (Hierbipiame), 244–45, 246–47, 248

Escobar, Geronimo, *Gobierno de Popayán: Calidades de la tierra*, 272
Estrella Bay (Santa Isabel island), 181, 184, 197
ethnicity, 22, 189, 267
ethnogenesis, 69, 216; Dagua River region, 273–74, 279
ethnonyms, of Dagua River Africans, 276–77
Europe, trade goods from, 14, 212–15
exchange systems, 7; on Hispaniola, 59–60, 62, 68–69. *See also* gift exchange; trade networks
exotic species (invasive species), introduction of, 143–44
extirpación de idolatrías, in Andes, 167, 168, 170

farming, Mariana Islands, 228–29, 234, 235–36
Fatherland site (Grand Village of the Natchez, Louisiana), 87
feasts: Coalhuitecan, 256–57; Ifugao, 208; Txē complex, 256–57
Festival of the Crosses, 169
Figueroa, Diego de, 120
Figueroa, Sancho de, 143
Filipinos, 14, 201; Europeanization of, 213–15, 216–17. *See also* Ifugao; Tagalog
Florida, 93; Apalachee chiefdom, 85–89; Calusa in, 89–90
food, 21, 62, 190; in El Salvador, 143–44; on Santa Isabel, 184–85; Txē celebrations, 256–57
foreign goods, 6, 9, 23, 203; in Philippines, 206, 211; Solomon Islands, 92–93; as symbolic capital, 212–15
forts, fortresses: in American South, 92–93; in Guam, 226; in La Florida, 92–93; in Nejapa Valley, 109–12, 113; West African, 35, 36–37
Fort San Juan (La Florida), 91, 92, 93, 95

Franciscans, on Mendaña expeditions, 179, 189
free blacks (*negros libres*), 277
free towns, in Dagua River region, 269, 273, 284, 285
French, 13, 36, 58, 189
Freycinet, Louis de, 229
funeral practices, 59; El Chorro de Maíta, 68–69

Gabrielino/Tongva, 17–18, 22
Gaghe (Estrella Bay, Santa Isabel island), 181, 184, 197
Gambia River, 38
García Bravo, Alonso, 133
García de Castro, Lope, 179
García Valdez, Pedro, 284, 285
gardening, Mariana Islands, 228–29
Georgia, 88, 93
Geuss Valley, 235
Ghana, 31, 35, 48, 276; Christianization efforts in, 42–43; European forts in, 36–37
ghosts, Spanish as disease-carrying, 184, 187
gift exchange, 21, 40; Hispaniola, 65, 67; Mendaña expeditions, 185–86, 189–90; Solomon Islands, 180, 182, 185–86
Gobierno de Popayán: Calidades de la tierra (Escobar), 272
gold: Hispaniola, 60, 71*f*, 74n2; West Africa, 35
Gold Coast, 35, 43*f*; enslaved people from, 276, 277, 278, 280
gold mines, 58, 276; Dagua River region, 268*f*, 270, 272, 277–78, 280; in Hispaniola, 62, 64, 74n2
gorgets, Mississippian elite, 85–86
Greater Antilles, 55, 57, 63
Greater La Amontonada (Oaxaca), El Órgano barrio in, 115, 122–23
Guadalcanal, 181–82, 187

Guam, 12, 222, 226; archaeology of, 230–35; early contact with, 224–25; *lånchos*, 235–36; *latte* sites on, 230–31, 234–35; Manila galleon trade and, 225–26; *reducción* in, 223, 226; Spanish colonialism, 226–28
Guaspet (Alta California), 17–18
Guatemala, 10, 11, 13, 15, 130; conquest of, 131, 132
Guiengola (Oaxaca), 109
Guinea, 49n1, 281; enslaved people from, 275, 276; Portuguese in, 32, 34, 36
Guiquisale Confederacy, 246
Hernández de Córdoba, Francisco, 178–79
Higüey Wars, 63
Hispaniola, 55, 65, 72, 74n2; settlement patterns, 60–61; Spanish on, 58, 59–60
hostage-taking, Mendaña expedition, 185
huacas, huanca-huacas, at Kipia, 11, 161–63, 167
Huari, 169
hunting parties/territories, 242–43, 245, 261; multination encampments, 246–49

Iberian Union, 10, 32, 36
identicide, 165
identity, identity formation, 3, 8, 20–21, 22, 64, 65, 138; of Caribbean peoples, 57, 70; at El Chorro de Maíta, 68–69; at Elmina, 44–45; material culture, 259–60, 261–62; Melanesian, 183–84; persistence of, 69–70; in Philippines, 201, 215–17; and place, 203–4; San Salvador, 139–40
idolatry, idols, 119, 167
Ifugao, 12, 201, 206, 217; rice terraces, 203, 204, 206, 207*f*, 208–9, 217
Igorot, 205

ilustrados, 201, 205; imported goods, 212–15; social status/identity, 212–13, 215–17

imported objects, as symbolic capital, 212–15

Inca, Inka, 21, 153, 159, 179

India, 20, 33

indigenous peoples, 12, 24, 275; Caribbean, 58–59, 62–64; Cauca Valley, 271–72; Plains bison hunters, 242, 243–49. *See also* by group name

indios, 19, 57, 65

indios chinos, 20, 22

intangible cultural heritage, 223–24; Chamorro, 230, 236

intermarriage, 3; among Texas-Mexico indigenous groups, 249–56, 261

Inti Raymi ceremony, 152

Island Carib. *See* Kalingo

Iximché (Guatemala), 131

Jamaica, 65, 132

Japanese, World War II, 236

Jesuits, in Mariana Islands, 222, 226

Joara chiefdom, 89, 90, 91, 92, 95

Jordan site (Louisiana), 87–88, 94

Juffure (Senegambia), 38

Jumanos, 245–46

Kaji' Imox, 134, 142

Kalinago, 57

Kaqchikel Maya: in Santiago en Almolonga, 137, 140; and Spanish conquest, 131, 132, 134, 137

Karankawa, 243–44, 249, 259

King site (Georgia), 88, 92, 94

Kipia (Peru), 11, 156*f*, 158*f*, 168, 169, 170; cosmological arrangement of, 151, 152[ck], 157–58; ecological setting, 155, 157; radiocarbon dates, 160–61; religious sector, 161–65, 166

Kommenda (West Africa), 37

Kostumbren Chamorro, 224

La Ballona (California), 17

labor, 14, 57; encomienda, 65, 74n2; San Salvador, 135–36; and Santiago en Almolonga, 136–37; slave, 58–59, 62–64, 272, 276, 279–81

La Florida, 83–84; Mississippian chiefdoms and, 89–91; Spanish forts in, 92–93

Lake Jackson mound site (Florida), 85, 86

lançado settlements, 48, 50n9

lânchos, 223, 224, 226, 228, 229, 230; archaeology of, 231, 234–35; use of, 235–36

land, land use, 121, 143, 151; on Guam, 226, 230, 231(table), 234, 235; Mariana Islands, 228–29; in Santiago en Almolonga, 140, 144

landscape, 7, 60, 94, 144, 213, 216; colonial, 200, 203; rice cultivation, 207*f*, 208; sacred, 17–18, 39–40, 152–53, 157–59, 161–65, 211; social, 250–56

La Pérouse, Jean-François de, 189

Las Juntas (Colombia), 269, 270, 280, 283, 284

latte buildings, 224, 225; sites with, 230–31, 234–35

Laws of the Indies, 209, 215

Legaspi, Miguel López de, 204–5, 225

León, Alonsó de, 246

Lesser Antilles, 55, 57–58, 63

Liano, Pedro de, 143

Lienzo de Quauhquehollan, 130, 134, 135*f*

lightning deity, Santiago as, 165, 166

livestock, introduction of, 143, 144

López Gordillo, Diego, 138

Los Picachos (Nejapa Valley), 111–12, 123

Lost River Village (Guam), 231, 234

Louisiana, Mississippian culture in, 87–88, 94

Lucayan Islands, 63

Luna, Tristán de, 89

Luso-Africans, 33–34, 36, 38, 44, 50n10
Luzon (Philippines), 205

Mabila (Alabama), 92, 95
Magellan, Ferdinand (Fernando de Magallanes), 12, 204, 224
Majaltepec (Maxaltepeque) (Oaxaca), 6, 23, 116–18, 120, 123
Maldonado, Francisco, 120
Malopé, 189–90, 191, 192, 196
Manila (Philippines), 12, 13, 15, 204–5
Manila-Acapulco galleon trade, 8, 12, 13, 14–15, 179, 204, 205; Guam and, 222, 225–26
Marapa, 187
Marees, Pieter de, 41, 42, 50n7
Margués the Aguayo, 247
Mariana Islands, 12, 14, 222, 223*f*, 224. *See also* Chamorros; Guam
marriages, 19, 42, 242, 279; in bison hunting groups, 249, 261; multicultural, 278–79; San Antonio River mission, 251–56
material culture, 6, 65, 106, 159, 201; in Caribbean, 71–72; El Chorro de Maíta, 68–69; at Elmina, 45–47; on Hispaniola, 61–62; and identity, 215–16; in Mississippian sites, 90, 94–95; Pinagbayanan, 211–12; at San Antonio missions, 258–60. *See also* by type
Maya, 137, 138, 140, 141, 146
Mayeye, 244, 247, 248, 249
megalithic pillars, Chamorro, 224, 225
Melanesians. *See* Solomon Islands, Islanders
Melilla (North Africa), 32
Mendaña, Álvaro de, 177; colonization, 188–92, 195–96; exploration, 176, 178*f*, 179–88; human sacrifice and, 183–84; negotiations, 185–86; rites of possession, 181–82
Menéndez de Avilés, Pedro, 90

mestizos, mestizas, 7, 19, 6 4, 73, 229, 286n2
Mexicanos, in Santiago en Almolonga, 137, 140, 142
Mexico, 6, 8, 10, 13, 14, 15, 19; indigenous groups in, 242–49
México-Tenochtitlan, 133, 141
military campaigns, 19; Guatemala and El Salvador, 131, 132, 137, 145; Portuguese-Elmina, 40
Mina (West Africa), 35, 36, 276, 277, 278, 280
mines, mining, 276; Dagua River region, 277–78, 279, 280
Misión Espíritu Santo de Zúñiga (Texas), 259
Misión Nuestra Señora de la Purísima Concepción (Texas), 249, 257; marriage records, 251–56
Misión Refugio (Texas), 259
Misión San Antonio de Valero (Alamo), 249; marriage records, 251–56
Misión San Francisco de la Espada (Texas), 249
Misión San Francisco de Solano (Texas), 249
Misión San Gabriel (Alta California), 17
Misión San José y San Miguel de Aguayo (Texas), 249
Misión San Juan Capistrano (Texas), 249, 260
missions, 6, 12–13, 261; in La Florida, 90, 93; at Mississippian mound centers, 86–87; *mitotes*, 257–58; in San Antonio River basin, 247, 249–56, 257–60
Mississippian culture, 6, 83; colonization of, 92–95; instability of, 88–89; persistence, 85–88
mitotes, 261; Coahuiltecan bands, 256–57; mission eradication of, 257–58
Mixe speakers, 105, 107, 109, 115, 121; in Nejapa Valley, 111, 113, 117, 120

Mollien, Gaspard-Theodore, 281, 283
Mori (Ghana), Dutch fort at, 36–37
Moscoso, Luis, 87
mound centers, 83; Mississippian, 85–
   89; Spanish colonization and, 92, 94
Mound Key (Florida), 90
mulattoes, 7, 42, 72
multiethnicity, of Nejapa Valley, 105–6
Muralla, Cerro de la (Nejapa Valley),
   112, 123
Muruame, 249

Nahua, 19; in Santiago en Almolonga,
   140, 142; with Spanish, 131, 132, 137,
   144–45, 146
Nahua speakers, 105–6
Nahuat Pipil, 131, 132, 135, 136, 137; in
   San Salvador, 138–39
Nahuizalco (Guatemala), 145
Narváez, Juan Pánfilo de, 86
Natá de los Caballeros (Panama), 133
Natchez chiefdom, 87
Nejapa Valley (Oaxaca), 6; colonial-
   ism in, 122–23; Dominicans in,
   115–17, 119; fortified sites in, 109–
   12; identity in, 117–18; pilgrimage
   to, 118–20; pluralism in, 105–6,
   123–24; settlements in, 112–13;
   Spanish conquest of, 120–21; trade,
   106–7
neophytes: identity, 261–62; San Anto-
   nio River missions, 250, 258
Nigeria, 35, 276
Niger River, 281
North Carolina, 90, 91
North Finegayan (Guam), 231
Nueva Cádiz de Cubagua (Venezuela),
   64, 67f
Nueva Granada, 13, 24, 267, 270–71; Africans in, 275–77; mixed-race society
   in, 274–75
Nuevo León, 243, 244

Oaxaca, 24, 108f; multiethnicity in, 105–
   6; trade networks in, 106–7
obsidian, in Nejapa Valley, 112, 113, 115,
   118
Ojeda, Alonso de, 60
Old Kiyyangan Village (Philippines),
   208
Olivares, Antonio de San Buenaven-
   tura, 249, 250
Ordinances for Settlement, 189, 190
Ouidah (West Africa), 277, 281
Ovando, Nicolás de, 63, 132

Pacaha, 87
Pachacamac, 152
Pachamama, 169
Pacheco, Gaspar, 120
Pajalache, 255
Palomo, José R., 235–36
Pamparomás (Peru), 159, 169
Pamua (San Cristobal Island), 192–93,
   197
papal decrees, 36, 43
Pardo, Juan, 88, 89, 91, 92, 93
Park, Mungo, 281
Parkin site (Arkansas), 92
Patumaca/o, 255
Payaya, 247, 252
Pearl Coast (Venezuela), 62
pearl fisheries, on Cubagua, 58, 62
persistence, 4; in Caribbean societies,
   69–72; Dagua River region, 285–86;
   of Mississippian culture, 85–89; in
   Nejapa Valley, 117–18
Perulapa (El Salvador), 143
Philippines, 9, 12, 19, 202f; coloniza-
   tion in, 200–201, 204–6, 209–12;
   Europeanization in, 212–15; identity
   in, 22, 215–17; Spanish trade with,
   179, 222
Phillip, II, Ordinances for Settlement,
   189

pigs, 9, 62, 143, 144; and Mendaña expedition, 184–85, 190

pilgrimages: in Andes, 169; to Cerro del Convento, 118–20, 123

Pinagbayanan (Philippines), 9, 201, 203; archaeology in, 209–11; identity formation in, 204, 216–17; imported objects in, 212–15; migrants in, 205–6

Pipil, 131, 132

place, place making, 3, 4, 6, 8, 10, 15–16, 22, 25, 187, 203–4, 211; access to, 260–61; colonial, 23–24; and identity, 203–4; Mendaña's expeditions, 196–97; Philippines, 200–201, 209–10; religion of, 152–53, 155; sacred, 17–18, 161–65

Plaza de España (Hagatña, Guam), 227

pluralism, 4, 6, 8, 11, 19, 25, 200; in Nejapa Valley, 105–7, 122, 123–24

Pobre de Zamora, Juan, 228, 229

polytheism, 153–54

Ponce de León, Juan, 90

Popo, 276, 277, 280, 281

porters, Dagua River region, 279, 280, 285

Portugal, Portuguese, 3, 7, 43, 50nn3–5, 10, 63; at Elmina, 41–42, 45, 46*f*, 50n6; settlements, 32–33; and West African trade, 31, 33–36, 37, 38–39, 47–49

pottery. *See* ceramics

prestige economies, in Philippines, 215, 216

Príncipe, as Portuguese colony, 31, 32, 35, 50n3

processions, Catholic, 155, 169

Puelles, Pedro de, 143

Puerto Rico, 55, 58, 65, 132

Pulantat (Guam), 234–35

Qsares Seghir (Morocco), 32

Quiroga y Losada, Governor, 226

Ramón, Domingo, 247

rancheria grande encampments, groups at, 247–49

ranches, in Nejapa Valley, 121. *See also lānchos*

Raposo (Nueva Granada), 276, 286n3

reducciones, 11, 167–68, 170; failures of, 150–51; and identity formation, 216–17; Mariana Islands, 223, 226, 229; in Philippines, 201, 211

Relación de Nexapa (Santamaría), 121

Relación Marroquín, 143

Remesal, Antonio de, 133

resistance: Calusa, 89–90; Ifugao, 204, 206; in Philippines, 200–201, 204

Ribeira Grande (Cabo Verde), 32

rice terraces, Ifugao, 201, 203, 204, 206, 207*f*, 208–9, 217

rites of possession, Mendaña expedition, 181–82, 187

rock outcrops, Kipia, 157, 159, 161–64

Rota, 226, 227, 228

Royal Council of the Indies, 13

Ruiz, Juan, 119

Ruta de Colón (Hispaniola), 60

sacrifice, human, 183–84

Saffray, Charles, 281, 283

St. Augustine (Florida), 92, 93

saints, and Andean deities, 152, 165–66, 168–69

Salcedo, Juan de, 205

Sana, 247, 252

Sanan, 244

San Antonio River Basin (Texas), missions in, 249–56, 259–60

San Cristobal (Makira) island, 187, 192–93

San Juan (Philippines), 205

San Luis (Florida), 92, 93; structure of, 86–87

San Salvador (El Salvador), 11, 130–31, 132, 141, 146; ceramics in, 139–40; demographics of, 138–39; design of, 133, 134, 145; expansion of, 142–43; foods at, 143–44; labor in, 135–36

Santa Barbara del Salto (Nueva Granada), 278, 283

Santa Cruz Islands (Nendo), Mendaña colonization, 176, 189–92, 195–96

Santa Elena (La Florida), 91, 92, 93

Santa Isabel (ship), 189, 192, 193,196, 197

Santa Isabel island (Solomon Islands), 176, 180, 181, 197; human sacrifice, 183–84; Spanish on, 184–85, 186

Santamaría, Bernardo de, *Relación de Nexapa*, 121

Santa Marta (Colombia), 270

Santiago: as Andean lightning deity, 165, 166; and Kipia, 168, 169

Santiago Nexapa (Oaxaca), 112–13, 120

Santiago en Almolonga (Guatemala), 11, 130, 131, 132, 144, 146; demographics in, 137–38, 140–42; design of, 133, 134–35, 145; labor in, 136–37

Santo Domingo (Hispaniola), 63

Santo Tomás (Hispaniola), 60

São Antonio (Axim), 37

São Jorge da Mina, Castelo (Elmina Castle), 35, 36, 40; Portuguese at, 41–42

São Tomé, 31, 32, 35, 42, 50n3

Sarmiento de Gamboa, Pedro, 179, 188

Senegambia, 34–35, 38, 48, 277

Señor de los Milagros, 152

settlement patterns: Chamorro, 224–25; Guam, 230–35; Hispaniola, 60–61; Mariana Islands, 228–29; Mississippian, 87–88, 94; Philippines, 204; Santa Cruz Island, 190

Shama (West Africa), 35

Siabane, 250

slavery, slaves. *See* enslaved peoples

slave trade, 14, 19, 24, 35, 141; Caribbean, 62–64; Nueva Granada and, 275–76

social status: Chamorro, 60, 91, 229; Ifugao, 208–9; *ilustrado*, 215–16; Pinagbayanan, 201, 212–13; of San Antonio missions, 251–56

Solomon Islands, Islanders, 12, 34, 176; cannibalism, 183–84; colonization of, 188–92, 195–96; exploration of, 176, 181–88; hostilities, 186–88; social and economic relationships, 194–95; trade networks, 180–81

Sombrerillo (Colombia), 269, 273, 284, 285

Soto, Hernando de, 88, 179; expedition of, 86, 87, 89, 91, 92, 95

South America, 15, 150. *See also* Dagua River region; Kipia

Southeast Asia, 3, 7, 8, 12, 15, 20

South Texas, 257; indigenous groups, 243–44, 245

space, 4, 16; and place, 203, 211; religion of, 152–53; sacred, 159, 161–65; symbolic, 261–62

Spanish, Spaniards, 7, 13, 57; in Andes, 150–51; exploration, 178–79; on Hispaniola, 59–60, 64; in Nejapa Valley, 105, 106, 115–20; in Santiago en Almolonga, 137, 142

stockades, Mississippian and Spanish, 92–93

symbolic capital, 9, 212–13

Tacame, 255

Taensa chiefdom, 87–88

Tagalog, 12, 201, 216, 217

Taíno culture, 61

Tapay (Peru), 169

Taqui Oncoy movement, 167

Tehuantepec, Isthmus of, Zapotecs in, 107, 109

Tejas, 245, 247, 249

Tennessee, 88, 89, 91

Texas, 12; indigenous groups in, 242–49
Texas-Mexico borderlands: bison herds in, 242–43; indigenous groups in, 243–49
Toledo, Francisco de, 151
Tonkawa, 244–45, 248
trade networks, 3, 12, 106, 212; Caribbean, 9, 60, 65, 67; Chamorro, 224–26; intercolony, 14–15; Manila-Acapulco, 14–15, 205; Nejapa Valley, 106–7, 109, 122–23; Solomon Islands, 180–81; West African-Portuguese, 31, 32, 33–35, 36, 37–39
transportation, Dagua River region, 279, 280, 285
trazas, 132–33, 146
Treaty of Alcáçovas, 32
Treaty of Tordesillas, 24, 32, 178
Triana de San Geronomo de las Benedicciones, 278
Txē complex celebrations, 256–57, 261

United States, 11, 13; and Guam, 227, 230. *See also* American South; *various states*

Vanikoro, 189
Venezuela, 62, 63, 64
Viday, 247
violence, 146; by Mendaña expeditions, 185, 186–87, 189, 190–91, 192

Virgin of the Candelaria, 169

Wadan (Senegambia), 35
warfare: in Africa, 274; in American South, 86, 95; in Central America, 131, 132, 133–34, 146
warriors: Apalachee, 86, 95; Mexican/Nahua, 15, 19
water rituals, 169; at Kipia, 162–63
West Africa, 7, 31, 49, 281; enslaved labor in, 35–36; Portuguese and, 10, 21, 33–35, 37, 38–39, 42–43, 47–49; slaves from, 275–76. *See also specific regions*
wheat, introduction of, 143, 144
Wolof territory, 35

Xarame, 247, 250, 252
Xinka, 137, 141
Xuala province (La Florida), 91

Yagul (Oaxaca), 112
Yojuane, 244, 247, 248, 249
Ypandi, 252

Zaachila (Oaxaca), 107
Zapotecs, 120, 142; fortresses, 109, 111; in Nejapa Valley, 105, 106, 107, 109, 112–13, 122, 123; and Spanish colonization, 121, 131
Zapotec speakers, 105, 107, 115
Zapotitlán (Oaxaca), 112